The Rationale Behind Change

Bi Fan

The Rationale Behind Change

Institutions, Development, and Principles of Economics Based on the China Paradigm

Translated by Qian Kunqiang

CTPH

Springer

Bi Fan
Beijing, China

Translated by
Qian Kunqiang
School of Foreign Studies
University of International Relations
Beijing, China

ISBN 978-981-97-8853-8 ISBN 978-981-97-8854-5 (eBook)
https://doi.org/10.1007/978-981-97-8854-5

Jointly published with China Translation & Publishing House
The print edition is not for sale in China (Mainland). Customers from China (Mainland) please order the print book from: China Translation & Publishing House.
ISBN of the Co-Publisher's edition: 978-701-02-4488-4

Translation from the Chinese Simplified language edition: "变革的逻辑" by Bi Fan, © People's Publishing House 2022. Published by People's Publishing House. All Rights Reserved.

The original submitted manuscript has been translated into English. A subsequent revision was performed by the author(s) to further refine the work and to ensure that the translation is appropriate concerning content and scientific correctness. It may, however, read stylistically different from a conventional translation.

This Springer imprint is published by the registered company Springer Nature Singapore Pte Ltd.
The registered company address is: 152 Beach Road, #21-01/04 Gateway East, Singapore 189721, Singapore

Preface: The Power of Institutions Re-conceptualized

The idea of comparative advantage as discussed by classical economists refers primarily to natural factors such as resource endowments and geographical locations. However, this does not necessarily mean that a country with naturally-endowed comparative advantages will automatically enjoy sound development. Many countries and regions, for all their resource scarcities and geographical disadvantages, have managed to become wealth-creating centers. Apart from the factor of accidental opportunities, the institutional factor definitely plays a determining role in economic development. It is a comparative advantage created through the human factor. The rapid economic development that China has undergone since its reform and opening-up campaign has been characterized as an achievement ascribable to institutional advantages. This then leads to a chain of questions. How does institution determine development? Are there any general laws underlying the institutional evolution itself? How can we choose the kind of institution that is most instrumental to development? These are the questions that ineluctably emerge in any analysis involving institutions. This book seeks to explore these issues from the perspective of the institutional theory in economics, in connection with China's practices in economic reform.

1

In the history of human civilization prior to the birth of economics, a vast array of politicians and intellectual thinkers both in the East and in the West had already realized the paramount importance of economic institutions to the growth of national wealth and to the rise and fall of the political reign. During that period, economic thoughts, largely embedded in philosophical and political thoughts, failed to develop into an independent intellectual scheme. The history spanning from the 16th century to the mid-18th century witnessed Britain entering the period of mercantilism, a period in which economic thoughts and economic policies underwent close interactions. As the political, business, and academic communities became concerned with the issue of how to construct a viable economic system, economists started to perform the mission of contributing to the governance of the country and enlightening the general public. The publication of *An Inquiry into the Nature and Causes of the Wealth of Nations* heralded the advent of the classical economics, producing a profound impact on the governance of individual nations. Influenced by Adam Smith's theory of liberal economics, European countries and the United States developed their architecture of modern economic institutions. With the advent of the neoclassical economics, economists started to rely heavily on the extensive use of quantitative tools, to such an extent that the study of economic institutions came to be neglected. It was not until the Keynesian revolution that economic institution re-asserted itself as a critical concept over the horizon of the mainstream economics.

However, those institutional issues were merely confined to discussions concerning specific institutional arrangements. It is the institutional economics that really started to treat institution as an independent academic subject by studying the rules underlying its inception and evolution. Institutional economics itself has evolved through three separate stages—the Institutional School, the Neo-Institutional School, and the New Institutional Economic School. The birth of new institutional economics coincided with the dominance of neoclassical economics as a mainstream school. Neoclassical economics purported that institutions could remain unchanged, believing that the collection of information, bargaining, the instituting of contracts, and the oversight of the honoring of contracts were free from costs. As institutions were excluded from neoclassical economic models, the result was that institutions were viewed as irrelevant to the practice of economic activities. Ronald H. Coase, the proponent of new institutional economics, proposed his theorem of transaction costs, subverting the hypothesis established by neoclassical economics about institutions as constants and disclosing the substitutive relationship between the enterprises and the market. In subsequent studies, new institutional economics developed three major theoretical tools, namely, the theory of property rights, the contract theory, and the theory of transaction costs, which have been used to analyze the transaction costs of the state, the enterprises, and the market in economic activities. One of the beliefs of the new institutional economics is that reducing transaction costs is the core objective of institutional reforms and any design and adjustment of property rights and contracts must be centered on the reduction of transaction costs. With Ronald H. Coase, Douglass C. North, and John Williamson being awarded the Nobel prizes in economic sciences over the years, new institutional economics emerged as a leading academic discipline in economic sciences.

Regrettably, however, in the transformation of many countries from the system of planned economy to that of market economy, and in the strategies pursued by some developing countries to catch up with and overtake developed countries, new institutional economics has failed to produce the expected role of shedding light on how to construct new institutions. This regret is somehow related to the limitations inherent in the studies performed by new institutional economics itself. First of all, new institutional economics has defined transactions too narrowly. Essentially, transactions involve the transfer of rights. New institutional economics only focuses on the property rights as the subject of transaction studies, denying the legitimacy of other rights as proper subjects for investigation. Secondly, new institutional economics tends to view all countries as homogeneous and undifferentiated, unable to offer an anatomical analysis, so to speak, of the state which is the largest provider of institutions. Such a view is surprisingly similar to neoclassical economics' view of enterprises as homogeneous and undifferentiated. Thirdly, no viable method was found to calculate transaction costs. Meanwhile, the practice of using money as the yardstick for measuring transaction costs has proved increasingly ineffectual. Fourthly, new institutional economics constructed an analytical framework in which the transaction costs were to be studied on the dimensions of the state, the enterprises, and the market. In actuality, however, only the transaction costs of the enterprises and the market were studied, leaving out the study of the transaction costs of the state.

2

In view of the inadequacies inherent in the existing institutional studies of economics, this book ventures to undertake some tentative explorations in an effort to push back the boundaries of research in this field. Transaction costs constitute the core of institutional studies in economics. As the state is the paramount provider of institutions, the transaction costs generated by its behavior must be brought into the realm of our scrutiny. The rights derived from the government's administrative actions are in essence equivalent to various rights linked up with property rights. Therefore, in transaction costs, the objects of transaction encompass not only the property rights but also the rights derived from administrative actions, such as the administrative licenses issued by the government to enterprises and the safety standards formulated by the government. These rights are of the same nature as the property rights in that they are the fundamental units of economic activities, equipped with the concomitant attribute of resource scarcity.

The next question to address is how to measure transaction costs. In the transactions of the rights other than the property right, it is highly difficult to quantify transaction costs by means of money. For instance, when an enterprise applies for administrative licenses from the government, the price that the applicant pays is primarily not money. Except for money, what else can serve as the criterion for measuring transaction costs? If we open up the coordinate system in economics, the variables that are available include price, value, quantity, and time. Among these four variables, both the price and the value can be gauged in terms of money. With regard to the quantitative indicators such as the production volume, the transaction volume, and the consumption volume of different categories of products, they can hardly be compared if not converted into the value of money, as different units of measurement are employed for different categories of products. Therefore, it seems now that the only variable left is time.

Time is a concept that is readily recognizable in the theoretical frameworks and key doctrines of economists ranging from Adam Smith, Karl Marx, Irving Fisher, Alfred Marshall to Paul A. Samuelson. Nevertheless, it seems that time has never been seriously and systematically discussed. Time is closely related to the value of labor, interest, and efficiency, and it is an objective way to include time as a means of calculating costs. It is subjected to observation and numerical description, exempt from the interferences by any external forces. Consequently, in the following analysis, time will be chosen as a key criterion for quantifying transaction costs. Studies have already indicated that this method is entirely feasible.

In shopping, one sometimes has to queue up. This act of queuing up is itself a way of using time as a transaction cost in exchange for the objects of commodity at the equivalent value. Queuing up for the government's administrative licensing is no different in nature from queuing up for purchasing commodities in that both acts would lead to the superimposition of the transaction costs, in the form of time, onto the price of commodities. Together, the cost of time and the price of the commodities constitute the overall transaction cost. Under the planned economy, the time consumed in waiting was virtually worthless. Under the market economy, money tends to be quite insignificant as compared with the time consumed in waiting, because an entity in possession of sufficient time is capable of creating tremendous financial outcomes and even achievements beyond our wildest imagination. In the transactions between different enterprises, except for paying for the goods according to prices, any transaction that might elongate the transaction duration must be curtailed. In a similar vein, the transaction cost in the form of time caused by the government's administration actions should be minimized.

Using time as a benchmark for measuring transaction costs is not meant to deny the role of money as a standard of measurement. Rather, the purpose is to enrich the modes of quantifying transaction costs. Although previous studies of economics have never used time as a means for computing transaction costs, all entities, be they the state actors engaged in the economic governance of a country or the enterprises engaged in business operations, have unanimously and spontaneously pursued the goal of saving time. For example, many countries, in seeking to improve the business environment and to enhance the efficiency of investment, have endeavored to reduce the time spent on the government's administrative licensing. If there is a totality of labor time in a given society, this sum necessarily comprises of the time of transaction costs. The less proportion the time of transaction costs accounts for in the totality of labor time, the higher proportion of time could be spent on the creation of material wealth. Once time is incorporated as one of the norms for calculating transaction costs, it would be fairly easy to evaluate both the strengths and the weaknesses of various institutional arrangements that produce transaction costs and thus to construct targeted institutions with lower transaction costs.

Once time is employed to determine transaction costs, it will shed refreshingly significant light on the studies of economic institutions. We can utilize this tool to explain many of the attributes manifested by institutional evolution and to uncover the rules underlying the evolution. For instance, we can determine which is better between the two modes of institutional evolution, the rational construction or the spontaneous evolution (which are sometimes termed as the sudden change and the gradual change). Controversies have surrounded this question in the academic community as well as in the circle of institutional formulators (who design and establish institutions) and the institutional operators (who implement and enforce institutions). When time is used for measuring transaction costs, it becomes apparent that as far as formal constraints in Douglass C. North's theory are concerned, rational construction tends to exhibit remarkable advantages in economizing transaction costs. This is because, under an established formal constraint, it will usually take more time to regulate the conflicts between the existing institution and the emerging institution if we merely rely on the spontaneous evolution of the institutions. As for the informal constraints in North's theory, spontaneous evolution might be a more universal phenomenon in addition to being a less time-consuming mode. This book will conduct a case analysis of China's unique Household Contract Responsibility System[1] for the sake of examining the respective advantages of rational construction and spontaneous evolution at different stages and in different contexts. For another instance, why does there exist such a thing as path dependence in the course of institutional evolution? Actually, path dependence can be accounted for by the fact that the operators of a given institution can avoid wasting time—time that might otherwise be spent on reconstructing an institution—by "making patches" in the existing institution.

Some of the new characteristics uncovered in the study of institutional evolution can also be explained by means of transaction costs. The first is the diminishing of the institutional efficiency. It is a general rule that the efficacy of a formal constraint will start to diminish the moment it is established. The reason lies in the fact that a new institution, once implemented, entails constant adjustments and improvements. Generally speaking, the marginal adjustments of an institution will render that institution increasingly complicated while the operation of that institution will become increasingly time-consuming. Most importantly, such augmentations are often irreversible. The second is institutional alienation. By institutional alienation, it means that, in the course of its evolution, an institution gradually deviates from the initial intent of its creation and ends up turning against itself. In the actual practice, it is often the case that many policies designed to promote social and economic development end up in the constant escalation of transaction costs until retro-regulation, or reverse regulation, occurs. Far from promoting development, an institution that suffers from alienation hampers development.

Both the gradual change and the sudden change of an institution are characterized by path dependence, diminishing efficiency, and institutional alienation. Each of these three characteristics does not exist in isolation; instead, they are closely interwoven and share a reciprocal causation. They are congruent with the three cardinal laws

[1] The Household Contract Responsibility System, or contract responsibility system, was a practice in China, first adopted in agriculture in 1979 and officially established in 1982, by which households are held responsible for the profits and losses of an enterprise. This system, which came to replace collective farming, maintained public ownership of land and some of the means of production, but made production the responsibility of households. Households still had to contribute to state quotas but could make their own decisions about what to plant on contracted land and could sell via a multi-tier price system that included the lowest price for payment to the state up until the quota, a higher rate for above-quota sales to the state, and market price for crops allowed to be sold at fairs.

of institutional evolution. The first is that, an institution evolves in the concomitant conditions of path dependence and diminishing efficiency, conditions which eventually lead to institutional alienation. The second is that an established institution will not incur demise prior to the complete release of its productive power. The third is that without the exogenous condition producing its due impact, the endogenous condition alone is insufficient to give rise to a sudden and fundamental change in a particular institution.

Once we have availed ourselves of the transaction costs as an analytical instrument, the next step is to construct an analytical framework with which to anatomize an institution. To enact a transaction of rights, there requires the presence of the objects, the rules, the costs, and the entities of the transaction. In terms of the specific contents of a transaction, the rights to be traded are the objects of transaction, the contract constitutes the rules that the transaction abides by, time and capital are the transaction costs, and the government, the enterprises, and the market are the entities of the transaction. To facilitate the analysis of a great variety of complicated institutions in a technically manageable manner, we employ the method of module analysis—each transaction will be posited as a module consisting of three components, the rights, the contract, and the costs. Transaction entities close a deal between themselves by means of a transaction module. A right is transferred between transaction entities in accordance with a certain contract, and the time and the capital that are spent constitute the transaction costs. The transactions that transaction entities complete among themselves via transaction modules include those between the government and enterprises, between the government and the market, between one government agency and another, and between the enterprises and the market. Among all these transactions, the existing institutional theories in economics have performed sufficiently in-depth studies regarding the transactions between the enterprises and the market. Hence, this book will refrain from any further treatment on the subject. Coase succeeded in offering an anatomy of corporate organizations by going beyond the neo-classical economics' assumption of corporate homogeneity. Similarly, by analyzing a full range of the transactions of rights between the government and various other transaction partners, we can go beyond the assumption of homogeneity postulated by both the neoclassical economics and the new institutional economics concerning the state by anatomizing the state behavior in its various manifestations.

3

To start with, it is possible to use a new analytical framework of economic institutions to investigate, on the macro level, the evolution of economic institutions in China. With the founding of the New China, that is, the People's Republic of China, in 1949, China created a brand-new economic architecture totally different from that of the Old China (the Republic of China before 1949). China modeled its economic pattern mainly after the system of the Soviet Union. It was assumed that the socialist economic system was characterized by public ownership, the planned economy, and the distribution of wealth on the basis of labor. In accordance with this guideline, China undertook rational construction of its economic institutions. During "the First 5-Year Plan" period, China made spectacular achievements in its economic development and, as time passed, gradually succeeded in setting up a complete and relatively independent industrial system as well as a national economic system. However, the flaws inherent in that economic system soon surfaced. The excessively extensive control and rigid regulation by the state resulted in insufficient economic vibrancy while, for a long time, the supply of the means of production and the consumer goods could not meet the demands. At best, only a low level of supply-and-demand equilibrium could be maintained. The critical reason for those problems could be attributed to the exorbitant transaction costs in economic activities.

Under the system of the planned economy, an enterprise was, at most, equivalent to a workshop owned by the government, with the production, management, and the supply and demand of products all planned and arranged by the government. The completion of a single inter-enterprise transaction had to go through repeated transactions between the enterprises and the government agencies and also between government agencies themselves. If an enterprise had a demand for a particular kind of products, the demand had to be reported from the most primary level all the way to the central planning department which, in return, issued the production plans back to the enterprise responsible for producing that particular product. To ensure the necessary connectivity between the production and the demand, the central planning department had to collect data concerning the categories and the quantities of the products demanded as well as the production capacity of the enterprises. Then, following the "two top-to-bottom processes and one bottom-to-top process" or the "two top-to-bottom processes and two bottom-to-top processes" of information feedback regarding annual production plans, the central planning department sought to maintain a supply-and-demand balance nationwide and arrange for production after finalizing the overall plans. The time consumed in all those processes would find its way into the final transaction costs. Under the market economy, enterprises can engage in direct transactions, eliminating the transactions of rights between the enterprises and the government, or between the government agencies themselves. Consequently, the transaction costs could be significantly reduced.

China commenced its reforms with the reform of the institutions of high transaction costs. In the wake of the so-called "Cultural Revolution (1966–1976)," China shifted the work focus of the nation from the highly politicized class struggle to the economic development. But the central government concentrated its time and energy primarily on modifying and improving the planned economy rather than on developing the market economy. It was in those parts of the country where the control from the planned economy was weak that the market-oriented transactions mushroomed by circumventing the state planning. Gradually, as the scale of state planning kept shrinking, a dual pattern in which the planned economy was paralleled by the market economy came into being. In the rivalry between the two economic systems, both the institutional constructors and the institutional operators recognized the fact that, with the market economy offering lower transaction costs and improving economic efficiency, the system of market economy would ultimately prevail. The 14th National

Congress of the Communist Party of China (CPC), convened in 1992, officially charted the system of socialist market economy as the direction of China's reform. In 1993, the Third Plenary Session of the 14th CPC Central Committee carried out the first large-scale rational construction of the system of market economy, re-constructing the three major transaction entities comprising of the enterprises, the market, and the government and recalibrating the rules of transactions among the transaction entities. With China's accession to the WTO in 2001, another round of large-scale marginal adjustments in institutions was launched.

This institutional change produced a whole range of significant impacts. After over four decades of reform and opening-up, China reconstructed its economic institutions by abolishing the bindings with its social system in three aspects of the relations of production. The first is that regarding the allocation of resources, the binding between the planned economy and the social system was removed. It was specified that the reform of the economic system must proceed in the direction of constructing a system of socialist market economy. This meant that China's reform would not be oriented toward a dual model in which the planned economy and the market economic would co-exist or toward the pattern of the planned economy, but a unified, single, and complete system of market economy under the socialist system. The second is that with respect to the system of ownership, the binding between the public ownership and the social system was removed, and it was specified that China's fundamental economic system would assert the predominance of public ownership while promoting the development of various forms of ownership alongside the public ownership. The third is that in terms of distribution, the binding between the distribution of income and the social system was removed; the conventional principle of distribution on the basis of labor was combined with the principle of distribution on the basis of production factors, allowing and encouraging production factors such as labor, capital, technology, and management to partake of the distribution of wealth in accordance with the contributions that they make.

While unfettering the three "bindings," China restored the status of the market and of the private sector as legitimate transaction entities. In addition, as the public sector gradually got rid of the constraints imposed by the planned economy, enterprises started to acquire ever-expanding autonomy. The transactions between corporate organizations and the transactions between the enterprises and the market could be completed directly, obviating the need for planning on many different levels by the central planning department. The factors of production, which used to be deprived of the right to partake of wealth distribution, could now become part of the distribution process. Meanwhile, egalitarian distribution of income came to be replaced by differential distribution according to varying degrees of contributions. This incentive mechanism spurred various market entities to maximize the production of value within minimal time spans, thus creating inner driving forces for reducing transaction costs. The abolition of the three "bindings" made it possible to the society as a whole to drastically increase the total transaction scale and lower the average costs of transaction. With the proliferation of economic activities lower in transaction costs, there emerged pronounced increase in China's economic vibrancy, resulting in the release of substantial institutional advantages. It is no exaggeration to assert that the removal of these bindings precisely constitutes the "secret" behind China's rapid economic development since the reform and opening-up.

4

It is not always the case that China's reform can reduce transaction costs. This is because the birth of a new institution means that the state is beginning to institute controls and constraints in a particular area. According to the law of path dependence, a new institution will undergo continuous diminishing of efficiency and alienation, both of which will contribute to increased transaction costs in the operation of an institution. As a consequence, we will witness the phenomenon called the spreading of constraints.

In this book, two patterns of change are described regarding the spreading of constraints—the change "from a particular segment through an entire industry chain" and the change from "a particular segment across an entire sector." For example, in the coal-electricity industry chain and the real-estates industry chain, any mismatching between the demand and the supply would call for government interventions and this mismatching would, in return, be extended to the supply-and-demand segments in the upstream or the downstream of the industry chain. Under such circumstances, the government is once again obligated to impose interventions on the supply-and-demand segments in the upstream or the downstream. The range of intervention would expand from a single segment to an increasing number of segments until the entire industry chain is subjected to the constraints of administrative controls and regulations. This is what is called the spreading of constraints from one particular node in an industry chain throughout the entire chain. For another example, the mechanism of credit monitoring was a measure initially designed to help enforce legal verdicts by including individuals who refuse to liquidate the money long overdue in a list of defaulters and by restricting their luxury consumption and a certain degree of their personal freedom of mobility. After this mechanism was established, a number of government departments formulated their own methods of penalizing credit violations, placing the administrative counterparts, that is, the individuals upon whom administrative actions are to be enforced for breaching the rules and regulations formulated by those departments, in the list of dishonest defaulters. Several government departments may even work together to impose sanctions on the defaulters by restricting a series of their civil rights like traveling, engaging in business activities, and launching companies. As there lack specific and strict norms for defining dishonest behavior, the individuals to be subjected to penalties, and the means of penalty, the spreading of constraints has happened from particular segments in a business sector across the entire business community.

This diffusion of constraints in China has occurred in the transactions of rights between the government and the market, between the government and the state-owned enterprises, between the government and the private sector, and between different departments of the government themselves. For example, in regulating the market by means of government planning, industrial policy, government pricing, market accessing, administrative licensing, the negative list, anti-monopoly measures, combatting against unfair competition, and credit monitoring, the government may impose excessive rules on the market in order to achieve the same policy objective, thus resulting in the accumulation of transaction costs. The state-owned enterprise is a case in point. For such an enterprise, apart from fulfilling business objectives, the top management has to comply with the central government's rules regarding the decision-making on major issues, the appointment of important officials, the decision-making on major investment projects, and the use of large amounts of fund. In addition, a state-owned enterprise has to meet the objectives in a number of domains, such as controlling both the total amount and the intensity of energy consumption, carbon peaking and carbon neutrality, autonomous innovations, social responsibility, developing and expanding business overseas, addressing production overcapacity, and disposing of zombie companies which are no longer solvent. A state-owned enterprise has to comply with all these transaction rules. The time and expenditure consumed outside the efforts to meet business objectives constitute costs of transaction between the government and the enterprise which, in return, affect the government's ability, as shareholder of the state-owned enterprises, to benefit from the proceeds of the state-owned enterprises. The private sector has to pay extra transaction costs in responding to discriminatory transaction rules such as market access, the acquisition of production factors, and administrative licenses. Among different government departments, they have to fulfill separate task objectives allocated to them and to meet an ever-growing number of supervisions, inspections, and performance assessments from above.

Many studies tend to attribute the above-mentioned problems to the system of planned economy. Such an ascription is somewhat reasonable, but it is not sufficiently convincing. Usually, economic systems fall into one of the three categories—the system of planned economy, the system of market economy, and the dual system incorporating both the planned economy and the market economy. Such a loose classification can hardly explain most of the economic phenomena arising from institutional factors. Therefore, it is necessary to analyze each category of institution by anatomizing an institution in considerable details. Inspired by the idea of the "subtype" in medical science which subsumes many physiological symptoms, this book employs the concept of "institutional subtype" to conduct institutional analysis, classifying the transactions of rights involving similar transaction entities and rules into a subtype. In this way, we can divide, in a tentative manner, the system of planned economy into two subtypes—the directly-planned institution and the indirectly-planned institution. The system of market economy can be categorized into four subtypes—complete competition, monopoly, monopolistic competition, and oligopoly. The dual system can be divided into four subtypes—shadow planning, monopolistic planning, exogenous planning, and differential regulation. The market-oriented reform has served to generate institutional dividends, but the spreading of constraints tends to erode such institutional dividends by permeating throughout an industry chain and across a whole industrial sector. An analysis of the system of planned economy, the system of market economy, and the dual system, along with an analysis of their subtypes, indicates that some of the economic institutions in China have, to a large extent, remained located within the dual system and the system of planned economy. A single, unified, and complete system of market economy under the socialist system is yet to be established. To further deepen the reform, we must endeavor to improve the system of market economy on one hand and to prevent the spreading of constraints. To accomplish this mission of reform, it is essential to adhere to the principles of reasonability and necessity, the principle of proportionality, and the principle of minimum damages and reform should be pursued along the path of low transaction costs. This means that the principles of reasonability and necessity, as two prerequisites, must dictate the establishment of transaction rights and the formulation of transaction rules. Any attempt to formulate and modify transaction rights and transaction rules must ensure that the transaction costs paid by the transaction entities are commensurate with the returns that they can derive from the transaction. When presented with a number of reform alternatives, the reformer should opt for the alternative that will cause minimum damages to the transaction entities in terms of the time and expenditure of the transaction. In other words, the reform program to be chosen should be the one with the lowest possible transaction costs. Reform could be undertaken on the following three fronts: (1) the institutional reform that can serve general purposes, like the reform of fiscal and taxation system, the financial system, the investment system, and market supervision system; (2) the reform in a particular field or region; and (3) the reform of an entire industry chain along the upstream and the downstream, like the coal-electricity industry chain, petroleum and gas industry chain, and the real-estates industry chain.

5

To put transaction costs into proper perspective, this book chooses to perform in-depth analyses in those areas that tend to exert significant impact on economic development, namely, the investment, the land use for construction projects, energy, and the business environment.

Investment is one of the three locomotives driving economic growth. The infrastructure development that commenced with the period of planned economy and the investment in fixed assets since the reform and opening-up have consistently constituted the critical objects of the state macroeconomic regulation. An enterprise files an application for government approval of a particular investment project and the government issues the license. The time and the expenses that the enterprise pays in this process comprise the transaction cost. When this licensing system was first established, China was still under the planned economy. As the projects requiring licensing were not that large in number, the licenses could be issued fairly quickly to allow the projects to be activated in a short time and the transaction costs were fairly low. However, as the reform and opening-up continued, there appeared a parallel increase in the scale of investment and in the number of investment entities. As a consequence, by subjecting all investment projects to mandatory government licensing, a rule framed by the government would force the investment activities of the entire society to pay huge amounts of meaningless transaction cost, an institution that posed severe barriers to economic growth. In 2004, the State Council promulgated the decision to introduce reform into the investment licensing system, replacing the review and approval system with the registration system and the verification system that exempted all the construction projects financed by non-government capital from administrative approval and licensing, thus drastically reducing the transaction of rights across various categories of investment activities. But it was not long before the ratification of the investment projects once again became an exceedingly time-consuming process. After 2013, with the continuous streamlining of the ratification procedures regarding investment projects, the overall time spent on ratification was somehow reduced. Nevertheless, up till now, 42 categories of investment projects are still preserved, which necessitate government review and ratification. Under each category, there are a number of sub-categories and prerequisite matters that call for administrative ratification. The cumulative transaction costs under all those categories of administrative ratifications still remain formidable.

In investment activities, land is an indispensable production factor. In recent years, investors complain that the administrative approval of land use poses the most significant constraint on their investment impulses. In the initial stage of reform and opening-up, land requisition was fairly easy and straightforward: the company which wanted to use land only had to make due compensations to the land owner and the deal was closed once the government approval was obtained. This mode of land requisition was characterized by simple procedures, relatively cheap compensations, and low transaction costs. However, in the requisition of lands, a number of problem soon emerged—the acquired land was used extensively without careful planning, arable lands were appropriated arbitrarily, and the rights of the farmers who were deprived of their lands were not adequately protected. In view of these problems, the government subsequently implemented a number of measures aimed at strengthening the protection of arable lands and ensuring the economical and intensive use of lands. Undoubtedly, such measures were appropriate. However, the constraints posed on investment by the resultant high transaction costs were far from negligible. The transaction costs arising from the land used for construction have escalated along two paths. The first is the increasing number of transaction modules. For over two decades, a considerable number of systems have gradually been established, including the system of land requisition, the system of paid use of land, the system of land and spatial planning, the regulatory system of land use, and the system of annual land use planning.The second is the increase in the number of transaction rules within a given transaction module, as the rules become increasingly complicated and detailed in contents. For example, in order to ensure that the requisition of arable lands is balanced by the reclamation of new arable lands, a series of policies have been implemented, such as pre-requisition reclamation, the requisition-reclamation balance regarding the arable lands in a given local area, and the requisition of high-quality arable lands balanced by the reclamation of equally high-quality arable lands.

For another example, the annual plans of land use, divided into separate categories, are issued by the central government vertically down to various levels of the local government. In 1999, there were only three indicators for evaluating the land use and now there are four indicators. Each indicator is sub-divided into more indicators. At the very outset, the control indicators or indexes were issued by the central government. Later on, the provincial and local governments were authorized to set up control indexes on their own. As a consequence, the constraints imposed on the land supply by the mandatory plans have become all the more potent. Although government agencies in charge of land administration have taken measures in recent years to lower transaction costs, the situation of high transaction costs in the land supply for construction projects, caused by the excessively complicated land administration system, has remained unchanged.

Energy is the material foundation for the subsistence and development of humanity. Under the planned economy, energy was a product subjected to the most stringent state control and planning. The plans regarding coal, electricity, and petroleum and their transportation served as the benchmark for formulating other plans. Through four decades of reform and opening-up, China has succeeded in reaching the leading positions in the world in terms of both energy technology and energy production. Nevertheless, the gap between the supply and the demand of energy is still rather serious, as severe shortages of electricity, gas, and coal do happen from time to time. The shortages have evolved progressively from constraints on the supply side, through the tight balance between the supply and the demand, to the more recent dual constraints on both the supply side and the demand side. The primary energy sources originate from nature. For energy to be made accessible to the end user, it has to pass through the phases of primary product, intermediate product, and final product. The entire process involves a multiplicity of institutions, ranging from the system of the property rights of the energy resource, the concentration ratio of the industry, the government's administrative system of the industry, forms of ownership, the circulation system, the fiscal and taxation system, and the supervisory and regulatory system. All these systems are interwoven with the transactions of rights between the government and the enterprises, between the government and the energy market, and between different government agencies. The formidable transaction costs could impose constraints on both the supply and the demand of the energy. This book uses the coal-electricity industry chain to illustrate how administrative constraints spread from a particular segment through an entire industry chain. The constraints imposed on the whole oil-gas industry chain have never been fundamentally eradicated since the planned economy.

The business environment is of paramount importance to a specific region in attracting investments and bringing together professional talents. International organizations like the World Bank, the World Economic Forum (WEF), and International Institute for Management Development (IMD, located in Lausanne, Switzerland) conduct annual or regular assessments of the business environments in various economies. The evaluations focus primarily on the cost of time and the financial cost that an enterprise has to incur in order to comply with the policies, laws, and regulations in its efforts to launch a company, engage in business, conduct trade, pay taxes, execute contracts, and shut down the company. Most of the evaluation norms are related to the amount of time consumed in each of these activities. Many local governments in China, by using the indexes developed by the international organizations as a frame of reference, have substantially reduced the time consumed on the transactions of rights between the government and the enterprises. It is even likely that some regions, whose investment environments are most repugnant to prospective investors, may boast stunning indicators in their business environments. As a plethora of rights are being traded in the transactions between the government and the enterprises, the selection of a small number of indexes can far from presenting a panorama of a given business environment. For instance, the commercial system involves a number of transactions between the government and the enterprises throughout three phases of an enterprise's existence—foundation, continuation, and withdrawal. There are many sub-modules under each of the main transaction modules. In most regions in China, the time to register a newly-founded enterprise has been reduced to 4 working days, which testifies to one of the highest degrees of administrative efficiency in the entire world. However, a broader view of an enterprise's entire life cycle reveals that, in recent years, instead of a decrease, there has been an increase in the already overly-high transaction costs in a whole sequence of steps that an enterprise has to go through—disclosing annual reports, acquiring business licenses, and cancelling the enterprise. The reduced transaction cost that an enterprise benefits from shortened registration time has been counteracted or even dwarfed by the increased transaction costs in other aspects. This book chooses to analyze a number of areas, including the commercial system, electricity supply, construction licensing, sanctions against credit violation, and administrative penalty, with a view to unveiling how the analytical method involving the use of transaction modules can help illuminate the secrets behind time.

All of the institutions in the above-mentioned areas did yield important institutional dividends in the course of reform and opening-up, but they have experienced diminishing efficiency and institutional alienation in the process as well. Subsequently, the rules of transaction have been subjected to constant modification and adjustment, and under the condition of path dependence, there have been varying degrees of fluctuations in the transaction costs. Currently, transaction costs have been generally found to be exceedingly high. The problems are to be worked out either through institutional restructuring or through marginal adjustments. In evaluating potential reform programs, the essential point is to use the transaction cost as a critical norm so that the effort to reduce transaction costs will develop from a spontaneous act into a self-conscious act.

From the measurement of transaction costs to the characteristics and rules of institutional evolution, and from institutional dividends arising from low transaction costs to the erosion of institutional dividends arising from increased transaction costs, my studies of these issues have allowed me to develop some new insights concerning how reform can be best undertaken. In enforcing any reform measures, it is vital to exercise utmost prudence toward institutional innovation because an institution will remain irreversible once it is framed and established. If an institution is found to have gone astray, we have to pay heavy prices by starting all over again. When uncertainties abound, it is inadvisable to engage in any reform modeled on the trial-and-error mechanism. To the extent that a practice, in seeking to achieve a common objective, leads to the superimposition of rules for the market, the enterprise, and the government—because of the government's impulse toward the formulation of rules and regulations— and results in increased transaction costs, such a practice should be avoided. At present, it is particularly important to pay serious attention to the spreading of constraints from a particular segment through an entire industry chain and from a particular segment across an entire sector, as these constraints will wear away institutional dividends. In any reform program, it is the qualified entities that should be made responsible for institutional construction in order to reduce the impact produced by the institutional operators on institutional construction. In the case of multiple reform alternatives, priority should be given to the one with the lowest transaction costs.

China's reform has benefited substantially from the rational construction of the superstructure. Genuine insights into the laws underlying institutional evolution are the key to the success of any reform program. By focusing on an in-depth study of economic institutions, this book is ideally meant for target audiences ranging from government officials at various levels, economists, to researchers of reform. It is particularly meant for a limited number of key policymakers in the largest institutional provider—the state. The success of China's reform won't be possible without the painstaking efforts of everyone involved in developing sound economic institutions.

All these thoughts of mine constitute this very preface.

Beijing, China
December 2021

Bi Fan

Introduction: Questions About Institutions

Four decades have passed since China first initiated its reform and opening-up campaign. In this process, many scholars, both Chinese and international, have sought to give theoretical explanations about how the campaign has proven successful. A general consensus amidst conflicting interpretations is that China's institutional advantages are a decisive determinant of China's successful development. Politicians and economists across the world sometimes call China's success in reform the "China Model." Nevertheless, they unanimously raise the following questions:

How institutions determine development?
What institutional reforms in the China Model have proven successful?
Does any reform have to be undertaken cautiously (as in the words of Deng Xiaoping, "to wade across a deep stream by groping for supporting stones")?
Of the two paradigms of reform, gradual change and abrupt change, which is preferable?
How to conduct top-level designs regarding reform programs?
How to evaluate different alternatives of reform plans?
Are there any laws governing the evolution of institutions?
Can theories of institution in economics provide useful guidelines for reform?
Are the reforms that have taken place in China applicable to other countries?
......

The China Model is rich in contents, ranging from the mode of development, political institutions, economic institutions, the mode of governance, ideology, to cultural traditions.With regard to economic institutions themselves, the current institutions are wholly different from those at the preliminary stage of the reform and opening-up. Even the current institutions are far from perfect and there is much room for their reform and amelioration. Therefore, in future reforms, we face an important question—among the existing institutions, what institutions should be preserved and what institutions should be abolished? This is a question that we have to answer when we proffer this narrative about the economic institutions in the China Model.

When Deng Xiaoping proposed his idea that reform should be undertaken with considerable prudence in the same way that we "wade across a deep stream by groping for supporting stones," what he had in his mind was that reform was a trial-and-error process. At a time when, in many areas, there lacked theories to back up the reform, or when there were no precedents to follow, Deng Xiaoping's idea was indeed a sensible one. The act of daring to venture into unknown waters and to grope for supporting stones was itself an unmistakable indication of the courage for reform and the spirit of adventure. However, after four decades, China has managed to create economic institutions in virtually all the spheres of economic activities. Under such circumstances, if we still undertake our reform on the basis of trials and errors and expect to start all over again once a reform program is found to have gone astray, this would indicate that we have failed to develop a genuine understanding about the target model of reform or about the laws underlying institutional evolution. An analogy can be made between the construction of institutions and the construction of infrastructure projects. Guided by theories of civil engineering, a civil engineer can design equipment that can work under changing working conditions and erect buildings that fit into various natural environments. Is it possible, then, for institutional framers to make their institutional designs in a similar fashion?

Reform in the mode of gradual change and reform in the mode of radical and sudden change, they are also the issues that have been frequently mentioned in the discussions about China's reform. In particular, in view of the lessons derived from the shock therapy in the former Soviet Union, China has demonstrated obvious preference for reform in the mode of gradual change. The paradigm of "pilot programs preceding large-scale implementation" has come to constitute a standard model for multiple-phase reforms because of its evolutionary nature. In such cases, any discussion about radical reform would seem to be unnecessary and extraneous. However, not all the reform practices are taken in an evolutionary and gradual manner. The reform of the system of electricity supply, carried out in 2002, was an abrupt and drastic action without any prior experiments, designed to break up the monopoly of the former National Electrical Power Corporation. That reform was viewed as a reform in the mode of sudden and radical change, whose success has been widely acknowledged. However, subsequent market-oriented reforms of the system of electricity supply have turned out to be extremely difficult, despite repeated pilot programs on a trial basis. If we examine all the reforms conducted in various segmented areas, there seems to be no definitive conclusion about the relative superiority between reform in the mode of gradual change and reform in the mode of sudden and radical change.

In the period spanning from the beginning of reform and opening-up to the 1990s, there used to heated discussions concerning the target model of reform, but these discussions have dwindled in the past decade. As economic institutions become unprecedentedly complicated, the difficulty to exercise overall manipulation by the central government over any given reform has become enormous. On one hand, the entire society calls for the strengthening of the top-level design regarding any specific reform programs in order to strengthen the sound coordination in the reforms carried out in various fields. On the other hand, the level of specialization in any reform has significantly increased, and it is often the case that a single reform in a particular sphere would affect an entire sector. Thus, it has become exceedingly difficult to set a reform program in motion. A question often posed by both the reformers and researchers is whether it is possible to develop a theory or methodology to help improve the overall design of reforms.

Nevertheless, any systematic design, however ideal and perfect, requires the reformers to deliver specific solutions to the reform in a specific area. But the fact is that there will be more than one alternative for any given reform. Now, a question thus arises—what are the norms for determining the relative strengths of all the alternative plans? For some time, new institutional economics was regarded as the prioritized option for studying reform. Ronald H. Coase, Douglass C. North, and John Williamson have been awarded the Nobel prizes in economic sciences over the years, and their theories have become beacons from which many reform researchers hope to find potential solutions. Regrettably, however, their theories have not proved sufficiently useful either in providing guidelines to China's reform or in helping China summarize the experiences and contributions from all reforms that it has undertaken. In addition, their theories are hardly helpful to the institutional development of other developing countries or to the countries going through institutional transformation. An overview of the history of mankind's development reveals that the practice of reform, the theory of reform, and the achievements of development have hardly happened in a synchronized manner. Even up till this very day, the absence of studies concerning the laws governing institutional development has caused reformers to continue to pay costs and prices for their trials and errors when blueprinting future reforms. For economics, this is definitely a major regret.

A retrospective view of history can easily help us recognize that there have been countless great minds, both in the past and at present, who have conducted broad and in-depth investigations into institutional issues. However, treating economic institutions as an independent subject of research was an academic development only in the early 20th century. All the leading thinkers of institutional economics acknowledge that the state is the largest provider of institutions, but they have failed to perform sufficient studies regarding the state's very act of providing institutions and how related mechanisms evolve. It is no exaggeration to claim that the four-decade history of China's reform and opening-up can provide a rich variety of cases for study in economic institutions and that the studies of the underlying laws that have governed China's reforms can perhaps make up for the aforesaid regret inherent in institutional economics.

Contents

Chapter 1
Institutional Issues that Perplex Mainstream Economics

Over the past, economists have constructed a grand mansion of economic theories. Most economists, no matter whether they focus on the allocation of resources, or on economic development, or on social reproduction, have found it impossible to study economic issues without studying institutions. In most of the historical periods, an enduring topic of economic studies has been how to build economic institutions that can bring prosperity to a nation and its people. In this sense, a history of economic thoughts is a history of constructing economic institutions. In the following parts, a brief overview is offered concerning the thoughts on economic institutions as presented by different schools of mainstream economics.

1 Ancient Sages: Thinking and Practice of Economic Institutions

In the history of human civilization prior to the birth of economics as an academic discipline, economic thoughts were largely incorporated in philosophical and political thoughts. For example, the ancient China witnessed the co-existence of a number of schools of thought, such as the Confucian School, the Taoist School, the Mohist School, and the Legalist School. Ancient Greek philosophers and medieval scholastic philosophers also advanced many interesting economic ideas. A number of ancient sages and monarchs had already realized that the institutions and policies in a given state could exert enormous impact on the growth of wealth in that particular state. Differences in policies and institutions could often account for the waxing and waning of the strength of different states and may even underlie the regime changes.

Despite the fact that our ancient sages developed many economic thoughts, only a small number of such thoughts could actually be materialized in the form of economic institutions. In ancient China, the most distinguished figures were Zhou Gong (the Duke of Zhou) and Guan Zhong (723 B.C.–645 B.C.), who were among a limited

B. Fan, *The Rationale Behind Change*, https://doi.org/10.1007/978-981-97-8854-5_1

number of practitioners of state governance equipped with rational thinking and pragmatic spirits. When the Zhou Dynasty was first established, the Duke of Zhou, during his regency, formulated systematic rules for rites and court music, all codified in the book entitled *Imperial Rites of the Zhou Dynasty*. The economic ideas contained in this book became the springhead from which various economic institutions in China subsequently evolved. The economic institutions designed in the *Imperial Rites of the Zhou Dynasty* involved a variety of fields, including heavy emphasis on agriculture, commerce, craftsmanship, famine relief, and the land system called "*jingtianzhi*."[1] The fact that the Zhou Dynasty managed to survive for 800 years (about 1046 B.C.–256 B.C.) was totally inseparable from the good governance based on a sound economic system. For example, the *Imperial Rites of the Zhou Dynasty* created a specialized financial institution and set up a government accounting system, which formed the prototype of public finance.

The Western Zhou Dynasty lasted from approximately 1046 B.C. to 771 B.C. Toward the end of the dynasty, the unified state structure gradually disintegrated. By the Spring and Autumn Period, the authority of the supreme monarch Emperor Zhou declined while the strength of various vassal states substantially enhanced. The dramatic changes in the geopolitical landscape stimulated a general development of economic thinking. Ideas such as "moral principles versus material interest," "lightness (depreciation) versus heaviness (appreciation)," and "rejecting extravagance in favor of frugality" became full-fledged guidelines, shaping the economic policies and institutional building in various vassal states. Acting as the chancellor of the State of Qi, Guan Zhong reconstructed a prosperous state and built a strong military, asserting the supremacy of the monarch while suppressing the surrounding alien states which were viewed as barbarian. Within a short span of 7 years, the State of Qi became the dominant state among all the vassal states and Emperor Qi Huangong became topmost among the five hegemonic monarchs during the Spring and Autumn Period. Guan Zhong's economic thoughts are primarily found in the book entitled *Guan Zi*, which involves multiple facets of the economic administration of a state, including finance, currency, agriculture, industry, and commerce. Among many of his thoughts, the ideas of "the lightness (depreciation)" and "heaviness (appreciation)"[2] still enjoy international reputation in the present-day world. Guan Zhong

[1] This is the system of land tenure that predominated in China in the Zhou and earlier dynasties. This system represents nine parcels of agricultural land that are controlled by a noble. The eight parcels on the margin are separately farmed by eight families for their personal support. The center parcel was farmed by the eight families jointly and the produce was given to the nobles for his support.

[2] The idea is that when a certain product is in sufficient supply, it would become "light in weight," that is, its value would depreciate and its price would drop. By contrast, when a certain product is in short supply, it would become "heavy in weight," that is, its value would appreciate and its price would increase. The ideas of "lightness" and "heaviness" were actually early descriptions of the relationship between the supply and the demand. According to this principle, Guan Zhong proposed the theory of monetary quantity, arguing that "all goods will become cheap when the value of money appreciates and all goods will become expensive when the value of money depreciates." This theory can be interpreted as signifying an inverse relationship or a negative correlation between the quantity of money in circulation and its actual value.

applied his ideas about "the lightness" and "heaviness" as well as his idea about currency to the efforts of famine alleviation. The state could purchase huge amounts of grains in bumper years when the prices were relatively low and sell them when prices were to surge in times of crop failure so that the government could not only stabilize the prices but also increase the state's fiscal revenue. Guan Zhong inherited some of these ideas from the Duke of Zhou, but he proposed his own innovative ideas that constituted the very foundations for the government policies in subsequent ages on price stabilization and state-coordinated transportation. By adopting Guan Zhong's ideas of political and economic reform, Emperor Qi Huangong achieved immense success in state governance. Even after Guan Zhong's death, the State of Qi continued to implement Guan Zhong's ideas of reform and managed to maintain a high level of state power.

During the Warring Period, most of the vassal states implemented the policies of alleviating taxation and promoting agriculture and commerce, policies that were much akin to what came to be called mercantilism in Europe from the sixteenth century to the eighteenth century. The State of Qin granted the business tycoon Lv Buwei the position of chancellor and recognized a number of other business magnates. After unifying all the six warring states, the State of Qin switched to the policy of prioritizing agriculture and suppressing commerce. In the early period of the Western Han Dynasty, many regulatory policies imposed by the Qin Dynasty came to be abolished, replaced by the policies of "governance through non-governance" and "rehabilitation and recuperation," reflecting a liberalist and laissez-faire economic philosophy. After the reign of Emperor Wudi of the Han Dynasty, the relationship between the government and the market went through dramatic changes. The wars waged on alien states made the government expenditure soar and fierce debates erupted between the Confucian School, represented by scholars of high culture, and the Legalist School represented by Sang Hongyang. Emperor Wudi embraced the policy proposals by Sang Hongyang and initiated the system of government-monopolized sales of salt, iron, and liquor. With the introduction of the government-manipulated transportation of commodities and the state-run trade, the state could buy at lower prices and sell at higher prices to create a considerable profit margin that ultimately contributed to fiscal surplus. Since the age of Emperor Wudi, the emphasis on agriculture over commerce and on state intervention became the predominant notions informing the economic thinking and policies of successive dynasties in China. These concepts were closely geared to the needs of the centralized rule and facilitated the development of the agricultural civilization. Such economic ideas and policies produced significant impact on Europe, as most strikingly evidenced in the economic tenets and policies of physiocracy in France during the seventeenth and the eighteenth century. With the rise of the Industrial Revolution, these tenets and policies were quickly abandoned in the West.[3]

The economic thoughts in ancient Greece exerted direct influence on the classical economics that developed after the eighteenth century. From the late eighth

[3] Tang Qingzeng, *A History of Chinese Economic Thoughts*, The Commercial Press, 2010 Edition, pp. 436–441.

century B.C to the early seventh century B.C., Hesiod proposed the idea of scarcity. Of course, he did not believe that scarcity was related to limited resources or to people's insatiable desires. Rather, he maintained that scarcity was an evil released by Pandora when he opened the magic box. He was the first to propose the idea of utility efficiency. Xenophon, who lived between 430 B.C. and 355 B.C, wrote a book entitled *Oeconomicus*, a name that was derived from the word "economics" in the Greek language. As a term, it refers to the effective management by an individual producer on the level of family. Today's English word "economy" is evolved exactly from this Greek word. Xenophon, Plato (427 B.C.–347 B.C.), and Democritus (about 460 B.C.–370 B.C.) all realized the importance of specialization and the division of labor in economic activities.

A further belief maintained by Democritus is that the private ownership of property can be a driving force spurring more and more economic activities. As for Aristotle (384 B.C.–322 B.C.), he condemns the pursuit of economic interests on one hand and, on the other hand, acknowledges the right to private property. Another major contribution that Aristotle makes to economic thoughts is his idea about the role played by currency in the exchange of commodities. Many concepts as are employed by modern economics, such as scarcity, the division of labor, efficiency, commodity, currency, private property, and public property, can all be traced back to the age of ancient Greece. The economic thought during that historical period perfectly paralleled the historical circumstances of slavery that existed at that time and the preliminary development of commodity economy under natural economic conditions.

From the decline of the Roman Empire to the advent of mercantilism (around the fifteenth century), the medieval Western Europe went through a long period of feudalism. The feudal economy was the dominant form of economy and the manorial economy flourished and then declined. In accordance with the feudal rule, religion played a dominant role in social life. Many clergymen not only grew into great feudal lords but also monopolized intellectual thinking. The economic thoughts in the Middle Ages were primarily reflected in the scholastic philosophy. Its theories were derived not from practical experiences but from the Bible or the works of the clergymen. The representative figure of the scholastic philosophy was St. Thomas Aquinas (1225–1274), who was esteemed as the most eminent theological authority. His economic thoughts cover the system of ownership, price, currency, commerce, and interest. St. Thomas Aquinas was strongly in favor of private ownership and against public ownership. He proposed the idea of "just price" (*justum pretium*) and believed that minting money and determining its purchasing power were the prerogatives of the sovereign ruler. He was very negative about commodity, contending that it is shameless to derive profits from business. However, with the development of the production capabilities, the manorial economic system, characterized by subsistence farming and land ownership by landlords or nobility, experienced a progressive decline against the irreversible waves of commodity economy. The tenets in the scholastic philosophy became increasingly out of tune with the economic and social reality. The entire society faced the pressing need to be liberated from the political and economic authority exerted by the Church. The scholastic philosophy did try to adapt itself to the changing developments but, ultimately, its reigning ideas were passed into oblivion along with the collapse of the feudal system which it served.

2 The Age of Mercantilism: Raising Issues about Economic Institutions

The two and a half centuries from 1500 and 1750 was the age of British mercantilism. Mercantilism is a term susceptible to different interpretations. Sometimes, it is taken to mean the mercantilist ideas or thoughts; at other times, it is taken to mean mercantilist policies. These interpretations tend to intermingle and become confused.[4] A close examination of this historical period reveals that part of the mercantilist ideas were transformed into mercantilist policies. The application of these policies, in return, contributed to the further development of mercantilist ideas. The close interactivity between mercantilist ideas and policies made it possible for Britain to develop an architecture of institutions that was geared to the needs of capitalism and the market economy. By facilitating the industrial revolution and economic development, mercantilism enabled Britain to significantly outcompete other Western powers. In the history of economics, mercantilism is generally defined as the doctrine that only hard currency like gold and silver is the real form of wealth and the purpose of engaging in any economic activities and of implementing economic policies is to acquire the hard currency of gold and silver. Trade surplus is the source of wealth, thus a country must endeavor to make its export outweigh the import in international trade. The state should impose active interventions on the economic life of its citizens by using legislative and administrative measures to encourage export and restrict import. More specifically, exorbitant tariff duties can be imposed to limit import whereas tax reimbursement or even subsidies can be introduced to stimulate the export of industrial products.[5] Both physiocracy and mercantilist policy have been labeled as government interventions and have often been viewed as typical doctrines of state control or trade protectionism. They become the objects of vehement criticism by liberalist economic theories that developed later.

But the real situation was far more complicated than the neat categorization in the textbooks of the history of economic theories. In his *The Wealth of Nations*, Adam Smith (1723–1790) devoted one fourth of the book to a pioneering analysis of mercantilism.[6] He regarded mercantilism as a holistic system so that it proved

[4] Li Xinkuan, *The State and the Market: A Historical Interpretation of the Age of British Mercantilism*, Central Compilation & Translation Press, 2013 Edition, p.6.

[5] Harry Landreth and David C. Colander, *History of Economic Thought*, trans. Zhou Wen, Posts and Telecom Press, 2014 Edition, pp. 48–59; Yin Bocheng, *A History of Western Economics: Observations from the Perspective of Market Economy*, Fudan University Press, 2005 Edition, pp.7–10.

[6] Adam Smith, *An Inquiry into the Nature and Causes of the Wealth of Nations*, trans. Guo Dali and Wang Yanan, The Commercial Press, 1974 Edition.

fairly convenient for him to criticize the economic thoughts during that period.[7] If we examine both the economic thoughts and the history of economic development from the sixteenth century to the mid-eighth century, we will discover that mercantilism did not remain static and unchanging. The mercantilist ideas and mercantilist policies had always been informed by controversies and rivalry between government intervention and liberal economy. The complexities of these contentions were almost beyond description.[8] In the age of mercantilism, British businessmen, capitalists, and aristocrats were fully aware of the importance of institutional building in securing their interests. Commercial capitalists (as distinguished from industrial capitalists) actively sought government protection, relying on the King's authority to protect their economic interests and to grant them chartered rights and royal commissions to reap monopolistic profits. On his part, the King also sought the support of the business community in order to expand the imperial authority and acquire wealth from overseas markets. Various stakeholders either used ideas to influence policies or used policies to seek material interests. As described by Joseph Alois Schumpeter (1883–1950), the parliament and the government held investigatory meetings, encouraging and training people to debate on a whole range of economic issues. The general public gave testimonies before various royal committees, delivered speeches, handed in petitions, and issued pamphlets concerning issues like land enclosure, industries, companies, market system, monopoly, taxation, currency, tariff, poverty relief, wages, and industrial management, etc.[9]

Schumpeter believes that all the issues discussed by mercantilists were issues faced by an emerging nation state. These issues were mostly practical issues directly related to economic policies and the general public presented their arguments primarily by relying on the power of common sense, thus making "a large amount of mercantilist literature pre-analytical in nature; additionally, such literature is crude—the work by nonprofessionals or even by uneducated individuals, who generally lack the skill to elucidate basic principles."[10] After presenting their arguments, they would hasten to make specific recommendations. For example, they would try to identify the most promising industries and recommend government support. They argued that, as far as Britain was concerned, special government support should be made accessible to fishery, metallurgical industry, linen fabric industry, improvement of waterways, or the exploitation of royal lands. Many of their works were merely fraught with development plans.[11]

---

[7] Fernand Braudel, *Civilisation materielle, economie et capitalisme, XVe-XVIIIe siecle*: Tome 2, trans. Gu Liang, SDX Joint Publishing Company, 1993 Edition, pp.599–600.

[8] Joseph Alois Schumpeter, *Economic Doctrine and Method: An Historical Sketch*, trans. Wu Huanggang, The Commercial Press, 2018 Edition, pp.80–82.

[9] Joseph Alois Schumpeter, *History of Economic Analysis*, Vol. 1, trans. Zhu Yang, The Commercial Press, 2001 Edition, p.260.

[10] Joseph Alois Schumpeter, *History of Economic Analysis*, Vol. 1, trans. Zhu Yang, The Commercial Press, 2001 Edition, p.531.

[11] Joseph Alois Schumpeter, *History of Economic Analysis*, Vol. 1, trans. Zhu Yang, The Commercial Press, 2001 Edition, pp. 536–537.

Many of the current policy studies in China share much in common with the British mercantilist policy debates three centuries ago. The research reports presented by many Chinese scholars tend to make policy recommendations immediately after mere description of a problem. Worse still, each report tends to be rather short. Admittedly, short reports can considerably save the time spent by the top policy makers on reading these reports, but studies of this kind tend to lack systematic theoretical reflections or detailed analysis of institutional mechanisms. The policy proposals are largely based on simple intuitive perceptions. Truly in-depth and insightful analysis capable of withstanding rigorous scrutiny needs to take into account comprehensive factors including price, wages, profit, currency, exchange rate, etc., instead of focusing simply on one isolated aspect. In Britain, many mercantilist ideas were adopted by the parliament and the government, and were then developed into mercantilist policies. These policies produced both positive and negative effects on British economy in different periods of time and were amended and adjusted from time to time. In terms of their positive outcomes, these policies served to expand the space of market operation with the strong support of the state and facilitated Britain's commercial prosperity, wealth accumulation, and economic growth. With regard to their negative effects, these mercantilist policies led to state controls that, in the face of growing scale of market economy, constrained and impeded the development of the market economy. In return, the market forces exerted manifold impacts on the functions of the state. For instance, the market forces were opposed to the King's granting of chartered or monopolistic rights, thus undermining the government's intervention in economy. As a consequence, the boundary between the state and the market economy gradually became well-defined.

In Britain, mercantilism evolved through approximately three stages, switching from the government-dominated mercantilism to the mercantilism dominated by the free market. The first stage was represented by the age of Tudor monarchy. The state intervention was both large-scaled and wide-ranged. Government intervention could be found across many fields, ranging from domestic industrial development and overseas trade to even daily life. The second stage spanned the period from the House of Stuart to the Glorious Revolution, during which antagonisms against state control and government intervention kept escalating. Government intervention and the monopolistic rights enjoyed by chartered companies all came under vehement attacks. Amidst these attacks, there emerged the mercantilist doctrine of free trade, insisting on the need to allow market mechanisms to play their independent role. The third stage covered the period from the Glorious Revolution to the mid-eighteenth century, during which Britain primarily resorted to tariffs and other intermediate measures to regulate the economy. As the state control over the general public's daily life gradually dwindled, a society where the market dominated the allocation of resources and regulated the economy came into existence.[12] Thus, the early mercantilist doctrines came to be challenged and subverted as mercantilism came to its final stage.

[12] Li Xinkuan, *The State and the Market: A Historical Interpretation of the Age of British Mercantilism*, Central Compilation & Translation Press, 2013 Edition, p.9.

3 Classical Economics: Building the Framework of Economic Institutions

The period of classical economics lasted from the mid-seventeenth century to the 1870's. Classical economics consists of economic theories developed in the context of the accelerated progress of the Industrial Revolution, based on economists' serious reflections on mercantilist and physiocratic doctrines and policies. Regarding the relationship between the government and the market, classical economics always insisted on the principle of economic freedom. Under the influence of this theory, many European countries and the U.S. kept adjusting and standardizing the role played by the government and developed a preliminary architecture of modern economic institutions. Classical economics produced its impact first on Britain, spurring it to become the first country to achieve the transition from the system of mercantilism to the system of free trade. This, in return, influenced Holland, Portugal, and countries in America which transformed toward free economy.

Classical economics furnished a crucial theoretic foundation for the Western countries to develop a political system characterized by "small government and big society." The age of classical economics began with the publication of Adam Smith's *The Wealth of Nations* in 1776 and its conceptual framework comprises of such economic notions as the division of labor, exchange, money, value, wages, profit, land rent, capital, etc. The idea of economic freedom remains at the center of Adam Smith's economic thinking. His conviction is that the growth in the wealth of nations depends on free institutions, a free order, and a government which protects such freedoms. To be more specific, he is opposed to feudalism, mercantilism, and the government's interventions into economic life and is a staunch advocate of free trade. He points out that, if a politician attempts to instruct individuals on how to use their capital, such an act would not only mean courting trouble insensibly but also, almost without any exception, prove futile or even detrimental.[13] Under economic freedom, the government has only a limited number of functions to perform, like the national defense, judicial and executive responsibilities, and the development of public projects and public utilities. In other words, the government's role is that of a "night watcher." Apart from that, he proposes a theory concerning fiscal revenue and expenditure that would fit a "small government." Classical economics kept developing in the works of David Ricardo (1772–1823), Thomas Robert Malthus (1766–1834), Jean-Baptiste Say (1767–1832), among others, and came to an end in the works of John Stuart Mill (1806–1873).

In the age of classical economics, economists focused their studies on the economic issues arising from the Industrial Revolution. By mid-eighteenth century, Britain had replaced Spain, Portugal, and Holland to become the world's largest colonial empire. However, Britain still implemented mercantilist policies, such as prohibiting the import of grains, imposing regional trade barriers, and preserving

---

[13] Adam Smith, *An Inquiry into the Nature and Causes of the Wealth of Nations,* Vol. 2, trans. Guo Dali and Wang Yanan, The Commercial Press, 1974 Edition, p. 31.

tariffs on foreign trade. Those measures constrained the development of the industrial capital and aggravated the discontent on the part of the industrial and commercial capital. While offering a systematic criticism of mercantilist policies in *The Wealth of Nations*, Adam Smith elaborated on the lucrativeness of free trade to both the buyer and the seller of a transaction. He insisted that the *Apprenticeship Act* should be abolished to allow for the free flow of laborers. He demanded that the government stop intervening into domestic trade and remove restrictions on overseas trade. Furthermore, he advocated the abolition of the *Corn Laws*, removal of the protection of tariffs, and extermination of the guild system and the monopolistic system in its various forms.[14] David Ricardo developed the idea of free trade and proposed the theory of comparative advantages. He contended that, under free trade, importing cheap corns and grains could help lower wages and enhance the profitability of the industrial and commercial sectors. Therefore, he called on Britain to expand foreign trade and eliminate laws like the *Corn Laws* that might impose constraints on free trade.

Classical economists resorted to their extensive political activities to exert influence on the government's policy making, translate their research findings into social practices, and facilitate changes in Britain's economic institutions. Adam Smith maintained close associations with prominent political figures like Henry Dundas, Carlisle, William Eden, and Sinclair[15] so that he could pitch to them his ideas of free trade. David Ricardo and John Stuart Mill were both members of the British parliament. Moreover, David Ricardo was a member of the Malthus Political Economy Club and the King's Club. The extensive social activities by classical economists made it possible for their ideas of free trade to produce vital impact on Britain's economic institutions. In his 1777 speech on budget, Prime Minister Frederick North acknowledged that *The Wealth of Nations* provided the theoretical basis for the newly-added tax collection projects.[16] Based on the ideas of free trade, the Irish parliament passed a resolution in 1779 aimed at liberating the Irish trade.[17] The Manchester

[14] Wang Zhanghui, *A History of British Economy*, China Social Sciences Press, 2013 Edition, pp. 264–265.

[15] Henry Dundas was appointed lord advocate in 1775 and was the main manipulator of the right to protect Scotland. In his letter to Adam Smith on Oct. 30, 1779, he expressed his approval to relax the restrictions on Irish trade. Carlisle was appointed chairman of the British Trade Commission in 1779 and in the next year was appointed the Irish Governor. In 1780, Eden was appointed secretary to the Governor. In his *Four Letters to the Earl of Carlisle* (1779), he explicitly adopted Adam Smith's idea regarding Ireland's freedom of trade.

[16] Ian Ross, *The Life of Adam Smith*, trans. Zhang Yaping, Zhejiang University Press, 2013 Edition, p. 483.

[17] Since 1698, Ireland was subjected to the most harsh trade restrictions by the Kingdom of Britain, over which the Irish people expressed their profound indignations. When Adam Smith's *The Wealth of Nations* was published, the idea that Smith expressed in the book, of giving Ireland the freedom of trade, won unanimous acclaim in Ireland. In a pamphlet he published, John Healy Hutchison, a member of the Irish National Parliament, gave a detailed account of the idea of free trade as expounded on in *The Wealth of Nations*. In addition, Hutchison expressed his full acceptance of the idea throughout his writings. Adam Smith's ideas were the direct driving force behind the Irish

School launched nationwide campaigns against the *Corn Laws*. By publishing newspapers, holding mass rallies, participating in political votes, running for members of the parliament, and exerting pressures on MPs, the Manchester School forced the Robert Peel administration to abolish the *Corn Laws* in 1846.[18] Within several years after the abolition of the *Corn Laws*, Britain enacted a series of laws eliminating tariffs imposed on various commodities. In 1849, the *Navigation Acts* was repealed and in 1852 the parliament issued a statement, proclaiming that the principle of free trade would be Britain's national policy. Thus, Britain became the first influential world power to implement, unilaterally, the free trade system. In the nineteenth century, Britain entered the golden age of free trade. By exploiting the institutional advantages, Britain became an empire on which the sun never set, whose economic aggregate accounted for 70% of the world economy. Britain's free trade policy exerted immense impact on the European continent and on countries in America. Holland, Portugal, and other countries soon followed suit and became countries of free trade.

4 Neoclassical Economics: Avoiding the Study of Economic Institutions

Since the beginning of mercantilism, economists tended to maintain close relations with those who governed the state and their doctrines exerted profound impacts on the state governance. They played an indispensible role in improving the governance of the country and enlightening the general public. The idea of economic freedom as propounded on by classical economics not only dominated the economics community for a long time but also evolved into a mainstream value that many countries adhered to in building their economic institutions and promoting the evolution of these institutions. However, things began to change with the advent of the neoclassical economics. In the studies performed by neoclassical economists, the focus began to shift toward uncovering the internal laws governing the operation of market economy under the system of free economy. Neoclassical economists emphasized the extensive use of quantitative tools over in-depth analysis of economic institutions. The attempt to turn economics into a scientific discipline came to replace economics' conventional mission of contributing to state governance and enlightening the general public.

Generally speaking, neoclassical economics commenced in the 1870's and ended in the 1930's.[19] Neoclassical economics focused on marginalism, rational expectations, and the strong policy assumption of market efficacy. Key figures of

---

National Parliament's passage of the resolution in 1779 that demanded the emancipation of the Irish trade.

[18] Wang Zhanghui, *A History of British Economy*, China Social Sciences Press, 2013 Edition, pp. 260–261.

[19] In the early 1870's, William Stanley Jevons, Carl Menger, and Léon Walras started to apply marginal analysis in their economic theories and they are generally regarded as marking the beginning of the neoclassical economics. By 1930's, Alfred Marshall's economic ideas started to decline. This entire period is usually seen as the age of neoclassical economics.

neoclassical economics included William Stanley Jevons (1835–1882), Carl Menger (1840–1921), Léon Walras (1834–1910), and Alfred Marshall (1842–1924).

Alfred Marshall formulated his neoclassical economic theories by inheriting and developing classical economics. Neoclassical economics synthesized the supply analysis in the classical economics and the demands analysis in the Marginal Utility School. By applying the method of mathematical analysis and developing a certain number of theoretical models, neoclassical economics achieved huge success technically. However, contrary to the ideals of contributing to the state governance and enlightening the general public pursued by mainstream schools of economics in the age of classical economics, leading neoclassical economists like Carl Menger and Alfred Marshall made extensive use of quantitative tools. As a result, economists virtually became mathematicians and economics seemed to have become a mathematical science. However, the abstract formulae and equations developed by neoclassical economics turned out to be rather weak in explaining the economic reality, unable to provide sufficiently useful guidance to actual economic operations. In particular, the university-based neoclassical economists spent huge amounts of their time and energy developing mathematical models, few of which could deliver valuable insights into microeconomic operations or into macroeconomic policy-making by the government.

As a leading figure of neoclassical economics, Alfred Marshall studied a number of issues in his *Principles of Economics*, such as desire and gratification, factors of production (such as land, labor, and capital) and their organization, the general relationship between the demand, the supply, and the mean value, the distribution of national income (salary, interest, and land rent), etc. However, he did not offer any analysis specifically focused on the relationship between the government and the market or on economic institutions. As he said himself, the work of economics is to collect, codify, and interpret facts and to derive conclusions from these facts. The purpose of economic research is to seek knowledge for the sake of knowledge. The reasoning in various aspects of economics is more accurate now than before, and this change marks the transition of the research methods of economics from the elementary stage to the advanced stage.[20] Marshall believed that economics should avoid discussing many political issues because it is a pure and pragmatic science; therefore, the term "economics" is more precise in meaning than the term "political economy."

In the age of mercantilism and the age of classical economics, institutions and policies were important subjects for economic studies. As economics acquired an increasingly scientific attribute, more and more mathematical tools were introduced into this science. In this process, the mainstream economics came to discover that it would be more and more difficult to use mathematical models to simulate economic institutions. When institutions were abstracted, it was indeed fairly easy to study many economic phenomena by applying mathematical tools. Therefore, economists assumed that economic institutions were constant. Of course, the institutions involved

[20] Alfred Marshall, *Principles of Economics*, trans. Zhu Zhitai and Chen Liangbi, The Commercial Press, 2019 Edition, p.17.

in this assumption were the institutions of free market economy. During the period of neoclassical economics, capitalist countries in the West achieved rapid economic growth under the system of free market economy. It was all the more natural that neoclassical economists taciturnly accepted the free market economy as their institutional assumption. However, starting from the neoclassical economics, it has virtually become a tradition for the mainstream Western economics to ignore the study of economic institutions and to assume institutions as constants. The impact of such a tendency was as extensive as it was negative.

5 Beyond the Keynesian Revolution: Back to Issues of Economic Institutions

Neoclassical economics was found totally nonplussed in the face of the Great Depression that descended on the Western capitalist countries in the 1930's. This dilemma gave rise to the Keynesian Revolution. John Maynard Keynes (1883–1946) contended that unemployment was due to the insufficiency of effective demands and effective demands consisted of both investment demands and consumption demands. He further argued that, in the case of severe unemployment, the pricing mechanism alone could not regulate the economy to yield sufficient employment, thus the state intervention in economy was required. He advocated that the central government should focus on implementing fiscal policies and should consciously seek to positively influence effective demands and overall employment by increasing fiscal revenue and expenditure. Monetary policy could be used by the central bank to consciously alter the quantity of supply and the interest rate, thus stimulating economic activities. Keynes insisted that an important means to implement fiscal policy was the debt-fueled spending and inflation. It was the Keynesian economics that delivered the Western countries out of the crisis of the Great Depression. They built a whole architecture of institutions whereby the government could intervene in economy, as evidenced most typically in the United States and Britain. For instance, in 1932, the British government announced the renunciation of free trade, the imposition of import tax, the creation of Imperial Preference (which became Commonwealth Preference after World War Two), and the protection of the domestic market. In 1945, Britain's Labor Party proposed the idea of the welfare state and the British government immediately issued economic policies featuring full employment, welfare state, and mixed economy, all based on large-scale government intervention as an important means. In 1948, the Labor Party announced the success of building a "welfare state." In the United States, President Franklin Roosevelt implemented the New Deal, developing a whole set of institutions that allowed the government to intervene in economy, featuring such important measures as fiscal policy (expanding public expenditure), monetary policy (relinquishing the gold standard and allowing money depreciation), industrial policy (regulating industrial and agricultural production), and social policy (creating unemployment and social security system). In addition, counter-cyclical adjustments were introduced. All these measures helped the United States gradually recover from the Great Depression.

When many Chinese scholars saw how Keynesianism came to be implemented in the Western capitalist countries under market economic conditions, they concluded, in a rather simplistic manner, that government intervention can be equated with the method of government planning. They argue that Keynesianism represents a perfect example of how the method of planning attained success in the Western countries. This success can serve as a strong proof that China can also implement the planning-based governance under the socialist market economic conditions. However, the precondition of this doctrine is itself unjustified. The government intervention and the welfare government under Keynesianism were essentially different from the so-called planned economy because they represent two diametrically opposite modes of allocating resources. The so-called planned economy is an approach in which the government exercises its executive power to achieve the allocation of resources. Thus, the planned economy can also be termed "the economy of executive orders." The government intervention as discussed in Keynesianism is based on the institutions of free market formulated by the neoclassical economics and the allocation of resources is dominated by the market itself rather than by the government. The government intervenes only in those domains where the market malfunctions. In other words, the government is never directly involved in the allocation of resources. Under the planned economy, the allocation of resources is specified by the government to such an extent that it covers every single industry, every single sector, and every single product. Under Keynesianism, the macroeconomic regulation sought to manipulate the total volume of supply and demand by means of fiscal policy and monetary policy. Such a manipulation was never targeted at specific microeconomic activities.

After John Maynard Keynes, Paul A. Samuelson (1915–2009) emerged as a representative of the neo-Keynesian economics. Neo-Keynesian economists insisted on the state intervention as a fundamental means of economic regulation, arguing that expansionary policies could be used to stimulate economy in times of depression whereas austerity measures could be instituted to restrain economy in times of economic boom. These two modes of policies could reduce fluctuations in the process of economic growth. Keynesianism laid special emphasis on fiscal policy whereas neo-Keynesian economics laid equal emphasis on both fiscal policy and monetary policy to maintain necessary magnitude of economic stimulation.

Keynesianism delivered capitalism out of the crisis. While putting Keynesianism into practice, some Western countries came under the influence of the Soviet Union's planned economy and adopted a number of measures to directly intervene into economic activities. These interventions resulted in larger government size, rigidity in institutional operation, and increased fiscal deficit. It was not long before the negative consequences arising from excessive state intervention surfaced. During 1970's and 1980's, the Western world was generally trapped in a "stagflation" crisis in which economy stagnated, coupled with inflation and serious unemployment. Other maladies included exorbitant welfare expenditure, rising taxation, and frequent energy and financial crises. In the wake of these crises, a wave of neo-liberalist economic schools emerged in the West that remained antagonistic to government intervention. They included the Neo-Austrian School, the Freiburg School, the Chicago School, the Monetarism, the Supply-side Economics, and the Rational Expectation School. All those schools of thought were united in their opposition to the direct state intervention in the production and business operation of individual enterprises. They were equally opposed to government pricing. They all insisted that the state intervention was justified only to the extent that such intervention could ensure competition and restrict monopoly. Soon, all those contentions produced their due impact on government policies in Europe and the United States.

Both Ronald Reagan and Mrs. Thatcher accepted the propositions championed by the supply-side economists and they launched their own supply-side revolutions. During the Reagan administration, a number of policies were implemented, including tax abatement, reduction of government expenditure, control of currency circulation, and the lessening of government regulation and control. The United States achieved sustained growth for 65 months in succession (from December 1982 to May 1988), with the inflation rate decreasing from 13.5% down to 5%.[21] On the other side of the Atlantic Ocean, Mrs. Thatcher became the British prime minister in 1979 and started to implement policies recommended by the Supply-side Economics and Modern Monetarism. Some of these policies featured the privatization of state-owned enterprises, control over currency issuance, reduction of welfare expenditure, and suppression of labor unions. As these liberal economic policies produced their due impact, Britain succeeded in addressing the "British disease" and came to accomplish what is often called the "Thatcher Miracle."

For Keynesianism and the subsequent mainstream economic schools, the relationship between the government and the market once again became the focus of their studies. Since 1970's, there have been many important changes and adjustments in the economic institutions in Western countries in response to changing circumstances. After the collapse of the former Soviet Union and the drastic changes in East Europe, China and a number of developing countries were embarked on the path of market economy and have achieved rapid economic growth. How to build the architecture of effective institutions conducive to economic growth has once again become a subject of study that has captured significant scholar attention. Of course, most of these studies are still focused on the formation and evolution of specific institutions rather than on the general laws governing the operation of institutions.

[21] Data source: the U.S. Bureau of Economic Analysis.

Chapter 2
Existing Studies on Institutions: The Pros and Cons

Since the age of mercantilism, the studies performed by most schools of economics have involved the issues of economic institution in varying degrees. As neoclassical economics excluded institution from their framework of theoretical assumptions, a critical flaw has been created in their economic studies.[1] It was the Institutional School, Neo-institutional Economic School, and New Institutional Economic School that really started to treat the subject of institution, that is, the formation of institutions and the laws governing institutional evolution, as their proper object of research. These schools are opposed to treating institutional factors as externalities in the analysis of economic activities, insisting that the operation of capitalism must be studied from the perspective of institution or structure. Such a study might even change the way capitalism operates. Among these three different schools of thought, the Institutional School and the Neo-institutional Economic School laid special emphasis on uncovering the laws underlying the operation of institutions. On the other hand, the New Institutional Economic School proposed the innovative idea of using transaction cost as a yardstick for measuring institutional costs. However, it is a regret that New Institutional Economics itself has failed to make any progress in measuring transaction costs, a fact which has in return hampered the practical application of New Institutional Economics.

1 Enlightenment from the Studies on Economic Institutions

Before the advent of the institutional economics, some economists had already focused their studies on institutional issues and had undertaken systematic investigations. Among these studies, the research performed by Karl Marx on economic institutions is most in-depth and exhaustive, developing a significant system of intellectual

[1] Wolfgang Kasper, Manfred E. Streit, *Institutional Economics: Social Order and Public Policy*, trans. Han Zhaohua, The Commercial Press, 2000 Edition, pp.5–6.

B. Fan, *The Rationale Behind Change*, https://doi.org/10.1007/978-981-97-8854-5_2

thoughts. Apart from the studies by Karl Marx, there were the studies conducted by the School of German History and the Austrian School. Although their research on economic institutions was not labeled as institutional economics in the history of economics, their theories and methodologies produced considerable impact on the studies of economic institutions in the subsequent generations. The following paragraphs will offer a synoptic account of the aforementioned theories according to their chronological order.

The first is the School of German History, which proposed the theory of national economics that reflected national and historical characteristics. This school had its inception in Germany during the 1840's and, by denying the existence of general laws underlying economic and social development, this school maintained that economics could be best studied by means of historical induction. The representative figures of this school included Friedrich List (1789–1846), William Roscher (1817–1894), and Gustav von Schmoller (1838–1917). The School of German History believed that classical economics was a cosmopolitan economics whose presumptions consisted of a world coalition and an enduring peace. However, these assumptions were actually invalid because the real world is divided into individual states and these diverse countries or nations differ from one another in terms of their history and conditions of economic development. All the economic policies are formulated within the physical boundaries of these countries. Therefore, the state plays a special role in economic development. Friedrich List argued that the backward countries must, first and foremost, build up their national strength and only then would they be equipped to engage in free competitions with advanced countries. Germany should implement economic policies that would remove tariffs among different regions and encourage free trade. Internationally, tariffs should be imposed to protect the development of Germany's fledgling national industry so that Germany could expect to catch up with the advanced and economically developed countries.[2] Gustav von Schmoller, on the other hand, proposed the idea of state supremacy, arguing that it would be difficult to imagine a highly developed national economy without a state authority equipped with full economic functions.[3] Those propositions raised by the School of German History were diametrically opposed to economic freedom insisted on by classical economics and they dominated Germany on a long-term basis as mainstream economic ideas. After World War I, Hitler came into power amidst economic depression and built a new economic system different from both the capitalism of Western countries and the socialism of the Soviet Union. This new system was a mixture of economic autonomy and comprehensive national manipulation.[4]

The second is Karl Marx, who generalized about the laws governing the evolution of the social system. In his theory of political economy, Marx constructed a grand

---

[2] Friedrich Liszt, *The National System of Political Economy*, trans. Chen Wanxu, The Commercial Press, 1983 Edition, pp.5–13.

[3] Ji Taoda, *Selected Readings in the Vulgar Capitalist Political Economy*, The Commercial Press, 1963 Edition, pp.344–345.

[4] Karl Hardach, *The Political Economy of Germany in the Twentieth Century*, trans. Yang Xu, The Commercial Press, 1984 Edition, pp.8–9.

conceptual framework with which he performed exceedingly profound studies of various social systems. According to Douglass C. North (1920–2015), Marx's analytical framework is the most convincing among all the theories aimed at describing the long-term institutional changes because the framework included all the factors that were absent from the neoclassical analytical framework, such as institution, property rights, state, and ideology.[5] Marx studied the laws underlying the changes of social system from the perspective of human history. He believed that, whatever the social system that is established in a given country, that system would not face demise before all the productive forces accommodated in a society are fully released. On the other hand, the more advanced form of production relations would never emerge before the conditions for its existence become ripe in the embryo of the existing social system.[6] To put it in another way, all institutions would change and a new institution would develop when the existing institution can no longer accommodate its own productive forces. It is generally believed by both Chinese and international scholars who study the history of economic theories that the planned economy of the Soviet Union was both a legacy and a practical example of the Marxist ideas of political economy. However, such a viewpoint can hardly be supported by evidence. On one hand, the works of Karl Marx and Friedrich Engels do not contain systemic theorizing concerning the relationship between the government and the market. On the other hand, neither of them proposed the idea that a socialist country must implement the planned economy. Therefore, it is extremely difficult to derive any definitive conclusion from the Marxist political economy that socialist countries must implement the planned economy.

The third is the Austrian School which advocated economic liberalism. The representative theorists of the Austrian School included Eugen von Bohm-Bawerk (1851–1914), Ludwig Heinrich Edler von Mises (1881–1973), and Friedrich August von Hayek (1899–1992). Returning to Adam Smith's theory about the inefficacy and low efficiency of the government intervention in economy, the Austrian School analyzed the reasons why the institution of free competition was more efficient than other forms of institution. With regard to the socialist system of the Soviet Union, the Austrian School believed that the central planning authority, in order to allocate limited resources reasonably to countless competing goals, would try to seek immediate solutions to a simultaneous equations matrix consisting of tens and thousands of equations. The real difficulty does not lie in the formal structure of these equations but in the overwhelmingly colossal information, statistics, and workload required for obtaining the solutions. As a matter of fact, the central planning authority could not acquire all the necessary information and statistics for working out the simultaneous equations matrix, nor could it manage to formulate decisions and policies efficiently. Therefore, the allocation of resources would be characterized by unreasonable wastes, making the economic efficiency of the planned economy lower than

[5] Douglass North, *Structure and Change in Economic History*, trans. Chen Yu and Luo Huaping, SDX Joint Publishing Company, 1994 Edition, p.68.

[6] Karl Marx, *Critique of Political Economy*, trans. Xu Jian, People's Publishing House, 1955 Edition, pp.1–4.

that of the market economy. Worse still, the central planning authority might frame seriously flawed policies, subjecting economy to serious damages worse than the depressions in capitalist countries. Friedrich August von Hayek maintained that the system of planned economy was better equipped to materialize certain objectives than the system of free competition. Also, the system of planned economy might adopt certain new technologies that are technically very advanced but might otherwise be rejected for being not so economical under the competition system. Such achievements were the results of concentrating huge quantities of resource on these particular goals by the central planning authority while disregarding the demands in many other areas. Instead of testifying to the success of the system of planned economy, this demonstrated that the resources had been erroneously allocated and thus had been wasted. The efficiency of the entire economy would be reduced because of the achievement of those particular goals.[7]

In the 1930's, regarding the pros and cons of the market and of the government planning, a heated debate happened between the Austrian School represented by Friedrich August von Hayek and the economists in favor of "the market socialism" represented by F. Taylor (1855–1932) and O. Lange (1904–1965). O. Lange argued that, under the socialist economy, the mechanism of the price determining the process was quite similar to the process under the system of market competition. Under the socialist economy, the central planning authority played the role of the market and worked out the allocation of resources by "simulating the market." Therefore, it was highly probable and also feasible that planning could replace the role of the market.[8] The collapse of the Soviet Union and the eventual switching of the East Europe to complete market economy testified to the failure of the state planning. It was absolutely impossible for the government to accurately calculate the demands of the entire society or the prices of all the commodities. Therefore, the economic plans formulated by the central planning authority could not keep abreast with the economic development of a society. Forcibly implementing economic plans would simply end up in long-term inefficient production, in shortages of supply, and in the failure to satisfy demands.

2 Breakthroughs by Institutional Economics in the Traditions of Economics

Institutional economics is a branch of economics which exclusively focuses on economic institution as its subject of research. Institutional economics comprises of three individual schools which can be listed as, according to their chronological sequence, the Institutional School, the Neo-institutional Economic School, and the

---

[7] Friedrich August von Hayek, *The Road to Serfdom*, trans. Wang Mingyi, Feng Xingyuan, et al, China Social Sciences Press, 1997 Edition, pp.39–46.

[8] Oskar Ryszard Lange, *The Economic Theory of Socialism*, China Social Sciences Press, 1981 Edition, pp.14–16.

New Institutional Economic School. These three schools have similar names and they developed in close chronological order, but they are widely different in their key propositions.

The Institutional School came into existence in the United States toward the end of the nineteenth century and at the beginning of the twentieth century. It is the first school of economics to specifically focus on economic institutions as its proper research targets. The Institutional School opposed any practice to treat institution as an external condition for analyzing economic activities. Economists of this school maintained that the root cause underpinning social and economic development is various forms of institution that are related to economic life. On the other hand, the social and economic development of any country is determined by the development of institutions.[9] These economists advocated the use of "historical induction" proposed by the School of German History to analyze the formation, development, and function of economic institutions. They insisted on the reform of capitalism institutionally or structurally. The chief figures representing the Institutional School included Thorstein B. Veblen (1857–1929), John R. Commons (1862–1945), Wesley C. Mitchell (1874–1948), and others. Thorstein B. Veblen defined institution as "social conventions in wide existence," believing that institution is not an organizational structure but some kind of "constant mental habits" shared by the majority of people.[10] John R. Commons maintained that institution refers to collective actions that impose constraints on individual behavior and legal institutions are the most important among all the institutions. Legal institutions not only existed prior to economic institutions but also played a determinant role in the evolution of economic institutions. The essence of economic relationship is transaction and the conflict of interests in the transaction process can only be solved by means of legal institutions. The government is the key factor behind the development and movement of economic regimes. It functions as the primary instrument in taking collective actions and in effecting changes.[11]

The Neo-institutional Economic School developed during the 1950's, focusing on examining how institution determines social life and how institution evolves. Methodologically, the Neo-institutional Economic School inherited, to some extent, the tradition of Thorstein B. Veblenn. By analyzing the structure of an institution, it proposed an evolutionary approach to the analysis of economic issues. The Neo-institutional Economic School is opposed to the method of quantitative analysis practiced by the neoclassical economics and sought to topple or replace the neoclassical economics. The Neo-institutional Economic School has two representative figures, John Kenneth Galbraith (1908–2006) and Gunnar Myrdal (1898–1987). They both

---

[9] Thorstein B. Veblen, *The Theory of the Leisure Class: An Economic Study of Institutions*, trans. Li Huaxia, Central Compilation and Translation Press, 2012 Edition, pp.143–145.

[10] Geoffrey M. Hodgson, *A Manifesto for a Modern Institutional Economics*, trans. Xiang Yibin, Peking University Press, 1993 Edition, p. 149.

[11] John R. Commons, *Institutional Economics: Its Place in Political Economy* (Vol.1), trans. Yu Shusheng, The Commercial Press, 1998 Edition.

believed that institution plays a determining role in social life and that technological changes are crucial to the evolution of institutions. The increase in the stock of knowledge is the primary motive force driving institutional changes. The contradiction and the reconciliation between the stock of knowledge and the structure of existing values determine the way institutions evolve.[12]

Both the Institutional School and the Neo-institutional Economic School, which emerged between the end of the nineteenth century and the outbreak of World War II, recognized the importance of institutions and analyzed how institutions could be impacted by the society, culture, psychology, customs and habits, law, and the progress in science and technology. In addition, those two schools proposed the use of empirical statistical analysis.[13] However, neither of the two schools succeeded in developing systematic theories on institution, or in making the relationship between the government and the market the focal point of their study. Their legacy was no more than a stack of practical materials without any theoretical value and little of this legacy could be handed down to future generations.[14]

The publication of the book *The Nature of the Firm* by Ronald H. Coase (1910–2013) in 1937 was a major event marking the birth of the New Institutional Economic School. With the publication of this book, the studies on property rights, contract, and transaction cost became increasingly enriched and deepened and they became important tools for explaining the real world. In 1975, Oliver Williamson (1932–2020) formally named this systemic theory as "New Institutional Economics."[15] New institutional economics inherited the legacy of neoclassical economics in a critical manner, making institution an important subject of scholarly inquiry. As maintained by new institutional economics, institution is an organized structure of the society which determines the allocation of resources.[16] New institutional economics has three basic theoretical tools—the theory of property rights, the theory of contract, and the theory of transaction cost. New institutional economics further believed that the reduction of transaction costs is the core objective of institutional reform. The design and the adjustment of property rights and of contract should all be centered on the reduction of transaction costs.

---

[12] Lu Xianxiang, Zhu Qiaoling, *New Institutional Economics*, Peking University Press, 2021 Edition, p.4.

[13] Thorstein B. Veblen, *The Theory of the Leisure Class: An Economic Study of Institutions*, trans. Li Huaxia, Central Compilation and Translation Press, 2012 Edition, p.2.

[14] Ronald H. Coase, Douglass North, Oliver Williamson, et al, *Institutions, Contracts and Organizations: Perspectives from New Institutional Economics*, trans. Liu Gang, et al, Economic Science Press, 2003 Edition, p.10.

[15] Oliver E. Williamson, "Markets and Hierarchies: Analysis and Antitrust Implications: A Study in the Economics of Internal Organization," *Accounting Review*, 1975.

[16] New institutional economics is not simply focused on the market. It is focused on a broad range of issues including the nature of the firm, its organizational structure, the substitutive relationship between the firm and the market, transaction cost, power distribution between the firm and social organizations, social contract relationship, the reasons for the formation of individual and collective psychology and their consequences, the formation of knowledge, the allocation of resources, income distribution, the determinants of organization and control, and institutional change.

3 New Institutional Economics: Understanding Institutions

The inception of new institutional economics coincided with neoclassical economics' reigning position in mainstream economics. There is an a priori hypothesis in *n*eoclassical economics that institution is a constant, obstinately believing that the collection of information, bargaining, signing of contracts and the supervision over the implementation of contracts would be free from costs. A comparison can be made between this and a phenomenon in physics—the motion of one physical object relative to another object. In the preliminary study, friction could be presumed not to exist in the idealized abstract situation. But friction has its objective existence. Therefore, when physics is applied to actual projects, the factor of friction must be taken into consideration. Similarly, neoclassical economics refused to regard human behavior as the product of particular institutions. It assumed that humans would simply react by following a pre-designed and optimized model. As the neoclassical economics excluded institution from its research model, this exclusion has resulted in a fatal gap between its theory and the reality of economic activities. The models developed by neoclassical economics cannot be used to make accurate predictions about the prospect of economic development or to generate policy recommendations for economic development in developing countries. With regard to the fatal flaw inherent in the neoclassical economics, Ronald H. Coase proposed that there exists no transaction that is without "friction" and that the "friction" in all the transactions constitutes the transaction cost.

When neoclassical economics' assumption about the "institution" as a constant was subverted, economics came to embrace a wave of new revolutions. Previously, both the Institutional School and the Neo-institutional Economic School resorted to the methods of historical induction and empirical statistics, but they all failed to develop any systemic theory about institution. Few of their ideas or arguments have been handed down to the succeeding generations. By contrast, through the relentless efforts of a number of scholars like Ronald H. Coase, Oliver Williamson, Douglass C. North, Armen Albert Alchian (1914–2013), Steven N. S. Cheung (1935–) and others, the New Institutional Economic School has gradually emerged out of its peripheral position in the past to enter the mainstream of economics. By focusing its scholarly investigations firmly on transaction cost, the new institutional economics has come up with new propositions regarding institutions, which can be summarized as follows.

To start with, the institution of property rights can be used as a starting point of the entire intellectual inquiry. It is generally believed by the new institutional economics that property rights constitute a constraint which can be used to solve the conflict of interests as a result of resource scarcities. According to the definition in the ancient Roman Law, the property rights refer to the rights enjoyed by individuals to the free disposal of their tangible assets. Scholars on the property rights have developed many classifications regarding the composition of the property rights. Generally speaking, complete property rights include the right of ownership, the right of utilization, the usufruct (right of income), and the right of alienation. Most scholars on property rights, based on the degree of exclusiveness of the property rights, classify property rights into three categories—private property rights, communal property rights, and state-owned property rights. In addition, property rights can also be divided into absolute property rights and relative property rights. Property rights are characterized by exclusiveness, divisibility, alienability (or disposability), and perpetuity (or security).

A clear definition of the property rights is a precondition for market transactions.[17] The price is the most critical factor for market transactions and the property rights determine the price. The issue of determining price is essentially an issue of how property rights are defined and exchanged and under what conditions the exchange happen.[18] Whether or not a country can develop a sound institution of property rights determines the economic development of that country. The establishment of private property rights can be seen as the very foundation on which the Western world achieved its rise in the modern period.[19] In a society suffering from resource scarcities, the conduct of each individual is subject to the constraints of the resources. The rules imposed on the way people acquire and exchange resources are tantamount to the institutional arrangements concerning property rights. Property rights have two functions—providing incentives and imposing constraints. In the words of Mencius (about 372 B.C.–289 B.C.), those who are not guaranteed the security of their property would demonstrate no perseverance in pursuing property. Simply put, it means that, when the property rights of individuals are subjected to jeopardy, these individuals will demonstrate significant uncertainties in their expectations about the future. As a result, investment would be reduced and the prices of assets would accordingly decline. By contrast, a stable and reasonable institution of property rights will deliver incentives for individuals to expand production and increase investment, thus stimulating economic growth. The institution of property rights directly determines the transaction cost. In the Coase theorem, special emphasis is placed on two crucial points—the initial allocation of property rights and the redistribution of property rights. Coase was convinced that a sound definition of the initial rights would be conducive to the enhancement of a society's overall welfare. A redistribution of the rights can also reduce the transaction cost and contribute to a society's overall welfare.[20]

---

[17] Ronald H. Coase, *The Institutional Structure of Production*, Springer Berlin Heidelberg, 2008.

[18] Armen Alchian, "Some Economics of Property Rights," *Political Economy*, 1965, pp.816–829.

[19] Douglass C. North, *The Rise of The Western World: A New Economic History*, trans. Li Yiping and Cai Lei, Huaxia Publishing House, 2009 Edition, pp.4–7. In this book, North concludes that the development of an efficient economic organization in Western Europe is the very reason for the rise of the Western world. An efficient organization needs to make institutional arrangements and to establish ownership in order to create an incentive. An individual may, through his own economic endeavors, make his private returns approximate social returns. Therefore, a sound institution of ownership can make social production a lucrative activity and thus make economic growth happen.

[20] According to a summary made by Joseph Field, a professor with Bradley University in the United States, the Coase Theorem consists of three individual theorems. The First Coase Theorem: is the initial definition of rights important? If the transaction cost is zero, then the answer is negative. The random allocation of rights will be efficiently corrected, without any cost, by the entities directly involved in the property rights. Therefore, in terms of economic efficiency, an initial allocation

The second is the use of reduced transaction cost as the aim of the contractual arrangements. The idea of contract can be found in the early history and culture of various countries. In the early Jewish Law, the *Bible* was considered as a contract between the Jewish people and the God. When the Roman Law was popularized across Europe, the idea of contract became a theoretical resource shared by all people. Due to its secular attribute and its implied principles of equality, freedom, practicality, and rationality, contract came to constitute one of the natural principles for dealing with the reciprocal relationship among people in their daily life. The contract theory has always occupied a very important position in the European political philosophy. The mainstream political philosophers during the Enlightenment, such as John Locke, Jean-Jacques Rousseau, and Immanuel Kant, believed that the power of the government was derived from the contract between the state and the people. All people enter a common contract, proclaiming to give up part of their natural rights and vest these rights in a public institution, which converts these rights into public powers to which all must defer.

New institutional economics inherited the idea and the theory of contract immanent in the European political philosophy and applied this idea and theory to institutional analysis. A contract consists of certain commitments made voluntarily by the parties in action and it is a form of property rights transfer that happens in the transaction process. Due to the transaction cost, people would choose different contractual arrangements in order to lower the transaction cost in the economic operation and to maximize their efficiency. A contract can help reduce transaction cost in one of the following five ways. The first is that the parties involved in a contract can resort to different modes of resource transfer or resource combination and, under certain constraints, sign a contract that is most favorable to them, thus achieving effective allocation of resources. The second is that the relevant stakeholders of a contract sign the contract under the condition of information symmetry and the contract can protect one stakeholder from possible damages arising from the deceptive frauds of other stakeholders, in accordance with the principles of law, the formal document, and self-liquidation. All the law-abiding stakeholders who honor the contract would benefit from the contract and the transaction cost is thus reduced. The third is that the third-party governance can be introduced. Disputes could be settled by means of the third party, who passes judgment on the behavior of the parties in action to ensure their long-term cooperation. The fourth is that, in the case of frequent transactions between the parties in action, such frequent transactions can be transferred from the market into the enterprises (organizations), thus lowering the transaction cost. The fifth is that simple governance structure is matched with simple transactions whereas

of rights is no different from another initial allocation. The Second Coase Theorem: is the initial definition of rights important? If the transaction cost is positive, then the answer is affirmative. When there does exist transaction cost, the initial allocation of the rights that can be transacted will influence the eventual allocation of rights and may also influence the overall welfare of a society. The Third Coase Theorem: when there does exist transaction cost, the improvement of the welfare that is achieved by re-distributing the already defined rights might be superior to the improvement of the welfare that is achieved through transactions.

complex governance structure is matched with complex transactions. An optimized governance structure is capable of minimizing the transaction cost.[21]

The third is the fundamental impact that transaction cost can have on economic development. There have been numerous studies by economists on the factors that impact economic development. A number of doctrines have been advanced, ranging from production factor determinism, technological determinism, and cultural determinism, etc. These theories can, to some extent, explain some economies for a certain period of time, but none of them can come up with universal explanations regarding the differences in different economies. It is a belief shared by all the scholars of institutional analysis, be they from the Institutional School or from the Neo-institutional Economic School, that different institutions are the ultimate reasons underlying the differences in economic development. Nevertheless, neither of these schools can come up with full-fledged methodologies for comparative institutional studies.

New institutional economics maintains that the transaction cost is the necessary cost for enforcing a contract. Transaction costs consist of the cost for measuring, defining, and guaranteeing property rights, the cost of finding transaction partners and transaction prices, the cost of bargaining and instituting a contract, and the cost of supervising the strict honoring of the contract, etc. New institutional economists classify transaction costs into three categories—market transaction cost, managerial transaction cost, and political transaction cost. More specifically, the market transaction cost comprises of the cost of collecting information, bargaining, decision making, supervision, and execution; the managerial transaction cost consists of the cost of establishing, maintaining, or changing the design of an organization and of the cost of operating the organization; the political transaction cost covers the cost of establishing, maintaining, and changing the formal or the informal organizations within an institution, plus the cost of operating political institutions. The inception of an enterprise, the formation and development of governance structure are all aimed at reducing transaction costs.

The fourth is the analysis on three separate dimensions—the state, the enterprise, and the market. No economic activities can be separated from these three crucial organizations, namely, the state, the enterprise, and the market. New institutional economics uses the theories of the property rights, the contract, and the transaction cost to analyze the transaction cost of the state, the enterprise, and the market in economic activities. The transaction cost determines the boundary and the scale of an enterprise. An enterprise is a substitute for the price mechanism—an enterprise comes into existence when the market transaction cost exceeds the cost of management and coordination within an enterprise. It can be safely asserted that an enterprise is created simply in order to reduce the market transaction cost. Conversely, when the market transaction cost is lower than the cost of an enterprise's internal management, the enterprise can, by means of splitting up, transform the internal management into market transactions, thus reducing the transaction cost. The market transaction cost

---

[21] Oliver E. Williamson, *The Economic Institutions of Capitalism: Firms, Markets, Relational Contracting*, trans. Duan Yicai and Wang Wei, The Commercial Press, 2002 Edition, pp.24–31; pp.101–144.

and an enterprise's organizational cost determine the quantity of the resources that the enterprise can allocate, thus determining the size of the enterprise.[22]

This substitutive relationship between the enterprise and the market is liable to the incentives and the constraints from particular economic institutions and the state is the biggest provider of institutions. According to Douglass C. North's definition of institution, there can be formal institutions and informal institutions, along with mechanisms of enforcement. The formulation of formal institutions and the operation of the enforcing mechanisms primarily fall within the responsibilities of the state. The rules and regulations framed by the state pertain to the defining and the protection of property rights, and also pertain to the coordination of different interest groups. The state has two objectives to pursue. On one hand, the state maximizes its rent by providing different property rights to different power groups. On the other hand, the state achieves the increase of wealth and social stability by reducing the transaction cost for the sake of maximizing the social output. The rules and regulations framed by the state determine a country's economic development and also determine the general direction of the choices that people make. The behavior of the state can serve as the key to economic growth, but it can also be the root cause for economic recessions.

4 The Difficulty of Measuring Transaction Costs

Since the transaction cost lies at the center of new institutional economics, how to define and measure this cost becomes a major task for new institutional economics. Toward this objective, new institutional economics made significant efforts to explore for potential solutions in order to work out the measurement of transaction costs.

Prior to the birth of new institutional economics, Karl Marx had already developed some explanations concerning transaction cost. In his *Das Kapital*, he discussed the circulation cost, arguing that the costs consumed in the circulation process mainly included the pure circulation cost, the custody cost, and transportation cost. The pure circulation cost included the time consumed in reaching a transaction, the book-keeping cost, and the monetary obsolescence cost.[23] The transaction cost discussed by economists in succeeding generations is fairly close to Marx's idea of the circulation cost. New institutional economists have defined the transaction cost from a multiplicity of perspectives. For instance, Coase defined the transaction cost as the "cost of institutional operation" while an enterprise is engaged in economic exchanges in the market, which subsumes the costs of finding out the price, negotiating, signing the contract, supervising and enforcing the contract. In actuality, Coase defined the transaction cost as "the cost of operating an entire economic institution." Kenneth J. Arrow (1921–2017), who was the first economist to have formally proposed the concept of "transaction cost," defined the transaction cost as

[22] Ronald H. Coase, "The Nature of the Firm," *Economica*, 1937, 4, pp.386–405.

[23] Karl Marx, *Das Kapital*, People's Publishing House, 1975 Edition, pp.147–150.

the cost of utilizing economic institutions.[24] Following the definition by Kenneth J. Arrow, Oliver Williamson sub-divided the transaction cost.[25] In North's definition, the transaction cost covers the totality of the transaction costs incurred by an enterprise, encompassing the cost of measuring the value of the commodities for exchange, the cost of protecting the enterprise's rights, and the cost of monitoring and enforcing the contract. Transaction costs originate from social, political, and economic institutions.[26] The transaction cost as defined by Steven N. S. Cheung features a series of institutional costs, including the costs of information, negotiation, drafting and implementing contracts, defining and exercising property rights, supervision and management, and the cost of changing institutional arrangements. As a matter of fact, he defines all the costs that do not directly happen during the process of physical production as transaction cost.[27] *The New Palgrave Dictionary of Economics* summarizes the idea of transaction cost as the cost arising from the transfer of property ownership and is the product of all the discrete ownerships, private properties, and their transactions. Transaction costs do not exist in a collective economy dominated by completely centralized decision-making; this is because they are replaced by administrative costs.[28]

A number of Chinese scholars have also endeavored to develop their definitions and interpretations of transaction cost. For example, Zhang Peigang proposed the idea of "pure commercial cost" during the 1930's when studying the economic issues in the period of China's resistance against the Japanese invasion. He observed that the Chinese farmers in inland provinces like Hunan and Jiangxi were exceedingly poor and their cost of grain production was rather low. By contrast, in the grains market in coastal cities like Ningbo, the rice from China's inland provinces was at a competitive disadvantage as compared with the rice imported all the way from Thailand. With due investigations, Zhang Peigang discovered that the sales channel from the inland rural areas to coastal cities was fraught with trade barriers that resulted in exorbitant business costs. Such barriers included local separatism, inordinate blackmailing at inter-provincial checkpoints, and many other man-made obstacles, thus excluding the highly competitive inland rice from the coastal markets. He argued that effective improvement of business channels could lessen business costs and help strengthen China's grains supply.[29] Scholars like Fan Gang view the transaction costs arising from China's reform as the economic damages caused by the conflicts of interests in

---

[24] Michael Dietrich, *The Economics of Transaction Costs: About New Economic Meaning of Firms*, trans. Wang Tiesheng and Ge Licheng, Economic Science Press, 2000 Edition, p.25.

[25] Michael Dietrich, *The Economics of Transaction Costs: About New Economic Meaning of Firms*, trans. Wang Tiesheng and Ge Licheng, Economic Science Press, 2000 Edition, p.29.

[26] Douglass C. North, *Institutions, Institutional Chang and Economic Performance*, trans. Hang Xing, Truth and Wisdom Press, SDX Joint Publishing Company, Shanghai People's Publishing House, 2014 Edition, p.37.

[27] Steven N.S. Cheung, *Economic Explanation: Selected Papers of Steven NS Cheung*, trans. Yi Xianrong and Zhang Weidong, The Commercial Press, 2000 Edition, p.407.

[28] John Eatwell, Murray Milgate, and Peter Newman, *The New Palgrave Dictionary of Economics*, Vol. 4, trans. Chen Daisun, et al, Economic Science Press, pp.730–733.

[29] Zhou Qiren, "Institutional Cost and the Chinese Economy," *Economics*, 2017, Issue 3.

the reform process or as the costs paid for such conflicts. The transaction cost would be lowered if reform programs could reduce either the number of individuals incurring the damages or the magnitude of the damages.[30] Consequently, reform should be undertaken, first and foremost, in those fields where the established institutions were the most vulnerable and the local reforms could produce positive external effects that might facilitate gradual institutional changes.[31] Qian Yingyi contends that the transaction costs are the costs related to the signing and enforcing of contracts and to the protection of property rights. He further argues that these costs are often not directly determined by price parameters but by institutional building, the development of the rule of law, and various regulations and systems of the government.[32] Scholars like Zhou Qiren maintain that the institutional costs are the prices that any economic actor has to pay in order to obtain gains. The prices can be monetary, non-monetary, temporal, mental, or spiritual. Any expenses that pertain to the consumption of resources in creating, operating, and changing institutions can be classified as institutional costs.[33]

The differences in both the denotation and the connotation of the transaction cost have contributed to the difficulty in measuring transaction costs. Between the existing two modes of measurement, the first method is the direct measurement. For example, scholars like North have tried to calculate the percentage of the transaction costs in the GDP in American economy. They divided the U.S. economic sectors into the transaction sector and the transformation sector and the total transaction cost is the sum of the transaction costs of the two sectors put together. The total value of the resources utilized by the transaction sector is used to indicate the transaction cost of this sector whereas, in the transformation sector, the product from the number of staff in transaction services multiplied by their salaries is used to estimate the transaction cost of this sector. Based on these statistics, they calculated that the proportion of the U.S. transaction cost in GDP has increased from 24.9 to 26% in 1870 to 46.66 to 54.71% in 1970.[34] The method of direct measurement proposed by North and other scholars has been adopted by a considerable number of researchers. However, the transaction costs calculated with this method only cover the transaction costs that are in market circulation, thus this method is fraught with limitations for ignoring the transaction costs that exist in the non-circulation sector.[35] E. Mettepenningen and other scholars applied the method of investigation to measure the transaction costs. They registered all the transaction costs that were spent on schemes related to the

---

[30] Fan Gang, *An Evolutionary Path: An Economics Analysis of Economic Reform*, China Social Sciences Press, 1993 Edition, p.3.

[31] Miao Zhuang, "Strategic Choices of Reform in Institutional Changes," *Economic Research Journal*, 1992, Issue 10.

[32] "Qian Yingyi: Reducing Transaction Cost as a Way of Reducing the Cost in Real Economy," http://www.xinhuanet.com//politics/2017-03/06/c_1120578334.htm.

[33] Zhou Qiren, "Institutional Cost and the Chinese Economy," *Economics*, 2017, Issue 3.

[34] See J. J. Wallis, D. North, L. Growth, "Measuring the Transaction Sector in the American Economy, 1870–1970," *Long-Term Factors in American Economic Growth.*

[35] L. McCann, K. W. Easter, "Estimates of Public Sector Transaction Costs in NRCS Programs," *Journal of Agricultural & Applied Economics*, 2000, 32(03), pp.555–563.

agricultural and environmental programs in a year and concluded that the transaction costs accounted for 14% in the total costs of the agricultural and environmental programs.[36] On the other hand, Pilling and other scholars developed a set of criteria which consisted of multiple variables for measuring the expected transaction costs. This set of criteria can be used to monitor the pre-event cost of developing relations and the post-event cost arising from monitoring the performance and dealing with opportunistic behavior.[37]

The second method was the indirect measurement. For example, Williamson proposed the use of ordinal comparison to measure transaction costs. A comparison of two institutions or two contracts is sufficient to reveal the volume of transaction costs.[38] S. Djankov and others used the varying levels of businesses being subjected to regulation to perform comparative analysis of the transaction costs in different countries.[39] In addition, Scholars have also explored the possibility of the indirect measurement of transaction costs by assessing market governance structures, asset specificity, environmental uncertainty, and behavioral uncertainty. They believed that the governance structure which is not market-oriented, higher asset specificity, higher environmental uncertainty, and higher behavioral uncertainty all mean higher transaction costs.

Since the 1980's, by applying these direct and indirect paradigms of measurement, economists in the U.S., European countries, Japan, India, China, Mexico, countries in South America, Australia, and New Zealand have performed a large quantity of empirical and applied studies.[40] Some Chinese scholars believed that the challenges in measuring transaction costs made it difficult to compare the efficiency of different institutions by means of the transaction cost theory. This strong concern with transaction costs was aimed at reducing transaction costs rather than measuring them accurately. There would be no need to make any measurement when inaccurate measurements themselves were sufficient to motivate people to reduce transaction costs. They thus conclude that, perhaps, it was both impossible and unnecessary to measure the sum total of the transaction costs of any given country or region.[41]

---

[36] E. Mettepenningen, A. Verspecht, G. V. Huylenbroeck, "Measuring Private Transaction Costs of European Agri-environmental Schemes," *Journal of Environmental Planning and Management*, 2009, 52 (5), pp.649–667.

[37] B. K. Pilling, L. A. Crosby, D. W. Jackson, "Relational Bonds in Industrial Exchange: An Experimental Test of the Transaction Cost Economic Framework," *Journal of Business Research*, 1994, 30 (3), pp.237–251.

[38] Oliver E. Williamson, *The Economic Institutions of Capitalism: Firms, Markets, Relational Contracting*, trans. Duan Yicai and Wang Wei, The Commercial Press, 2002 Edition, pp.315–316; pp.543–546.

[39] S. Djankov, R. L. Porta, L. Shleifer, "The Regulation of Entry," *Quarterly Journal of Economics*, 2002, 117(1), pp. 1–37.

[40] Oliver E. Williamson, "The New Institutional Economics: Taking Stock, Looking Ahead," *Journal of Economic Literature*, 2000, 38(3), pp. 596–613.

[41] Huang Xiaoan, "A New Interpretation of Six Basic Theoretical Issues in Institutional Economics," *Academic Monthly*, 2007, Issue 1.

5 Limitations in the Studies by New Institutional Economics

New institutional economics took institution as its proper subject of study. This was virtually an intellectual revolution in the mainstream economics at that time. The dissemination of this doctrine made people aware of the importance of institution to development. However, from a global perspective, since the 1980's and 1990's, a large number of countries practicing the planned economy have started to transform toward market economy and many developing countries have reached the phase where they have started to catch up with and surpass developed countries. They all faced the urgent need to restructure their economic institutions. Yet, a singular regret is that, in the face of those great historical opportunities, new institutional economics has failed to play its role in guiding the institutional changes in those countries. New institutional economics did realize that the state is the paramount provider of institutions, but in those academic disciplines that are directly related to state governance, such as public administration and administrative law, we can rarely find the application of the methodology and the research findings of new institutional economics. Since the 1990's, with Coase, North, and Williamson winning the Nobel Prizes in Economic Sciences, most of the important publications in new institutional economics have been translated into Chinese and introduced to the Chinese academic community. But over the past decade, there has been an obvious decline in the enthusiasm with which people, both in China and abroad, have reacted to the new institutional economics. On the other hand, there have been few new publications that carry weight. As a branch of economics which exclusively focuses on institution as its subject of study, new institutional economics has produced practical effects that fall far short of the expectations of the theoretical circle as a whole and of the institutional practitioners, that is, those who are engaged in formulating and operating institutions. Scholars of new institutional economics have already offered many discussions concerning the limitations of this doctrine. Some further observations and comments seem to be necessary here.

The first deficiency in new institutional economics is an overly narrow definition of transaction entities. New institutional economics treats the institution of property rights as the starting point of its intellectual reasoning, believing that transactions are essentially the transfer or the alienation of rights. However, according to new institutional economics, the rights being alienated only include various physical and service rights derived from the property rights in market economic activities. As a matter of fact, the rights involved in economic activities are not restricted to the rights outlined above. In any given country, the visible hand of the government would intervene in economic activities. For example, the administrative governance by the Chinese government covers ten categories, including administrative licensing, administrative penalty, administrative compulsion, administrative planning, administrative arbitration, and administrative contracting. Apart from these formal administrative measures, many informal administrative actions would happen to the contacts between the enterprises and the administrative departments, which are often termed "unwritten rules." Even in developed countries boasting a high level of the rule of law, such "unwritten rules" also exist. The state, through its administrative actions, formulates rules and regulations regarding the enterprises and deals with the rights derived from the specific matters related to the enterprise. Enterprises acquire these rights and in this process both the government and the enterprises have to pay various prices such as time, money, and energy. This process of deriving and acquiring rights is in itself a process of the alienation of rights, which is also a form of transaction. When discussing transactions, new institutional economics tends to ignore this form of transaction that is actually in widespread existence.[42] The absence of studies regarding this form of transactions imposes limitations on new institutional economics in its understanding about the state, leaving this theory particularly weak in explaining and addressing the realistic problems in the state governance system, especially the problems that the government encounters in the reform of its economic institutions.

Secondly, new institutional economics has failed to perform a perceptive anatomy of the state, which is the largest provider of institutions. New institutional economics is similar to neoclassical economics in that they have both demonstrated considerable partiality in their understanding—the new institutional economics' understanding of the state and the neoclassical economics' understanding about the enterprise. Neoclassical economics treated enterprises as homogeneous and undifferentiated market entities, presupposing that the behavior of all enterprises is uniform and identical. One of the most important contributions that Coase made was his subversion of neoclassical economics' assumption about "complete rationality," emphasizing that not all the enterprises are identical and that there is a substitutive relationship between the enterprise and the market. The state as depicted by new institutional economics is quite similar to the enterprise as described by neoclassical economics since it is also characterized by homogeneity. It can design institutions, define and protect property rights, orchestrate the relationship between different interest groups, and act as a third-party enforcer. However, new institutional economics fails to open up the treasure house which is the state, the largest provider of institutions, and fails to offer any insightful analysis. How does the state provide institutions? What are some of the laws behind the state's providing of institutions? Delivering answers to these questions might have been the most important contributions that economic theories on institution can make, but new institutional economics merely treats the state as a fixed premise and leaves it at that.

[42] Douglass C. North is the most representative scholar of new institutional economics who studied institutional changes on the macro level. The idea of "institution" as discussed by Douglass C. North has broader meanings than the word "system" in Chinese. His studies cover the enterprise, the state, and various economic organizations. His analysis of the state includes studies on the executive, the legislative, and the judiciary. Other new institutional economists like Ronald H. Coase and Oliver Williamson focused their studies on the enterprise. Douglass C. North's studies on institutions have been widely accepted, as these studies conformed to people's perceptual knowledge. But he failed to make full use of the transaction cost, which is a core analytical tool in new institutional economics, to substantiate his conclusions in a rigorous manner. The economic institutions as discussed in this book are restricted to those only related to the government, the enterprise, and the market.

Thirdly, new institutional economics has failed to find a viable method for gauging transaction costs. Regarding transaction costs, a conceptual definition that is acceptable to the majority of new institutional economists has not yet been developed. Worse still, none of the existing definitions demonstrates effective operability. As a matter of fact, transaction costs not only cover the products in people's daily life and the physical exchanges in the service sector, but also extend beyond the traditional boundary dividing the production sector and the transaction sector. Transaction costs can be observed in virtually all forms of economic and social activities.

In its early days, new institutional economics was merely concerned with studying the transaction costs in simple economic activities. Hence, it was entirely feasible to measure transaction costs in terms of the monetary value. In his *The Nature of the Firm*, Coase cites an example which is truly a case in point. Whether or not Firm A decides to merge with Firm B with which it has business connections depends entirely on a comparison between the transaction cost of the merging process and the cost of having direct market transactions with Firm B. When the former is higher, Firm A would not choose to merge with Firm B. By contrast, if the former is lower, Firm A would choose to merge with Firm B. As new institutional economics kept developing, the idea of transaction cost came to encompass an increasing variety of costs and it became increasingly ineffectual to measure transaction costs based on the monetary value. For example, in managing economy, the government tends to resort to administrative approval, which is mostly free of charge. However, some enterprises prefer to pay significantly higher prices in order to obtain administrative approval the soonest possible. This is because, for such enterprises, the earlier they acquire the necessary administrative approval, the greater the benefits yielded by early business operation, far greater than the cost of capital that is otherwise consumed in waiting for the administrative approval. Meanwhile, although the administrative approval established by the government is gratuitous, the transaction cost for the enterprise is obviously not. The longer it takes to secure the required administrative approval, the greater the transaction costs for the enterprise, which are often beyond measurement.

Furthermore, at present, transaction costs have mostly been calculated in terms of money. This makes it impossible to use money to quantify the transaction costs that occur in the non-transaction sectors or in non-transaction activities. As these problems have long remained unsolved over the past, scholars had to mainly resort to qualitative descriptions to discuss the idea of transaction cost in their actual research. As a consequence, some new institutional economists have already downplayed or even discarded the notion of transaction cost in their research.

Fourthly, institutional studies have failed to cover a sufficiently wide range of research areas. With respect to the three dimensions of the state, the enterprise, and the market, new institutional economics has focused primarily on the transaction cost between the enterprises and the market. It has overlooked the transaction cost between the state and the market, and the transaction cost between the state and the enterprises. The transaction costs on the latter two dimensions are precisely the issues that should be most urgently addressed in a country's building of new economic institutions and in the reform of the existing economic institutions. The institution of planned economy and the institution of market economy are the most representative among modern economic institutions and they were pitted against one another in fierce rivalry throughout the twentieth century. In this process, there were instances in which the countries of market economy tried to introduce the mechanisms of state planning; meanwhile, there were also instances in which the institution of planned economy sought to switch to the institution of market economy. New institutional economics has consistently failed to use its own analytical framework to perform effective analysis and raise interpretations concerning the evolution of these two types of institutions, along with the laws behind their reciprocal transformation. New institutional economists have merely been telling politicians that economic institutions are important, without proposing any constructive opinions regarding the specific measures of building or reforming economic institutions.

Chapter 3
Reconstructing the Analytical Framework of Institutions

It is true that new institutional economics achieved breakthroughs in the research on property rights, contracts, and transaction costs. Nevertheless, it has manifested limitations in defining the range of transactions, measuring transaction costs, anatomizing the government behavior, and determining the contents of institutional studies. These limitations have in return hampered its application to real-world issues. Over the four decades of reform and opening-up, China has accumulated a large number of valuable cases in institutional evolution, of which Western economists who engage in institutional studies are totally unaware. Therefore, in order to work out the problems that confront institutional economics, it is necessary to further expand our conceptual horizon and develop a new understanding about transactions and transaction costs. It is also imperative to broaden our vision about the practical endeavors in institutional building. In this way, it will be possible to uncover the laws underlying institutional evolution as demonstrated by China's reform and opening-up. Based on the theories have matured in the institutional studies in economics, we can expect to further construct an institutional analytical framework that would prove instrumental to diverse areas of social and economic development.

1 Expanding the Understanding of Transactions

The analysis performed in the preceding chapter has already illuminated some of the deficiencies inherent in new institutional economics regarding the determination of the range of transactions. Essentially speaking, transaction involves the transfer or alienation of rights. The transaction discussed by new institutional economics only cover the alienation of property rights, not the alienation of the derivative rights ensuing from the government's administrative action. The rights that are derived from the government's administrative action are essentially equivalent to the individual rights associated with the property rights. They demonstrate attributes that conform

B. Fan, *The Rationale Behind Change*, https://doi.org/10.1007/978-981-97-8854-5_3

to new institutional economics' general understanding about transaction. Therefore, it is completely justified to regard such an alienation of rights as a kind of transaction.

Concerning the source of rights, we can identify two sources—the source of the state and the source of the government. The state possesses a broad range of rights, including the administrative rights, the legislative rights, the judiciary rights, national defense, and other supervisory functions. As far as economic activities are concerned, the execution of the legislative, judiciary, and supervisory functions will ultimately have to depend on the government's administrative departments. A government's administrative actions represent the will of the state. Therefore, when the concept of the state is mentioned in this chapter and in succeeding chapters of this book, it primarily refers to the government.

First and foremost, administrative actions constitute the fundamental unit of economic activities. In the history of economic theories, John R. Commons was the first to describe transaction strictly as a concept of economics. When elucidating how transaction came to constitute a basic unit of mankind's economic activities, he pointed out that transaction is an interpersonal relation, a transfer of property rights. Transaction is different from exchange, because exchange is a process of labor involving the giving and taking of physical objects whereas transaction is not targeted at physical substances. Rather, transaction is targeted at property rights and is a form of interpersonal relation, which involves the yielding and the acquisition of the rights of natural objects. These ideas raised by John R. Commons came to be widely accepted by new institutional economists after John R. Commons.

In John R. Commons' analysis, the entities of transaction are human individuals, the objects of transaction are property rights, and the act of transaction consists of the transfer of property rights. According to the understanding of John R. Commons at the time when he proposed his theory, the participants involved in a market transaction only consist of human beings, including the natural person and the corporation (the legal person). As a matter of fact, however, the government is also a participant in the market transaction activities. Furthermore, all the transactions participated by the natural person and the corporation are inseparable from the government. Therefore, any discussions concerning transaction would be incomplete if such discussions exclude the government from the transaction entities. The government imposes rules and regulations on corporate organizations by means of administrative actions and a considerable number of rights can be derived from administrative actions. The rights that are made accessible to corporate organizations tend to have the same status as other forms of property rights. If rights are the objects of transaction, then, the rights derived from administrative actions should not be excluded from the scope of transaction. The deriving of the rights by the administrative departments from their administrative actions is also a form of the transfer of rights and this process of transfer also necessitates expenses on the part of both the government and the corporation, which is essentially the same as the transfer of property rights.

Through its administrative actions, the government is involved in transaction activities in an all-encompassing manner. For example, a certain gas company is to supply gas to a particular residential compound. The gas company signs agreements with the residents in the residential compound regarding the selling of gas, and with the gas supplier regarding the supply of gas, and with the construction company regarding the construction of the necessary facilities. All these activities are transactions. It should also be noted that, when the government grants the franchise, a form of privileged license, to the gas company, it means that the government allows the rights derived from its administrative actions to be transferred to that gas company. The rights derived from the government's administrative actions include the gap company's right to supply gas to particular areas and keep supplying the gas for a specific period of time. In the process of the transfer, the government has to organize bidding sessions whereas the gas company has to submit a tender. Both the government and the company have to pay prices—time, money, and physical and mental energy. This process of transfer is an act of transaction whose nature is identical with any other business activity. The franchise that the gas company acquires becomes part of the overall property rights of the company itself. The government's administrative decision to grant the franchise to the gas company is an indispensible part of the gas supply transaction of the gas company.

Many transaction activities that seem to have nothing to do with the government are actually subject to the constraints arising from the government's administrative rules and regulations. For instance, for most enterprises, the manufacturing and the sales of their products would not require the government's franchise as does the gas supply of the gas company. However, the government does develop and impose safety and environmental standards on all kinds of products. The fact that an enterprise engages in the manufacturing and the sales of these products implies that the enterprise and the government enter a contract and the enterprise automatically subjects itself to government's rules and regulations. The enterprise will have to pay prices in accordance with the rules and regulations once it violates the contract. Therefore, nothing in an enterprise's production and sales is entirely free. The government is actually involved in an enterprise's rights of manufacturing and selling of products, even though these rights do not seem to entail government licensing.

Secondly, the rights derived from administrative actions are characterized by scarcity as are the property rights. In neoclassical economics, it was taken for granted that transactions could be automatically completed on the market. Thus, in studying the efficiency of the allocation of resources, neoclassical economics tended to exclude transaction from the impacting factors. Ronald H. Coase inherited John R. Commons' idea of transaction as a basic unit of mankind's economic activities and used transaction as a basic unit of analysis. Ronald H. Coase believed that transaction is characterized by scarcity and, like production activities, transaction activities also have to consume resources that are largely scarce, such as time, energy, leisure, and property. On the other hand, the act of deriving rights from the government's administrative actions is also characterized by scarcity, which is closely related to the limitedness of the government's administrative resources and its administrative capacity. For example, both in China and elsewhere in the world, governments generally only allow the medicines that have been tested to be sold on the market. Not all the products which purport to possess therapeutic effects could be marketed in the name of medicines. Due to the government's limited abilities in medicine testing, it usually takes a long time for medicines to pass the government's testing. In some countries, the pharmaceutical corporations might even have to pay exorbitant fees for having their medicines tested.

Based on the foregoing analysis, we can conclude that the act of deriving rights from the government's administrative actions can also be viewed as a form of transaction. The deriving of rights from the government's administrative actions is an act of signing a contract between the administrative department and the administrative counterpart, that is, a corporate organization or an individual who are the object of the government's administrative action. This act allows an administrative department to transfer the rights whereas the corporation or the individual can gain access to the transferred rights and then honors the concomitant obligations. Both sides have to pay certain prices. Such a transfer of rights is the outcome of satisfying the reciprocal demands of both the government and the corporation or the individual and it is essentially the same as the transaction between firms. Therefore, whenever economics addresses the subject of transaction, it should be understood that transaction entities include not only firms but also the government. Similarly, the objects of transaction include not only property rights but also the rights derived from the administrative actions of the government. In this chapter and the chapters that follow, this book establishes rights as the object of transaction, which not only cover the rights attached to the property rights in the traditional sense but also feature the rights derived from the administrative actions of the government.

2 Measuring Transaction Costs by Means of Time

For a long time, new institutional economics has failed to find a viable means to measure transaction costs. When the scope of transaction is expanded to include property rights, it becomes all the more difficult to gauge transaction costs based on monetary value. Transaction costs are the prices paid during the transaction process, which include time, energy, leisure, and property. Then, apart from money and currency, is there any possibility to find another way of measuring transaction costs? If we open up the coordinates in economics, we have multiple variables to choose from, which feature price, value, quantity, and time. Among these four variables, price (including commodity price, wages or salary, interest rate, etc.) and value (including sales volume, profit, GDP, etc.) are measured in terms of money. Quantity (the production volume, transaction volume, and consumption volume across various categories of commodities) is calculated with different units of measurement regarding different categories of commodities. If quantity is not multiplied with unit-price and converted into monetary value, it is difficult to make value comparisons between different quantities of physical commodities. Now, the only option left is time.

Time is a magic power implicit in the world of economic studies. We can find that time is a concept that Adam Smith, Karl Marx, Irving Fisher, Alfred Marshall, and Paul A. Samuelson referred to from time to time in their theoretical frameworks and key doctrines. However, there have never been any serious or systemic discussions concerning time as a norm for measuring value. It is high time that we examine the role that time can play in the conceptual schemes of economics.

The first is the relationship between time and value. Ancient Greek thinkers had already developed ideas concerning the two uses of commodity, that of utility and that of exchange. In the history of economics, Adam Smith was the first to differentiate the commodity's value of utility and the value of exchange. This idea was further elaborated by Karl Marx. However, the criterion for measuring a commodity's value of utility and value of exchange was money. However, the fact is that a commodity's value of utility and value of exchange both contain time and any analysis that excludes the time factor will ultimately remain idealized and abstract in its examination of a commodity's value. Hence, there is always a significant gap between such an investigation and the economic reality it studies. It is true that labor determines the value and the price, but time plays a crucial role in the entire process. As pointed by Marx, value is the crystallization of the time spent on labor and is the labor in material form. Marx divided labor into two categories—the necessary labor and the surplus labor. Within a certain period of time in the entire process of production, a worker only produces the value to cover his necessary subsistence and this period of labor is called the time of necessary labor. Beyond this period of necessary labor, the worker engages in his labor and produces surplus value; hence, this period of time is called the time of surplus labor.[1] The accumulation of labor over time creates value and contributes to prices. The socially necessary labor time determines the volume of the value of the commodities.[2] Marx further argued that there exists a total amount of labor for a society and he also discussed the distribution of the necessary labor time for different categories of commodities.[3]

The second is the relationship between time and the interest rate. Time has a monetary value. This value exists in a society's social and economic life, but it has taken a long time to prove, theoretically, the monetary value of time. In the 1880's, Eugen von Böhm-Bawerk (1851–1914), a member of the Austrian School, proposed his "time lag theory of interest," arguing that the commodities that one currently purchases are generally more valuable than the same quantity of commodities in the same categories that one might purchase in the future.[4] He insisted that time, as a factor for generalizing about all truth, tends to impact on our evaluation of property and commodities.[5] Based on this theory, Irving Fisher proposed the theory that time

---

[1] Please refer to *The Selected Works of Marx and Engels*, Vol. 2, People's Publishing House, 1995 Edition, pp.193–194.

[2] The socially necessary labor time, or Gesellschaftlich notwendige Arbejtszeit, refers to the labor time needed for creating certain utility under the existing normal production conditions of a society, based on the society's average labor skillfulness and labor magnitude.

[3] Please refer to *The Complete Works of Marx and Engels*, Vol. 25, People's Publishing House, 1975 Edition, pp.716–717.

[4] Eugen von Böhm-Bawerk, *PositiVe Theorie Deskapitalcs*, trans. Chen Duan, The Commercial Press, 1964 Edition, p.11.

[5] Eugen von Böhm-Bawerk, *Capital and Interest*, trans. He Kunzeng and Gao Dechao, The Commercial Press, 2010 Edition, p.12.

preference determines the interest rate. According to this theory, different individuals have different time preferences. Those individuals who have preference for the present might choose to borrow money at present and those who have preference for the future might choose to lend money at present. The so-called investment is to acquire future income at the expense of the current income.[6] Alfred Marshall believed that the interest is a form of compensation for the time spent on waiting. Paul A. Samuelson believed that capital is the current monetary value of the income flow in the future.[7]

The third is the relationship between time and efficiency. Adam Smith believed that the division of labor is the source of wealth and the division of labor is essentially aimed at reducing the time consumed in creating wealth. Both the improvement of a worker's skillfulness and the invention of machines are essentially aimed at increasing the speed of production. The acceleration of production and the reduction of the time loss caused by the transitions among different production operations share the same objective—to reduce the time consumed in creating the equal amount of wealth.

Time is inextricably intertwined with the value of labor, the interest rate, and efficiency. There have been instances in the history of economic theories in which time was used as a means for calculating costs. When Karl Marx discussed the circulation cost in his *Das Kapital*, his discussions had already included time as a necessary factor for closing a deal. He argued that it would take time for both the seller and the buyer to complete a transaction, especially because there would be bargaining between both sides in order to secure the most favorable terms possible. The time spent on the transaction is a form of circulation cost that would not increase the already converted value.[8]

There are a number of obvious advantages in using time as a means for calculating the transaction cost.

The first is the objectivity of time. Time is the greatest and the fairest arbiter. Time has its objective existence that can be observed and numerically described, immune from the interference by external forces and fair to all human individuals. Time represents a kind of regular fluidity that cannot be accelerated or retarded. Every moment in the fluidity can be divided and differentiated and all the temporal moments are identical. The past and the present have no essential difference in their dynamic changes. Time is characterized by a singular dimensional existence, as no one knows its origin and no one can predict about its conclusion. Currencies might vanish, so might commodities, but time wouldn't. On the time's axis are recorded all the events that have happened. All these objective attributes of time makes its universality and applicability far beyond other variables of measurement.

The second is the intrinsic unity between the temporal norm and the monetary norm. Labor, interest rate, and efficiency can all be measured according to monetary

---

[6] Irving Fisher, *The Theory of Interest*, trans. Chen Biaoru, The Commercial Press, 2013 Edition,

[7] Paul A. Samuelson and William D. Nordhaus, *Economics*, trans. Xiao Chen, et al, The Commercial Press, 2013 Edition, p.261.

[8] Karl Marx, *Das Kapital*, Vol. 2, People's Publishing House, 1975 Edition, pp. 147–150.

value and all the measurements will have to involve time. The time spent on labor will yield value only through due accumulation. Interest is the compensation for the period of time in which money is lent and awaits being returned. The reduction in the production time means the increased efficiency of creating wealth. As for efficiency, it forms a negative correlation with time. The shorter the time spent on achieving the same extent of growth, the higher the efficiency. In the discussions on many economic issues, time is an indispensible parameter whenever monetary value is used as a standard of measurement. On other occasions, some measurements which necessarily involve time may not necessarily involve money. Using time as a yardstick for measuring transaction costs, far from denying money as a means of measurement, expands the modes of measuring transaction costs.

The third is that it is easy and convenient to use time as a standard of measurement. If money is used as a standard of measurement, comparative studies among different countries will have to involve the conversion of exchange rates, and comparative studies regarding different periods of time will have to involve fluctuations in the interest rates and prices. Their calculation tends to rely on complicated models and the setting of all kinds of hypothetical conditions. Compared with the money standard, the time standard will incur no interferences arising from interests, the interest rates, and the prices. This temporal standard of measurement remains uniform for all countries and for all historical periods. Being easy and convenient, it is highly operable and is prone to acceptance by all parties.

If there is a total sum of labor time for any given society, this labor time must perforce include the time of transaction costs. Among the total sum of labor time, the less time is spent on transaction costs, the more time is saved for the creation of wealth. Throughout human history, mankind has always sought to create more wealth within a shorter span of time. During the twentieth century, the Soviet Union achieved industrialization within a relatively short period of time by implementing the planned economy and its economic aggregate was ranked No. 2 in the world. Many countries and economists enthusiastically embraced the system of planned economy. However, as time passed, there was a striking decline in the speed at which the planned economy created wealth. As a consequence, the Soviet Union, East European countries, and countries in other parts of the world that enforced the planned economy gradually gave up this economic system. Such an outcome was directly connected with transaction costs. In the early days of the planned economy, the supply side and the demand side came together under the direct arrangement of the state, thus reducing the time that both sides spent on closing a transaction on the market. In this mode of transaction, the transaction costs were relatively low. However, as the size of the entire economy expanded, there was a drastic increase in the number of supply-and-demand relationships that called for balancing. It became excessively time-consuming for the supply side and the demand side to complete a transaction simply by relying on government arrangements. In the year the Soviet Union collapsed, its planning commission had to fix prices for a total of 24 million commodities in the entire country[9] and there was no way to calculate how many products should be manufactured in the following year. The result was that people had to queue up for hours outside supermarkets merely in order to buy some eggs whereas factories kept producing, around the clock, the iron and steel that were already in over-supply. With the dramatic increase in transaction costs and the consumption of disproportionate time in transactions out of the total labor time of the society, the time was significantly lessened for the creation of wealth so that the entire economy of the society could no longer maintain normal cycles of reproduction.

Although time was never used as a means for measuring transaction costs in previous economic theories, all the countries have unanimously and voluntarily sought to save time and reduce related transaction costs in the governance endeavors of the government. This is exactly what corporate organizations have sought to do in their business operations. To improve the business environment and enhance investment efficiency, many governments have tried their best to decrease the time spent on issuing administrative approval. On their own part, corporations have resorted to state-of-the-art technologies, the optimized management, and easy access to sound investment environment in order to increase the time for creating wealth and save the time irrelevant to production. When an enterprise evaluates government efficiency and the soundness of the business environments, it tends to prioritize on the time input far above the capital input. In many cases, in seeking government approval, a corporation may find that, compared with the time cost, the capital cost is truly insignificant. When time is employed as a means of quantifying transaction costs, it would become quite easy to assess the relative efficacy of various institutional arrangements that are themselves sources of transaction costs. In this way, it becomes likely to construct, with clear purposes, institutions of low transaction costs or to undertake targeted reforms. Accordingly, both the government and the enterprises will turn the efforts to reduce transaction costs from a spontaneous act into a self-motivated act.

3 Explaining Institutional Evolution with Transaction Costs

New institutional economics has realized that all transactions are conducted under certain institutional arrangements and institutions determine economic performance. Regarding what is meant by "institution," Douglass C. North argues that institutions are artificially designed constraints shaping the interactive relationship between individuals. An institution consists of three parts: formal constraints, informal constraints (codes of behavior, conventions, and self–imposed behavioral standards), and their enforcement. In North's conceptual framework, the notion of "institution" carries a broader range of meanings than the idea of "system" in the Chinese language. It covers corporations, the state, and all kinds of economic organizations. In addition,

[9] Tian Xiudong, "Price Subsidies in the Soviet Union and Debates on Price Subsidies," *Price Theory and Practice*, 1987, Issue 2.

the concept of the "state" consists of the executive, the legislative, and the judiciary.[10] Other leading scholars of new institutional economics, such as Ronald H. Coase and Oliver Williamson, have focused their studies on firms. In the studies performed by Ronald H. Coase, the idea of institution covers an overly broad scope. By contrast, other economists have defined the notion of institution too narrowly, overlooking the state which is the largest supplier of institutions. The institution as discussed in this book refers to a whole complex that consists of a series of formal constraints, informal constraints, and modes of enforcement that, within the range of the government, firms, and the market, complete the transactions of rights and pay transaction costs in accordance with certain contracts.

All institutions go through a process of genesis, operation, and demise. This process can be called institutional evolution. According to the observations made by new institutional economics, institutional evolution is characterized by path dependence. The process of institutional formation incorporates both rational construction and spontaneous evolution, but the modes of institutional evolution are not merely restricted to those two modes. In terms of the entire life cycle of an institution encompassing inception, operation, and demise, institutional evolution goes through the following stages: an institution is formed or terminated by virtue of rational construction or spontaneous evolution; and an institution maintains its operation through phases of path dependence, diminishing efficiency, and institutional alienation. Transaction costs can be used to analyze these attributes and their causes.

The first are rational construction and spontaneous evolution. Rational construction and spontaneous evolution represent two diametrically opposite viewpoints maintained by the economics community regarding the inception of institutions. Scholars of new institutional economics are convinced that an institution is constructed by an actor through rational calculations. These arguments belong to the rational construction theory. The generation and transformation of an institution is guided and shaped by the "visible hand." The decision maker is capable of choosing the optimum or the relatively satisfactory institutional paradigms as targets for active construction. For example, in 1994 China launched the reform of the revenue-sharing fiscal system. This fiscal system was a newly-designed taxation institution modeled after its Western counterparts. For another example, in 2015 China instituted the reform of the administrative approval system regarding pharmaceutics and medical equipment. Through this reform, China formulated standards regarding new drugs that are entirely consistent with the standards in developed countries and initiated the drug consistency evaluation regarding generic drugs.[11] The Institutional

---

[10] Douglass C. North, *Institutions, Institutional Change and Economic Performance*, trans. Hang Xing, Truth and Wisdom Press, SDX Joint Publishing Company, Shanghai People's Publishing House, 2014 Edition, pp. 3,6,–7,33. North defines institution as consisting of formal constraints and informal constraints (codes of behavior, conventions, and self-imposed behavioral norms) and in Chapter 7 of this book he discusses the "enforcement" of these constraints.

[11] Please refer to "The State Council's Policy Proposals Concerning the Reform of the Review and Approval System of Drugs and Medical Equipment." [State Development and Reform Commission [2015] No. 44]

School as represented by Thorstein B. Veblen and John R. Commons, and the Neo-institutional Economic School as represented by John Kenneth Galbraith, and the Austrian School as represented by Friedrich August von Hayek, these three schools of thought believed that institutions develop as a result of long-term unconscious evolution and selection. These three schools can be classified as proponents of the theory of spontaneous evolution.[12] They believed that institutions are the result of the interactions and reciprocal learning among all the participants. The genesis of institutions is guided by the "invisible hand" instead of due to the intentional rational design by a certain participant in advance.

Superficially, rational construction and spontaneous evolution seem to belong to two mutually opposed intellectual schools. Essentially, they describe two modes of institutional generation and these two modes co-exist instead of being mutually repulsive. As there are absolutely no institutions whose spontaneous evolution has been fully validated, such institutions have hardly found their way into the research by the proponents of rational construction. A sound institution which comes into existence entirely through spontaneous evolution and totally independent of rational construction will have to go through a long cycle in order to become improved and propagated. Therefore, pure spontaneous evolution without rational construction is incongruent with the reality of institutional change. For example, after the period of the People's Commune (from 1958 to late 1970's) in China, a number of regions in the country tried to implement the Household Contract Responsibility System, which was repeatedly disapproved by the CPC (the Communist Party of China) Central Committee. The system was popularized throughout the country only when it was approved by the Central Committee until after 1980. Without the rational construction coming from the endorsement by the Central Committee, the spontaneous evolution of the Household Contract Responsibility System was bound to be difficult in addition to being illegal. It was the Central Committee's decision in favor of the system that the system has come to constitute a basic system of agrarian business operation across China's rural areas. The rational construction of this institution cannot be separated from the previous foundation of spontaneous evolution. The above-mentioned policies of primary drug review and the consistency evaluation of the generic drugs, both of which are subjected to medical products supervision and administration, have already been enforced in Europe and the United States. In China, these policies had been under discussion for years and were tentatively formulated. When these policies were formally enforced, their rational construction seemed to be fairly abrupt, but it was essentially firmly based on spontaneous evolution that had already been going on.

The rational construction and the spontaneous evolution of institutions happen independently, and they may also occur in a synchronized fashion. The rational

[12] The evolutionary economic growth theory derived its inspirations from the theory of biological evolution, treating economic growth as a dynamic non-equilibrium evolutionary process. Joseph Alois Schumpeter's theory of innovation made important contributions to the development of this theory. The evolutionary economic growth theory developed during the 1980's and Thorstein B. Veblen, John R. Commons, and John Kenneth Galbraith are generally considered as the forerunners of the theory.

construction of formal constraints has the obvious advantage of saving transaction costs. Under the existing formal constraints, it will generally consume more transaction costs to depend on the spontaneous evolution of an institution with which to regulate the conflicts between the existing institution and the new institution. For example, if the CPC Central Committee had refused to allow the Household Contract Responsibility System to be implemented on a nationwide scale, local governmental officials and the farmers who privately put this system into practice would have to devise ways to evade the inspections by government officials from higher levels and to protect from possible hazards to their personal safety. The time consumed on these activities could be viewed as the transaction costs to the unofficial Household Contract Responsibility System. However, once the Household Contract Responsibility System became a formal constraint, all the transaction costs of the informal system could be annulled. As far as informal constraints and various measures of their enforcement are concerned, spontaneous evolution represents a more widespread phenomenon and also a mode of institution with lower transaction costs. Here, we can still cite the Household Contract Responsibility System as an example. When implementing this system, different regions in China resorted to different measures. For instance, should the land be distributed in accordance with the household as a unit or in accordance with the number of individuals in a household? Should the daughters who live in other villages after getting married still be eligible for the distribution of land? How to distribute the land in good conditions and the land in poor conditions? In addition, how to distribute the land in large stretches and the land that was isolated and fragmented? Regarding those problems, different areas came up with different solutions. It was not until the second round of land contracting in 1997 that the household land contracting became relatively well-defined in rural areas. Eventually, in 2015, the state started to reaffirm the farmers' contractual rights to the distributed lands and to issue certificates. If formal constraints had been imposed on such a plethora of widely different cases of land distribution, the government would have to devote huge amounts of time and energy to solving land disputes and the speed of land distribution would have been seriously retarded. The transaction costs arising from by early imposition of formal constraints would be significantly far greater than if the autonomy was relegated to the basic-level rural organizations.

The second is path dependence, which is sometimes called technological lock-in. By path dependence, it is meant that it becomes difficult to make radical changes in an economic institution once it is established. As the returns from patching up an existing institution are greater than the costs, the institution is likely to be maintained on a relatively long-term basis. W. Brain Arthur (1946–) summarized the chief reasons for the technological lock-in. Huge amounts of fixed cost have been invested in the existing institution and building a new institution means new investments. By contrast, making modifications and improvements along the established path may still increase output and reduce costs.[13] According to the evolutionary economic theory, path dependence is somehow analogous to the phenomenon of inertia in physics.

[13] See W. B. Arthur, A. Ruszczynski, "Strategic Pricing in Markets with Increasing Returns," *Increasing Returns and Path-Dependence in the Economy*, 1994.

Once a physical object moves along a certain path, it will grow dependent on that path. Path dependence exists in economics because economic life shares something in common with the physical world, where one can find mechanisms of increasing returns and self-reinforcement.[14] The previous studies performed by economists on the reasons of path dependence will remain equally valid if the path dependence is substituted by transaction costs. "Patching up" the existing institution helps avoid spending time on institutional restructuring and requires only a very limited amount of transaction cost. As a consequence, path dependence becomes rather widespread.

The third is the diminishing of efficiency. It is a general rule that formal constraints will experience the diminishing of efficiency once they are established. The chief reason for the efficiency decline is the rigid increase in transaction costs, that is, the increase in transaction time. Formal constraints are usually the results of rational construction, but the implementation of an institution may run counter to the original intention with which it was created. As analyzed by Douglass C. North, the enforcement of an institution is usually imperfect and one reason for the imperfection is that the enforcement is executed by agents.[15] The moment a new institution is enforced, it faces the need to make constant adjustments and improvements and the marginal adjustments in an institution will generally contribute to rising transaction costs. Ronald H. Coase also pointed out that an increase in the complexity of an institution leads to a decrease in returns.[16] This rule applies not only to firms but also to the government. For instance, in some places in China, the government might set up a trans-departmental coordination mechanism—a certain so-called "leading group"—for the sake of solving a major problem. Once this leading group is established, there must be an office. Once there is an office, more divisions will have to be set up, such as the functional division, the comprehensive division, the supporting division, and the logistics division. The functional division and the comprehensive division might have to formulate a series of workflow procedures, both internally and externally. When the government on a higher level establishes a leading group and an office, the government on a lower level will have to set up a corresponding coordination mechanism and functional agencies. Under such circumstances, an administrative action taken in order to solve a major problem ends up in a gradual increase in the transaction costs in the entire hierarchy. The more specific are the rules contained in this temporary coordination mechanism for solving the problem, the more transaction costs the administrative counterparts have to pay. To make matters worse, once such a functional department is created, it is very likely to evolve from a temporary institution into a permanent institution and the temporary policies that it implements may evolve in long-term policies. The increase in the transaction costs imposed on the administrative counterparts and the government tends to remain irreversible.

---

[14] Douglass C. North, *Structure and Change in Economic History*, trans. Chen Yu and Luo Huaping, SDX Joint Publishing Company, 1991 Edition, p.150.

[15] Douglass C. North, *Institutions, Institutional Change and Economic Performance*, trans. Hang Xing, Truth and Wisdom Press, SDX Joint Publishing Company, Shanghai People's Publishing House, 2014 Edition, p. 65.

[16] R. H. Coase, "The Nature of the Firm," *Economica*, 1937, 4, pp.386–405.

The fourth is the institutional alienation. In his *Economic and Philosophic Manuscripts of 1844*, Karl Marxist proposed the pioneering idea of alienated labor. According to Marx, a worker in a capitalist society would become increasingly poor if he or she produced increasing amounts of wealth, because the worker might be alienated from the products that he or she manufactured.[17] Although the phenomena that Marx described happened in capitalist societies, the law of alienation is ubiquitous in all forms of institutions.[18] Many institutions, over a period of evolution, tend to depart or deviate from the pristine intention with which it was created. They turn against themselves or become their opposites. Many policies designed to promote growth and development end up in the real world in constantly accumulating transaction costs until reverse regulation happens, which proves obstructive to development. For instance, coal and electricity are located respectively in the upper and lower streams of the energy industry chain. With the advent of the twenty-first century, coal production in China gradually became market-oriented, but the price of electricity and the supply and demand of electricity were still under the control of the state. An examination of the relationship between coal and electricity revealed that coal was frequently in short supply so that the price of electricity had all the likelihood of rapid surge. Nevertheless, the state was woefully slow in adjusting the price of electricity, resulting in enormous losses on the part of the power plants. To address this paradox, China framed a series of policies that featured the alignment between the coal price and the electricity price, the long-term negotiated price of coal, and the adjustment in coal production capacity. The designing of these policies seemed to be ideal and perfect, but such a practice still resorted to man-made efforts instead of market forces to control the supply and demand of coal and electricity and their prices, and to respond to market fluctuations. The distortions in the supply and demand of coal and electricity as well as in their pricing remained unresolved. The prices of coal and electricity kept escalating in a spiral manner, resulting in increasingly serious supply-and-demand paradoxes between coal and electricity. A policy designed to work out the conflicts between coal and electricity ended up turning against itself.[19]

When analyzing the institutional changes that happened during China's reform, Chinese scholars have shown special preference for analyzing two modes of change—the sudden and radical change and the gradual change. They prefer gradual change after comparing the pros and cons of both modes of change. The foregoing analysis that I have performed is sufficient to show that institutional change is far more complicated than a neat dichotomy. Abrupt and radical institutional change

[17] Based on his idea that a worker is alienated from his own products and his own labor, Marx demonstrated that an individual is essentially alienated from his own nature as part of mankind and from other individuals. See Karl Marx, *Economic and Philosophic Manuscripts of 1844*, People's Publishing House, 2015 Edition, p.1.

[18] QingMU Changyan concluded in his book *A Comparative Institutional Analysis of Economic Systems* that an economic system is a complicated evolutionary institution. At the time of large-scale economic reform, even though the overall objectives have been clearly defined, the outcome and the process of the reform might be filled with uncertainties and alienation might occur in that particular economic system.

[19] Please refer to Sect. 2 of Chapter 8 in this book.

tends to be the result of rational construction and such construction is intimately related to the exemplary effects that are generated out of the spontaneous evolution. Gradual changes primarily consist of spontaneous evolution. But in the evolutionary reform driven by formal constraints, every push by formal constraints is a small-scale revolutionary change. Both evolutionary change and the revolutionary change are interwoven with cases of path dependence, efficiency diminishing, and institutional alienation. A close examination of China's reform practice can reveal at least three general rules governing institutional evolution.

Rule No. 1: under the condition of path dependence, an institution evolves in concomitant conditions of efficiency diminishing and institutional alienation. Due to the law of efficiency diminishing, an institution will incur increasing transaction costs in its marginal adjustment the moment the institution is established. In addition, due to the law of institutional alienation, an institution may deviate from its envisioned goal in the process of implementation. Governed by those two laws, an institution evolves in the direction of growing transaction costs and, as the transaction costs reach a certain point, the positive impact of the institution on promoting development will decrease and may even become a factor obstructing development. Obviously, the operators of an institution would not allow efficiency diminishing and institutional alienation to continue unchecked. They would stick to the existing institutional path and make marginal adjustments in the institution by "patching it up." In so doing, they try to keep the institution developing along the established path.

Rule No. 2: the existing institution will not incur demise before its productive force is fully released. As pointed out by Karl Marx, whatever its social system, a society would not experience demise before all the productive forces it accommodates are fully released. On the other hand, a more advanced form of production relations would never come into existence before the conditions of its physical existence become mature in the embryo of the existing social system.[20] This doctrine proposed by Marx is most applicable to the study of social systems. History has demonstrated that this doctrine is equally applicable to the study of the changes of economic institutions within a given social system. The life cycle of an institution, ranging from genesis, evolution to demise, usually comprises of a number of phases—initial flourishing, subsequent improvement, regression, degradation, alienation, and eventual dysfunction and decease. An institution comes into existence either by means of rational construction or by means of spontaneous evolution. In the preliminary stage of an institution, its transaction costs tend to be relatively low and its efficiency tends to be relatively high. However, impacted by diminishing efficiency and institutional alienation, an institution's efficacy keeps decreasing. By the time the institutional costs exceed the institutional returns and an institution releases all its productive force, the institution will lose its existential necessity and will face demise. For instance, China used to have many government institutions, like the ministry of machinery industry, the ministry of textile industry, and the ministry of

[20] Please refer to *The Selected Works of Marx and Engels*, Vol. 13, People's Publishing House, 1995 Edition, p.9.

electronic industry. Each ministry had a complicated hierarchy of functional departments extending all the way from the central government to provincial governments, consisting of a colossal administrative structure and a network of countless enterprises. Within a particular period of history, those administrative institutions played an important role in organizing production. But, as the market economy kept developing, the role of those institutions in China's national economy kept declining. By the time when the cost to maintain those administrative institutions far exceeded their returns, they were eventually abolished in their entirety.

Rule No. 3: without exogenous conditions, institutional revolutions cannot be accomplished solely by means of endogenous conditions. Just as an individual cannot lift himself above the surface of the ground by grabbing up his own hair, an institution is unable to effect any fundamental change simply by resorting to its endogenous forces. All the countries across the world follow this rule of institutional change. For Western countries, their economic institutions evolved from mercantilism, liberalism (represented by classical economics and neoclassical economics), Keynesianism, to the supply-side economics. In China, reform was conducted both in particular industrial sectors and throughout industry chains. In all these cases, the rule has dominated. In most circumstances, institutional operators are not institutional formulators or constructors. Institutional operators do not have the fundamental willpower to set up a brand-new institution. The *raison d'etre* for every institution is determined by the institution that created it. Even if the institutional operators have the intention to make drastic changes, these changes are likely to be disapproved by the institutional formulators. Therefore, all the changes that institutional operators can introduce into the existing institution are local modifications by way of "patching things up." Every single modification means an increase in transaction costs. The driving force for drastic institutional revolution will develop only under the impact of powerful exogenous factors. For instance, China conducted reform in 2002 in the electricity institution. The National Electrical Power Corporation which monopolized both the upstream and the downstream of the electrical power industry was split up. Before this splitting up, the National Electrical Power Corporation itself conducted extensive studies concerning its own reform, but the corporation's own reform agenda could never have formulated a splitting-up program of such magnitude. It was the decisions by the CPC Central Committee and the State Council that led to the breakup of the monopoly. For another example, according to the statistics of China's Ministry of Commerce, after China joined the WTO in 2001, China amended and removed, in accordance with the WTO rules, over 190,000 policies, regulations, and measures formulated by regional and local governments. Without the pressures exerted by the central government and by a whole range of exogenous factors, various departments under the central government and the local governments on different levels would not have had the motivation to eradicate all the outmoded normative documents.

4 Analytical Framework and Process of Institutional Evolution

By now, we have observed various phenomena in institutional evolution, gained understanding about the laws underlying institutional evolution, and realized the role played by transaction costs in institutional evolution. Confronted with such a plethora of complicated institutions in our social and economic life, institutional economists have a further problem to address—how to analyze the mechanisms of institutional evolution, determine institutional efficiency, and eventually take active steps to optimize institutions. Toward this objective, it is imperative to develop an analytical framework that can be universally applied to diverse forms of institutions.

In the foregoing analysis, it is pointed out that all transactions are completed under certain institutions. The unceasing transactions are the drivers of institutional evolutions. The completion of every single transaction necessarily involves the objects of transaction, the rules of transaction, the costs of transaction, and the entities of transaction. The analysis has already revealed that rights are the objects of transaction, contracts the rules of transaction, time and capital the costs of transaction, and the government, firms, and the market the entities of transaction. For the sake of analytical convenience, every transaction can be viewed as a module which comprises of three components—the rights, contracts, and costs (please refer to Table 1). Transaction entities complete transactions between each other by means of the transaction module, and transactions include the transactions between the government and corporations, between the government and the market, between different government departments, and between the corporations and the market.

Between transaction entities, rights are transferred or alienated in accordance with the terms and conditions set in a contract. Time has to be spent in order to satisfy every single transaction rule, and sometimes the satisfaction of transaction rules involves

Table 1 The structure of the transaction module

Transaction entities	××× Rights		
	Transaction rules	Transaction costs	
××× Corporation | ××× Government	1	t 1	P 1
	2	t 2	P 2
	3	t 3	P 3
	…	…	
		$\sum$t	$\sum P$

Remarks: 1. The grey part represents a complete transaction module
2. t represents the time spent on completing a transaction
3. P represents the costs paid to satisfy the rules of each transaction, that is, the price of a transaction
4. $\sum$ t represents the amount of time in the total transaction costs
5. $\sum$ P represents the capital consumed in the total transaction costs

the payment of money according to certain prices. Put together, all the time and money spent on the satisfaction of all the transaction rules constitute the transaction costs indispensible to the transfer of rights. When all the costs of transactions are put together, they constitute the costs of operating an institution on the macro level. Generally speaking, every time the government creates and establishes a right, a transaction module comes into existence. The creation, establishment, and transfer of rights will generate transaction costs. Any institutional analysis must delve deep into transaction modules, investigating how the design of rights and of contracts produces impacts on transaction costs. The optimization of an institution must focus on improving the design of rights and the design of contracts so as to discover ways for lowering transaction costs. The good thing about module-based analysis is that the otherwise highly complicated relations of rights are simplified. Many seemingly complicated structures of rights, once converted into modules, present very clear relations among diverse rights. The process of institutional analysis consists of the following steps: defining the transaction module, identifying transaction entities, establishing transaction rights, specifying transaction rules, quantifying transaction costs, investigating factors affecting transaction costs, and proposing solutions to institutional optimization.

In any study of institutional evolution based on transaction costs, the key lies in the analysis of transaction rules. As the largest provider of institutions, the state maintains contractual relationship with the market, the corporations, and government organizations. Such a relationship is primarily reflected in policies, rules, regulations, decisions, public notices and other normative documents. To understand these documents, one has to develop the ability to interpret the complicated verbal expressions and gain insights into the relations, as well as the changes in these relations, between the rights and the obligations of the transaction entities. In addition, one has to understand the impact that all these factors can have on transaction costs. Studies of this whole process can help chart out the trajectory of institutional evolution.

In the triangular relationship among the government, the market, and the enterprises, Coase and subsequent new institutional economists have conducted sufficient studies concerning the relationship between the enterprises and the market, obviating the need for further analysis. This book will focus on the relationship between the government and the market, between the government and the enterprises, and between different government departments. The first is the relationship between the government and the market. Regarding this relationship, this book will analyze the boundary between the government and the market in the same way that Coase analyzed the boundary between the firms and the market. By analyzing the transfer of rights and the transaction costs spent on honoring contracts, this book seeks to answer two questions—what are the responsibilities that the government should perform, and what are the responsibilities that the market has to perform. The second is the relationship between the government and the enterprises. My studies will be focused on the relationship between the enterprises and the rights that are generated out of the government's administrative actions. By examining the transaction costs that happen to the transfer of rights, this book attempts to answer another two questions—what are reasonable transaction costs and what are unreasonable costs? Finding answers to these questions can help find ways to improve the mechanisms of deriving rights from administrative actions, to optimize transaction contracts, and to reduce transaction costs. The third is the relationship between different government organizations. In all countries across the world, the government usually consists of a central government and many local governments. A government on a particular level can be divided into many different functional departments. The transactions between the government and the market and between the government and the enterprises are intertwined with large numbers of transactions of rights between different government departments. For instance, many items that require government approval may seem to be the transactions of rights between the government and the enterprises, but behind such transactions there are many transactions of rights between diverse functional departments of the government. In economics, no previous studies have done systemic analysis on this subject. In China, this class of transactions of rights account for a sizable proportion in the government's administrative actions and are a major factor contributing to the growing costs of institutional operation.

Chapter 4
How Institutions Determine Development: The Case of China's Reform and Opening-Up

China's reform and opening-up campaign constitutes a history of creating economic miracles. It is also a history in which different economic institutions competed against one another to promote growth and development. The planned economy and the market economy represent two entirely different technical routes in the government's economic governance. They co-existed and rivaled with each other and experienced waxing and waning throughout the competition cycle. Eventually, China chose the market economy which is lower in transaction costs and gave up the planned economy which was higher in transaction costs. This process has profoundly changed China's understanding about the production relations and how such relations could be most profitably put into practice. For a long time after the founding of the People's Republic of China, the Chinese government was convinced that the socialist production relations were fundamentally characterized by the public ownership, the planned economy, and the labor-based distribution of income. It was the reform and opening-up campaign that led to de-bindings with China's social system in those three spheres. The first is that, regarding the allocation of resources, a de-binding was created between the planned economy and the social system, the result being the creation of the socialist market economy. The second is that, regarding ownership, a de-binding was created between the public ownership and the social system, the result being the creation of a basic economic system dominated by public ownership under which many different forms of economic ownership can achieve common development. The third is that, regarding the distribution of wealth, a de-binding was created between the distribution based on labor and the social system, the result being the creation of a system under which labor, capital, technology, management, and other factors of production all participate in wealth distribution based on their respective contributions. In seeking to accomplish these three de-bindings, China restored the status of the market and private economy as transaction entities and created incentive mechanisms for reducing transaction costs. These endeavors have reduced the average transaction costs, spurring widespread economic activities of

B. Fan, *The Rationale Behind Change*, https://doi.org/10.1007/978-981-97-8854-5_4

low transaction costs and dramatically increasing the society's overall scale of transactions. As a result, the Chinese economy has been experiencing enduring vigor and vibrancy.

1 Reform Commencing with Institutions of High Transaction Costs

In 1928, the Soviet Union started to enforce its first 5-year plan. During that period, complete agricultural collectivization and mandatory plans were enforced, and the heavy industry and the military industry were developed at super-rapid speed. Ultimately, in the 1930's, a system of planned economy developed, characterized by high centralization and concentration, mandatory directives, and military mobilization. With the establishment of that system, the Soviet Union maintained its position as the world's second largest economy over a long period of time and succeeded in influencing the economic development of some other countries through the medium of the Council for Mutual Economic Assistance (Comecon). This made the Soviet Model the world's most influential and most important model of planned economy. In this section, analysis will be carried out to illuminate why the planned economy could lead to higher transaction costs.

1. **China built its system of planned economy in imitation of the Soviet Union**

Influenced by the Soviet Model, China built its own system of planned economy immediately after the founding of the People's Republic of China in 1949. In 1952, the state formally issued the annual control statistics for developing national economy. In the same year, the State Development Planning Commission (SDPC) was established. Starting from 1953, SDPC was responsible for formulating annual draft plans and 5-year draft plans for developing national economy. These plans covered almost all the segments in the economic and social operation that included production, distribution, exchange, consumption, and all the major facets of social reproduction, as well as science, education, culture, sports, health, and other programs of social development. From the founding of the People's Republic of China in 1949 to 1978, although China enforced the system of planned economy, all the successive 5-year plans failed to be effectively implemented except for the first 5-year plan. Since the reform and opening-up campaign in 1978, China still adhered to the planned economy for a considerable period of time. From 1978 to 1984, the year when the 3rd Plenary Session of the 12th CPC Central Committee was held, the planning-based governance was somehow reinforced[1] and the evils of the planned economy were rendered all the more pronounced. "China adhered to the planned economy during

[1] In the first "5-Year plan" period, there were a total of 16 categories of plans covering agriculture, industry, transportation, posts and telecommunication, commerce, geological survey, infrastructure, scientific research, culture, education and public health, urban public utilities, public finance, etc. In the wake of the 3rd Plenary Session of the 11th CPC Central Committee, the planned economy was strengthened. For example, the 6th "5-year plan" covered such content areas as the direction, the

that particular period of history primarily because China saw how, after the founding of the new republic, China could make spectacular achievements by enforcing the planned economy, in which large-scale programs of socialist economic development were undertaken by means of a high concentration of financial resources, material resources, and human resources. At the same time, a whole range of problems—vast territory, large population, undeveloped transportation networks, malfunctioning information communication, unbalanced regional economic and cultural development—could not be completely solved on a short-term basis. Furthermore, China lacked well-developed commodity economy at that time." Therefore, in view of all those factors, "it was all the more imperative to build such a system of planned economy."[2]

According to the understanding that people developed during that particular historical period, the idea of planning as used in the context of the planned economy did not refer to the planning of an individual economic unit or functional department, but to the planning of the reproduction of an entire society. Such planning had to use a unified national economic program to regulate the proportion of the total labor time distributed to individual production organizations in order to achieve a balance between social production and social demands and a well-coordinated development of the entire national economy. This unified planning must exercise a certain degree of binding force instead of being purely an economic forecast.

The traditional system of planned economy followed the principle of "unified planning plus administration on multiple levels." This principle meant that the state brought major social and economic activities into a unified program in which the development and the exploitation of the human resource, material resource, financial resource, and natural resource must be coordinated and arranged in a comprehensive and balanced manner on a nationwide scale. Various departments, regions, and economic units on basic levels must engage in economic activities entirely under the unified planning of the state. The responsibilities and administrative powers of the central government and the provincial governments were clearly defined. The planning departments at the basic levels were given due planning autonomy so that the provincial governments, departments, and the units at basic levels could exercise their initiative and proactivity.

Based on different time sequences, the national economic planning scheme was categorized into long-term plans (over 10 years), medium-term plans (approximately

---

objective, basic tasks, and comprehensive targets regarding national economy and social development, the distribution and deployment of production forces, the development programs of various economic departments of the government, regional economic development plans, programs for scientific research and educational development, and programs of social development, etc. Basic tasks and comprehensive targets included plans concerning the average annual growth rate of industrial and agricultural production, the overall quantity of products of the society, national income and economic outcomes, finance and credit loans, and investment in fixed assets, as well as objectives of scientific and technological development and human talents development, and the objectives of developing people's livelihood and social causes.

[2] Please refer to "The CPC Central Committee's Decision on the Reform of Economic System (Oct. 21, 1984)," *Selections of Important Documents since the 12th CPC National Congress* (Part 1), People's Publishing House, 1986 Edition.

5 years), and short-term plans (annual and quarterly plans). Based on the hierarchical sequence of administration, three categories could be differentiated. The first were the central plans, that is, the national plans and the plans for various ministries under the central government, formulated by the State Development Planning Commission (SDPC). The second were the regional plans, that is, the plans for provinces (and autonomous regions, municipalities) and counties. The third were plans for basic levels, that is, the plans for enterprises which practiced independent accounting and for independently-operating public institutions. In order to include all the activities of national economy within the range of central planning, the state, based on the sequence of social reproduction, framed production plans, circulation plans, distribution plans, and consumption plans. In addition, parallel to economic plans, the state developed scientific and technological plans as well as social plans.

The state planning primarily took the form of either mandatory plans or recommended plans. (1) Mandatory plans were issued, from top to lower administrative levels, to the planning units on basic levels by the central government and the planning commissions on various levels. The units at basic levels must implement such plans and ensure their full completion. Relevant personnel would be held accountable for failing to accomplish these plans due to their incompetent personal performance. Generally speaking, the state imposed mandatory plans only on products that were vital to national economy and the livelihood of ordinary people (i.e., products which required state allocation) and on major economic activities critical to national governance.[3] (2) The recommended plans were issued by the State Council and by various planning commissions on various levels and they were not mandatory in nature. The units for implementing the plans could develop their own plans based on the changing circumstances in the supply-and-demand relationship of the market and on the actual conditions of the units themselves. These plans must be submitted to and registered at the departments in charge.

The targets in the formulated plans were classified into the following categories. The first were the quantitative and qualitative targets. The quantitative targets were the objectives reflecting the scale of the national economic development, such as the output of the industrial and agricultural products and the volume of infrastructure investment. The qualitative targets were the goals reflecting the quality, efficiency, and economic results of production, business operation, and management, such as the yield rate of industrial products and the labor productivity. With regard to qualitative targets, those which reflected the use of production means like equipment, raw materials, fuel, and power were usually called techno-economic targets. The second were the physical targets and value targets. The physical targets referred to the targets that employed physical measurement units like weight, volume, length, and pieces to signify utility, such as tons of steel and cast iron, meters of cloth, or pieces of machinery. The value targets were the targets expressed in the form of money as measurement units. The third were the mandatory targets and recommended targets.

---

[3] Please refer to "The CPC Central Committee's Decision on the Reform of Economic System (Oct. 21, 1984)," *Selections of Important Documents since the 12th CPC National Congress* (Part 1), People's Publishing House, 1986 Edition.

The fourth were the performance evaluation targets and accounting targets. Performance evaluation targets were issued vertically to the basic levels and were used as a basis for assessing how well the units at basic levels had implemented the plans. Accounting targets were those used by the central government for analysis, research, feasibility study, and comprehensive balancing in the process of formulating plans. This category of targets would not be issued to organizations at subordinate levels.

In real-world economic practices, plans could be divided into several major categories as follows. The first comprised of production development plans, including the reproduction plans of agriculture, industry, energy, transportation, post, and fixed assets. The second comprised of circulation plans, including the plans regarding the means of production, the means of livelihood, and foreign trade. The third comprised of plans for population and labor, including the plans for population, labor force, and labor productivity. The fourth comprised of plans for science and education, including the plans for the development of science, technology, and the cause of education. The fifth comprised of distribution plans, including the plans for national income, the rewards for labor, cost, and price. The sixth comprised of consumption plans, which were mainly the plans for the consumption and the livelihood of the general public. The seventh were the comprehensive balancing of the national economy. All the above-mentioned contents constituted the system of national economic planning in that particular historical period of planned economy.

In that given period of traditional planned economy, the state's economic governance was primarily reflected in the formulation of annual plans. Those plans included the output of most products, the connection between the production and sales, the supply of raw materials, the scale of investment and arrangements for construction projects, the scale of fiscal revenue and expenditure as well as their structural arrangements, credit loans from banks, cash scale and structural arrangements, the scale of import and export in foreign trade and arrangements regarding categories and quantities, the number of people to be employed and the total wage arrangements, the number of students to be admitted into colleges, and the assignment of jobs to college graduates. Most of the targets were the targets in mandatory plans. It is generally believed that, under the system of planned economy, the behavior of the government and enterprises demonstrated typical characteristics, such as the unified control over revenue and expenditure, excessive-concentration, rigidity in unified control, an excessive proportion of mandatory plans, the non-separation of government administration and enterprise management, ill-defined property rights, inter-departmental division and isolation, and insufficient autonomy for enterprises. The exercise of administrative power by the government lied at the heart of the system of planned economy, whereby the government allocated resources by means of mandatory plans. Under the system of planned economy, the state-owned enterprises were deprived of their autonomy to manage their own business, lacked necessary flexibility, and were under the unified administration of the state which assumed responsibility for all the profits and losses of the enterprises. An overview of the research findings concerning the system of planned economy indicates that, under the system of planned economy, both the government and the enterprises demonstrated the following major characteristics.

The first characteristic was the imposition of state-formulated plans on the allocation of resources. All the social resources, including the human resource, financial resource, and physical resource, must be distributed and coordinated primarily in accordance with the targets in the plans. Generally speaking, such plans excluded the regulatory function of the supply-and-demand relationship and of economic levers. In terms of finance, unified state control over revenue and expenditure was implemented according to national plans, in which case banks were in reality the cashier or the treasurer of the State Planning Commission and the Ministry of Finance. The investment in fixed assets had to be conducted according to the state plans, ranging from feasibility study, project initiation, construction activation, construction completion, to inspection for acceptance. The pricing of most production means and of consumer products was performed by the state, most of the production means and the means of livelihood were purchased and distributed by the state, and the assignment of labor and wages was also conducted according to state plans, all in a centralized manner.

Secondly, an enterprise was merely a production unit under a certain state planning department. Most of the enterprises were enterprises of national ownership rather than entities representing independent interests. They were subordinated to an administrative department in a certain industrial sector. To those enterprises, state plans were equivalent to mandatory laws and were the tasks that must be accomplished by all means. An enterprise's human resource, financial resource, material resource, production, supply, and sales were all subjected to the government control according to the targets in the state plans.

Thirdly, the state planning was primarily focused on the control of material objects. The plans formulated by the state mainly sought to balance and manage the production, circulation, distribution, and consumption of various material resources. The management of value was only of secondary importance. In addition, under the planned economy, the state divided the entire society into two fundamental sectors—the material production sector and non-material production sector. It was believed that only the material production sector could create value whereas the tertiary industry, which encompasses science and technology, education, culture, public health, and government administration, had nothing to do with the creation of value. One of the consequences of this division between the material production sector and non-material production sector was that the development of the tertiary industry seriously lagged behind the development of other industries during the period of planned economy.

Fourthly, the government and the enterprises were not clearly separated. The government was not only the owner but also the business operator of state-owned assets. The government was involved not only in macro economy but also in microeconomic activities.

Fifthly, the interests of various economic entities were ignored. Under the system of planned economy, it was assumed that the interests of the state, enterprises, and individuals were highly unified and integrated, thus overlooking the interests of various economic entities. The state-formulated plans were the embodiment of the state will, unlikely to reflect the concerns and the will of various economic entities. As a result, it was difficult to bring the proactive initiative of the enterprises and individuals into full play. The traditional theory of planned economy maintained that such an economic model could boost the development of national economy most effectively and efficiently, capable of maximizing the interests of the entire society and fulfilling the principle of maximum frugality. It was also assumed that all the potential wastes and losses ensuing from the uncontrollable irregularities of the market could be obviated. However, the reality was that the planned economy, in ignoring the role played by the law of value and the principle of material interests, resulted in the severe gaps between the supply and the demand and, worse still, in low efficiency.[4]

2. **Economic activities organized "in accordance with plans and proportions"**

The idea of developing economy "in accordance with plans and proportions" was the central concept underpinning the planned economy. The Soviet Union was the first to apply this theory to its socialist development and the theory came to be the sole option for almost all the other countries which chose the path of socialism ever since. The key foundation for this theory came from some of the ideas that Marx expressed in a letter that he wrote to Ludwig Kugelmann in 1868. In the letter, Marx pointed out that, in order to obtain the quantity of products commensurate with the quantity of demands, it was necessary to put in a certain amount of aggregate social labor in various fields. It was self-evident that this necessity for the distribution of social labor according to certain proportions would never be abolished by any particular form of social production; the only change that would happen was in the way this necessity was manifested.[5] Marx further pointed out say that a socialist society was "a self-conscious and well-planned coalition."[6] Engels believed that a socialist country should be "a self-conscious organization of social production which engages in production and distribution in accordance with plans."[7] The economists of the Soviet Union contended that all those views implied that Marx and Engels believed that socialism must be planned. In fact, however, the comments made by Marx and Engels on the planning in a socialist society were all too sporadic and fragmentary, without any systemic elaboration on the need for planned economy.

---

[4] Some of the analyses in this section contain information from the following research: *Selected Works of Gui Shiyong*, China Yan Shi Press, 2007 Edition; *Manual of the Planning Work*, ed. Chen Xianzhu, China Financial and Economic Press, 1984 Edition; *Planned Economics*, ed. Li Zhenzhong, China Renmin University Press, 1985 Edition; *Issues in China's Plan-Based Governance*, ed. He Jianzhang and Wang Jiye, China Social Sciences Press, 1984 Edition; *Principles of National Economic Planning*, China Renmin University Press, 1983 Edition; *Introduction to Socialist Market Economy*, ed. The Textbook Editing and Review Committee of National Government Official Training Program, People's Publishing House, 2002 Edition; *Introduction to Socialist Market Economy*, ed. Song Xingming, Economy and Management Publishing House, 1998 Edition; *Introduction to Market Economy*, ed. Zhou Yuheng, China Wu Zi Press, 2001 Edition.

[5] Please refer to *The Complete Works of Marx and Engels*, Vol. 32, People's Publishing House, 1956 Edition, p. 541.

[6] Please refer to *The Complete Works of Marx and Engels*, Vol. 25 (Part II), People's Publishing House, 1974 Edition, p.745.

[7] Please refer to *The Complete Works of Marx and Engels*, Vol. 9, People's Publishing House, 2009 Edition, p. 422.

Vladimir Lenin believed that maintaining proportionality in a frequent and self-conscious manner was in reality a form of planning. Based on this, Stalin explicitly proposed that the "law of developing national economy in accordance with plans (and proportions)" constituted the economic law of socialism.[8]

China, having established its own system of planned economy, sought to organize economic activities according to plans and the principle of proportionality. In the first "5-year plan" period, China developed the idea of "four major proportions" and "three major balances." The "four major proportions" referred to the proportions between agriculture and industry, between light industry and heavy industry, between different sectors of heavy industry, and between the development of industry and the transportation of railway systems. The "three major balances" referred to the need to maintain balances between fiscal revenue and expenditure, between purchasing power and commodity supply, and between the supply and the demand of key material resources. A general understanding at that time was that the principle of "proportioned development" must be strictly abided by, but the specific proportions between different sectors might vary in different countries and in different periods even within the selfsame country. The only way to determine the proportionality was to assess whether different sectors were in balance. To be proportionate was to be balanced; vice versa, being balanced implied, in general, that everything was in proper proportion.

During the period of planned economy, the planning commissions of the state were responsible for drawing up a plethora of plans, resorting to a number of specific approaches such as the control of aggregate quantity, the control of quotas, government pricing, segmentation and assignment of tasks from top to lower levels, and performance evaluation to determine whether various targets had been met. The purpose of planning was to ensure an overall balance, that is, a proper distribution of the human resource, the material resource, and the financial resource in the entire society, and to achieve equilibrium between social production and social demands. In this way, within the entire national economic machinery, all the sectors and all the segments in social reproduction could be effectively geared to one another.[9] For instance, by aligning the material supply to the demands of economic development, the state imposed a plan-based distribution system on key material resources (the system of unified distribution) to ensure supply. In China, the material resources

---

[8] In 1952, *Issues in Soviet Union's Socialist Economy* was published. This was a book written by Stalin about the rules governing the socialist economy. He argued that national economy was governed by the rules of planned development and those rules came into existence as the opposites to the rules of competition and production anarchy under the capitalist system. The socialist economy developed on the basis of the public ownership of the production means. The rules governing the planned development of national economy could allow the planning departments of the Soviet Union to have the possibility to make correct plans about social production. However, it was wrong to confuse the possibility with reality, as possibility and reality were entirely two different things. In order to translate the possibility into a reality, it was necessary to study these economic rules, grasp them, and learn to skillfully put these rules into practice. It was necessary to formulate plans that could fully reflect the requirements of these rules.

[9] *Manual of the Planning Work*, ed. Chen Xianzhu, China Financial and Economic Press, 1984 Edition, p. 478 & p. 659.

distributed according to state plans covered 227 categories in 1953; in 1957, that figure rose to 532 categories. In the process, the industrial products that fell under direct state planning and administration reached 115 categories in 1953 and in 1956 that figure rose to 380 categories, accounting for approximately 60% of the aggregate industrial output. Prior to 1979, the State Planning Commission imposed state planning and management, in the form of mandatory plans, on the production of agricultural products in 25 key categories.[10]

Since the reform and opening-up, the categories of material resources subjected to the unified distribution of the state somehow declined in number, but still accounted for a rather high percentage. In 1979, the State Planning Commission was responsible for distributing 256 categories of materials that were subjected to unified state distribution. According to statistics, such materials accounted for different proportions in the overall domestic output, namely, 77.1% for iron and steel, 85% for timber, 35.7% for cement, and 58.9% for coal. In 1980, the State Planning Commission was in charge of administrating 120 categories of industrial products that fell under mandatory plans, and these categories of industrial products accounted for 40% of the country's aggregate industrial output.[11] In 1984, the State Planning Commission issued mandatory plans covering a total of 123 categories of products, whose output accounted for 40% of the entire industrial output. There were 1700 categories of industrial products under the administration of various ministries, accounting for approximately 30%. In addition, provincial and local governments imposed their own mandatory plans. Put together, all the categories of industrial products included in mandatory plans might reach up to 80% of the total industrial output.[12]

On the other hand, the government assumed the responsibility to fix prices on a broad range of material resources and commodities. For example, in 1978, in the retail business, the prices fixed by the government accounted for 97%. In the government's purchasing of agricultural products, the government-fixed prices accounted for 92.2% and the government-recommended prices accounted for 2.2%. The government imposed ex-factory prices on 100% of the production means. As the reform made headway, government pricing was significantly reduced. In 1997, in the retail sector, government pricing accounted for 5.5%, and the government-recommended pricing accounted for only 1.3%. In terms of the government purchasing of agricultural products, the government pricing accounted for 16.1% whereas the government-recommended pricing accounted for only 3.4%. The government imposed ex-factory prices on 13.6% of the production means and recommended ex-factory prices on 4.8% of the production means.[13]

Under the planned economy, each segment in the planning process could be seen as a transaction of rights and too many segments in planning would render it exceedingly costly to make and implement economic decisions. Plans were formulated according to the procedure of "coordination between the central government and

[10] *Selected Works of Gui Shiyong* (Vol. 8), China Yan Shi Press, 2007 Edition, pp.2–3.

[11] *Selected Works of Zheng Xinli*, China Social Sciences Press, 2016 Edition, pp. 152–153.

[12] *Selected Works of Gui Shiyong* (Vol. 3), China Yan Shi Press, 2007 Edition, p. 228.

[13] Zheng Xinli, *Studies in the Development Planning*, China Planning Press, 1999 Edition, p. 294.

local governments." First of all, the State Council would issue, in a top-to-bottom manner, control figures (or the suggested figures). Then, governments and planning departments on subordinate levels would develop draft plans and submit those plans, in a bottom-to-top manner, to the State Council. Finally, the State Council would issue the finalized official plans, in a top-to-bottom manner, to relevant subordinate departments and units for the plans to be implemented. This approach of formulating plans was called the procedure of "two top-to-bottom processes and one bottom-to-top process." In the first "top-to-bottom" process, the State Planning Commission would first propose key targets and undertake preliminary balancing. Those statistical targets, once approved and ratified by the State Council, would be issued to various departments and provinces (regions and municipalities). The regional and local governments would then assign those targets, that is, production goals, to enterprises. Then, in the "bottom-to-top" process, the enterprises would develop their own draft plans and submit these plans to provincial and local governments and finally to various departments under the State Council. Local governments and various departments under the State Council, after collecting all the submitted plans and making balances, would develop draft plans in their respective regions and departments and then submit the plans to the State Planning Commission once again. Based on the draft plans that had been submitted, the State Planning Commission would make overall balancing on a nationwide scale, developing draft plans for the national economic and social development. The State Council would call for and preside over national planning meetings and various provinces (regions and municipalities) and departments under the State Council would discuss the draft plans for the national economic and social development and then give feedback for revisions and modifications. After making necessary revisions and improvements, the State Planning Commission, with the review and approval by the State Council, submit the plans to the National People's Congress for the final review and approval. Finally, in the second "top-to-bottom" process, all the draft plans, once approved and ratified, would be finalized into official plans and would be issued, in a top-to-bottom manner, to various units on basic levels for implementation. In some cases, it was necessary for the local governments and enterprises to first submit information concerning their production and demands, and the State Planning Commission would, after making balances, develop preliminary plans and then issue the plans to local governments and enterprises to solicit feedback. If this process was to be included, then the whole procedure would consist of "two top-to-bottom processes and two bottom-to-top processes."[14] Consequently,

[14] In 1952, the Financial and Economic Committee under the Government Administration Council of the Central People's Government, known as FEC, issued the document "The Method of Formulating National Economic Plans," which stipulated that the formulation of the plans must go through "two top-to-bottom processes and two bottom-to-top processes." First, the government departments on the basic level must propose possible figures in the plans that were to be formulated. Then, the government departments on the higher levels must propose control figures in the plans to be formulated after making overall balancing. After receiving the control figures, the government departments on the basic levels would formulate draft plans in accordance with actual production circumstances. Finally, after discussions and demonstrations, the government departments on the higher levels would approve and publish the plans.

the entire planning process was exceedingly time-consuming, as the formulation of the plans would have to go through a number of phases, ranging from drafting plans, submitting plans to government departments on upper levels, collecting all the plans, making necessary balances among various plans, reviewing and approving the plans, assigning plans to relevant enterprises to be implemented, inspecting and evaluating the implementation of the plans. For example, the development of China's first "5-year plan" took a total of five years—the preliminary drafting of the plan commenced in 1951 and the finalized official plans were passed by the National People's Congress in July 1955.[15]

Here, we can simulate the entire process whereby two enterprises completed their transactions during the period of the planned economy. Suppose Enterprise A in a certain county needed a particular kind of steel, which could be produced by Enterprise B in another county. The completion of this supply-and-demand relationship would have to go through the following procedures (please refer to Fig. 1). First, the State Planning Commission would estimate the nationwide supply-and-demand situation of this steel via the coefficient-based analysis method,[16] the quota method,[17] the dynamic method,[18] and the factor analysis method.[19] This estimation would help develop an umbrella framework about the nationwide supply-and-demand situation (sometimes known as a "cage") concerning this product. Then, through the planning commissions in provinces, municipalities, and counties, documents were issued to collect to collect information concerning the production and the demands of the product. Next, Enterprise A would have to submit the demand information, through different levels from bottom to top, whereas Enterprise B would have to submit information about its production capacity in the same way from bottom to top. Finally, the State Planning Commission would make overall balancing and develop the final supply-and-demand plans. After that, the supply-and-demand

---

[15] Su Xing, *The Economic History of the People's Republic of China*, Party School Press of the CPC Central Committee, 2007 Edition, p. 148.

[16] The coefficient-based analysis method is also known as the proportion method. Coefficient refers to the numerical expression of the relatively stable interdependence between two or more economic variables. This numerical relationship can be used to estimate the targets for relevant plans during a particular period of economic plan. As the coefficient was derived from the past economic operations, the practice to develop future plans based on past coefficient would necessarily be filled with considerable uncertainties due to technological changes. These uncertainties tended to produce negative impacts on the overall plan as a result of chain effects.

[17] The quota method was used to develop targets based on various technological and economic quotas and plans within a particular period of economic plan. It was rather difficult to fix the quotas in a scientific manner and unreasonable quotas would negatively impact the development of relevant plan targets.

[18] The dynamic method was used to estimate the growth dynamics in the future 5-year period based on the growth dynamics of a single target in the past 5-Year Plan period. In formulating its own plans, China made use of the dynamic method on a more extensive scale. However, when it came to adjusting the targets, the adjustments might be too heavily based on past experiences or might prove heavily subjective.

[19] The factor analysis method was a method used to formulate targets in the plans by combining qualitative analysis and quantitative calculation. It was more complicated to apply this method to actual analysis.

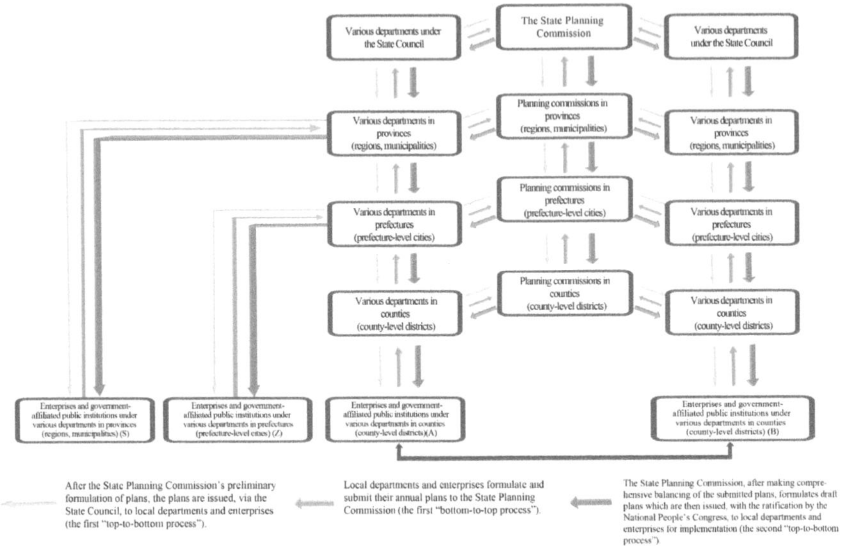

Fig. 1 The procedure of "two top-to-bottom processes and one bottom-to-top process" in formulating annual plans during the period of planned economy[20]

targets would be issued, according to the existing procedures, to Enterprise A and Enterprise B respectively. On their own part, Enterprise A and Enterprise B would have to complete their respective tasks of procurement and production in accordance with the plans formulated by governments on various levels. Therefore, what stated as a simple transaction between two local enterprises would actually have to require the communication and balancing among governments on five or six different levels and all those administrative work would necessitate huge amounts of human labor. If the supply and the demand between enterprises were mismatched and if there were supply shortages, there would require adjustments in the plans according to the established procedures. Worse still, it was very common to make adjustments in the plans. As the relationship among different segments of the economic activities of the entire society had already been locked up in advance according to plans, the failure to achieve balance by any single segment in the supply-and-demand chain would trigger chain reactions, affecting other segments in both the upstream and the downstream of a given industrial chain or, horizontally, affecting other industries and sectors. The efforts to achieve equilibrium in national economy by making adjustments in plans were bound to be extremely time-consuming and labor-consuming. Therefore, the transaction cost under the system of planned economy was extremely high.

---

[20] Data Source: Li Zhenzhong, *Planned Economy*, China Renmin University Press, 1983 Edition; *Principles of National Economic Planning*, China Renmin University Press, 1983 Edition.

3. **Exorbitant transaction costs rendering it difficult for the planned economy to continue**

From the founding of the People's Republic of China in 1949 to the time when the 14th CPC National Congress was held in 1992, the planning departments of China, the economic departments, and the governments on various levels were engaged in developing and implementing plans according to the guiding principles of planning and proportion—the overarching guidelines in that period. Many planners sincerely believed that the meticulous execution of their planning responsibilities would enable China to achieve sound economic development. However, there were quite a few planners and economists who realized, at the very beginning of the reform and opening-up, that the system of planned economy was fraught with evils and their views developed into a basic consensus. According to them, the main evil of the system was its partial and excessive emphasis on the role of planning at the expense of the market, denying and rejecting the role played by the market. With its overemphasis on planning and proportionality, the planned economy tended to overlook or underrate the role played by the law of value, rejecting the competitions among enterprises and the law of the survival of the fittest, and ignoring the low efficiency and low economic effects inherent in the system. The system placed one-sided emphasis on centralized government administration, depriving the microeconomic activities of their vitality and vibrancy. It excluded and restricted the development of economic sectors other than the state-owned sector, resulting in the virtual absence of private economy and of small businesses by self-employed individuals in the cities. On the other hand, excessive and overly-rigid control was imposed on the state-owned enterprises, depriving them of their autonomy in managing their own businesses. The top-to-bottom one-directional macro administration lacked constraints from micro autonomy as the enterprises only had the obligation to implement state plans, with no right to resist plan targets even though such targets were misaligned with their actual circumstances. Finally, in terms of the industrial structure, the emphasis laid on agriculture, light industry, and heavy industry was disproportionate, overemphasizing heavy industry at the expense of agriculture and light industry. The under-development of agriculture and light industry resulted in the long-standing shortages of agricultural products and light industry products. Other consequences included slow technological progress, ineffectual economic management, poor economic outcomes, and insignificant improvement in people's living standards.

The intrinsic reasons underpinning these problems can be explained in the light of transaction cost. Under the market economy, an enterprise engages in direct transactions with other enterprises. Under the planned economy, the precondition for an enterprise to complete a transaction with another enterprise is that there must be an administrative plan assigned the state. The so-called plan was in fact a form of administrative licensing which gave enterprises the permission to engage in transactions. It was a form of the transfer of rights. This cycle of formulating and issuing plans was summarized as "two top-to-bottom processes and one bottom-to-top process" or, in some cases, "two top-to-bottom processes and two bottom-to-top processes." In some special circumstances, there even had to be "several top-to-bottom processes and several bottom-to-top processes," as plans were submitted, revised, and issued among many government organizations, involving a number of repeated transactions of rights. The cycle of using plans to allocate resources involved more transaction steps than the cycle of using the market to allocate resources, consuming more time and thus having to pay considerably higher transaction costs. For example, during the period of planned economy, the annual planning meetings held by the State Planning Commission would usually last three months. Quite often, by the time all the plans were finalized, it was already half way through a "5-year period." As the plans were highly mandatory, making adjustments in the plans would have to repeat the entire cycle of existing procedures, which meant that the transaction costs would be doubled. Since the founding of the People's Republic of China, the country's planning efforts were fraught with setbacks. In those years when the targets were set unrealistically high, the economy would experience roller-coaster fluctuations. Even in the years when plans were executed smoothly, there existed problems like excessive and overly-rigid administrative control by the government, resulting in the low vibrancy and low efficiency of enterprises. Chinese planners already came to recognize the evils inherent in the planned economy at the beginning of the reform and opening-up. Admittedly, to some extent, the method of formulating plans based on "several top-to-bottom processes and several bottom-to-top processes" could help make plans more closely geared to social and economic realities. Nevertheless, the efficacy of such practices was limited, unable to fundamentally eradicate the deficiencies inherent in the system of planning. In order to make the plans more efficient, the planners would try their best to reduce product categories and standardize product specifications so that all the products would be easier to allocate and distribute. This explains why the products for daily use during the period of planned economy were so limited in categories and monotonous in styles.

Under the market economy, the transaction entities in the allocation of resources are usually not fixed, therefore the market is often said to demonstrate a certain degree of irregularity or randomness. Under the planned economy, the transaction entities in the allocation of resources were usually fixed. Although the carefully-planned arrangements could serve to eliminate the irregularity and randomness of the market, the transaction costs were formidable and the allocation of resources was inefficient. On the macro level, the entire national economy demonstrated a low-level equilibrium due to high costs and low efficiency. When it became difficult to maintain this low-level equilibrium, more and more non-planned transactions with lower transaction costs would happen outside the sphere of state planning. This directly explains the emergence of the such transactions in the form of "double-track system" in the initial stage of China's reform and opening-up campaign.

2 Institutions of Lower Transaction Costs Prevail in Competitions

Since the 3rd Plenary Session of the 11th CPC Central Committee in 1978, China's reforms achieved breakthroughs in the system of planned economy, notorious for its high transaction costs, by introducing market mechanisms of lower transaction costs. However, the market mechanisms failed to be generally embraced at the very outset. For some time, there was a co-existence of the planned economy and the market economy, often known as the "double-track system." Both the formulators and the operators of China's economic institutions realized that the market economy could prove more efficient than the planned economy in creating wealth and boosting social and economic development. This ultimately led to China's choice of the system of market economy, which represents an institution with lower transaction costs. This entire process happened through three major stages—the co-existence and competition of two economic institutions, the development of transaction entities and transaction rules, and the marginal adjustments in the new institutions. At each stage, there was a constant spiral movement between spontaneous evolution and rational construction. Reform tended to arise from the explorations on the basic levels and in local areas. Informal constraints would first be generated and then came to be recognized by the state. In the due course, the state would formulate formal constraints, and undertake rational construction of a particular institution, and finally implement the institution on a nationwide scale.

1. **The competition of two systems amidst co-existence**

After the founding of the People's Republic of China, the country immediately established the system of planned economy which required high transaction costs. As analyzed in the first section of this chapter, under such a system, a transaction must first be completed between an enterprise and a certain government department, or between one government department and another government department. It was only with the approval of government department(s) that an enterprise could engage in transactions with another enterprise. Under the system of market economy, a major characteristic of the transactions between enterprises is that enterprises can engage in direct transactions with one another, bypassing all the transaction steps between an enterprise and relevant government departments. In this way, transaction costs are significantly reduced.

In the history of China's reform and opening-up, the system of planned economy and the system of market economy were not mutually exclusive or absolutely incompatible. Instead, they co-existed in the country's economic life, and even in the selfsame industry or in the selfsame enterprise. This institutional phenomenon was called the "dual system" and, with regard to pricing, it became the so-called "double-track system." Many scholars believe that the double-track system was an important institutional invention unique to China's reform campaign, an institutional presence that accorded with the actual circumstances of the country. However, an overview of the entire historical process of the reform demonstrates that the double-track system came into existence not because the state adopted certain policy recommendations and implemented the system; rather, it was because in the real-world economic life there had always been competitions between the system of planned economy and the system of market economy.

In the initial stage of the reform campaign, China shifted the focus of the state governance from class struggle in the political sphere to economic development. At that time, the formal constraints in the economic field were represented by the system of planned economy and the central government focused on how to properly manage the planned economy. Yet, unlike the Soviet Union, China did not allow the planned economy to cover all the economic activities. There were some weak links or loopholes in the planned economy, that is, instances in which transaction entities bypassed the government intervention to engage in direct transactions with each other. Some of these transactions happened between individuals, and some happened between enterprises. The transactions were completed entirely autonomously by the individuals or by the enterprises, without any need for the unified planning by the government departments. All those transactions could be classified as informal constraints at that time, in sharp contradiction to the formal constraints. Any individual who chose to engage in private transactions would be viewed as being guilty of illegal speculations and profiteering, which was punishable by criminal liabilities. As market-oriented transactions kept increasing, the state gradually recognized this pattern of transaction and rejected the system of planned economy, making the establishment of the market-oriented economic system an unequivocal reform objective. Ever since then, top-to-bottom government campaigns were activated to comprehensively promote the market-oriented reforms.

In the rural areas, the formal institutional constraints under the planned economy were represented by the system of the People's Commune. Farmers engaged in farm work on a collective basis, and agricultural products were distributed by the production brigade in a unified manner.[21] There was an exceedingly long time before the farmers could receive the recompenses for the labor that they put into the farm work. A writer once wrote that, for a farmer working in the brigade, out of every 100 shovelfuls of earth that were shoveled, only one shovelful was linked to the farmer's personal interests; whereas if the farmer labored on the small plot of land allocated for his private use as a commune member, every shovelful was for his personal interests. This tellingly reflected the relationship between the labor input and the material reward of a farmer. The Household Contract Responsibility System, as a model of rural economy, shortened the cycle whereby farmers obtained remunerations from their labor input, which constituted a mode of transaction with lower transaction

[21] In 1961, the Central Government promulgated the *Regulations on the Work of People's Commune in Rural Areas* (Draft Version), which stipulated that "the three-tier ownership based on the ownership of the production brigade is the fundamental system of the People's Commune at the present stage." In 1962, the CPC Central Committee issued administrative instructions, specifying that the production brigade was the basic accounting unit of the People's Commune, a rule that would remain unchanged for at least 30 years. Please refer to *The History of the Communist Party of China* (Vol. 2), ed. the Research Institute of the CPC Central Committee, CPC History Press, 2011 Edition, pp. 583–585.

costs than that under the system of the People's Commune. In the early stage of the reform campaign, this model of household contract responsibility system evolved autonomously in places across a number of provinces, including Zhejiang Province, Sichuan Province, Shanxi Province, Guangdong Province, Jiangsu Province, and Anhui Province. At first, the government cracked down on the informal constraints as represented by this system, as it was clearly in violation of the predominant formal constraints. Nevertheless, in the early stage of the reform campaign, the household contract responsibility system posed a rivalry to the system of the People's Commune and it eventually came to be recognized by the CPC Central Committee for its higher efficiency and lower transaction costs. In 1981, the system was formally acknowledged and approved.[22] Later, in 1984, the state formally abolished the system of the People's Commune and promoted, on a nationwide scale, the household contract responsibility system as a formal constraint.[23] With regard to the rules of transaction, the competition between the system of planned economy and the system of market economy witnessed the ever-shrinking magnitude of the plan-based pricing and the ever-expanding scale of market-oriented pricing. From 1979 to 1984, while preserving the plan-based pricing, the state lifted restrictions on the prices of a proportion of commodities, which were to be regulated by the market. According to the new policy, a proportion of agricultural and sideline products were open to the purchasing and selling via bargaining, based on the negotiated price. In addition, a proportion of industrial products could be transacted according to floating prices based on the unified state pricing. For example, in 1980, the government department in charge of machinery fixed floating prices, on a trial basis, on 16 categories of mechanical products like the lathe and the air compressor, and also on a certain proportion of the farm machinery. The government department in charge of chemical engineering allowed the prices of the products in oversupply, like rubber pipes and rubber bags,

---

[22] In 1980, the Central Government issued the Document No. 75, entitled "*Several Issues Regarding Further Strengthening and Improving the Responsibility System of Agricultural Production*," which acknowledged that the household contract responsibility system was a responsibility system readily accepted by the farmers and that the farmers had the right to free choices. In 1982, the Central Government re-issued the minutes of the National Rural Work Conference held at the end of 1981. According to the conference minutes, the contract labor for particular phases of a construction project, remuneration paid on completing a particular production quota, payment according to output under the contract system of special rural industries, the practice of linking output quotas to labor power, the practice of fixing farm output quotas for each household or for each production team, and the practice of fixing labor quotas for each household or for each production team, all those were different forms of the production responsibility system under the socialist collective economy. All those forms should remain unchanged as long as the farmers made no demands for change. This was the first time that the practice of fixing farm output quotas for individual households was formally acknowledged in the name of the Central Government.

[23] In October 1983, the CPC Central Committee and the State Council jointly issued the *Notice Concerning the Implementation of the Separation between the Government and the Rural Society and the Establishment of Township Government*, requiring local rural areas across the country to establish township governments by the end of 1984. By the end of 1984, over 99% of the People's Communes in the rural areas completed their separation between the government and the rural society and established over 91,000 township governments, along with 92,600 rural residents committees.

to float downward. After 1981, the float pricing was extended to the purchasing of staple farm products and sideline products, and covered the ex-factory price and the sales price of a proportion of light industrial and textile products. In 1982, the state set free the pricing of 160 kinds of small commodities in 6 categories and in 1983 the relaxed pricing covered 350 kinds of small commodities in 8 major categories. Put together, a total of 510 kinds of small commodities broke free from the planned prices and were entirely priced by market mechanisms.[24] A close examination of this process shows that the plan-based government administration was first shattered in the realms of farm products, small commodities, and part of the industrial products in oversupply. In these fields, market-oriented transactions were set in motion. Immediately following this, market mechanisms started to extend to the upstream of the industrial chain. In May 1984, the State Council promulgated regulations regarding the selling of several categories of key industrial production means that were previously subjected to the unified distribution by the state. Enterprises could autonomously sell 2% of the steel products that fell within the state plans and sell all the surplus steel products outside the state plans. Enterprises could not autonomously sell products of cast iron, copper, aluminum, tin, zinc, coal, cement, sulfuric acid, concentrated nitric acid, caustic soda, sodium carbonate, and rubber that fell within the state plans, but could sell all the surplus products outside the state plans. Enterprises could autonomously sell all the mechanical and electrical products except for those for which the state provided raw materials and which were to be allocated by the state. When it came to pricing, regarding the proportion of industrial production means that an enterprise could sell autonomously and the surplus proportion outside the state plans, an enterprise was entitled to making independent pricing decisions as long as the prices floated within a range of 20% of their original prices. It was also possible for the supplier and the buyer to negotiate a price within the range of price floating. Later on, all the restrictions imposed on raising the prices of the production means were also removed.[25] In this way, even within a single enterprise, there existed the double-track system, under which the enterprise manufactured products both according the state plans and according to market demands, and according to state-fixed prices and according to the market-regulated prices.

In the early competitions between the two systems, in view of the fact that China had long been suffering from shortages of industrial and agricultural products, an enterprise could usually gain greater profits by selling at market-regulated prices than at the prices fixed by government plans. This profitability gave enterprises greater incentive to manufacture products according to market demands than according to government plans, thus rendering the government-formulated plans increasingly difficult to implement. Consequently, under the double-track system, the transaction costs arising from the production and exchange of the products that fell within the government plans turned out to be even higher than the single-track system of

[24] Su Xing, *The Economic History of the People's Republic of China*, Party School Press of the CPC Central Committee, 2007 Edition, pp. 581–582.

[25] Su Xing, *The Economic History of the People's Republic of China*, Party School Press of the CPC Central Committee, 2007 Edition, p. 583.

the planned economy. Some enterprises and individuals in positions of power could acquire lower-priced products manufactured under the planned economy and then sell them on the market according to higher market-oriented prices, thus making profits out of the price gaps. This economic phenomenon came to be called "profiteering, or black-marketing, on the part of government officials." When the government-fixed price was combined with the added price by the profiteering officials, the actual prices of the products that consumers purchased were virtually equivalent to the market-regulated prices. If a consumer made up his mind to acquire products manufactured according to the state plans, the consumer had to spend more time waiting for the acquisition of the products than if he tried to buy the same products on the market. Therefore, it became less and less meaningful to keep producing products according to government plans. Hence, it became imperative to convert the double-track system into a single-track system. Starting from September 1, 1992, the state removed the nationwide unified upper limits that used to be imposed on the ex-factory prices and the sales prices of a whole range of production means, including crude oil, refined oil, steel, and cast iron, that were produced outside the government plans. In 1993 and 1994, the double-track prices of the key production means, including steel, machinery, coal, and petroleum, were merged into one single track. In 1996, as China formally terminated the double-track system, the double-track pricing became a past history.[26] In the entire process of the competition between the system with higher transaction costs and the system with lower transaction costs, the two systems co-existed for a certain period of time until, ultimately, the system of planned economy was abolished due to its high transaction costs and the system of market economy prevailed due to its lower transaction costs. In the waxing and waning of the two rivaling systems, it was the powerful endorsement by the central government that expedited the institutional change.

If we re-examine the entire process in which the two systems co-existed and competed against each other, we would find several critical turning points in the construction of the formal constraints. The first turning point was September 1982, when the 12th CPC National Congress passed the resolution that "the planned economy shall remain the predominant economic model, supported by market-oriented regulations."[27] That was the first time when the CPC, having corrected the "leftist" party line, acknowledged the positive role of the market in national economy. The second turning point came in October 1984, when the 3rd Plenary Session of the 12th CPC Central Committee passed the resolution that "the socialist economy is the commodity economy based on public ownership, with necessary state planning."[28]

---

[26] Peng Sen, Chen Li, *Major Events in the Reform of China's Economic System*, China Renmin University Press, 2008 Edition, pp. 408–409.

[27] "Opening a New Chapter of Socialist Modernization Development in an All-Round Manner," *Selections of Important Documents since the 12th CPC National Congress* (Part 1), People's Publishing House, 1986 Edition.

[28] "The CPC Central Committee's Decision Concerning the Reform of Economic System (passed at the 3rd Plenary Session of the 12th CPC Central Committee on October 20, 1984)," *Selections of Important Documents since the 12th CPC National Congress* (Part 1), People's Publishing House, 1986 Edition.

The third turning point was October 1987, when the 13th CPC National Congress passed the resolution that "the system of socialist market economy with necessary state planning should be a system with intrinsic unity between the planning and the market."[29] These resolutions perfectly paralleled the rising importance of market regulation in the real-world economic life. The mode of transaction based on market economy kept rising in status until it ceased playing a merely supporting role and became on a par with the mode of transaction based on the planned economy. The fourth turning point came in October 1992, when the 14th CPC National Congress passed the resolution that the system of socialist market economy was to be established as the key objective of the reform. Thus, to supersede the system of planned economy with the system of market economy came to constitute a formally-defined objective of China's reform campaign.

2. **Reconstructing transaction entities and transaction rules**

In the wake of the 14th CPC National Congress, based on careful and in-depth discussions and analyses over a period of one year, the 3rd Plenary Session of the 14th CPC Central Committee passed a resolution in 1993, which purported to carry out a new round of rational construction of the system of market economy.[30] By defining the functions and the boundaries of both the enterprise and the government, the resolution re-shaped two transaction entities—the enterprise and the government. The resolution also proposed targets of market development that covered the reform of the capital, the land, and the labor force. It was also proposed that the mode of macroeconomic manipulation was to be reformed and the rules of the transactions between the government and the enterprises, as well as between the government and the market, were to be adjusted. Through this entire series of administrative measures, some of the informal restraints that had already existed in the past were elevated in their status and were transformed into formal constraints. Meanwhile, more and more rights could be transacted on the market, with the result of expanding the transaction volume and invigorating the economy nationwide.

(1) **Reconstructing transaction entities (I): the enterprise**

An enterprise is the most fundamental unit of economic activities. When we talk about enterprises today, such concepts as "companies of limited shares," "companies of limited liabilities," "partnership companies," and "private enterprises" would immediately come to our mind. However, for a considerable period of time at the beginning of the reform, China only had a superficial understanding about the nature and the management of enterprises. From the start of the reform and opening-up campaign until 1990's, in the official documents of the National Bureau of Statistics of China, market entities were classified into three categories—the ownership by the

---

[29] "Marching Forward along the Road of Socialism with Chinese Characteristics," *Selections of Important Documents since the 13th CPC National Congress* (Part 1), People's Publishing House, 1991 Edition.

[30] Please refer to "The CPC Central Committee's Decision Concerning Certain Issues in Establishing the System of Socialist Market Economy," *Selections of Important Documents since the 14th CPC National Congress*, People's Publishing House, 1996 Edition.

whole people, urban collective ownership, and the business of self-employed individuals. In economic activities, the business of self-employed individuals was a synonym for poor credibility, poor quality, and bribery. Compared with the ownership by the whole people and urban collective ownership, the business of self-employed individuals was subjected to all forms of discrimination and unequal treatment. In order to promote their businesses, many entities which engaged in private economy resorted to various measures, such as "affiliation to" or "joint operation with" the enterprises in the other two categories of ownership. In this way, they managed to put on a "red hat," meaning that they found legitimacy and legal protection for their businesses because they operated their businesses in the name of the enterprises that belonged to the other two forms of public ownership. As part of the enterprises of public ownership, the private businesses implemented independent accounting and paid a certain quantity of fees to the enterprises to which they were affiliated or networked. In 1992, only 140,000 private enterprises were registered with the National Bureau of Statistics, but the real number of the entities engaged in private businesses far exceeded that figure. During that period, the enterprises in China could hardly be viewed as enterprises in the true sense of the word because, in the name of ownership by the whole people and the collective ownership, there was the co-existence of the public ownership and the private ownership, and also the co-existence of the planned economy and the market economy. To promote market economy under such an institutional framework, there must be fully qualified enterprises to act as market entities. In the modern market economy, the fundamental operating units are companies or firms. Globally speaking, companies originated from partnerships. With the increasing need for the freedom to transfer shares, companies replaced partnerships. In order to ensure "that the actions of a company will not be viewed as the actions of its owners"[31] and, meanwhile, in order to guarantee the rights and the interests of the investors, the modern company system came to be established, under which two corporate architectures developed—the architecture of limited liability and the architecture of legal personality. In order to balance the distribution of interests, the investors and the company evolved the internal governance structure, that is, the delegated management under the investor ownership, equipped with a board structure. Generally speaking, a modern company demonstrates five essential attributes, i.e. legal personality, limited liability, transferable shares, delegated management with a board structure, and investor ownership.[32] A key advantage of the modern company system lies in the fact that it can answer to a full range of the needs of economic development, including socialized mass production and multiple-channel financing.

[31] Leonard W. Hein, "The British Business Company: Its Origins and Its Control," *The University of Toronto Law Journal*, 1963, pp.137–138.

[32] Please refer to Reinier Kraakman, et al, *The Anatomy of Corporate Law: A Comparative and Functional Approach,* trans. Liu Junhai, Xu Haiyan, et al., Peking University Press, 2007 Edition, pp. 6–7.

For countries which adopt either the Common Law System or the Civil Law System, the modern company system has been a universal option.[33]

The 3rd Plenary Session of the 14th CPC Central Committee proposed the establishment of the "modern enterprise system," a term which is virtually absent in any existing Chinese or international literature. Nevertheless, the system represented an innovative design which not only conformed to the institutional background of China during that particular historical period but also matched the commercial system of the countries practicing modern market economy. Under the modern enterprise system, an enterprise in China is both an entity with legal personality and an entity of market competition, which engages in independent business operations, is responsible for its own profits and losses, pursues its autonomous development, and is legally self-disciplined. The system's characteristics can be summarized as follows: "well-defined property rights, well-defined rights and responsibilities, separation between the government and the enterprise, and effective management." The modern enterprise system focuses on the solution of a number of fundamental issues faced by enterprises as market entities. The first is the personalization of the enterprise. An enterprise is an entity of legal personality which is entitled to civil rights and assumes civil responsibilities. Secondly, an enterprise is owned by investors. Based on the entire property of the legal person, an enterprise engages in independent business activities and, in accordance with the law, assumes full responsibilities for its own profits and losses, pays taxes according to government regulations, and remains accountable to investors with regard to the obligation to preserve and increase the value of corporate assets. Thirdly, an enterprise is allowed to go bankrupt. Following the principle of the survival of the fittest in market competitions, an enterprise can file for bankruptcy when it suffers from business losses on a long-term basis and is unable to offset its debts with its assets. Fourthly, it is clearly established that the government follows the principle of non-intervention, eliminating all the direct interventions by the government in the production and business operations of the enterprises. Fifthly, the relationship among the government, the state-owned enterprises, and the state becomes clearly demarcated. The state retains the ownership of all the state-owned assets within an enterprise whereas the enterprise owns the right to all the property of the legal person, arising from the investments by all the investors including the state. Sixthly, investors assume limited liabilities. A state-owned enterprise owns the rights and interests as an owner according to the amount of capital invested in the enterprise. These rights and interests include the right to the returns on the assets, the right to participation in major decision making, and the right to the selection of the management personnel. Investors assume limited responsibilities for corporate debts only in accordance with the amount of capital that they invest in the enterprise. Seventhly, a tentative form of modern enterprise governance structure is proposed, including the establishment of an effective corporate leadership system and organizational management system to regulate the relationship among the owner, the

[33] Gan Peizhong, Zhou You, "On the Convergence and Integration of the Changing Organizational Structures of Modern Enterprises: With the Congruity between the State Demands and Private Innovations as the Axle," *Law Review*, Issue 6, 2013.

management, and the employees and to develop mechanisms of business operations that incorporate both incentives and constraints.

This modern enterprise system applies to all the enterprises engaged in market economic activities at that time. According to this system, all enterprises, disregarding the types of ownership that they belonged to, that is, whether the investor is the state, individual, or any other organization, are equal market entities which operate business independently and assume full responsibilities for their own profits and losses. They must all pay taxes in accordance with government regulations and seek to outperform their rivals in market competitions. The state no longer assumes unlimited liabilities for the state-owned enterprises. Instead, it only assumes limited liabilities according to the proportion of the capital that it invests in the enterprise. A state-owned enterprise is a market entity with legal personality, who is responsible for maintaining and increasing the value of the assets on behalf of the state. The separation of the enterprise from the government further reinforces the enterprise's role as an economic entity. In addition, the establishment of the non-intervention principle indicates that the government has terminated the previous transaction rules that employed state plans to determine the output and the prices of the products manufactured by an enterprise. Another important role played by the establishment of the modern enterprise system is that this system provides institutional guarantee for the private economic sector to legally engage in business activities.

The proposal raised by the 3rd Plenary Session of the 14th CPC Central Committee to establish this innovative enterprise system was a major decision made by the ruling party. A number of institutional supplies were required in the legislative and administrative spheres in order for the system to be actually implemented. In 1993, the National People's Congress formulated the Company Law, specifying that companies include both the companies of limited liabilities and companies of limited shares. The state also framed a series of laws and regulations with respect to the registration of companies, their accounting system, and their human resource management. All those laws and regulations constitute the general architecture underpinning the modern enterprise system. For example, according to the Company Law, the government department in charge of industrial and commercial administration relaxed the conditions for registering enterprises by increasing the categories of enterprises to be registered. This allowed many enterprises which used to "wear red hats," that is, the enterprises which used to be affiliated to or jointly operate business with enterprises of public ownership, to be registered as independent companies. During that period, there was a huge wave of incorporating share-holding companies across the country. A large number of urban enterprises of collective ownership, as well as township enterprises, underwent a restructuring process. Starting from 1994, the state chose 100 state-owned enterprises in which to establish the modern enterprise system on an experimental basis. Various provinces and regions, along with government departments, also chose a number of enterprises to carry out the same restructuring process on a trial basis. In accordance with the requirements as stipulated in the Company Law, these enterprises defined their corporate shareholding structure and established relatively formal corporate governance structure. In 1998, as the Zhu Rongji administration took office, reform of the state-owned enterprises was carried out on a nationwide scale. The large and medium-sized state-owned enterprises with sufficient conditions to adopt the share-holding system, especially those enjoying cutting-edge advantages in the industry, were transformed into share-holding enterprises in one of the three forms—as publicly listed companies through formal procedures, as Sino-foreign joint ventures, or as enterprises with mutual equity participation. The state-owned enterprise could have access to both Chinese and international capital markets to attract investments from enterprises of various kinds of ownership and to develop into economic entities of mixed ownerships. In the present-day China, all forms of capital, be they the state-owned capital, the private capital, the domestic capital, or the international capital, are qualified for making investments and creating corporate market entities that conform to the rules of market economic operation and to government regulations. This achievement is precisely the outcome ensuing from the creative efforts made by the 3rd Plenary Session of the 14th CPC Central Committee to develop the modern enterprise system.

(2) **Reconstructing transaction entities (II): the market**

One of the beliefs maintained by Friedrich August Hayek is that the market developed out of the spontaneous order rather than out of the artificial design. This is a viewpoint that has been widely accepted in the community of economists. To some extent, this viewpoint has been demonstrated by China's practice of reform and opening-up. For example, commodity market emerged even when planned economy had predominated national economy. However, China's practice of reform and opening-up has also rendered manifest the one-sidedness of Hayak's viewpoint. After the 3rd Plenary Session of the 14th CPC Central Committee proposed to foster and develop the market system, China's market system was immediately established and its scale kept expanding rapidly. This demonstrated that the market, apart from developing out of the spontaneous order, could also develop out of rational construction.

From the late 1980's to the early 1990's, a certain degree of achievements were made in China's efforts to develop the market system. The restrictions on the prices of most consumer products were removed, and their market prices came to be determined by the supply-and-demand relationship. However, if measured by the standard of the market system in developed countries, China's market system remains markedly under-developed. Its main deficiencies are as follows. The level of the commodity market is relatively low as most commodities are traded by means of over-the-counter transactions. A large number of organizations participate in the market of the production means but the modes of transaction they use are quite primitive. In a certain proportion of this market, the double-track pricing system still exists. With regard to the market of production factors, despite a certain degree of development of the capital market, the land market, the labor market, and the technology market have not yet been developed. Under such circumstances, it will be an extremely long time before these markets can develop out of the spontaneous order. Rational construction can be seen as a model of institutional evolution capable of saving transaction costs.

The proposition by the 3rd Plenary Session of the 14th CPC Central Committee to foster and develop the market system comprised of the following objectives. The first was to develop the commodity market. In those places of the production, sales, or concentration and distribution of important products, wholesale markets dealing in bulk agricultural commodities, industrial consumer products, and production means were to be established. The second was to foster the markets of production factors and important commodities, including the financial market, the labor market, the real-estates market, the technology market, and the information market. The third was the development of the market of intermediary agency, focusing on the development of accounting firms, auditing firms, law firms, notary and arbitrating agencies, authorities in metrology, institutions in quality inspection and certification, information consulting agencies, and assets and credit rating agencies. The fourth was the creation of mechanisms in which prices are primarily determined by the market. The price restrictions imposed on competing commodities and services were removed and the double-track pricing system regarding the production means was abolished to facilitate the marketization of the prices of production factors. The fifth was to impose government regulation and supervision on the market to ensure fair trade and equal competition and to protect the legitimate rights and interests of both the businesses and the consumers.

The decision made by the 3rd Plenary Session of the 14th CPC Central Committee to foster and develop the market system proved immensely successful. Starting from 1993, the year in which the 3rd Plenary Session of the 14th CPC Central Committee was held, waves of government officials and ordinary individuals entering the business world swept across the country. In the retail market, various business models proliferated, including department stores, large supermarkets, monopoly stores, specialized stores, etc. Chain-store operations soon became widespread across the whole country. In the field of production means and bulk commodities, a large number of enterprises dealing in wholesale business and specialized wholesale markets mushroomed, and the futures market was created. Rapid progress was also made in the development of the market of production factors, as the number and the business scale of the enterprises listed on the Shanghai Stock Exchange and Shenzhen Stock Exchange quickly increased. By the end of 1993, there were 170 institutions engaged in the trading of property rights in the whole country. In 1995, the Commercial Bank Law was promulgated, establishing formal rules for the founding, market access, and standardized operations of various kinds of banking institutions. This legislation speeded up the development of the financial market with regard to credit loans, loans at call, and bonds. In 1998, reform was carried out regarding the urban housing system. The welfare-oriented distribution of houses was abolished, replaced by money-based distribution of houses. This measure promoted the quick development of the real-estates market. In 2001, reform was implemented concerning the urban state-owned land system, which offered the bidding, auction, and listing of the land transfer right. This expedited the market-oriented allocation of the lands for business purposes.[34]

[34] The Market Economy Research Institute of the Development Research Center under the State Council, *Four Decades of Reform and Opening-up: Establishment, Development and Prospect of the Market System*, China Development Press, 2019 Edition, p. 5.

(3) Reconstructing transaction entities (III): the government

During the period of planned economy, the government was supposed to be an omnipotent one that dominated the entire cycle of social reproduction covering production, exchange, distribution, and consumption. Plans were formulated by government departments, and the transactions between two enterprises required additional costs arising from the transactions between government departments and between the government and the enterprises. The system of market economy was established in order to minimize all those additional transaction costs. Toward this objective, it was necessary to reshape the government's function in economic governance.

In defining the function of the government, classical economic theory maintained that the government should act as a "night watcher," only assuming the responsibilities of national defense, judicial and executive responsibilities, as well as the responsibilities of developing and maintaining infrastructure and public utilities. However, the government in developing countries, including China, generally assumes the responsibility of economic development. The 3rd Plenary Session of the 14th CPC Central Committee terminated the government's direct intervention in economic activities under the system of planned economy, defining the government's economic function only as that of indirect management. The government is mainly responsible for formulating and implementing macroeconomic regulatory policies, developing infrastructure, and creating a sound environment for economic development. The government manages national economy by applying economic measures, legal measures, and necessary administrative measures but should never directly intervene in the production and business operations of the enterprises. Through this reform, the rights which the government can trade with the market and with the enterprises were significantly decreased, thus considerably reducing transaction costs.

Also, in the wake of the 3rd Plenary Session of the 14th CPC Central Committee, China implemented radical reforms of government organizations that failed to separate themselves from enterprises.[35] Under the State Council, there were many special economic institutions in the industrial sector which, as products of the age of planned economy, were the backbone for enforcing the country's economic plans under the historical conditions of that particular period. However, with the passage of time, these government institutions demonstrated obvious problems during the reform and opening-up, such as institutional oversize, overstaffing, mixture of the government and enterprise, and serious bureaucracy. They came to constitute the obstacles and the main organizational foundations that intervened in the business operations of the enterprises, posing severe impediments to the development of the market economy. Starting from 1998, China implemented reforms of the government's administrative system, which lasted for four and half years. In March 1998, the 1st Session of the 9th National People's Congress approved the institutional reform plan of the State Council, abolishing the special economic organizations in the industrial sector almost all at once. A total of 10 such organizations were terminated, which

[35] Please refer to Song Shiming, "Seven Decades of Reform of China's Administrative System: Retrospection and Reflections," *Administration Reform Journal*, Issue 9, 2019.

included the Ministry of Electric Power Industry, the Ministry of Coal Industry, the Ministry of Metallurgical Industry, the Ministry of Machinery Industry, the Ministry of Electronics Industry, the Ministry of Chemical Industry, the Ministry of Geology and Mineral Resources, the Ministry of Forestry, China National Council of Light Industry, and China National Council of Textile Industry. The number of ministries which made up of the State Council was reduced from 40 to 29, formally eradicating the system of direct intervention by special economic institutions in the management of enterprises. Immediately after this, a full range of reforms were conducted regarding various institutions under the CPC Central Committee, in other state departments, in the army, and in social organizations and institutions. After 1999, reform was carried out concerning the governments and CPC committees on the provincial level and, in 2000, concerning the governments and CPC committees at county and township levels. By June 2002, the institutional reform from central government to local governments was completed on a nationwide scale.

(4) **Reconstructing transaction rules: between the government and enterprises, between the government and the market, and between government departments**

While re-shaping transaction entities and defining the behavioral boundary of various entities, the 3rd Plenary Session of the 14th CPC Central Committee also embarked on the mission of restructuring the transaction rules among various entities. The rules governing the transactions of rights between the government and the enterprises and between the government and the market used to be dominated by direct government intervention. Now, such rules came to be dominated by indirect government manipulation. In the transaction of rights between two government organizations, the fiscal relationship between the central government and local governments was changed through the defining of their respective executive powers. By specifying the functions of the planning department, the fiscal department, and the financial department, the reform helped to reconstruct the transaction rules between one government organization and another.

First, regarding the relationship between the government and the enterprises, it was stipulated that the government must follow the principle of not directly intervening in the business operations of the enterprises. This principle fundamentally eradicated the mode of transaction regarding the government's right to issue production targets to enterprises in the form of government plans.

Secondly, regarding the relationship between the government and the market, it was specified that the prices of commodities and services were to be determined primarily by the market. This reflected the principle that the market-based prices are a general rule whereas government-fixed prices are an exception. At the same time, it was specified that the government bears the responsibilities of fostering the market, disciplining the market behavior, eliminating protectionism within particular regions and industries, and penalizing unfair competitions.

Thirdly, regarding the relationship between different government departments, it was specified that the state can seek to influence the behavior of the enterprises and the market only through macroeconomic manipulation. The authority to undertake macro manipulation is invested in the Central Government, including the power to issue currency, determine the benchmark interest rate, regulate the exchange rate, and adjust tax rates in key taxation categories. It was also specified that the number of the special economic institutions were to be reduced gradually and the departments in charge of comprehensive economic management would conduct overall coordination and establish mechanisms of mutual support and mutual check among the planning, financial, and fiscal departments. Governments at the provincial level were also vested with necessary authorities to formulate local laws, policies, and plans in accordance with the laws, regulations, and macro policies of the state.

According to the adjusted rules of transaction, the government was no longer authorized to directly issue production and sales plans to enterprises or to fix prices on commodities and services. The cost arising from the transactions between the government and the enterprises, and between the government and the market, was reduced almost to zero. Through reform of the system of government administration and gradual reduction of the number of special economic institutions, there were no more transactions between different governmental departments aimed at balancing the plan targets. The costs regarding such transactions were all reduced to zero. Those two cases of "reduction to zero costs" fundamentally solved the problems that rendered the planned economy impossible to continue due to excessive transaction costs. Thus, the obstacles to the development of market economy were cleared up.

3. **Marginal adjustments of institutions**

From the 1980's to the 1990's, Chinese economists made comprehensive studies of the system of market economy in developed countries. The 3rd Plenary Session of the 14th CPC Central Committee proposed building the architecture of the socialist market economic system, a model which was borrowed from many of the general practices in countries enforcing the market economy. Based on this framework, China reshaped three major entities, i.e. the enterprises, the market, and the government, along with rules of transaction among these three separate entities. These reform measures allowed China to be effectively aligned with the system of the countries practicing the market economy, not only in matters of foreign trade but also in the matters of introducing foreign capital into China. Since then, China has created new institutions in some areas but the country's overall institutional architecture has remained unchanged. All the institutions have been undergoing evolution through marginal adjustments and the institutional reforms since China's accession into the World Trade Organization (WTO) in 2001 represented a wave of adjustments with the largest magnitude and intensity.

Without exaggeration, the WTO rules, when put together, constitute an operation manual of the market economy which makes many otherwise abstract principles of the market economy concrete and specific. China's negotiation for joining the WTO and the pledges that China has delivered on after the WTO accession led to new adjustments in the entities of the enterprise, the market, and the government which had already been developed, along with adjustments in the rules of transaction among them. First, regarding the enterprises, China pledged that, in terms of the tariffs and domestic taxes imposed on imported commodities, the treatment accorded to foreign products would be no lower than that accorded to domestic products in the same categories. Any practices and policies in China that ran counter to the WTO national treatment principle must be revised and adjusted. The state-owned enterprises and state-invested enterprises can engage in the purchasing and selling only in accordance with commercial considerations; and the state-run trade companies should operate their businesses only according to commercial principles. Secondly, with regard to the market, China pledged that uniform trade policies would be implemented in the entire territory covered by the Chinese tariffs. China clearly defined the range of the products and services to which the state-fixed prices and the government-recommended prices would be applied respectively. In addition, China pledged to maximize efforts to minimize and abolish such executive controls. China also vowed that it would gradually lift restrictions on the enterprises' right to engage in import and export business and would terminate the approval system of the enterprises' right to foreign trade three years after joining the WTO. Finally, China promised to remove, prior to 2005, all the non-tariff measures (the quota, licensing, and targeted bidding regarding electromechanical products) that had been imposed on products in 400 categories. Thirdly, with respect to the government, China declared that the government would not, either directly or indirectly, exert influence on the commercial decisions in the state-owned or the state-invested enterprises. The central government pledged that China's laws, regulations, and other measures would conform to the duties that China was to assume according to the WTO Agreement and the related protocols. Local governments in China had no right to formulate trade policies related to the WTO Agreement and related protocols. Any local laws, government regulations, and other local measures that were incongruent with the duties that China vowed to perform would be eliminated. Finally, concerning the rules of transaction, China promised to publish all the laws, regulations, and the rules within particular administrative departments regarding foreign trade and business and China would not enforce any laws, regulations, or rules that were not publicly announced. Furthermore, China promised to remove non-tariff measures related to trade, such as the requirement to balance trade and foreign exchange, the requirement of local content, and the technology transfer. Finally, China promised that the laws, regulations, and the rules within particular administrative departments would not contain mandatory requirements of export performance and technology transfer, both of which were to be decided jointly by investing enterprises through negotiations.[36]

During the WTO negotiations and after joining the WTO, China carried out a large number of reforms in accordance with the WTO standards, formulating, revising, and eliminating a great number of laws, regulations, and the rules within particular

[36] Please refer to the "Circular of the General Office of the State Council on the Issuance of the Summary Table of China's Commitments upon Accession to the World Trade Organization" (State Council General Office Circular [2001] No. 69).

administrative departments.[37] In the actual process of implementing the WTO standards, China outperformed some of the WTO standards.[38] Although some of the key developed countries in the West still refuse to acknowledge China's status as a country of market economy up till this very day, China's accession into the WTO has undoubtedly played an important role in promoting China's system of market economy.

The period from the 1970's to the early 1990's marked China's experimental stage of undertaking reforms in the economic system. These reforms were characterized primarily by spontaneous evolution and gradual processes. After paying the transaction expenses for the trial and error of the reforms, the institutional formulators opted for the system of market economy, which is lower in transaction costs, in the rivalry between the planned economy and the market economy. Starting from the 14th CPC National Congress in 1992, China's reform embarked on the stage of rational construction regarding the institutional framework of the market economy. Within a short period of time and with relatively low transaction costs, China built new institutions and re-structured the long-established institutions and in doing so unleashed leapfrog development in the production capacity. In their own development, the newly created institutions also followed the general laws of institutional evolution, demonstrating tendencies of path dependence, diminishing efficiency, and

---

[37] According to the article "Making Domestic Legislation Conform to WTO Rules: China's Decade-Long Consistent Efforts to Eliminate Laws Contradictory to WTO Rules" (http://www.lawyers.org.cn/info/9d678d42628350754c36553b9bee3214), during the negotiations from July 2000 to December 2002, in order to align the Chinese laws with WTO rules, the Standing Committee of the National People's Congress formulated and revised 14 relevant laws; the State Council abolished 12 administrative laws, formulated and revised 38 relevant laws. The relevant ministries under the State Council formulated, revised, and abolished over 1,000 ministry-specific regulations and other policy measures. A total of 3,370 local laws and local government regulations were abolished, and 1,126 were revised. It was decided that provincial governments and their relevant departments, as well as important municipal governments and their relevant departments, must terminate implementing approximately 188,000 other policy measures. In addition, the implementation of 34 documents issued by the State Council and its General Office were to be terminated. According to the article "The Ministry of Commerce: China Has Completely Delivered on its Commitments for Joining the WTO" (http://www.news.cn/politics/2021-10/28/c_1128007033.htm), after China gained access into the WTO, the Central Government eliminated a total of 2,000 laws and ministry-specific regulations while local governments eliminated a total of 190,000 local laws, regulations, and policy measures.

[38] According to the article "The Ministry of Commerce: China Has Completely Delivered on its Commitments for Joining the WTO" (http://www.news.cn/politics/2021-10/28/c_1128007033.htm), regarding market access, China imposed a 15.3% tariff on imported commodities at the time of joining the WTO and pledged to reduce the tariff to 9.8% after joining the WTO. At present, China's overall level of import tariff is merely 7.4%, "lower than that of all the developing member countries, and close to that of developed member countries." In the service sector, China promised to open 100 sub-areas across 9 major categories by 2007, but actually about 120 sub-areas have been opened, "exceeding the commitments that were made." Furthermore, in terms of the compliance to the rules, China stepped up efforts to protect the intellectual property rights by establishing intellectual property courts or tribunals in many parts of the country. In addition, China has kept the WTO informed, in a timely manner, of the adjustment and implementation of the Chinese domestic laws and regulations.

institutional alienation. In most cases, the marginal adjustments in an institution would raise transaction costs. In the preliminary stage of these newly established institutions, the newly added transaction costs could be ignored as the new institutions could yield enormous social and economic benefits. However, as the transaction costs kept increasing, some of the transaction costs could prove too formidable for the transaction entities to withstand and the efficiency would inevitably decrease in the operation of an institution. Of course, there were undeniable instances in which some marginal institutional adjustments could serve to reduce transaction costs, such as a series of reforms that China undertook before and after its accession into the WTO.

Marginal institutional adjustments could trigger two conflicting tendencies in the transaction costs and this is largely the outcome of the impact generated by reform entities. When marginal adjustments were undertaken by institutional formulators, the formulators tended to make the maximization of the positive effects of an institution as the aim of the reform. This objective would motivate them to reduce the transaction costs of the proposed institution. By contrast, when the marginal adjustments were undertaken by institutional operators, i.e., people who enforce and implement the institution, the transaction costs were likely to increase as the interests of the operators themselves were closely connected with a given institution. When there was a potential conflict of interest between the institutional operators and the adjusted institution, the interest of the institution would have to give way to the interest of the operators.

In China, it is the CPC Central Committee and the State Council that make decisions regarding institutional building and major marginal adjustments. The 3rd Plenary Session of the 11th CPC Central Committee made the decision of reform and opening-up. The 3rd Plenary Session of the 14th CPC Central Committee made the decision concerning the construction of the institutional framework of the socialist market economy. There was also the decision to join the WTO. Under the decision-making mechanism of the CPC Central Committee, local interests had to give way to overriding national interests, thus institutional construction or adjustment aimed at reducing transaction costs could proceed without any barrier. By contrast, the reform promoted by specific government departments or by local governments tended to be hampered by various barriers arising from local interests, making it difficult for the reform to go very far. Instead of producing the desired outcomes, such reform might even prove counterproductive. It was true that, after the 3rd Plenary Session of the 14th CPC Central Committee, China removed the government's special economic departments that engaged in direct transactions of rights with the enterprises. However, the government still retained its supervisory function and indirect manipulative function. Consequently, there still existed transactions of rights between the government and the enterprises, and between the government and the market. The supervision and the manipulation were mainly carried out by government departments and local governments for the sake of marginal institutional adjustments. In the chapters that are to follow, this book will discuss reforms regarding the investment institution, the system of land use for construction purpose, the energy institution, and the commercial institution. In those reforms, there were cases in which some newly-constructed institutions, having undergone marginal adjustments performed by institutional operators, gradually deteriorated from institutions of high efficiency and low costs into institutions of low efficiency and high costs.

3 Unraveling the "Three Bindings" to Create Institutional Dividends

In the rivalry between the system of planned economy and the system of market economy, it was the market economy that has prevailed. This triumph on the part of the market economy made it possible for people to develop a brand new understanding about the production relations in China and to implement a new pattern of such relations. Under the traditional system of planned economy, in order to achieve development in accordance with plans and proportions, there must be people responsible for formulating and implementing the plans. The government was the sole entity capable of taking up the responsibility of blueprinting national plans. To ensure that the government was well-equipped to formulate and implement plans, it followed that the government must have all the resources, assets, and even labor force under its control. This meant that the state must implement the system of public ownership. Under this system, the state imposed public ownership on property, economy and society operated according to government plans, and the reward for the labor of individuals must also reflect the will of the state. As the property gaps among individuals were minimal, there was virtually no possibility of distributing reward according to property (i.e.; according to capital). There only existed the distribution of reward according to the labor that individuals contributed. The state was the sole employer of labor and all the production and demands were brought under the control of the government plans. The state was not quite sensitive to the differences of the labor that individuals contributed, nor could such differences be accurately measured. The distribution according to labor evolved into distribution according to the time of labor and according to social ranks, which ultimately evolved into an equalitarian pattern of distribution. China's market-oriented reforms encompassed almost all economic spheres and all the reform measures, diverse and complicated as they were, were essentially targeted at three facets of the production relations—ownership system, the allocation of resources, and the pattern of distribution. Enormous institutional bonus was created by unraveling the bindings of three elements—the public ownership, the planned economy, and the pattern of distribution according to labor—with China's social system as a socialist country. Un-binding these three bindings served to reduce the exorbitant transaction costs under the planned economy and stimulate the market entities to engage in increasing number of economic activities at lower transaction costs. As a result, the wealth of the entire society increased exponentially within a short stretch of time. This is exactly the underlying secret to the China Miracle.

Firstly, the abolition of the planned economy served to decrease the cost of transactions between the enterprises and the government, and between different government departments. In the production of all the consumer products and in the production of the majority of production means, China obliterated mandatory plans and government pricing, thus reducing the constraints exerted by annual plans and development programs. With regard to macroeconomic manipulation, direct manipulation was transformed into indirect manipulation. By affirming the decisive role of the market in the allocation of resources,[39] China managed to get rid of the restrictions exerted by the system of the planned economy. After the reform, in most cases, the transactions between enterprises no longer required prior transactions of rights with the government, nor was there any need to engage in transactions of rights between different government departments through the "two top-to-bottom processes and one bottom-to-top process" or through the "two top-to-bottom processes and two bottom-to-top processes," thus substantially lowering the transaction costs of economic activities. The government could dedicate more and more energy to the creation of a sound environment for investment and business operation instead of intervening in the specific business activities of the enterprises. On the other hand, the enterprises could increasingly concentrate on creating wealth instead of dealing with the government.

Secondly, enabling the enterprise and the market to resume their status as transaction entities served to create economic activities with lower transaction costs. Prior to the reform and opening-up, China's ownership structure was essentially dominated by the economy of the ownership by the whole people and the economy of collective ownership. The institutions representing those two forms of economy were the main transaction entities. After the reform, a basic economic architecture was created, in which the economy based on public ownership played a dominant role while a multiple other forms of economy based on different ownership models pursued common development. The economy of private ownership enjoyed the equal status as transaction entity as other forms of economy that belonged to the system of public ownership, including the state ownership, the collective ownership, and the mixed ownership. China also established the modern system of property rights which guarantees the equal legal status of all the market entities and their right to development. Furthermore, China established the multiple-tier market of consumer commodities as well as the market of production factors covering labor, land, capital, and technology. As enterprises of various ownerships and the market were accorded the status as transaction entities, the steps in the allocation of resources became remarkably simplified. Because the right to conduct the allocation of resources was

---

[39] In dealing with the relationship between the government and the market, the 14th CPC National Congress held in 1992 proposed "to make the market play a fundamental role in deciding the allocation of resources under the state macroeconomic manipulation." The 16th CPC National Congress held in 2002 proposed "to make the market play a fundamental role in deciding the allocation of resources on a heightened level." The 3rd Plenary Session of the 18th CPC Central Committee held in 2013 further made it clear "to enable the market to play a decisive role in the allocation of resources and allow the government to play a better role." The role of the market was elevated from the previous "fundamental role" to "the decisive role." This reform objective was reaffirmed by the 19th CPC National Congress held in 2017.

delegated to the market from the government, China developed new and highly efficient modules of transaction. Among those new transaction modules, the enterprise has become both a producer and a business operator, who exercises self-management, assumes independent responsibilities for its own profits and losses, and autonomously assumes all possible business risks. The enterprise makes its decisions independently, without any need to report its plans to any government departments to be approved or balanced. In this way, the decision-making process becomes expedited. The enterprise can quickly adjust its strategies of production and business management according market demands, thus producing the products and supplying the services that are closely geared to the market demands. The enhanced transaction efficiency helps to lessen transaction costs. The highly-efficient transaction modules have allowed the economic scale to expand and have unleashed strong momentum of economic growth. By now, China has completely got rid of the age of commodity scarcity and, for most commodities, the supply and the demand are well-balanced and in some cases the supply exceeds the demand. The Chinese people are no longer satisfied with the mere quantity of products; instead, they have been making increasing efforts to improve the quality and the profitability of products.

Thirdly, the participation of the production factors in distribution has contributed to the creation of internal incentive mechanisms for reducing transaction costs. Previously, China practiced the distribution of income according to labor. The system remained largely nominal because, in actuality, distribution was made on an equalitarian basis. Then came the changed pattern of distribution, in which distribution according to labor still predominates, but with the co-existence of multiple other modes of distribution. This marks a major adjustment in transaction rules. Apart from labor, other production factors including capital, land, knowledge, technology, management, and data participate in production as they used to; moreover, they also participate in distribution. In this way, a new mechanism of distribution has developed, with flexible and diversified rules of distribution, timely feedback, and fairness and efficiency. The new pattern of distribution shattered the equalitarian distribution, spurring individual initiative in production, innovation, and entrepreneurship. By introducing new production factors into the realm of distribution, the new mechanism stimulates input into production factors. On the other hand, the rules of distribution and the outcomes of distribution have been altered. Previously, they were decided by the state, and there had to be repeated transactions between the enterprises and the government, and also between different government departments. Now, an enterprise can directly participate in distribution by means of input and reward. The relationship between the input and reward becomes more direct and transparent and the distance between input and reward is shortened, lessening the transaction costs for obtaining the recompenses. This institutional change produced immense incentives for various factors to exercise their initiative and creativity in developing economy and accomplishing scientific and technological innovations.

The entire historical process of China's reform and opening-up demonstrates that, in the rivalry between the institution of lower transaction costs and the institution of higher transaction costs, it is the institution with lower transaction costs that ultimately prevails. This can explain why the shock therapy of the former Soviet Union failed to succeed and why China's overall reform program is gradual and evolutionary whereas the reforms in specific areas tend to be radical, abrupt, and drastic. This is because an institution of lower transaction costs usually has to go through a full cycle—growing full-fledged through gradual evolution, getting promoted on a nationwide scale through rational construction, making marginal adjustments while being promoted, and ultimately replacing the institution of higher transaction costs with the institution of lower transaction costs. Without this step-by-step process, once the system of planned economy, with its high transaction costs, is terminated, the system of market economy might be unlikely to be established. Worse still, the existing low-level economic equilibrium could be devastated and the overall economic situation would become worse than that of the planned economy. Nevertheless, when it comes to the specific areas of reform, it is difficult to generalize about what kind of reform is to be adopted, the radical, abrupt, and drastic reform or the gradual and evolutionary reform. The choice of either of these two modes of reform depends entirely on which reform is lower in transaction costs.

Chapter 5
How to Optimize the Supply of Institutions

The reform and opening-up campaign has allowed China to reconstruct three transaction entities, namely, the enterprise, the market, and the government. In this process, the transaction rules have also undergone important changes. Both in theory and in practice, in three major areas, the system of ownership, the allocation of resources, and the system of distribution respectively, China succeeded in de-binding three elements, namely, the public ownership, the planned economy, and the distribution of rewards according to labor, from its social system. Although such a series of changes were well-defined as objectives of reform, they have not yet been fully realized in reality. In the process of institutional evolution, the planned economy and the market economy tend to overlap, and a whole range of conflicts and problems exist between these two modes of economy with regard to macro manipulation, industrial development, regional development, and the supply-and-demand relationship. In seeking to solve these conflicts and problems, the state, as the most important institutional supplier, has to keep modifying the existing institutions and building new institutions. Governed by the law of path dependence, new institutions tend to demonstrate diminishing efficiency and institutional alienation that result in the spreading of constraints. Transaction costs keep escalating as increasingly complicated transaction rules combine to make the governance structure complicated. With regard to the methodology of reform, there require new explorations in order to enable China to achieve, through the reform process, objectives of marketization on one hand and to avoid the spreading of constraints on the other. Just as Ronald H. Coase pursued beyond neoclassical economics' abstract understanding about firms by conducting an anatomic analysis of the firms, we have endeavored, in the preceding chapter, to depart from neoclassical economics' assumption about the homogeneity of the state by offering an anatomy of the government. In this chapter, the author will attempt to anatomize the planned institution, the market institution, and the dual institution and, by introducing the idea of institutional subtypes, to develop new perspectives concerning economic institutions. Based on the analysis, the author will propose

B. Fan, *The Rationale Behind Change*, https://doi.org/10.1007/978-981-97-8854-5_5

ways concerning how institutional subtypes with higher transaction costs can be transformed into institutional subtypes with lower transaction costs.

1 The Spreading of Constraints in Institutional Evolution

Once the government imposes rules and constraints on a particular field, rights are generated as tradable objects and there will be transaction costs to any transaction between the government and the market, or between the government and the enterprises. In the transactions between the government and the market, or between the government and the enterprises, the government enjoys a privileged status, as the state is both the provider of institutions and the formulator of rules. As a consequence, a common phenomenon comes into existence. As the rules of transaction become increasingly complicated and the cost of transaction gradually increases, the constraints arising from the government's regulation of the market and the enterprises will keep increasing. This phenomenon can be characterized as "the growth of constraints." The government's regulation of a given domain does not exist in isolation; instead, one regulation tends to become the extension or the precondition of other forms of regulation. When an emergency situation or a conflict forces the government to take actions to intensify the regulation of a particular field, a possible outcome is that other related fields would also be subjected to heightened regulation. This means that the government would impose constraints on the market or the enterprises in a more comprehensive manner. This phenomenon can be characterized as "the spreading of constraints." Regulatory constraints often initiate from the regulations imposed by the departments of the central government and of the local governments targeting certain types of market entities and economic activities. When the constraints are extended to the upstream and the downstream of an industry chain or to broader market entities, the spreading of constraints happens vertically, throughout a given industry chain, or horizontally, throughout a particular industrial sector.

Here, the misalignment in the supply-and-demand relationship can be cited as an example to illustrate how the spreading of constraints happens vertically throughout an industry chain. For instance, in a certain period of time, coal, electricity, natural gas, real estates, pork, and even the garlic are in short supply, leading to rapid surges in prices. This will court direct government intervention. In the case of supply shortages, supply is stimulated while demands are restricted. By contrast, in the event of over-supply, supply will be restricted whereas demands are encouraged. Such interventions might seem necessary on the surface, but when intervention policies are actually implemented, the policies are highly likely to lag behind the fluctuations in the supply-and-demand relationship in the market. Even when the market is already in over-supply, the government might still be stimulating production. Conversely, when the market is already experiencing short supply, the government might still be restricting supply. The consequence is escalating gaps between the supply and the demand. As intervention tends to lag behind the changing circumstances of the market, the ill-matched supply-and-demand relationship might overflow into the upstream or the downstream of an industry chain. In this case, the government once again has to enforce similar interventions into the supply-and-demand relationship in the upstream or the downstream of an industry chain. The intervention expands from one particular segment to an ever-increasing number of segments. The more segments are subjected to government intervention, the more disparities will emerge in the supply-and-demand relationship. Eventually, the government will be obliged to place the entire industry chain under regulatory control, or merge enterprises in the upstream and the downstream into a single enterprise until the entire supply-and-demand relationship stabilizes.

Of course, such an outcome can still be viewed as an ideal one. The reality is that, more often than not, not all the information that the government has at hand about the supply-and-demand relationship is accurate. The fact that the government intervention tends to lag behind market fluctuations and demonstrate considerable randomness would sometimes give rise to the recession of an entire industry chain. Most of the contradictions and problems in modern economic life can be attributed to a certain industry chain and many problems happen in the transaction segment. The reasons underlying the occurrence of such problems can be traced to many segments in both the upstream and the downstream of an industry chain. Therefore, the spreading of constraints is most likely to happen along an industry chain. In China's coal-electricity industry chain, there was a time when "segment-specific constraints" (government interventions in a particular segment) spiraled into "chain-specific constraints" (government interventions in an entire industry chain), resulting in "the reverse marketization in a whole industry chain." This means that the entire industry chain faces the risk of returning to the traditional model of planned economy.[1] The high transaction costs resulting from planned administration would finally trigger a "regression of the whole industry chain" and there would be constraints over the product supply.

Here, another example can be cited regarding the government's regulatory measures and total quantity control to demonstrate how the spreading of constraints happens horizontally, across an entire industrial sector. As the government engages in its administrative process, some of its regulatory measures might be initially targeted at the behavior of particular groups. However, in the pursuit of regulatory magnitude or efficiency, these local regulatory measures might end up being widely expanded, developing into regulatory measures targeted at all the market entities. We can take credit supervision as an example. The mechanism of credit supervision was initially instituted as a punitive measure in law enforcement aimed at solving the difficulty of implementing legal verdicts. This measure, by enacting the system of publishing the list of defaulters who refuse to abide by legal verdicts, did indeed significantly increase the total number of cases of verdict enforcement and promote the voluntary performance of the obligations stipulated in the verdicts. In order to further enhance

[1] Please refer to Sect. 2 in Chap. 8 in this book.

the magnitude of law enforcement, the Supreme People's Court signed memorandums of joint administering of legal penalties with a number of government departments. The joint penalty is still targeted at the defaulters listed by the Supreme People's Court, but the specific measures of punishment were expanded to cover 55 items, restricting the defaulters from establishing financial institutions, engaging in civil and commercial activities, enjoying preferential policies, or assuming important positions. From then on, in building China's credit system, various government departments kept promulgating their own measures of penalizing defaulting behavior. The defining of defaulting action, the defaulters to be subjected to penalty, and the means of penalty, all of these factors become increasingly generalized. For example, a list of seriously law-violating and defaulting enterprises was established, serious law-violating and defaulting behavior was defined, and mechanisms of warning and regulatory talks aimed at admonishment was created against potential defaulting. With the introduction of these and other measures, a system of penalizing violation of business honesty was instituted in an all-round manner.[2]

Furthermore, in its administrative management, the government tends to resort to the so-called "total quantity control" in order to ensure that the scale of an industry does not exceed a certain limit. Production capacity replacement at an equal or reduced level was implemented in high energy-consuming sectors such as steel, electrolytic aluminum, cement, flat glass, and shipbuilding. In the financial sector, companies have to acquire necessary financial licenses in order to engage in business across 19 categories, including banking, securities, insurance, credit, futures, public offering of funds, third-party payment, etc. All these licenses are issued by the Central Bank, China Banking and Insurance Regulatory Commission, China Securities Regulatory Commission, Asset Management Association of China and other institutions in accordance with the principle of total quantity control. At present, only 236 licenses of third-party payment and only 19 licenses of private banking have been issued. In addition, excessive safety inspections in public places that exceed necessary and reasonable bounds, as well as the demarcation of overly large risk areas in epidemic prevention and control, practices like these are also typical examples of the spreading of constraints.

As a common phenomenon, the spreading of constraints exists not only in China but also in many other countries around the world. Britain experienced the excessive regulation of economic activities by the government in the age of mercantilism, so did the United States and European countries in the age of Keynesianism. In these cases, the spreading of constraints was inevitable. Under the impact of opposing forces, the spreading of constraints might be held in check to some extent; however, after a certain period of time, the diffusion of constraints would re-emerge. The government's economic governance could be characterized as a cycle consisting of "the spreading of constraints," "regulation relaxation," and "the re-spreading of constraints." Of course, what happens in each round of regulation relaxation and the spreading of constraints might be different in specific contents, but the internal impulses of the government to strengthen regulatory control remains identical.

[2] Please refer to Sect. 5 in Chap. 9 in this book.

China did enjoy the bonus of low transaction costs after initiating the reform and opening-up campaign. But it should be noted that, since the government's regulatory control of the market and the enterprises has been instituted in all the spheres of economic activity, the spreading of constraints has become inevitable in varying degrees. The regulatory measures include administrative licenses, administrative orders, administrative approval, administrative arbitrations, administrative certification, administrative penalty, mandatory administrative enforcement, as well as formulation of plans and programs. Only by gaining a comprehensive understanding of the manifold phenomena of the spreading of constraints can we take proactive measures to optimize the government regulation and reduce the transaction costs of institutions in the future reform undertakings. The following is an analysis of the necessity to optimize the government's regulatory control in four major aspects.

The first need arises from the transactions between the government and the market. The regulatory control imposed by the Chinese government on the market takes the form of the following measures: administrative programs and plans, industrial policy, government pricing, market access, administrative licensing, negative list, anti-monopoly, anti-unfair competition, credit monitoring, etc. These regulatory measures have indeed played their positive role in standardizing economic activities of the market. Recent years have witnessed many government institutions promulgating an increasing number of measures aimed at market regulation. These measures might seem reasonable individually. However, when put together, they create alarming institutional transaction costs. For example, the Development and Reform Commission would first reduce the total energy consumption volume and the energy consumption of per unit of GDP (the so-called dual control of total energy consumption and energy intensity) and break these two major targets into a multitude of sub-targets and distribute those targets to the administrative regions on the provincial level and the latter would in return assign the targets to the governments and enterprises on the more basic levels. As a result, a large number of potential investment projects had to be postponed for failing to obtain the necessary energy consumption quotas. For another example, every year, the Central Bank would issue decrees concerning the total loan scale for a particular period to various individual banks. The loan quotas cannot be transferred from one year to another within the same bank; neither can they be circulated and borrowed among different banks. Similarly, the government department in charge of investment approves investment projects according to the 5-year program and any potential investment projects that exceed the program would not be accepted for approval. In various regions, the government departments in charge of economic operation would issue plans concerning the utilization hour of the power-generating unit to the power plants, imposing plans of the orderly use of electricity on the major electricity-consuming enterprises.

The second need arises from the transactions between the government and the state-owned enterprises. Under the modern enterprise system, the ownership of an enterprise is separated from the right to enterprise management. The rules of transaction between the investors and the management can be simplified as a pattern in which the investors supply the capital whereas the management provides the investors with the returns on the investment. However, the government, as the capital-provider of the state-owned enterprises, follows very complicated rules when engaging in transactions with the state-owned enterprises and is entitled to rights far beyond an ordinary investor. Apart from accomplishing business objectives, the state-owned enterprises have to comply with a whole range of rules regarding the decision-making on major issues, the appointment of important officials, the decision-making on major investment projects, and the use of large amounts of fund. In addition, they have to meet the objectives in a number of domains, such as saving energy and reducing emission, controlling both the total amount and the intensity of energy consumption, carbon peaking and carbon neutrality, autonomous innovations, social responsibility, developing and expanding business overseas, coordinated development of the Beijing-Tianjin-Hebei region, the national strategy of the Yangtze River Economic Belt, addressing production overcapacity, and disposing of zombie companies which are no longer solvent. Fulfilling those goals is part of the transaction of rights between the government and the state-owned enterprises. The time and the capital invested in accomplishing the objectives other than business objectives all contribute to the transaction costs between the government and these enterprises. The gigantic transaction costs undermine the ability of the massive state-owned assets to provide the state, as share-holder, with the returns on the investment. We can cite the example of the central state-owned enterprises and the state-owned share-holding enterprises[3] (henceforward referred to as the "centrally-managed enterprises"). In 2018 and 2019, the total volume of assets of the centrally-managed enterprises amounted to 80.8 trillion RMB and 87 trillion RMB respectively.[4] The business revenue from the central government's state capital operations that was turned over in the same period totaled 132.638 billion RMB and 163.596 billion RMB respectively,[5] the ratio between the turned over profits of the state-owned capital budget and the total assets was 0.16% and 0.19% respectively, lower than the interest rate of the bank deposits and loans in the same period and also lower than the inflation rate in the same period. In 2019, the central government spending registered 35,115.15 billion RMB[6] and the expenditure

---

[3] They include the centrally-managed enterprises financed by the State-owned Assets Supervision and Administration Commission (SASAC) and the Ministry of Finance and the enterprises affiliated to the institutions and departments under the Central Government, excluding the state-owned class-A financial enterprises.

[4] Please refer to "The General Report on the Administration of the State-owned Assets in 2018 by the State Council" (http://www.npc.gov.cn/npc/c30834/201910/9b41e133a8cb45abaebbb448 93a2eb55.shtml) and to "The General Report on the Administration of the State-owned Assets in 2019 by the State Council" (http://www.npc.gov.cn/npc/c30834/202010/845921 0b544e4b9dba 931e5b4682e9fa.shtml).

[5] Please refer to Liu Kun, Minister of Finance: "Report on the Final Accounts of the Central Government in 2018: at the 11th Meeting of the Standing Committee of the 13th National People's Congress on June 26, 2019" (http://www.npc.gov.cn/npc/c30834/201906/341b59d78d3242e891a82543cdc b98bf.shtml).

[6] Please refer to Liu Kun, Minister of Finance: "The State Council's Report on the Final Accounts of the Central Government in 2019: at the 11th Meeting of the Standing Committee of the 13th National People's Congress on June 18, 2020" (http://www.npc.gov.cn/npc/c30834/202006/c6b4e1 f6afa348dc8ea9e020dd1ebb80.shtml).

supplied by the central state-owned assets worth nearly 100 trillion RMB accounted for merely 4.6%.

The third need arises from the transactions between the government and the private economic sector. In their business operations, the entities of the private sector face much higher transaction costs than do the entities of the public sector and even than the entities of the foreign capital. In their business management, the private sector has to withstand not only all the costs of transaction between the government and the market, but also the transaction costs arising from the government's policy discriminations against the private sector. The government's discriminatory policies constitute new transaction rules. For example, the state stipulates that only the state-owned sole-proprietary or share-controlling enterprises can engage in business operations in certain particular areas. At the same time, the government promises to open some business areas to the private sector. However, in the actual enforcement of the government policies, the business areas that the government promised to open would remain long closed. In some areas, although there have been measures designed to allow the private sector to operate business, the state fixes exceedingly high thresholds with regard to the capital size, professional qualifications, business scale, and performance evaluation, thus excluding a large number of private enterprises from engaging in business in those fields. Another example is that, with regard to the acquisition and use of production factors like land, capital, and energy, we can witness too many cases of double standards and dual institutional arrangements. The primary market of land is monopolized by the government, which allows the state-owned enterprises to use the land allocated to them by the government whereas private companies can acquire the use of lands only from the secondary market, by means of bidding, auction, and listing of the land transfer right.

China's three petroleum and gas giants, namely, China National Petroleum Corporation, China Petrochemical Corporation, and China National Offshore Oil Corporation, can obtain the right to exploit petroleum and gas gratuitously simply by registering with the Ministry of Naturel Resources. By contrast, private companies are all denied access to the right to petroleum and gas extraction. Some other measures of government control include the control of both the total amount and the intensity of energy consumption, the total quantity control of coal consumption in some regions, and restricted approval of the maritime spaces in sea use projects.[7] These control targets and measures are more or less designed to ensure that the key national development projects and a portion of state-owned enterprises could enjoy privileges and preferential treatment. By contrast, private companies are excluded from government protections. In the financial sector, the state-owned banks issue loans to the state-owned enterprises usually according to the benchmark interest rate. By contrast, these banks treat private enterprises with an extremely cautious attitude, demonstrating considerable prudence, fear, and stinginess in issuing loans. In addition, these banks may seek to postpone the granting of loans, force corporate

[7] In 2017, China's marine administrative department suspended the approval of reclamation projects in the Bohai Sea and in 2018 suspended the quota allocation of local reclamation projects of the year and the approval of regional sea use plans across the country.

organizations to pay back the loans in advance, and discontinue the issuing of loans. In addition, the existing legal system cannot provide sufficiently strong protection of the personal and property rights of individuals in the private sector. In the practices of criminal justice and administrative law enforcement, there have been many arbitrary and random transgressions against the rights and interests of the private economic entities. For instance, there are more than 1200 items whereby the government agencies in charge of market supervision can impose administrative penalties on corporate organizations. The penalties are enforced primarily by market supervisory departments on the basic levels of regions and counties and there are virtually no state-owned enterprises on these basic levels. Therefore, the penalties are primarily targeted at private enterprises and at small and micro enterprises. As a result, many entities of private economy have to pay higher transaction costs in order to protect their personal safety as well their property safety.[8]

The fourth need arises from the transactions between different government departments. During the period of traditional planned economy, enterprises completed their allocation of material resources and their purchasing activities in accordance with the government's administrative orders. Those transactions might seem to have happened between different enterprises, but they were actually transactions between different government departments. With the market-oriented reforms, the allocation of resources is determined by the market and enterprises operate their businesses autonomously and assume responsibilities for their own gains and losses. There is a significant decrease in the transaction of rights between different government departments in the process of resource allocation. However, such transactions have not been completely eliminated. In particular, in recent years, regarding a series of critical steps in the government's administration of investment projects, such as project review and approval, market access, administrative licensing, the scale of the bonds to be issued and the scale of bank loans to be distributed, the transactions between different government departments have kept growing and have produced appreciable restrictions on economic activities. For example, the land use planning and the overall urban and township planning tend to exert very strong control over the land use for construction investment projects. Enterprises have to first file applications for adjustments in the land use programs and the applications have to be submitted to the planning departments from basic levels up to higher levels. Once these applications are approved, the approvals would be delivered back to the enterprises.[9] For another example, the review and the approval of special bonds also have to go through processes similar to the "two top-to-bottom processes and two bottom-to-top processes" in the period of planned economy.[10] The issuing of bonds may seem to be a transaction between the enterprise and the market, but in reality the completion of the bond issuance necessitates transactions between the enterprise and the government as well as between different government agencies. Moreover, the

[8] Please refer to Sect. 2 in Chap. 9 of this book.

[9] Please refer to Sects. 2 and 3 in Chap. 7 of this book.

[10] Please refer to Sect. 2 in this chapter of this book.

transactions between these different government agencies far exceed the transactions between the enterprise and the market in terms of quantity and time.

2 An Anatomy of Economic Institutions Based on Institutional Subtypes

The spreading of constraints that has happened in China's reform and opening-up process is partly the result of the institutional evolution extending from the tradition system of planned economy and partly the result of the evolution of the newly-created institutions. Obviously, for the spreading of constraints in these two modes of institutional evolution, the causes are different. Many new institutions were created in the name of reform and were promoted for the purpose of establishing the socialist system of market economy, but the actual outcomes of these institutional changes have fallen far short of the expected results of reform. Therefore, it is particularly important to determine whether a certain institution can be classified as belonging to the planned economy or to the market economy. This classification can help shape the future direction of reform.

Regrettably, economists have so far been unable to define any widely-accepted norms with which to determine the kind of economic institutions that enterprises belong to. For instance, as part of the effort to develop the modern enterprise system, most state-owned enterprises were converted into share-holding corporate organizations which established their corporate governance structure. Equipped with expanding autonomy to operate their own businesses, they engage in transactions according to market-decided prices and conduct business activities such as bidding and tendering. The government does not issue any mandatory plans to the enterprises, neither does the government intervene in the allocation of the products manufactured by the enterprises. On the surface, the state-owned enterprises, having undergone market-oriented reform, have become transaction entities of market economy. The reality, however, is that many of such enterprises do not follow the rules of the market economy. Generally speaking, companies of market economy are extremely sensitive to the fluctuations in the interest rate. When the interest rate surges, enterprises tend to reduce their size of investment; by contrast, when the interest rate declines, they would expand their investment scale. But a large number of state-owned enterprises in China are insensitive to fluctuations in the interest rate. Even as the interest rate rises, they choose not to reduce their investment; on the contrary, they choose to increase their investment. To classify enterprises like these faces an essential dilemma because it is exceedingly hard to classify them and decide whether they belong to the planned economy or to the market economy.

In the traditional sense, economic institutions could be divided into two categories—the planned economy and the market economy. On the other hand, the system in which the planned economy and the market economy co-exist is categorized as the dual system. Among those three different categories, it is not very common in China to witness cases of purely market economic system and purely planned economic system. The dual system is a much more common condition of the Chinese economic institution. The reform objective of the market economic institution, established at the 14th CPC National Congress, could be interpreted as developing a single and complete system of market economy under the socialist condition. The objective meant that, through reform, the system of planned economy and the dual system were to be converted into the system of market economy. However, classifying economic institutions into these three categories is an over-simplification, unable to illuminate the institutional nature of many government departments and enterprises. Based on Ronald H. Coase's anatomy of companies and the anatomy of the government institutions in the preceding chapter of this book, we can also conduct an anatomy of the economic institution itself when attempting to analyze the problems of economic institutions. In this way, we may expect to elucidate the reasons underlying the spreading of constraints under different types of economic institutions and undertake reforms of these economic institutions. In classifying economic institutions, an important inspiration comes from medical science in which many physiological conditions can be divided into "subtypes." In medical science, when classifying blood types, we can differentiate a number of subtypes even within the Blood Type A, which includes A1, A2, A3, AX, AM, etc. Inspired by this idea of "subtype," we can also employ the notion of "institutional subtype" in our institutional analysis. In anatomizing the system of planned economy, the system of market economy, and the dual system, we can classify a transaction activity of rights consisting of similar transaction entities and transaction rules as a subtype.

The first is the system of planned economy and its subtypes. The system of planned economy refers to the kind of economic system in which the government imposes plans and arrangements on the allocation of resources including production, distribution, exchange, and consumption. Even after China set the reform goal of establishing the system of the socialist market economy, the system of planned economy continued to exist in the country's economic life on a considerable scale. This fact was reflected in the following aspects. The transactions of rights between enterprises were the results of the transactions of rights between the enterprise and the government, and between different government departments. The main contents of the transaction rules were various arrangements formulated by the government regarding the size of an enterprise, the categories of products, production output, commodity price, and the trading partner. The transaction cost was the sum of the costs ensuing from the transaction of rights in three spheres—the transaction between the enterprises, between the enterprise and the government, and between government departments. There were two main subtypes of the planned economic system.

(1) Direct plans. Direct plans include mandatory plans and recommended plans, and the mode of transaction consists of control of targets, project review and approval, and government pricing, etc. Government planning is demonstrated mostly in the relevant department's regulatory control over such fields as the fiscal funds (bonds and transfer payments), investments within the central budget, the loan size, and the quotas in the land plans. In the subtype of the

direct plans, the transaction entities and the transaction rules are quite similar to those in the transactions between the government and the enterprises under the traditional planned economy.[11] In China at present, there are two cases regarding the formulation and the issuance of direct plans. In the first case, what happens is somewhat similar to the "two top-to-bottom processes and one bottom-to-top process" or the "two top-to-bottom processes and two bottom-to-top processes." Sometimes, "several top-to-bottom processes and several bottom-to-top processes" are required. Plans are submitted to a multiplicity of government departments, revised, and then re-submitted to the government departments and in the process they engage in repeated transactions of rights. For example, when issuing special bonds, China still resorts to the procedure of the "two top-to-bottom processes and two bottom-to-top processes," very much akin to those during the period of planned economy. As local governments are not authorized to issue bonds autonomously, the Central Government issues the bonds on behalf of the local governments. According to the proper procedure, the enterprises and government-affiliated public institutions at the basic levels first submit reports concerning the demands for special bonds. Then, the governments on the levels of county (prefecture), municipality, and province quantify all the data and then submit reports to the Central Government. This constitutes the first "bottom-to-top process." After determining the overall size of the bonds, the Central Government makes comprehensive adjustments and balances to form an overall plan of bond issuance and assigns the plan in varying proportions to individual provinces for execution. With the due adjustments and balances by the provincial, municipal, and county governments, the final plan concerning the need of bond issuance is developed (the first "top-to-bottom process"). The final plan regarding the need of bond issuance is then submitted, through multiple upward administrative levels, to the provincial government (the second "bottom-to-top process"), and the provincial government commissions specialized agencies (or platforms) to underwrite and financial institutions like banks would participate in the purchase of the bonds (the second "top-to-bottom process").[12] The entire cycle of bond issuance comes to an end only at this point. In the market-oriented bond-issuing model, enterprises and government-affiliated public institutions issue bonds directly with the help of the underwriting platforms and both the buyer and the seller come into direct business deals. With shorter execution chain and higher efficiency, the interest rate of the bonds can more accurately reflect the economic value of the bond project. As good projects tend to have lower interest rates while bad projects higher interest rates, market mechanisms can be adopted to create sound mechanisms of incentive and constraint with regard to the bond issuance of the local governments.

---

[11] Please refer to Sect. 1 in Chap. 4 of this book.

[12] Please refer to the "Notice of the Ministry of Finance on Issuing the 'Management Measures for Local Government Special Debt Budget'" and "Management Measures for the Issuance of Local Government Bonds".

In the second case, the targets contained in the plans, broken into different proportions, are issued to the local governments and enterprises without soliciting their feedback. Some government departments would issue planned targets, compulsory targets, and even projected targets to local governments in different proportions and would make performance evaluation. The results would be presented in the form of a list of rankings. When issuing those targets, it would be specified that the government officials in charge of implementing the plans would be held accountable for failing to meet the set objectives. Evidently, plans of this kind must be implemented more strictly than the mandatory plans in the period of planned economy. For example, the Chinese government launched the action plan of the prevention and control of air pollution in 2013 and, as part of this action plan, the methods of performance evaluation were specified. Each administrative region would be assigned a portion of the pollution combat objective. The results of the performance evaluation would be made public to the entire society and would be registered and recorded by the government departments on higher levels, serving as valuable basis in the overall performance evaluation of individual officials and the leadership committees. In 2016, China started to implement energy consumption programs in the 13th "5-Year plan," including the dual control objectives regarding the total volume and the magnitude of energy consumption in various regions, the plan of total emission control of chemical oxygen demand (COD) in various regions, and the plan of total ammonia and nitrogen emission control in various regions. Each of the plans were broken into varying component proportions and the provincial governments were made responsible for issuing the plans to governments on the more basic levels for implementation, along with the terms and provisions for holding officials accountable for their potential failures to enforce the plans. As the formulation of those plans did not involve either the "bottom-to-top processes" or the "top-to-bottom processes," the transaction costs of distributing control targets among different government departments on different levels were not very high, but the transaction costs between the government department and the enterprises were exceedingly high. For example, as many enterprises were denied quotas for energy consumption or for pollution emission, the construction of investment projects could not be activated and the normal production and business operations had to be discontinued, resulting in huge transaction costs due to long periods of waiting.

During the period of planned economy, direct plans were characterized by a high level of centralization, as all the targets were strictly under the control of the planning commission of the Central Government, which conducts the balancing of the targets. Different from the high-level concentration in the traditional planned economy, the current form of planned economy is more discrete. As the central and local government departments have their own "fields where they impose their regulatory control," they ended up being "independent kingdoms" under the planned economy. Many government officials mistake the planning in their administrative work for planned economy. It is true that the central and local government departments have the responsibility to conduct planning of their administrative work, but it is totally inadvisable for them to impose plans on enterprises and other administrative agencies. Every target in a plan, and the breakdown and implementation of each planned target at different administrative levels would produce costs of transaction between the enterprise and the government agencies, and between different government agencies themselves. All the evils characteristic of the traditional planned economy, such as excessive and overly-rigid administrative control, low inefficiency, and bureaucracy of the opinionated senior officials, have resurged under the system of discrete planned economy. To address these institutional evils is no less difficult than to overcome problems in the traditional system of planned economy. In the traditional planned economy, the pattern of "several bottom-to-top processes and top-to-bottom processes" and "comprehensive balancing," though unable to eradicate the institutional evils of the planned economy, could nevertheless reflect the efforts of the planning commissions to match plans with the objective reality, testifying to the democratic nature of the economic decision-making. This attribute was a major factor that differentiated China's planned economic system from that of the Soviet Union. At present, many government departments tend to divide the plan targets into specific components and assign them to governments on the more basic levels in a once-and-for-all manner, without soliciting the feedback from local governments and enterprises. The nature of "mandatory economy" inherent in this new pattern is even more pronounced than the direct plans during the period of traditional planned economy. Some economists have pointed out that, in seeking economic development, it is necessary to prevent the occurrence of the "fallacy of composition," avoiding the situation where partially rational policies, when combined, create negative effects. On the other hand, it is also essential to guard against the "fallacy of division." It is inadvisable for planning commissions simply to divide overall tasks into smaller segments and impose them on government departments and enterprises on the basic levels for compulsory implementation. It is even more unacceptable for government departments on higher levels to add extra tasks when requiring government departments on the lower levels to implement the plans, which will create serious dilemmas for the government departments on the basic levels. It can be concluded that the accumulation of transaction costs is the intrinsic reason behind both the fallacy of composition and the fallacy of division.

(2) Indirect plans. Administrative measures based on such indirect plans are sometimes called economic levers, which include economic programs, interest rate, exchange rate, price, and other means that the state employs to regulate the economy. After China established the reform objective of building the socialist market economic system, these measures of administrative manipulation are no longer called plan-based administration. Nevertheless, they are essentially not different from those during the period of planned commodity economy in terms of the contents and the objects of regulation, thus necessitating relatively high transaction costs in the transaction process. For instance, it has been a long-standing practice for the Chinese government to fix prices on electricity—the price for electricity accessing the power grid and the price for electricity sold to end users. When the prices of electricity and coal rise significantly, there is always a delay in the rise of electricity price, which in return causes

gaps in the prices of coal and electricity and in their supply-and-demand relationship. The transaction costs generated by the entire period of delay in the electricity price adjustment would force power-generating enterprises to incur enormous losses.[13] For another instance, in some parts of China, local governments would impose recommended prices on the transactions of real estates, stipulating that all the real-estates transactions should not exceed the recommended prices. However, the gaps between the recommended prices fixed by the local governments and the actual market prices are huge. Therefore, in the actual real-estates transactions, the developer tends to sign multiple contracts with the buyer and create multiple transaction modules in order to close the deal according to the market price. Some developers would first sign a contract with the client according to the government's recommended price. Apart from this contract, the developers would require the buyers to sign an additional contract concerning the selling of a parking space or concerning the intensive interior decoration. These additional contracts could make up for the gaps in the prices between the government-fixed price and the market price. In many cases, in order to meet the requirements stipulated in the government's price supervision and inspection, the developers would create a highly complicated concatenation of transaction modules. In those circumstances, both the developer and the customer have to spend considerable time dealing with the regulations imposed by the government and pay extra transaction prices outside the costs of normal market transactions.

Drawing up development programs is a common means of indirect plans. Since the beginning of the reform and opening-up, fundamental changes have happened in China's mid-term and long-term development programs with regard to the nature, contents, and methods. Mandatory plans were eliminated, gradually replaced by recommended plans of indirect government regulation. The original purpose of drawing up mid-term and long-term programs was to propose visions for social and economic development and make projections concerning future trends. These programs were entirely non-mandatory in nature. However, from the very outset of the twenty-first century, there have been some new developments. Some government departments have been taking advantage of the authoritative nature of those programs. Under the pretext of government programs, they secretly seek to expand their administrative power. As a result, the phenomenon of implementing the programs in a dogmatic and rigid manner has become increasingly widespread. Plans as well as programs have all been employed by some government departments as an excuse for intervening in market operations. Some departments create bindings between the programs and the administrative licenses. For instance, before applying for construction licenses, enterprises would be required to first secure a land use planning permit, a construction project planning permit, and a rural construction planning permit. Some government departments use the program planning as a basis for reviewing and approving investment projects, rejecting all the projects that are not listed in the development programs. In order to bring their projects into the development

[13] Please refer to Sect. 2 in Chap. 8 of this book.

program, the enterprises would have to spend large amounts of time seeking to have their projects included in the program. This means that, before activating the construction of their projects, the enterprises would have to engage in transactions with the government in order to obtain the government's approval to have their projects included in the development programs. Enterprises can undertake their own preliminary work in construction projects only after completing above steps. In real-world situations, there lacks a consistently high level of professionalism in special programs or industry programs, with many programs being formulated early, of low quality, and deficient in foresight. In the transition from old development drivers to new development drivers in which low-quality development is to be replaced by high-quality development, a large number of new projects characterized by advanced production capacity, state-of-art technologies, and industry-leading prospects could not be approved for construction as a result of rigid implementation of the existing programs. In such cases, the new projects face huge transaction costs because the entities of those projects would have to wait for an exceedingly long time.

The second is the system of market economy and its subtypes. The system of market economy is the kind of economic system in which market mechanisms serve as the basic means in the allocation of resources. The system's basic attribute is that companies engage in direct transactions of rights and their transaction costs only encompass the time spent on acquiring information, conducting negotiations, and signing contracts. In such transactions, there is no cost arising from the transactions of rights between the enterprises and the government, or between different government departments. The rules of transaction are simple as the supply-and-demand relationship determines the categories, quantities, and prices of the products to be transacted. Here, I will continue to use the classification of the markets made by the neoclassical economics and divide the market economic system into four subtypes: the market of complete competition, the market of monopoly, the market of monopolistic competition, and the market of oligarchical monopoly.

(1) The market of complete competition. In such a market, there is a high level of competition and a low level of concentration, with a large number of buyers and sellers. Both the supplier and the buyer can enter and leave the market with utter freedom, and everyone is a recipient of prices. In this transaction module, there is virtually no government intervention and both the supplier and the buyer, as law-abiding entities, engage in transactions according to the rules of the market without any need to engage in prior transactions with the government. There are no extra transaction costs. The chain of transaction is short and the cost of transaction is low.
(2) The market of monopoly. This type of market is the opposite of the market of complete competition. In a monopolized market, the level of competition is low and the level of concentration is high. There is usually only a single seller or buyer and the price is determined by either the seller or the buyer who monopolizes. The monopolized market develops either due to natural factors or due to artificial factors such as technology and access. To maximize public welfare, the government will have to intervene in some monopolistic markets,

for instance, by adopting measures such as granting franchises, implementing price controls, and sharing profits.

(3) The market of monopolistic competition and the market of oligarchical monopoly. These two types of market transactions come in between the market of complete competition and the market of monopoly in terms of the degree of market competition and concentration. Of the two, the market of monopolistic competition demonstrates a higher degree of market competition and a lower degree of concentration than the market of oligarchical monopoly. In these two types of transactions informed by monopolistic competition and by oligarchical monopoly, the level of government intervention also comes in between the two other modules of transaction, namely, the market of complete competition and the market of monopoly. In many cases, the intervention in oligarchical monopoly is even stronger. The government intervention is reflected in the setting of rules for these transaction modules, forever seeking to strike a balance between safeguarding fairness and maintaining efficiency.

The third is the dual system and its subtypes. The dual system is a form of institution in which the allocation of resources is fulfilled by means of both the system of planned economy and the system of market economy. Under this dual system, a portion of product transactions between two enterprises have to pay costs of transaction between the enterprise and the government and between different government departments. For the rest of the products, they can be traded directly between the enterprises. For example, under the double-track system of product prices, some products are sold according to the prices fixed by government plans while other products are sold at the market prices. Another important case about this dual system is that, in order to complete the transactions of product rights, enterprises would have to pay the costs in the above-mentioned two modes of transactions. In producing and selling certain products like coal and petroleum, the state-owned enterprises must meet the requirements of various performance evaluations imposed on the state-owned enterprises by the government departments on the higher level. On the other hand, they must also participate in market competition. As a result, the state-owned enterprises have to pay dual transaction costs. At present, the following four subtypes can be identified in the dual system.

(1) The shadow plan. Shadow plans are a manifestation of the government's intervention in the state-owned enterprises by means of performance evaluation. Although the government does not assign direct mandatory plans or even recommended plans to the state-owned enterprises, the requirements in their performance evaluations serve as the objectives of the government-formulated plans. For state-owned enterprises, they now no longer rely on the government's allocation of products as they used to during the period of traditional planned economy. Instead, they engage in transactions with other enterprises according to market principles. However, the purpose of their transactions is not to maximize the interests of the shareholders, but primarily to meet the criteria or standards specified in the performance evaluations by the administrative departments on the higher level. In this particular institutional subtype, the entities of transactions

are the state-owned enterprises and other market entities, and the rules of transaction are a mixture of the criteria of performance evaluation and the market rules, with the criteria of performance evaluation taking precedence over the market rules. Therefore, many of the business operations by the state-owned enterprises cannot be assessed according to the market economic thinking. The criteria contained in the performance evaluations outside the market rules have certainly added to the internal management costs for the state-owned enterprises.

(2) The monopolistic plan. Some of the industries in China used to be the sectors which fell under the administration of mandatory plans in the traditional planned economy. Although the entities in those industries have been converted into enterprises through the reform process, their mechanisms of business operation have remained largely unchanged. In this institutional subtype, the rules of transaction demonstrate the characteristics of both the monopolistic industries in the market economy and the plan-based administration under the system of planned economy. However, China has so far failed to develop effective government supervisions of these monopolistic industries comparable to the supervisions which have been developed in the countries of developed market economy. For example, China's "Big 3" petroleum and gas giants (i.e. China National Petroleum Corporation, China Petrochemical Corporation, and China National Offshore Oil Corporation), the State Grid Corporation, the PipeChina, China Tobacco, and China National Salt Industry Corporation, they all belong to monopolistic industries. These state-owned enterprises still retain the quasi-government nature so that other market entities which engage in transactions with these state-owned enterprises are virtually engaging in transactions with the government. This is because these market entities, prior to their market transactions with the state-owned enterprises, have to apply for relevant rights from these enterprises and can enter market transactions with these enterprises only after securing necessary approvals. For instance, when an enterprise applies to the grid corporation for access into its power grid or to the petroleum and gas corporation for pipeline transportation, and when a private vendor applies to the state-controlled salt corporation or tobacco corporation for retail business in salt or tobacco, they all have to engage in preliminary transactions which are akin to the transactions between market entities and the government. Only after obtaining the necessary licenses and approvals can market entities have access to the related services. This entire process creates additional transaction costs outside the regular business activities.

(3) The exogenous plan. In recent years, in addition to economic targets, the Chinese government has imposed on enterprises other administrative requirements with respect to environmental protection, energy conservation, pollution reduction, and carbon reduction. Like mandatory plans, these targets are broken into component portions and then assigned through various administrative levels down to enterprises, thus imposing constraints on their economic behavior. However, these targets belong to exogenous plans as they are not aimed at the control over economic objectives. In this institutional subtype, the inter-enterprise transactions demonstrate similar characteristics to those in

the subtype of direct plans under the system of planned economy. Before enterprises complete their transactions of rights, they must first complete transactions of rights with the government. The only difference is that, in the transactions between the enterprise and the government, the direction intervention imposed by the government on product quantities and prices in the subtype of direct plans has been replaced by the requirements concerning energy consumption and environmental protection. Together, the exogenous plans and market rules constitute the rules of transaction in the inter-enterprise transaction module. Like mandatory plans, the exogenous plans tend to be contradictory to market rules and it is precisely this contradiction that forces enterprises to establish a set of new transaction modules to meet the demands of various stakeholders. The inevitable result is a rise in transaction costs.

(4) The differential administration. The government imposes different modes of regulation on different enterprises or on different products in the same industry. This is another way indicative of the transactions between the enterprise and the government. This differential treatment is sometimes reflected in the system of ownership and sometimes in the government's determination of the direction and the level of sophistication of a given industry. The double-track pricing system is precisely a manifestation of the differential treatment of product prices. With the implementation of differential administration, the same act of transaction follows different rules of transaction, thus giving rise to different transaction modules. Among all the modules, the one into which the government intervenes more vehemently requires that the enterprises have to engage in transactions of rights with the government before transactions in the market. Enterprises have to obtain the license or the approval and other related rights that fall under the government administration.

3 Reshaping the Reform Path with Low Transaction Costs

The foregoing analysis of the transaction costs shows that, although reform has succeeded in generating institutional bonuses, the spreading of constraints has seriously eroded these bonuses throughout an industry chain and across an entire industrial sector. On the other hand, the analysis of the system of planned economy, the system of market economy, and the dual system, along with their respective subtypes, indicate that some of the economic institutions in China are still confined to the dual system and the system of planned economy. A single system of complete market economy is far from being established. The further deepening of reform means that China should not only keep developing the system of market economy but also should prevent the spreading of constraints. To fulfill the mission of deepening the reform, it is imperative to follow the path of reduced transaction costs and choose a reform program of low transaction costs according to three major principles—the reasonable and necessary principle, the principle of proportion, and the principle of minimal detriment. In this way, a transformation can be achieved from the subtypes of the system of planned economy and the dual system to the subtypes of the system of market economy. More specifically, the reform can take the following steps.

The first step is to determine the transaction modules. Various economic systems and various official documents of government policies might seem bewilderingly complex, but they are ultimately concerned with completing the transactions of rights. In studying the path of any reform, we can simplify a complicated institution into a number of transaction modules and determine what rights are being traded in each transaction module, between the government and the market, between the government and the enterprise, and between different government departments. It is also crucial to understand what rules the government has formulated concerning any given right. In addition, a single transaction module can be divided into a number of sub-modules of transaction.

The second step is to analyze the transaction costs. Having defined transaction modules, it is important to calculate the transaction costs that will be incurred in the transaction of any single right, that is, the time and the capital that transaction entities have to invest in a transaction. The time spent on completing a transaction should definitely be counted as part of the transaction costs for all the entities involved. Different transaction rules will lead to different transaction costs. A comparison of these different transaction costs will help determine the institutional efficiency under different reform programs. When there are a number of alternative reform programs to choose from, it is always possible to choose the optimum one by applying relatively objective norms.

The third step is to formulate objectives for different institutional subtypes. The so-called institution is a complex consisting of a series of transaction modules. A cluster analysis of each module in an institution can help determine which subtype in the system of planned economy or in the dual system that institution belongs to. Based on this analysis, it is possible to propose how to transform to a particular subtype in the market economy and to formulate the overall objective of the reform.

The fourth step is to optimize the transaction rights and the transaction rules. Institutional changes are primarily aimed at changing the transaction rights and transaction rules. Guided by the overall reform objectives, decisions should be made concerning every single transaction right that deserves to be preserved or added, and adjustments need to be introduced into the rules of transaction of every single right, all according to the principle of reduced transaction costs. The aim of reform is to reduce the transaction costs, but in certain circumstances, the increase in transaction costs is inevitable. The optimization of the transaction rights and the transaction rules should follow the following three principles. (1) The reasonable and necessary principle. The state should define, within reasonable and necessary bounds, the transaction rights and transaction rules between the government and the enterprise, between the government and the market, and between different government departments. Any transaction rights or transaction rules that are unreasonable and unnecessary or have gone beyond the reasonable and necessary bounds should be eliminated or duly adjusted. (2) The principle of proportion. The formulation and adjustment of the transaction rights and transaction rules should ensure that the time and the capital that transaction entities invest in a particular transaction should be proportionate to the gains that they can acquire from that transaction. (3) The principle of minimal detriment. As transaction costs stemming from any transaction of rights are to the detriment of the interests of the transaction entities, minimizing transaction costs should be pursued as an optimum solution in creating transaction rights and transaction rules. When a number of alternative reform programs are available, the reformer should opt for the one with the lowest transaction costs.

The aim of reform is to tackle prominent problems in economic and social development. The spreading of constraints is indeed quite extensive, but it is unrealistic to address the constraints all at once. Instead, it is necessary to analyze the rationale behind those constraints and overcome them in a step-by-step manner, according to the order of priority. Basically speaking, reform can be undertaken in three domains. The first is general reform, which can also be called general-purpose reform, akin to the general purpose technology (GPT) in scientific and technological development. The government programs in certain areas of social and economic development tend to produce overall impact on the entire country and the government's administrative actions can affect many fields, such as the fiscal and taxation system, the financial system, the investment system, and the market supervision system, etc. The second is the reform in focus areas. Institutionally, some industries tend to enjoy a relatively high level of autonomy, such as the tobacco industry and the salt industry. As different regions across China undergo different stages of development and reform, reform must be undertaken by moving from one particular area to the next, in a step-by-step manner. The third is the reform in a whole industry chain. For some industries where there is serious imbalance between the supply and demand, comprehensive reform should be conducted along both the upstream and the downstream of an industry chain, such as the "coal-electricity" industry chain, the petroleum-gas industry chain, and the real-estates industry chain. To further deepen the reform, it is necessary to comprehensively define the relationship between the government and the market, between the government and the enterprise, and between different government departments in all the segments of an industry chain. Beyond that, it is necessary to adjust transaction rights and transaction rules. In this way, the spreading of constraints might be fundamentally stopped. The following paragraphs will offer an analysis of how to deepen reform, taking the marketization of an entire industry chain as an example.

There are three types of paths to follow in a reform designed to transform an industry chain of incomplete marketization into an industry chain of complete marketization. The first is the further improvement of the subtypes of the market economic system. The second is the transformation of the subtypes of planned economic system to the subtypes of the market economic system. The third is the transformation of the subtypes of the dual system to the subtypes of the market economic system (please refer to Fig. 1). When China first embarked on the reform and opening-up campaign, practically none of the industry chains were completely market-oriented. After four decades of reform and opening-up, some industry chains have achieved full marketization while others have merely achieved quasi-marketization. The existence of industry chains of incomplete marketization constitutes serious hurdles to China's stable economic growth and to structural adjustments. It needs to be pointed out that the development of industry chains of complete marketization does not deny the role that the government plays; rather, the transaction of rights between the government and the enterprise and between the government and the market should be minimized. Even under the market economic system of full competition, the government bears the responsibility to supervise enterprises' external behavior and the industries of natural monopoly while at the same time providing public services to enterprises. These are the duties that the government is meant to perform under market economic system.

Following the principle that the path of reform is shaped by low transaction costs, we can draw up the following process whereby to transform an industry chain of incomplete marketization into an industry chain of complete marketization (please refer to Fig. 2). The first step is the identification of the problems. For an industry chain of incomplete marketization, the most common problems are mainly the worsening discrepancy between the supply and the demand and the diminishing profits of an industry as a whole. For example, in the "coal-electricity" industry chain, the first thing that proves very puzzling to many people is that the power plants would suffer massive losses in times of power supply shortages when the prices of electricity and coal actually significantly escalate. The underlying reason is that the power plants

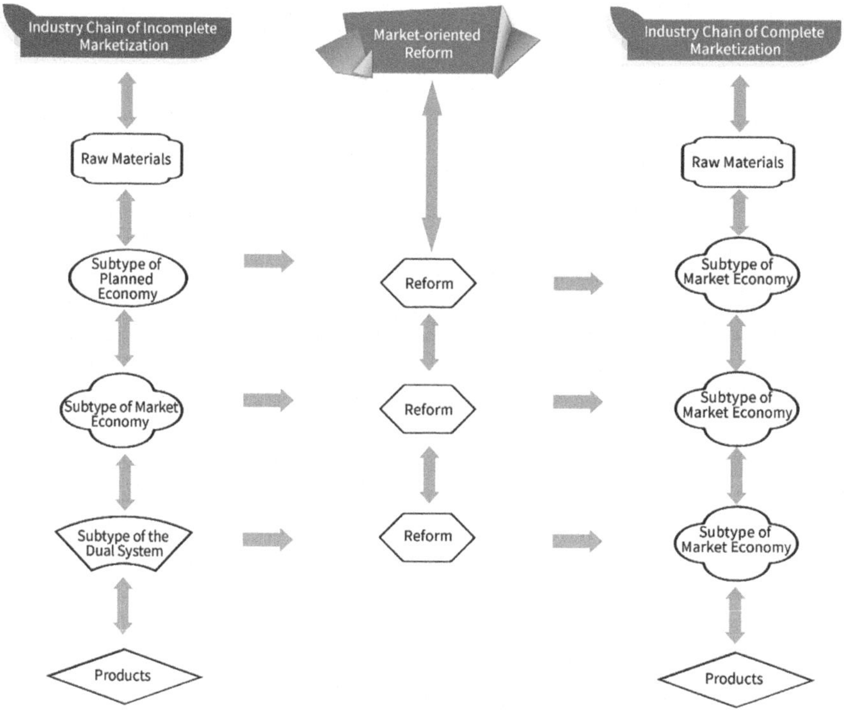

Fig. 1 The path of evolution from the industry chain of incomplete marketization to the industry chain of complete marketization

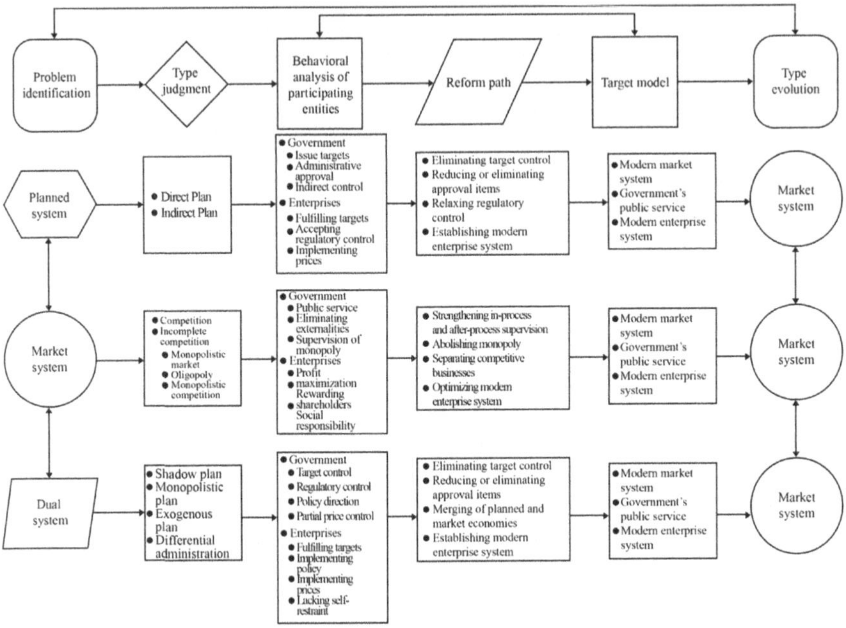

Fig. 2 The process of constructing industry chains of complete marketization

are in position to remove the factors behind the rising costs. It is only by determining the problems that we can understand the necessity and the importance of reform.

The second step is type judgment. This step requires the determination of the institutional nature of an industry chain and whether a given segment in an industry chain belongs to the system of planned economy, to the system of market economy, or to the dual system. After four decades of reform and opening-up, we now seldom witness many complete and typical institutions of planned economy. Nevertheless, it is crucial to identify atypical institutions and institutional subtypes. For example, we should investigate whether there exists natural monopoly, whether the government's regulatory control and supervision are justified, as well as other issues like the extent of concentration in a particular industry and the degree of competitiveness, etc.

The third step is to analyze transaction modules. To determine the transaction module in an industry chain, it is necessary to first determine the transaction entities in each transaction module, whether a transaction happens between the government and the market, between the government and the enterprise, or between different government departments. At the same time, it is necessary to determine the rights of transaction and the rules of transaction. There can be several transaction modules for each segment in an industry chain and each transaction module can be divided into several sub-modules. Finally, the transaction costs in each module should be calculated.

The fourth step is to propose the target model of the reform. The target model of industry chain reform is to be proposed according to the special characteristics of an industry and the principle of a fully competitive market. The transaction costs should be used as a yardstick with which to choose the target model of low transaction costs from among a number of alternative institutional models. For example, in the "coal-electricity" industry chain, the target institution to be proposed should include the creation of a fully competitive coal-electricity market, the market of transportation capacity, and the market of electric power. In this way, a pattern of electricity transaction characterized by "multiple buyers and multiple sellers" will be formed.

The fifth step is to develop the reform path. This means that specific reform measures must be proposed, a step which can be approached from two aspects—the government and the enterprise. For the government, its reform measures should mainly include eliminating the control over plan targets, reducing or eliminating administrative approval, lifting restrictions on prices, and transforming the double-track (plan-oriented and market-oriented) system into a single-track (purely market-oriented) system. For the enterprises, their reform measures should mainly include establishing and improving the modern enterprise system and enhancing their ability of self-restraint. For example, in the "coal-electricity" industry chain, the reform path should consist of a unified coal-electricity price, the separation between the management of railway infrastructure and the business operation of the railway system, the opening up of competitive businesses, the separation between electric power transmission and distribution, the withdrawal of power grid enterprises from the business of electricity buying and selling, and the establishment of a cash market of electric power.

The sixth step is to implement the reform. The government can undertake reform by increasing or decreasing the transaction rights and by adjusting transaction rules. Through a series of reform efforts, an industry chain will evolve to acquire the institutional nature of a fully market-oriented industry chain.

The seventh step is to repeat the entire process. It is highly unlikely that a single reform can accomplish all the reform goals. Therefore, it is necessary to launch a new round of reform to repeat the entire cycle, starting with the identification of problems. The reform objective of marketization will be fulfilled only through several rounds of such reforms.

Chapter 6
Reform of the Investment System

The term "investment" in the investment system refers to the investment in fixed assets. By the time the People's Republic of China was established, the country inherited pathetically scanty fixed assets for production purpose from the old China, and the newly formed fixed assets mainly derived from new construction, reconstruction, and expansion. At that time, such investments in fixed assets was called "basic construction." During the period of planned economy, China's economic growth was primarily driven by basic construction, and the source of funds was mainly fiscal funds, similar to the capital budget of the countries that implement a double-entry budget system. The state's control over the scale of basic construction constituted the primary measure of regulating the economic cycle. In the process of the reform and opening up, a pattern of diversified funding sources and investment entities came to be gradually established in China's investment sector. Having established the reform goal of building the socialist market economy, China has embraced the modern thinking of macroeconomic management and viewed investment as one of the three key locomotives driving economic growth. Regulation of the investment scale still remains the primary means of macroeconomic regulation. Given the important role of investment in the entire macro-economy, it is of particular significance to investigate the system of fixed assets investment when we discuss the impact exerted by the evolution of China's economic institutions on the social and economic development since the start of the reform and opening-up.

1 From Basic Construction to Investment in Fixed Assets

China's system of planned economy was modeled after that of the former Soviet Union, and the system of basic construction was an important component of the planned economy, deriving its theoretical foundation from Marx's theory of reproduction. However, Marx himself did not propose any concept of basic construction.

B. Fan, *The Rationale Behind Change*, https://doi.org/10.1007/978-981-97-8854-5_6

What Marx did was simply dividing reproduction into two distinct categories, the simple reproduction and the expanded reproduction. In the expanded reproduction, he divided capital into variable capital and constant capital. The Soviet economists also classified the reproduction of fixed assets into two categories, the simple reproduction and the expanded reproduction, both of which were to be realized through basic construction. In managing its planned economy, China classified the new construction, reconstruction, and expansion of fixed assets as basic construction, which was utilized for the expanded reproduction of fixed assets. The upgrading and renovation of the existing fixed assets were separately listed outside of basic construction for the purpose of the simple reproduction of the fixed assets, whose source of funding came from drawing of the depreciation fund.[1] During the "First Five-Year Plan" period (1953–1957), China merely invested 55 billion yuan in the basic construction,[2] but by 1979, the investment had reached 651.7 billion yuan.[3] The scale of construction reached by the investment from the depreciation fund each year was already quite considerable. The scope of investment covered by the existing basic construction could no longer reflect the actual construction scale. In the early 1980s, China introduced the concept of "fixed asset investment" which consists of two parts: the basic construction and the technological renovation (which was then called "tapping the production potential and upgrading technology").[4]

Between 1952 and 1984, the growth rate of China's investment in basic construction demonstrated obvious cyclical fluctuations, with a decline for one or two years following a period of consecutive growth for three or four years. Each rapid expansion in the investment scale would result in a comprehensive shortage of materials and resources such as coal, electricity, oil, and transportation, followed by significant surges in in prices. Eventually, the government had to intervene and make adjustments. Such roller-coaster fluctuations in investment had a significant negative impact on economic development. During that period, the primary measure to control investment inflation was through the approval of investment projects. Since all the projects of basic construction were subjected to the control imposed by national planning, the state had stipulated specific provisions governing a whole range of procedures ranging from the preparation of the plan books to the design, construction, completion, and check for acceptance.[5] When the investments became overheated,

[1] Please refer to Li Zhenzhong (ed.)'s "Planned Economy" published by Renmin University Press in 1985, pages 249–250.

[2] Please refer to Liu Suinian and Wu Qungan (eds.)'s "A Brief History of China's Socialist Economy (1949–1983)" published by Heilongjiang People's Publishing House in 1985, pages 177–181.

[3] Please refer to Wang Tongsan's "The Development Path of China's Investment System" published by Economic Management Press in 2013, page 39.

[4] In the fourth session of the Fifth National People's Congress in 1981, the "Government Work Report" proposed: "Investments in fixed assets used in the future should be arranged and used uniformly for both infrastructure construction and technological transformation." Starting from 1982, the country decided to compile a unified plan for fixed asset investment, including both infrastructure construction and technological transformation.

[5] In the "Several Provisions on the Procedures for Infrastructure Construction" issued by the State Planning Commission, State Construction Commission, and Ministry of Finance on April 22, 1978,

the government could use the approval mechanism to control the size of new projects and the progress of ongoing projects. In the case of a slowdown in economic growth that created a need to expand investment, all the central government had to do was to relax the administrative approval, which would provide significant ventilation to the investment impulses of the local governments and a large number of construction projects would consequently be launched.

During the market-oriented reforms in the 1990s, China gradually adjusted its regulation method, shifting from direct manipulation to indirect manipulation. In addition, China expanded its scope of regulation, shifting from the administration of merely state-owned enterprises to the administration of all types of ownerships and of market entities. Of the three major engines driving economic growth, the state lacked effective means to manipulate the consumer demands, and the net exports were subject to the impact from many uncontrollable external factors. Therefore, after establishing the overarching reform goal of building the socialist market economy in 1992, China continued to treat investment as one of the key mechanisms to regulate economic growth. With the outbreak of the Asian financial crisis in 1997, China was confronted with a severe situation of insufficient demand. As a result, in 1998, measures were taken to expand domestic demand and strengthen infrastructure construction, leading to the issuance of 660 billion yuan in long-term construction bonds by 2002.[6] Later, in response to the 2008 global financial crisis and to the pressure of economic downturn after entering the "new normal" in 2012, China all resorted to the measure of expanding investment.

Although China recorded significant growth in investment scale in each round of macroeconomic manipulation, the impact of investment on driving economic growth has been increasingly below expectations. Based on this phenomenon, many scholars believed that it was no longer viable to use the expansion of investment as a means to stimulate economic growth. If we merely analyze the correlation between investment and the statistics of China's GDP, such a conclusion that scholars reached would seem to be tenable. However, the conclusion might be completely different if we take institutional factors into consideration. Prior to 2002, every time the country adopted the policy of expanding investment, physical output could be quickly generated immediately after the funds were in place. However, over the past 20 years, the cycle of generating physical output has become increasingly longer, a fact that has affected the driving effect of investment. This is not because the multiplier effect of investment has failed; rather, it is because the approval process for investment projects has become increasingly complex, transaction costs have risen sharply, and project progress has been delayed.

the plan and task book for all large and medium-sized projects should be reviewed by the competent department of the State Council or province (autonomous region or municipality) according to their affiliation, and then submitted to the State Planning Commission for approval. Some major projects are subject to the approval of the State Council by the State Planning Commission.

[6] Please refer to "Zeng Peiyan on Development and Reform" (Volume I), published by People's Publishing House in 2014, page 564.

2 The Evolution of Investment System Creates Changes in Transaction Costs

The investment system, like other systems, keeps evolving through transaction activities over time. We can use a hypothetical investment project to examine how transaction activities are conducted within the system.

Firstly, it is necessary to define the transaction modules of fixed asset investment activities. A transaction module should comprise three major components: rights, contracts, and transaction costs.

(1) Rights. When an enterprise files an application to the government to obtain the necessary administrative approval for a construction project, the government grants the approval if the enterprise meets certain requirements. The government's administrative action gives rise to the right which is the "construction project permit."
(2) Contracts. When the government grants the right of the permit and the enterprise acquires that right, a contract is reached between the two parties accordingly. The document approved by the government constitutes the content covered by the contract. A contract should generally include: the owner of the construction project, investment scale, source of funds, construction site, construction duration, quality and technical standards, etc. In addition, the creation of this contract should also include some implied conditions, that is, both the government and the enterprise should comply with other laws and regulations of the country as well as technical standards and pollution discharge standards stipulated by the country.
(3) Transaction costs. When an enterprise applies to the government for the approval of construction project and receives the government approval, the costs incurred in this process are transaction costs, which primarily include the time and the money consumed in the process. For an enterprise, time is something that it values greatly. This is because the more time that it spends on waiting for the government approval, the more delayed the production becomes. This will trigger a chain reaction in which the enterprise will have to bear greater financial costs and face greater risks of forfeiting market opportunities. For government agencies engaged in administrative approval, they will also incur transaction costs, including the time of making decisions, the salaries to be paid to civil servants, on-site inspection expenses. The entire approval process would definitely consume significant administrative resources on the part of the government.

Secondly, it is essential to identify the transaction entities of fixed asset investment. Here, three main entities can be differentiated—the government, the market, and the enterprise. The government departments that engage in transactions with the market and the enterprises are specific administrative agencies, which include various development and reform departments (the former National Development and Planning Commission and individual planning departments), various planning departments, the natural resource departments (the former land management departments), the ecological environment departments (the former environmental protection departments), and the housing and urban–rural development departments (the former housing and construction departments and construction departments). Generally speaking, a construction project has to go through all the necessary approval procedures by all these separate government agencies: the ratification of a project, land planning and land transfer, meeting environmental standards, and granting construction permits. In the following paragraphs, a discussion will be offered concerning the transaction activities among the three transaction entities according to three different scenarios.

(1) The transaction between the government and the market. The transaction between the government and the market is reflected in the government's use of contracts to delineate the respective boundaries of activities for both the government and the market. In the early stage of fixed asset investment, the investment projects were fully funded by the state. The funding of those projects fell under the sphere of the government's functional responsibilities. With the deepening of reforms, multiple investment entities have been introduced into various construction projects. The government defines its own boundaries and those of the market in the form of normative official documents, allowing various qualified investment entities in the market to make investments within the prescribed spheres. This type of normative official document serves as the contracts between the government and the market. We can witness an obvious transformation when the government moves from prohibiting investments by various market entities in a given field to allowing these entities to access construction projects in the field. In this process of transformation, the government completes a transaction with the market, and the transaction cost incurred is mainly time. Similar situations occur when the US government prohibits the export of certain products to a country but then, after efforts by all parties, opens up the export to that country. This is equivalent to completing a transaction between the US government and the market. The contract of the transaction is the export license, which may be fully open or conditionally open to the transaction partners involved. The time consumed from prohibiting exports to allowing exports constitutes the transaction cost.

(2) The transaction between the government and the enterprise. The various rights generated through the administrative actions of the government institutions are transferred to the enterprises, and each transfer of rights constitutes a transaction between the government and the enterprise. The transaction involves the administrative approval, inclusion of enterprises in construction investment plans, the permit of land use, the permit of pollutants discharge, and the permit of construction, etc. The documents of approval issued to enterprises by the government agencies are the transaction contracts, in which the rights and obligations of both parties are stipulated. The time and the money spent by an enterprise on acquiring these documents of approval constitute the transaction costs.

(3) The government-to-government transaction. Governments on different levels are vested with different approval and administration authorities according to the size of the investment. Generally speaking, projects of larger scale require approval from higher-level government agencies, in the order of the county/prefecture-level, the city-level, the provincial-level, and the national-level. For the government on the same level, different agencies equipped with different functional powers are vested with different approval authorities over investment projects. When an enterprise submits an application for a particular investment project to a government agency on the basic level, in some cases the application requires the government agency on the basic level to report the application for approval to higher-level government agencies in a hierarchical manner; in other cases, the application must seek approval from all the relevant government agencies on the same level in accordance with certain procedures. It is also quite common for a particular construction investment project to seek approval both from government agencies on different levels and from multiple government agencies on the same level. Going through all the approval procedures requires transactions of rights between and among multiple government agencies. For example, an enterprise may seek to obtain government approval of its investment project by first applying to the city-level development and reform commission. The city-level commission needs to report this project to the provincial-level commission for approval, and then the provincial commission reports it to the national-level commission for approval. A transaction of rights thus develops between the lower-level and upper-level development and reform commissions. Similar transactions also exist between government agencies at the same administrative level.

Thirdly, it is necessary to calculate transaction costs. Based on the analysis of the foregoing two steps, we can see that all the transactions between the government and the market, between the government and enterprises, and between different government agencies have their transaction costs. If we calculate all the costs of the transactions between the government and individual enterprises, we can obtain statistics concerning the overall transaction costs of this particular kind of transactions. The average transaction costs of such projects can also be calculated. A comparative study of the transaction costs for the approval of individual items can be conducted with regard to all the categories of construction projects that require government approval. Such comparisons can also be undertaken between different regions or even between different countries. Additionally, the transaction costs for the approval of the same item can be listed according to according to chronological sequence for comparative analysis in a vertical manner.

Having developed analytical tools consisting of transaction modules, transaction entities, and transaction activities, we can use them to analyze the evolution process of China's investment system. In the process of implementing a construction investment project, enterprises and government agencies do not just engage in a single transaction. At a given point in time, multiple transaction modules are often operating simultaneously. For instance, during the preliminary phase of a project, transactions

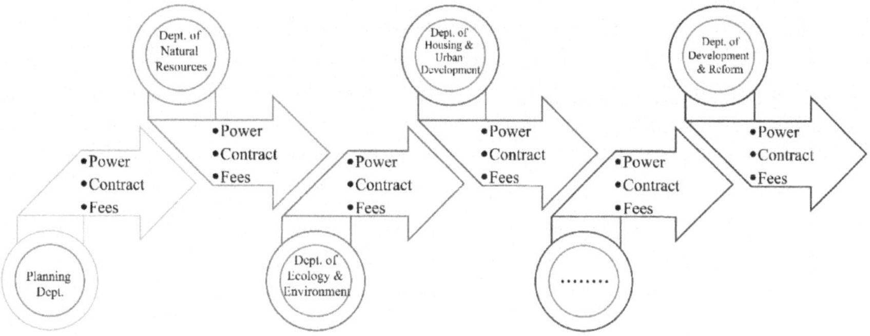

Fig. 1 Diagram of the transaction modules in the preliminary phase of investment projects

need to be conducted with government agencies such as the development and reform commission, the planning department, natural resources department, ecological and environment department, and housing and urban development department (please refer to Fig. 1).

We can analyze how the institutional evolution impacts on transaction costs by focusing on one particular type of transaction, the transaction of rights between the enterprise and the development and reform commission. We will examine a whole range of changes that have happened in terms of the rights, contracts, and transaction costs since the period of the "first five-year plan" to the present, in the manner of a time-series analysis.

Firstly, in the "first five-year plan" period, a highly centralized system for administrating basic construction was established. Important material resources and facilities related to national economy and people's livelihood, including mechanical and electrical equipment required for new construction projects, were managed by the National Planning Commission and by various central authorities in charge. All such resources and facilities were subject to the planned distribution. At the level of the central government, the National Planning Commission, the National Basic Construction Commission, the National First Machinery Industry Department, and various central authorities in charge were established. Below the central level, the government at all local levels also had planning commissions, basic construction commissions, and various administrative authorities in various industries. In the transaction between the planning department[7] and the enterprises, the administrative actions by the planning department generated the right to arrange for investment plans for large and medium-sized construction projects and to issue task plans. These

[7] Investment projects in China are generally managed according to their scale. Large-scale investment projects are submitted by local planning commissions to the planning departments of the relevant national ministries or the National Planning Commission for approval and issuance after approval by the National Planning Commission. Medium and small-scale investment projects are approved and issued by local planning departments. For the sake of analysis, the planning departments at all levels are collectively referred to as planning departments.

plans and documents constitute the contracts between the government and the enterprises. As there weren't a large number of projects scheduled by the government during that period, the proposed plans could be implemented fairly quickly and the transaction costs were thus not high.

Secondly, in the initial stage of the reform and opening-up campaign, the scale of basic construction was under effective control. After the end of the Cultural Revolution, local government authorities demonstrated an exceedingly high level of enthusiasm for social and economic development, and there was a new campaign of "Great Leap Forward" in which Western technologies was introduced massively into China to boost development. Under such circumstances, the government took measures to tighten the scale of investments in basic construction. In 1978, the planning departments began to review and approve construction projects with considerable strictness, requiring that all types of projects, apart from undergoing the existing procedures, be first evaluated by the relevant departments for product design, resource and geological conditions, and supporting conditions such as coal, electricity, oil and transportation. Feasibility reports must be submitted before the National Planning Commission could possibly review for approval. Although the investment plan continued to be the right in the transaction between the planning department and enterprises at that time, the contract had changed. The increased items in the pre-approval procedures prolonged the overall approval time and increased transaction costs.

Thirdly, in 2001, the review and approval process regarding investment projects was simplified. The State Planning Commission announced the cancellation of the first batch of investment project approvals in five categories.[8] The cancellation was conducted according to the following principle. For the projects which did not require investment by the central government investment, which were encouraged by the country's industrial policies, and whose total investment limit was below a certain threshold, those which were funded by local governments were to be approved by the local planning department, while those funded by enterprises were to be autonomously decided by the enterprises themselves.

[8] The first batch of five types of approval items cancelled include: (1) urban infrastructure construction projects, mainly including urban water supply facilities, urban sewage treatment facilities, urban garbage treatment facilities, urban gas facilities, urban central heating facilities, urban roads and bridges and tunnels, except for urban rail transit, thermal power plants, bridges and tunnels crossing major rivers, and inter-provincial urban water diversion projects; (2) agricultural, forestry, and water conservancy projects that do not require central investment, including construction projects in planting, animal husbandry, fisheries, and agricultural and sideline product processing, as well as various bundled projects in forestry and water conservancy facilities construction; (3) social welfare projects constructed with local and enterprise self-raised funds, including construction projects for culture, radio, film and television, education, health, sports, and large-scale tourism and entertainment facilities; (4) real estate development projects, mainly including high-end office buildings, high-end residential communities, high-end tourist hotels and restaurants, etc.; (5) commercial and trade facility projects, including commercial facilities and market facilities.

During that period of time, the planning department transferred part of the investment approval authority to the market, thus reducing the transaction costs for this part of the construction projects. However, for construction projects that still required administrative approval, both the approval process and the transaction costs remained unchanged.

Fourthly, in 2004, the investment approval process was significantly adjusted. The State Council made a decision on investment system reform, equipping enterprises with greater autonomy to make investments. For construction projects that do not involve the government investments, these projects would be no longer subjected to administrative approval. They were brought under authorization system or registration system depending on specific circumstances that they belonged to. The "Catalogue of Investment Projects Subject to Government Authorization" was developed, and the government authorized projects that fell within the range of the catalogue. With regard to the construction projects invested by an enterprise, the enterprise could seek government authorization merely by submitting application documents to the government, without having to go through the previous approval process of submitting project proposal, feasibility study report, and construction commencement report. With regard to the construction projects invested by an enterprise that were outside the catalogue, the enterprise could seek government authorization merely by having the project registered with relevant government agencies. Prior to 2004, after the investment projects were approved by the planning commission, other government agencies would cooperate with the planning commission. The planning commission's approval process could take a long time, but other government departments would shorten the process by acting quickly. With the implementation of the authorization system, relevant government agencies would activate their ratification process first. What an enterprise needed to do would be to collect all the documents ratified by various government agencies and submit these documents to the development and reform commission (formerly the planning department). In this new flow chart, some ratification procedures which used to happen in the latter stage of the process were rescheduled into procedures at the preliminary stage of the authorization process. However, the ratification by one government agency tended to be the precondition for the ratification by another government agency, therefore, the ratification of a construction project by all the individual government agencies tended to incur serious bureaucratic procrastinations and delays. As a result, the project ratification by government agencies might take significantly longer, but the process could be shorter with the development and reform commissions. For construction projects that required ratification, the transaction cost arising from the development and reform commission alone manifested an obvious decrease. However, if the overall transaction cost was calculated, there was certainly an increase.

Fifthly, the period from 2013 to 2016 witnessed the government's continued efforts to streamline administration and to delegate power. For three times, the State Council revised the "Catalogue of Investment Projects Subject to Government Authorization," reducing the number of the centrally authorized projects by 90%. It promoted the cancellation and the relegation of the preconditions for ratifying construction projects invested by enterprises, and modified 50 preconditions for project authorization that involved 15 departments. Also canceled were 18 items that fell within the range of the enterprises' own autonomous business operations, such as the pledges from banks to grant loans. Among the remaining 32 pre-authorization conditions, only two were preserved, namely, the proposed construction site and the preliminary authorization of land use. In an effort to streamline and standardize the procedures for investment project reporting and authorization, the number of pre-construction reporting and authorizing matters involving 15 government agencies was reduced from 65 to 42, as long as the report of the investment project or the feasibility study report had been authorized.[9] After this round of reform, the development and reform department only retained the right to make energy-saving reviews and recommendations in investment project authorization. Other government agencies followed suit, streamlining and standardizing most of their respective reviewing and authorizing procedures regarding construction investment projects. As a result, the overall time required for authorizing investment projects decreased, and transaction costs were reduced accordingly.

The fore-going analysis indicates that, as seen from the perspective of the enterprise, the transaction costs that enterprises had to pay in order to obtain authorization for their construction projects from the development and reform commission tended to fluctuate. Initially, the transaction costs were relatively low, but gradually increased over time. After the reform, they decreased again. The process of this institutional transformation is congruent with the actual circumstances of economic development during that period. Since 2010, there was a consistent decline in the growth rate of China's fixed asset investments. In 2012, infrastructure investment even experienced negative growth. One of the important reasons for this was that the authorization process for new investment projects was too long, and the transaction costs were too high, both of which hindered the implementation of expansionary fiscal policies aimed at increasing investment. This explains why the reform of the authorization system of construction investment projects after 2013 was persistently focused on reducing transaction costs. According to a a sampling survey in 2016, the average cycle for authorizing new investment projects was around 420 working days. After the reform, transaction costs were somehow reduced. In 2020, among all types of investment project authorizations, the authorization period for construction projects was reduced to within 120 working days.[10]

Following the above reform trajectory, we can also analyze the changes in the transaction costs between the government and the market. From the "First Five-Year Plan" period to the beginning of the reform and opening up, the investments in fixed assets were almost exclusively government investments, hence no transaction would happen between the government and the market. However, with the deepening of market-oriented reforms, multiple investment entities were introduced into

[9] Please refer to "Creating a Good Investment Environment with the "Three Measures"—Summary of the State Council's Special Inspection on the "Streamlining Administration and Delegating Power and Improving Regulation" Reform, Investment Approval Reform Chapter", Xinhua News Agency, June 16, 2017.

[10] Please refer to the "Implementation Opinions of the State Council Office on the Comprehensive Reform of the Approval System for Construction Projects" (GuoBanFa [2019] No. 11).

the sector. Nevertheless, construction projects were still subjected to government approval. In 2001, the approval authority in five categories of fixed assets investment was abolished, defining for the first time the range of approval for investment projects, undertaken by the planning departments on behalf of the government in the form formal constraints. Projects outside this range no longer required administrative approval, thus reducing the transaction costs for the market to engage in such investment projects. In the reform of the investment system in 2004, the authorization system and the registration system were introduced, with the government publishing a catalogue of projects subject to government authorization and expanding the range of projects invested by market entities that could be exempted from administrative authorization. In this way, transaction costs were once again reduced. In 2015, the system of the negative list of market access began to be implemented, categorizing the industries, sectors, and businesses that were prohibited or restricted for investment and business operation by non-government entities. All the industries, sectors, and businesses outside this negative list were open to various market entities, which can access businesses in those areas legally and on an equal basis. This policy further expanded the scope of market investment and reduced transaction costs. In the abovementioned process, the contracts between the government and the market underwent continuous changes, moving from small-scale opening of the market and exemption from administrative approval to the establishment of the negative list which authorized the government to approve only a small proportion of investment projects. With those changes in the contracts, the transaction costs between the government and the market were gradually reduced (please refer to Table 1).

3 Investment Troubled by Transaction Costs

In the previous two sections, by examining China's development and reform scheme over the past few decades, we have conducted a historical analysis regarding the relationship between the government and enterprises, and between the government and the market. In the field of investment activities, the government's administrative actions tended to give rise to a large number of rights, which invariably generated costs in the transactions between the government and enterprises, between the government and the market, and between one government institution and another. Put together, these costs, when calculated in the form of time that was consumed, were still very significant. Currently, the state has still preserved investment approvals and administration across 42 categories (please refer to Table 2 in Appendix).[11] To complete an investment activity, it is imperative for an enterprise to go through, with varying numbers of administrative approval. For example, for undertake a construction project in Shenzhen, if the project is funded by the government, it requires

[11] Please refer to the "Notice on Issuing the Unified Names of Investment Approval Management Matters and the List of Application Materials for the National Investment Project Online Approval and Supervision Platform" (Development and Reform Commission Investment [2019] No. 268).

Table 1 The evolution of the transaction modules concerning the investment approval since the "first 5-year plan" period

Transaction between the government and the enterprise	During the "first 5-year plan" period	At the beginning of the reform and opening-up	In 2001	In 2004	From 2013 to 2016
Rights	Approval of investment projects and the allocation of material resources	Approval of investment projects, the allocation of material resources, & approval of investment within the budget of the central government	Project approval	Project approval	Project approval
Contracts	Arrangement for the large- and medium-scale investment plans, and issuing the document of the plans and tasks	In addition to existing procedures, various projects are required to be first studied and compared by the departments in charge concerning product plans, resource geological conditions, as well as supporting conditions for coal, electricity, oil transportation, etc. A feasibility report should be submitted, followed by approval from the National Development and Reform Commission	For projects not requiring central government investment, encouraged for development by national industrial policies, and below the total investment limit, those funded by local governments are subject to approval by local planning departments, while those funded by enterprises are subject to autonomous decision-making by the enterprises themselves	Projects within the scope of the "Catalogue of Investment Projects Approved by the Government" are subject to approval. For enterprise-invested construction projects that require approval, only a project application report needs to be submitted to the government, bypassing the procedures of approving project proposal, feasibility study report, and commencement report. Enterprise-invested projects outside the catalogue are subject to a filing system	The cancellation of 18 items, including bank loan commitments, which fall under the autonomy of enterprise operation, has been executed. Of the other 32 pre-approval conditions, only two—planning and site selection, and land use pre-examination—are retained. The number of construction application and approval items involving 15 departments between the approval of investment project reports or feasibility study reports and the start of construction has been reduced from 65 to 42 items
Costs	Low	Relatively high	Relatively high	High	Reduced

(continued)

Table 1 (continued)

Transaction between the government and the market	During the "first 5-year plan" period	At the beginning of the reform and opening up	In 2001	In 2004	From 2013 to 2016
Rights			The range of investment	The range of investment	The range of investment
Contracts					
Costs			Reduced	Reduced	Reduced

government approval in 50 items whereas, if the project is funded by the private sector, it requires government approval in 63 items (please refer to Table 3 in Appendix).[12] In Shanghai, there have been a number of reforms in the administrative approval of investment projects for industrial purposes. Apart from the regular items subject to administrative approval, 23 items are subjected to government evaluation and review, and only when all the paperwork is ready will the related administrative review and ratification process be activated (please refer to Fig. 2 in Appendix).

The tables and diagrams in the foregoing paragraphs indicate that the development and reform commission is a relatively comprehensive department, and an enterprise has to engage in transactions with many government departments in order to actually embark on an investment project. Many local governments claim that they have abided by the reform requirements imposed by the State Council by having all the items requiring administrative approval handled in the government service hall, and that there is no item for approval outside the hall. In addition, the time for approval has been shortened within 120 working days. However, the reality is that the 120 days merely means the time the documents submitted by the enterprise stay are kept for approval at a particular administrative division which receives the documents in the service hall, and a large amount of preliminary work still needs to be completed outside the service hall. This is exactly what has been criticized by many people in a sarcastic remark which goes like this, "the 120-day countdown happens inside the service hall but the all the extra hard efforts happen outside the hall." These announced 120 days of approval time does not accurately reflect the entire transaction cost.

Any analysis of the transaction costs for companies to undertake a construction project can be conducted according to the following steps. Firstly, it is necessary to define the transaction module according to formal constraints. Each item requiring government approval can be seen as a right generated from government administrative actions, and this right can be used to name the transaction module. Secondly, it is necessary to identify the transaction entities by clarifying the particular government agency which is to engage in the transaction of rights with the company. In this way, the government agency and the enterprise can be defined as two transaction entities. Thirdly, it is important to elucidate transaction rules by developing a full knowledge about the normative documents that need to be complied with for the completion of a particular transaction. Fourthly, it is also important to calculate the transaction costs. The entire time spent on every step of obtaining government approval, ranging from the initial communication between the company and the government agency, the compliance with the transaction rules that need to be implemented, to the government's eventual transfer of rights, should be counted as transaction costs.

However, this still does not represent the entire transaction cost. Among the 42 reserved administrative items that require investment approval, the completion of the transaction in each of the transaction modules often requires obtaining other approvals as a prerequisite according to the transaction rules that must be observed.

[12] Please refer to the "Notice of the General Office of the Shenzhen Municipal People's Government on Issuing the List of Approval Items for Social Investment Construction Projects in Shenzhen" (Shenfu Office Document [2018] No. 190).

Thus, a single transaction module can be divided into multiple sub-modules of transaction, and completing these sub-modules also requires paying transaction costs. These transaction costs should also be added to the total transaction cost of completing an investment project.

In the following paragraphs, several transaction modules will be chosen for further analysis.

The first module is the approval of land use. In the process of approving an investment project, the rights derived from the administrative actions of the natural resources department include the preliminary examination of project land use and the issuance of the land use permit for construction purpose (including the temporary use of land). With regard to some special projects, approval of soil and water conservation plans and the issuance of rural construction planning permits are also required. If each approval item is seen as a transaction module, then each module can be further divided into a number of sub-modules of transaction. For example, before any project involving land use is officially approved, it must go through the preliminary examination of construction land use. In such a transaction, the local natural resources department and the enterprise are the trading entities, and the right being transacted is the administrative approval of the preliminary examination of construction land use, with the transaction contract being the relevant regulations listed by the natural resources department. To complete this transaction of preliminary examination, several sub-modules must be completed in advance. If we use the approval process which happens in a certain county as an example, we will see that the enterprise which applies for land use has to complete a certain number of transactions of rights with the following government departments. The first transaction of right is the written judgment, to be presented by the urban and rural planning and construction bureau, concerning the site selection of the construction project planning and the related redline map. The second is the technical report, to be presented by the county land survey and planning team, of land surveying and demarcation and a map of the current status of land use. The third is the certificate concerning land ownership and land category, to be presented by the basic-level division of the natural resources bureau and land ownership division. The fourth is the written ratification of the project proposal or project registration, to be presented by the relevant government agency in charge. The fifth is the assessment report of potential geological disasters and hazards, to be presented by relevant intermediaries. The sixth is the written proof, to be presented by the land ownership and environment division affiliated to the land and resources bureau, of whether an independently located construction project overlays important mineral resources. Finally, there is the overall planning map of land use, to be presented by the planning division under the natural resources bureau. Each of the above-mentioned sub-modules could be further divided into sub-modules on the next tier. For example, concerning the overall planning map of land use, any adjustments in the plan is not something that can be accomplished solely by the planning division under the natural resources bureau. If the proposed project needs to overpass or overlay the ecological protection zone, the permanent basic farmland, the cultivated land, ecological forests for the public interests, wetlands, nature reserves, scenic spots, geological parks, etc., then adjustments must be made in the original planning, which must be submitted according to the original administrative procedure and must seek approval by the relevant departments. Usually, a plan is adjusted once a year or every few years. Generally speaking, local governments only allow 3–5 days for approval regarding the preliminary examination of land use. However, the transaction cost for completing this transaction of preliminary examination of land use should include the total transaction fees arising from all the sub-modules. Obviously, the total transaction costs far exceeds the time that seems to have been spent on individual sub-modules themselves.[13]

The second module is the energy conservation review. The government agency responsible for energy conservation review is the development and reform department in some places and, in other places, the energy management authority. Only by passing the energy conservation review can an enterprise acquire the government's evaluation report of energy conservation. For the investment projects funded by the government, the evaluation report of energy conservation is a prerequisite for the construction company to submit a feasibility study report. For the investment projects funded by private enterprises, it is a prerequisite for activating the construction process. Currently, except for projects with low energy consumption and the classified projects, all types of investment projects[14] need to go through energy conservation review. If we treat energy conservation review and assessment as a transaction module, both the energy conservation review authority and the construction company are the transaction entities, the written document of energy conservation review and assessment is the right derived by of reviewing authority from its administrative action, and the "Method for Energy Conservation Review of Fixed Assets Investment Projects" is the transaction contract. Different local governments may give different pledges regarding the time for completing the reviewing process and closing the transaction in this module, ranging from 2 or 3 days to 1 or 2 weeks. If we examine more closely this transaction module of energy conservation review, the review regarding the dual control of the total energy consumption volume and the energy consumption intensity are the most stringent, making the dual control the most difficult goal to achieve. According to the government regulations, any project's energy consumption volume and energy efficiency must meet the dual control requirements regarding the total energy consumption and the level of consumption intensity in the local area. This single transaction alone might render it impossible for many investment projects to achieve any progress over long periods of time.

The third module is the environmental protection approval. For the ecological and environment department, its most important authority in the investment project approval process is the approval of the environmental impact assessment (EIA) of the

[13] Please refer to Sects. 3 and 4 in Chap. 7 of this book.

[14] Fixed asset investment projects with an annual comprehensive energy consumption of less than 1000 tons of standard coal and an annual electricity consumption of less than 5 million kilowatt-hours, as well as projects outside the "Industry Catalogue that Does Not Require Separate Energy Efficiency Review" (NDRC-MEP No. 2017[1975]).

construction project.[15] In this transaction module, the local environmental protection bureau and the enterprise are the transaction entities, and the right involved in the transaction is the administrative license of the EIA. The formal constraints in the transaction contract are the acceptance conditions listed by the environmental protection department. A closer examination of this transaction module indicates that a number of sub-modules can be differentiated, such as excess production capacity review. If an enterprise is engaged in business operations in an industry with excess capacity, it is mandatory for the enterprise to obtain, from relevant departments, the additional approval for launching the construction project or to secure certificates of project registration. In the sub-module of excess capacity review, the enterprise and the relevant department are the transaction entities, and the government department's document of construction approval is the right of transaction. Generally speaking, the contract of transaction in this module consists not of formal laws or regulations, but of a certain number of policies or official documents. Sometimes, the contract may simply comprise of the department's perceptions and judgments concerning these issues, which can be classified as informal constraints. In addition, the time spent on communication between an enterprise and government departments is characterized by high uncertainties.

In the transactions in three major modules involving land use, energy conservation, and environmental impact assessment, and in each of their sub-modules, it is necessary for an enterprise to invest a certain amount of time. The time includes: (1) the time needed for searching for relevant information in a specific field and arranging for staff to gain sufficient knowledge about process approval process and about relevant rules and procedures; (2) the time for submitting applications; (3) the time for government agency to undertake reviews, including the preliminary review by specific personnel, the joint internal signing of documents by related functional departments, submitting reports hierarchically to government departments on higher levels for approval (in some cases, on-site inspections, experts confirmation, and evaluation by third-party organizations are required); (4) and the time for government agencies on higher levels to issue the approval. Many approval items are required to be completed within a few days or a dozen days within the prescribed 120 working days. However, if we conduct a close examination of each of the three major modules, and if the transaction time spent on each of the three modules and on each of their sub-modules is added together, we will find that the total transaction cost far exceeds 120 days.

Regarding the reform of the investment system in China, the reform is undoubtedly moving in the right direction when the reform is targeted at the approval process, seeking to streamline approval procedures and reduce the approval time. However, methodologically, the reform demonstrates obvious shortcomings. The first major shortcoming is path dependence, which allows each administrative agency to take reform actions on its own. In such a reform, usually the government agency which

[15] Please refer to the "Classification and Management List of Environmental Impact Assessment for Construction Projects (2021 Edition)" (Departmental Meeting No. 16) by the Ministry of Ecology and Environment.

initiates the reform would have consultations with the government agency with the approval authority. It is the government agency with the approval authority has a greater say in whether to retain the approval items or not. The approval authority is repeatedly transferred between the same department at the central and local levels or transferred between departments at the same level, making it difficult for the approval authority to be fundamentally eliminated. In each reform, there would be changes in the quantity of transaction costs, but it has been virtually impossible to achieve a qualitative breakthrough. The second shortcoming is the potential conflicts of transaction rules between the main module and its sub-modules. If we treat the approval of an investment project as a main transaction module, we will see that the central government, on behalf of the state, has formulated rules designed to simplify the approval process and reduce transaction costs. However, it is the various government agencies that are in charge of formulating the transaction rules in various sub-modules. The addition of a sub-module will create a new set of rules, resulting in the inevitable increase in the transaction costs. In addition, every time the rules are adjusted, there would often be an increase in the transaction costs. The third shortcoming is the incomplete calculation of transaction costs. The time spent in the government service hall for completing all the approval procedures does not adequately reflect the real transaction cost. Once we probe into each transaction module, we will discover that a large number of new sub-modules of transaction need to be completed and that each sub-module could be further divided into several sub-modules. The transaction rules contained in the sub-modules at all levels are not only numerous and interlocked but also in constant change. As a consequence, there exists a tendency of diminishing efficiency and institutional alienation, resulting in an increase in the overall transaction costs arising from the 42 reserved items that still require government administration and approval if enterprises seek to undertake the construction of investment projects.

Appendix

See Tables 2, 3 and 4.

Table 2 List of standard names of the matters in investment approval and management on the national platform of online approval and management of investment projects (2018 edition)

Serial No.	Name of the matters for review & approval	Applicable cases
1	Review and approval of the recommendation document of government investment projects	Government direct investment or capital injection projects
2	Review and approval of the feasibility study report of government investment projects	Government direct investment or capital injection projects
3	Review and approval of the preliminary design of government investment projects	Government direct investment or capital injection projects
4	Ratification of enterprise investment projects	Enterprise-invested fixed asset investment projects listed in the "Government-Approved Investment Project Catalog" (including fixed asset investment projects constructed by non-corporate organizations using their own funds, without applying for government investment)
5	Registration of enterprise investment projects	Enterprise-invested fixed asset investment projects not listed in the "Government-Approved Investment Project Catalog" (including fixed asset investment projects constructed by non-corporate organizations using their own funds, without applying for government investment)
6	Preliminary review of the land use for construction projects	Construction projects that do not involve new construction land and are within the urban construction land area determined by the overall land use plan, using the construction land which has already been approved, may be exempted from preliminary review of the land use for construction projects
7	Site selection evaluation document	Construction projects that require approval or certification by the relevant departments in accordance with national regulations, in which the right to use the state-owned land is provided by means of government allocation
8	Review and approval of the use of ports and shorelines	The use of ports and shorelines for the construction of docks and other port facilities within the overall planning area of the port
9	Review and approval of applications for the development and utilization of uninhabited islands	The development and utilization of uninhabited islands, where it involves the use of islands for special purposes, or the necessity of land reclamation to connect islands and other activities that significantly alter the natural topography and landforms of the islands, shall be approved by the State Council

(continued)

Table 2 (continued)

Serial No.	Name of the matters for review & approval	Applicable cases
10	Review and approval of construction projects overlying important mineral resources	The construction of railways, factories, reservoirs, oil pipelines, power transmission lines, and various large-scale buildings or building complexes overlying important mineral deposits
11	Review and certification of the right to use sea areas	Construction projects that involve the use of sea areas
12	Review and approval of the evaluation of the environmental impact of construction projects	Implemented in accordance with the "Catalogue for the Class-Based Management of Environmental Impact Assessment of Construction Projects"
13	Energy efficiency review	Excluding fixed asset investment projects with an annual comprehensive energy consumption of less than 1000 tons of standard coal and an annual electricity consumption of less than 5 million kilowatt-hours, fixed asset investment projects involving state secrets, and fixed asset investment projects outside the "Catalogue of Industries Not Subject to Separate Energy Conservation Review"
14	Review of the construction, modification, or expansion of sewage outlets in rivers, lakes, and reservoirs	Construction units constructing, modifying, or expanding sewage outlets in rivers, lakes, and reservoirs
15	Approval of flood impact assessment	(1) Construction, expansion, and modification of hydraulic projects on rivers and lakes that also involve adjusting the original functions of the existing water projects (review of the consent document of original hydraulic project planning); (2) Construction of bridges, docks, roads, ferries, pipelines, cables, water intakes, drainage, and other engineering facilities that cross rivers, pass through dikes, or are adjacent to rivers (approval of construction project schemes within the original river management area); (3) Construction of non-flood control projects in flood-prone and flood storage areas (approval of flood impact assessment reports for original non-flood control projects); (4) Construction of projects affecting hydrological monitoring upstream and downstream of national basic hydrological stations (approval of projects affecting hydrological monitoring upstream and downstream of original national basic hydrological stations)

(continued)

Table 2 (continued)

Serial No.	Name of the matters for review & approval	Applicable cases
16	Review of the assessment of waterway navigability and related impacts	The construction of projects related to waterways encompasses various structures and installations, including: (1) buildings and constructions that span or traverse waterways, such as bridges, tunnels, pipelines, ferries, cable lines, and similar structures; (2) permanent river control dams and barrages located on navigable rivers; (3) structures and installations situated within the protected zone of waterways, which may include buildings and constructions along rivers, lakes, or coastlines. This category encompasses facilities like docks, intake and outfall structures, jetties, revetments, boat ramps, slipways, shipyards, and enclosure works, among others
17	Review and approval of soil and water conservation plans for production and construction projects	Production and construction projects in mountainous areas, hilly regions, windy and sandy areas, as well as other regions prone to soil erosion as identified in soil and water conservation plans, whose activation may lead to soil erosion
18	Review and approval of water extraction permits	Construction projects that utilize water intake engineering or facilities to directly extract water resources from rivers, lakes, or the underground
19	Agricultural irrigation and drainage impact evaluation document (review and approval of compensation projects that occupy agricultural irrigation water sources and of irrigation and drainage facilitates)	In cases where engineering construction projects occupy agricultural irrigation water sources, irrigation and drainage engineering facilities, or have adverse impacts on existing irrigation water sources and water supply, if the engineering construction project requires the construction of replacement facilities to fulfill the original functions, it is necessary to undergo approval for compensation projects occupying agricultural irrigation water sources and irrigation and drainage facilities. If it is not feasible to construct replacement facilities, an assessment is required, and relevant fees for compensation shall be remitted to the treasury for the reconstruction and construction of irrigation and drainage facilities
20	Review of immigration resettlement plan	Large and medium-sized water conservancy and hydropower projects involving immigrant resettlement
21	Review and approval for the construction, expansion, and renovation of projects to avoid harm to the meteorological detection environment	New construction, expansion, and renovation projects within the protection range of meteorological stations

(continued)

Table 2 (continued)

Serial No.	Name of the matters for review & approval	Applicable cases
22	Review of the design of lightning protection device	Oil depots, gas depots, ammunition depots, chemical warehouses, fireworks and firecrackers, petrochemical and other flammable and explosive construction projects and sites, mining areas in lightning-prone areas, tourist attractions, or buildings (structures) and facilities that have been put into use and require separate installation of lightning protection devices, as well as large-scale projects with high lightning risk and no standard lightning protection norms, requiring special demonstration, are under the responsibility of the meteorological department for lightning protection device design review. The design review of lightning protection devices for residential building projects and municipal infrastructure projects is integrated into the construction drawing review process; the lightning protection management of professional construction projects such as highways, waterways, railways, civil aviation, water conservancy, electric power, nuclear power, and telecommunications is the responsibility of the respective professional departments
23	Review and approval (certification) of construction projects using forest land and construction in forests and national nature reserves of wildlife	(1) If the area of protective forest land or special-purpose forest land used exceeds 10 hectares, or the area of timber, economic, and fuelwood forest land and their logging sites exceeds 35 hectares, or if other types of forest land exceed 70 hectares; when using forest land in key state-owned forest areas (under the review of forest land use for the original construction projects); (2) Constructing facilities in forests and national nature reserves of wildlife
24	Review of mineral exploitation, engineering construction requisition, expropriation or the use of grasslands	Review of mineral development, engineering construction requisition, expropriation, or the use of grassland over 70 hectares

(continued)

Table 2 (continued)

Serial No.	Name of the matters for review & approval	Applicable cases
25	Review and approval of construction activities within scenic and historic areas	Construction projects within scenic and historic areas, excluding the following prohibited activities: (1) Activities that damage the landscape, vegetation, and topography such as opening mountains, quarrying, mining, reclaiming, and building graves or erecting monuments; (2) Constructing facilities for storing explosive, flammable, radioactive, toxic, or corrosive substances; (3) Violating the scenic and historic area planning by establishing various types of development zones within the scenic and historic area; (4) Constructing hotels, guesthouses, training centers, sanatoriums, and other buildings unrelated to the protection of scenic and historic resources in the core scenic area
26	Permission for construction project involving cultural relics protection and archaeological activities	(1) Construction of other projects within the range of protection exercised by cultural relics protection units, or construction projects involving blasting, drilling, excavation, etc. (approval for other construction projects or blasting, drilling, excavation, etc. within the original protection range of cultural relics protection units); (2) Construction projects within the construction control zone of cultural relics protection units (approval for construction project design schemes within the original construction control zone of cultural relics protection units); (3) Large-scale basic construction projects (permission for archaeological surveys and exploration in areas within the original project scope where cultural relics might be buried before undertaking large-scale basic construction projects); (4) After archaeological surveys and exploration, if underground cultural relics remain within the construction project scope (the original permission for archaeological excavation in coordination with construction projects)
27	Review and issuance of planning permit for construction land (including temporary land)	For construction projects provided with the right to use the state-owned land by means of administrative allocation within urban and town planning areas, after being approved, certified, or registered by the relevant departments, an application for a construction land planning permit should be submitted. The location, area, and permitted construction scope of the construction land should be determined based on the detailed regulatory planning

(continued)

Table 2 (continued)

Serial No.	Name of the matters for review & approval	Applicable cases
28	Issuance of rural construction planning permit	Construction of rural residences, township enterprises, rural public facilities, and public welfare projects within the planning areas of villages and rural Settlements
29	Review and issuance of permits in the category of construction project planning	(1) For construction of buildings, structures, roads, pipelines, and other engineering projects within urban and town planning areas, construction units or individuals must apply for a construction project planning permit, submitting relevant land use documents, construction project design schemes; and for projects requiring the preparation of detailed renovation plans by the construction unit, the detailed renovation plans must also be submitted; (2) Concerning the demolition of buildings, structures, and other facilities other than historical buildings within the core protection areas of historical and cultural districts, famous towns, and villages; (3) Involving the implementation of measures for the in-situ protection of historical buildings, as well as relocation to different locations for protection or demolition due to public interest; (4) Involving the external renovation and decoration of historical buildings, addition of facilities, and changes in the structure or the use of historical buildings
30	Seismic fortification approval of projects for high-rise buildings exceeding the limit	Projects of high-rise buildings exceeding the limit

(continued)

Table 2 (continued)

Serial No.	Name of the matters for review & approval	Applicable cases
31	Review and certification of fire protection design for construction projects	1. Public places of high human concentration with the following cases: (1) Sports stadiums and halls with a total building area of more than 20,000 m^2, public exhibition halls, and exhibition halls of museums; (2) Civil airport terminal buildings, passenger station waiting rooms, and passenger terminal waiting rooms with a total building area of more than 15,000 m^2; (3) Hotels, restaurants, shopping malls, and markets with a total building area of more than 10,000 m^2; (4) Cinemas and theaters, public library reading rooms, commercial indoor fitness and leisure venues, outpatient buildings of hospitals, teaching buildings, libraries, canteens of colleges and universities, production and processing workshops of labor-intensive enterprises, temples, and churches with a total building area of more than 2500 m^2; (5) Nurseries, kindergartens with children's rooms, indoor children's playrooms, nursing homes, welfare homes, hospital wards, teaching buildings, libraries, canteens of primary and secondary schools, dormitories of schools, and employee dormitories of labor-intensive enterprises with a total building area of more than 1000 m^2; (6) Dance halls, video halls, projection halls, karaoke rooms, nightclubs, game rooms, saunas, internet cafes, and bars with a total building area of more than 500 m^2, restaurants, teahouses, and coffee shops with entertainment functions. 2. Special construction projects with one of the following cases: (1) Construction projects with the above-mentioned public places with high human concentration; (2) Office buildings of state organs, power dispatch buildings, telecommunication buildings, postal buildings, disaster prevention command and dispatch buildings, radio and television buildings, and archive buildings; (3) Public buildings with a single building area of more than 40,000 m^2 or a building height exceeding fifty meters; (4) Class I high-rise residential buildings as stipulated by national standards; (5) Urban rail transit, tunnel projects, large-scale power generation and distribution projects; (6) Factories, warehouses, and special stations, docks for production, storage, loading and unloading of flammable and explosive dangerous goods, filling stations, supply stations, pressure regulation stations for flammable and explosive gases and liquids

(continued)

Table 2 (continued)

Serial No.	Name of the matters for review & approval	Applicable cases
32	Approval of construction projects involving urban green spaces and trees	Construction projects involving the occupation of urban green spaces, and the felling or relocating of trees
33	Review and approval of the construction in the category of municipal facilities	Construction projects involving the occupation and excavation of urban roads, construction of various pipelines, pole lines, and other facilities attached to urban roads, and the installation of various municipal pipelines on urban bridges
34	Review of the demolition, alteration, or relocation of water supply, drainage, and sewage treatment facilities due to construction project requirements	The modification, demolition, or relocation of urban public water supply facilities, and the demolition or movement of urban drainage and sewage treatment facilities due to construction project requirements
35	Review and issuance of construction permits for building projects	Construction of various types of housing and their ancillary facilities, interior decoration, and installation of associated lines, pipes, and equipment, as well as construction of urban municipal infrastructure projects
36	Review of the design document of water transport projects	Review of the preliminary design and construction drawing design of water transport projects
37	Approval of the design for highway construction projects	Construction projects for highways (including highways of various administrative and technical grades)
38	Approval of the construction of highway development projects	Construction projects for highways (including highways of various administrative and technical grades)
39	Approval of preliminary design documents for water conservancy infrastructure projects	Water conservancy infrastructure projects
40	Approval of preliminary design for special projects of civil aviation and civil aviation construction projects with central-government investment	Construction of special projects of civil aviation and construction of civil aviation projects with central-government investment

(continued)

Table 2 (continued)

Serial No.	Name of the matters for review & approval	Applicable cases
41	The approval of construction projects involving national security matters	(1) New construction, alteration, or expansion of projects within the security control zones surrounding important national institutions, military facilities, national defense and military industrial units, and other critical sensitive entities; (2) New construction, alteration, or expansion of projects specified in certain local regulations and rules that explicitly pertain to international airports, entry and exit ports, railway stations, important mail (express) processing sites, telecommunications hub locations, as well as construction projects involving overseas institutions, organizations, individuals' investments, residences, utilization of hotels, guesthouses, hotels, and office buildings
42	Approval of civilian nuclear facility construction activities	Construction projects of civilian nuclear facilities

Table 3 Catalogue of approval items for government-invested construction projects in Shenzhen municipality

Serial No.	Enforcement agency	Item names	Time limit	Category	Fees	Phase of execution
1	Municipal development and reform commission	The first allocation of the initial phase of the project's funding	2 working days	Public service	No	Approval of project initiation and land use planning
2	Municipal development and reform commission	Approval of the feasibility study report	20 working days	Public service	No	Permission of construction project planning and approval of budget
3	Municipal development and reform commission	Filing or approval of the project's preliminary budget	Approval: 20 working days; Registration: 5 working days	Public service	No	Permission of construction project planning and approval of budget
4	Municipal development and reform commission	Review and approval of funding application report	20 working days	Public service	No	Permission of construction project planning and approval of budget
5	Municipal development and reform commission	Energy efficiency review of fixed asset investment projects	20 working days	Administrative licensing	No	Permission of construction project planning and approval of budget
6	Municipal planning and land resources committee and administrative bureaus	Issuance of preliminary opinions on site selection and land use, and key points for planning and design	25 working days	Administrative licensing	No	Approval of project initiation and land use planning
7	Municipal planning and land resources committee and administrative bureaus	Issuance of construction land planning permit	20 working days	Administrative licensing	No	Approval of project initiation and land use planning

(continued)

Table 3 (continued)

Serial No.	Enforcement agency	Item names	Time limit	Category	Fees	Phase of execution
8	Municipal planning and land resources committee	Review and approval of maritime space usage rights	12 working days	Administrative licensing	No	Approval of project initiation and land use planning
9	Municipal planning and land resources committee	Approval of marine environmental impact reports for marine construction projects	20 working days	Administrative licensing	No	Approval of project initiation and land use planning
10	Municipal planning and land resources committee and administrative bureaus	Issuance of land allocation decisions or signing of land use rights transfer contracts	5 working days	Public service	No	Approval of project initiation and land use planning
11	Municipal planning and land resources committee and administrative bureaus	Issuance of review opinions on construction project scheme design (municipal linear projects)	15 working days	Public service	No	Approval of project initiation and land use planning
12	Municipal planning and land resources committee and administrative bureaus	Issuance of approval opinions for the opening of intersections and for municipal pipeline interface approval	15 working days	Administrative licensing	No	Permission of construction project planning and approval of budget
13	Municipal planning and land resources committee and administrative bureaus	Issuance of construction project planning permits (residential construction category)	15 working days	Administrative licensing	No	Permission of construction project planning and approval of budget

(continued)

Table 3 (continued)

Serial No.	Enforcement agency	Item names	Time limit	Category	Fees	Phase of execution
14	Municipal planning and land resources committee and administrative bureaus	Issuance of construction project planning permits (municipal linear projects)	15 working days	Administrative licensing	No	Permission of construction project planning and approval of budget
15	Municipal planning and land resources committee and administrative bureaus	Filing of tender records for construction project scheme design	10 working days	Public service	No	Permission of construction project planning and approval of budget
16	Municipal planning and land resources committee and administrative bureaus	Approval of place names (approval of the naming of buildings/ approval of the names of public facilities/filing of the names of special facilities)	5 working days	Public service	No	Permission of construction project planning and approval of budget
17	Municipal planning and land resources committee	Approval for dismantling or idling marine environmental protection facilities	10 working days	Administrative licensing	No	Construction permission
18	Municipal housing and construction bureau	Approval for changing from public tendering to invited tendering, competitive negotiation, or direct contracting in construction projects	3 working days	Administrative licensing	No	Permission of construction project planning and approval of budget

(continued)

Table 3 (continued)

Serial No.	Enforcement agency	Item names	Time limit	Category	Fees	Phase of execution
19	Municipal housing and construction bureau	Approval of the seismic fortification of high-rise buildings exceeding designated limits	20 working days	Administrative licensing	No	Permission of construction project planning and approval of budget
20	Municipal housing and construction bureau	Issuance of construction permits for building projects	3 working days	Administrative licensing	No	Construction permission
21	Municipal housing and construction bureau	Filing of construction project tender notices (invitations for bidding) and filing of tender organization	2 working days	Public service	No	Construction permission
22	Municipal and district environmental protection department	Approval of environmental impact assessment documents for construction projects	Report book: 20 working days; Report tables: 10 working days	Administrative licensing	No	Construction permission
23	Municipal human settlements commission	Technical review of environmental impact assessments	12 working days	Public service	No	Construction permission
24	Municipal transport committee	Review of scheme design for transportation construction projects	10 working days	Public service	No	Approval of project initiation and land use planning
25	Municipal transport committee	Filing of tender records for road and port construction projects	2 working days	Public service	No	Approval of project initiation and land use planning

(continued)

Table 3 (continued)

Serial No.	Enforcement agency	Item names	Time limit	Category	Fees	Phase of execution
26	Municipal transport committee	Review of the preliminary design of medium and large construction projects	5 working days	Administrative licensing	No	Permission of construction project planning and approval of budget
27	Municipal transport committee; municipal traffic police bureau	Approval for occupation and excavation of roads	Traffic department: 12 working days; Traffic police: 10 working days	Administrative licensing	Yes	Permission of construction project planning and approval of budget
28	Municipal transport committee	Issuance of construction permits for building projects (municipal roads and associated projects)	3 working days	Administrative licensing	No	Construction permission
29	Municipal transport committee	Filing for the commencement of special projects	2 working days	Public service	No	Construction permission
30	Municipal water resources bureau	Approval of construction schemes for the development and utilization of tidal flats in the Pearl River Estuary not involving two or more municipal administrative regions	20 working days	Administrative licensing	No	Permission of construction project planning and approval of budget

(continued)

Table 3 (continued)

Serial No.	Enforcement agency	Item names	Time limit	Category	Fees	Phase of execution
31	Municipal and district water resources department	Approval for the demolition or modification of urban drainage and sewage treatment facilities	20 working days	Administrative licensing	No	Permission of construction project planning and approval of budget
32	Municipal and district water resources department	Approval of construction schemes within river management areas	20 working days	Administrative licensing	No	Permission of construction project planning and approval of budget
33	Municipal and district water resources department	Filing of water conservation assessment reports for construction projects	On-the-spot processing	Public service	No	Permission of construction project planning and approval of budget
34	Municipal and district water resources department	Approval of soil and water conservation plans for production and construction projects	Approval: 20 working days; Registration: on-the-spot processing	Administrative licensing	No	Permission of construction project planning and approval of budget
35	Municipal and district water resources department	Approval of construction schemes within the scope of hydraulic projects	20 working days	Administrative licensing	No	Permission of construction project planning and approval of budget
36	Municipal water resources bureau	Issuance of building permits for new construction, expansion, and upgrading of water purification plants	3 working days	Administrative licensing	No	Construction permission

(continued)

Table 3 (continued)

Serial No.	Enforcement agency	Item names	Time limit	Category	Fees	Phase of execution
37	Municipal and district water resources department	Filing for the commencement of water conservancy projects	3 working days	Public service	No	Construction permission
38	Municipal and district water resources department	Issuance of urban drainage permit	12 working days	Administrative licensing	No	Construction permission
39	Municipal and district urban management bureau	Review and approval of forest land use for construction projects (including temporary occupation of forest land)	15 working days	Administrative licensing	Yes	Approval of project initiation and land use planning
40	Municipal and district urban management bureau	Approval for the occupation of urban green spaces and the felling or relocation of urban trees	10 working days	Administrative licensing	Yes	Permission of construction project planning and approval of budget
41	Municipal fire department	Review of fire safety design or spot check of the filing of such designs	10 working days	Administrative licensing	No	Permission of construction project planning and approval of budget
42	Municipal and district civil defense department	Submission and review of civil defense project scheme	5 working days	Administrative licensing	Yes	Permission of construction project planning and approval of budget
43	Municipal meteorological bureau	Review of the design of lightning protection device	5 working days	Administrative licensing	No	Permission of construction project planning and approval of budget

(continued)

Table 3 (continued)

Serial No.	Enforcement agency	Item names	Time limit	Category	Fees	Phase of execution
44	District cultural relics department	Review of other construction projects within the protection scope of district-level cultural relics protection units	8 working days	Administrative licensing	No	Permission of construction project planning and approval of budget
45	District cultural relics department	Approval of construction project design schemes within the construction control zone of district-level cultural relics protection units	8 working days	Administrative licensing	No	Permission of construction project planning and approval of budget
46	Municipal culture, sports, and tourism bureau	Approval of construction project design schemes within the construction control zone of municipal-level cultural relics protection units	8 working days	Administrative licensing	No	Permission of construction project planning and approval of budget
47	Municipal health, population, and family planning committee	Review of the occupational disease hazard pre-assessment report for radiodiagnosis and treatment construction projects	8 working days	Administrative licensing	No	Permission of construction project planning and approval of budget
48	Municipal market and quality supervision committee	Special equipment construction notification	On-the-spot processing	Public service	No	Construction permission

(continued)

Table 3 (continued)

Serial No.	Enforcement agency	Item names	Time limit	Category	Fees	Phase of execution
49	Municipal safety supervision bureau	Safety condition review of hazardous chemical construction projects	Regular Cases: 12 working days; Simplified Cases: on-the-spot processing	Administrative licensing	No	Permission of construction project planning and approval of budget
50	Municipal safety supervision bureau	Review of safety facility design for hazardous chemical construction projects	Regular Cases: 8 working days; Simplified Cases: on-the-spot processing	Administrative licensing	No	Permission of construction project planning and approval of budget

Catalogue Description:

1. There are a total of 50 construction permission approval items for government-invested construction projects in Shenzhen Municipality, of which 15 items require approval, and there are 35 items that may involve approval.
2. The approval process for construction permission of government-invested construction projects is divided into three stages, including the following required approval items. The first stage is the project initiation and land use planning permission which includes four items, namely, the initial allocation of preliminary funds, issuance of site selection and land pre-examination opinions and planning design essentials, issuance of construction land planning permission, and decision on land allocation or signing of the land use right transfer contract. The second stage is the construction planning permission and budget approval which includes six items, namely, feasibility study report approval, project budget record or approval, issuance of construction project planning permission (building construction)/issuance of construction project planning permission (municipal linear projects), approval of soil and water conservation plans for production and construction projects, record of water use and water-saving assessment report for construction projects. The third stage is the construction permission which includes five items, namely, issuance of construction project permission/ issuance of construction project permission (municipal roads and ancillary projects), record of construction project tender announcement (invitation to bid) and tender organization form, approval of construction project environmental impact assessment document, and technical review of environmental impact assessment.

Table 4 Catalogue of approval items for socially-invested construction projects in Shenzhen Municipality

Serial No.	Enforcement agency	Item names	Time limit	Category	Fees	Execution phase
1	Municipal and district development and reform department	Filing of socially-invested projects	2 working days	Public service	No	Land transfer and land use planning permission
2	Municipal development and reform commission	Review of energy efficiency in fixed asset investment projects	20 working days	Administrative licensing	No	Construction projects planning permission
3	Municipal planning and land resources committee and administrative bureaus	Signing of contract for transferring the right of land use	5 working days	Public service	No	Land transfer and land use planning permission
4	Municipal planning and land resources committee and administrative bureaus	Signing of contract for transferring the right of land use (urban renewal project)	5 working days	Public service	No	Land transfer and land use planning permission
5	Municipal planning and land resources committee and administrative bureaus	Issuance of construction land planning permit	20 working days	Administrative licensing	No	Land transfer and land use planning permission
6	Municipal planning and land resources committee and administrative bureaus	Issuance of a construction land planning permit (urban renewal project)	20 working days	Administrative licensing	No	Land transfer and land use planning permission
7	Municipal planning and land resources committee	Review and approval of the right to use maritime spaces	12 working days	Administrative licensing	No	Land transfer and land use planning permission

(continued)

Table 4 (continued)

Serial No.	Enforcement agency	Item names	Time limit	Category	Fees	Execution phase
8	Municipal planning and land resources committee	Approval of marine environmental impact report for marine construction projects	20 working days	Administrative licensing	No	Land transfer and land use planning permission
9	Municipal planning and land resources committee and administrative bureaus	Issuance of examination opinions on construction project scheme design (building category)	15 working days	Public service	No	Construction projects planning permission
10	Municipal planning and land resources committee and administrative bureaus	Issuance of examination opinions on construction project scheme design (building category) (urban renewal project)	15 working days	Public service	No	Construction projects planning permission
11	Municipal planning and land resources committee and administrative bureaus	Issuance of construction project planning permit (building category)	10 working days	Administrative licensing	No	Construction projects planning permission
12	Municipal planning and land resources committee and administrative bureaus	Issuance of construction project planning permit (building category) (urban renewal project)	10 working days	Administrative licensing	No	Construction projects planning permission
13	Municipal planning and land resources committee and administrative bureaus	Filing of tender for construction project scheme design	10 working days	Public service	No	Construction projects planning permission

(continued)

Table 4 (continued)

Serial No.	Enforcement agency	Item names	Time limit	Category	Fees	Execution phase
14	Municipal planning and land resources committee and administrative bureaus	Filing of tender for construction project scheme design (urban renewal project)	10 working days	Public service	No	Construction projects planning permission
15	Municipal planning and land resources committee and administrative bureaus	Approval of place names (approval of the naming of buildings/ approval of the names of public facilities/filing of the names of special facilities)	5 working days	Administrative licensing or public service	No	Construction projects planning permission
16	Municipal planning and land resources committee and administrative bureaus	Issuance of approval opinions for the opening of intersections and for municipal pipeline interface approval	15 working days	Administrative licensing	No	Construction projects planning permission
17	Municipal planning and land resources committee and administrative bureaus	Issuance of approval opinions for the opening of intersections and for municipal pipeline interface approval (urban renewal project)	15 working days	Administrative licensing	No	Construction projects planning permission

(continued)

Table 4 (continued)

Serial No.	Enforcement agency	Item names	Time limit	Category	Fees	Execution phase
18	Municipal planning and land resources committee and administrative bureaus	Issuance of certificate for registering construction project pile foundations	10 working days	Administrative licensing	No	Construction permission
19	Municipal planning and land resources committee and administrative bureaus	Issuance of certificate for registering construction project pile foundations (urban renewal project)	10 working days	Administrative licensing	No	Construction permission
20	Municipal planning and land resources committee and administrative bureaus	Inspection of property line upon the initiation of construction project (cuilding category)	5 working days	Public service	No	Construction permission
21	Municipal planning and land resources committee and administrative bureaus	Inspection of property line upon the initiation of construction project (urban renewal project)	5 working days	Public service	No	Construction permission
22	Municipal planning and land resources committee	Approval of dismantling or idling maritime environmental protection facilities	10 working days	Administrative licensing	No	Construction permission
23	Municipal planning and land resources committee and administrative bureaus	Inspection for acceptance of construction project planning (building category)	10 working days	Administrative licensing	No	Inspection for acceptance upon completion and fixed asset registration

(continued)

Table 4 (continued)

Serial No.	Enforcement agency	Item names	Time limit	Category	Fees	Execution phase
24	Municipal planning and land resources committee and administrative bureaus	Inspection for acceptance of construction project planning (building category) (urban renewal project)	10 working days	Administrative confirmation	No	Inspection for acceptance upon completion and fixed asset registration
25	Municipal planning and land resources committee	Inspection for acceptance of maritime environmental protection facilities	15 working days	Administrative licensing	No	Inspection for acceptance upon completion and fixed asset registration
26	Municipal planning and land resources committee	Initial registration of land use rights	5 working days	Public service	No	Inspection for acceptance upon completion and fixed asset registration
27	Municipal planning and land resources committee	Initial registration of land use rights and house ownership	5 working days	Public service	Yes	Inspection for acceptance upon completion and fixed asset registration

(continued)

Table 4 (continued)

Serial No.	Enforcement agency	Item names	Time limit	Category	Fees	Execution phase
28	Municipal planning and land resources committee	Registration of changes in land use rights and house ownership	5 working days	Public service	Yes	Inspection for acceptance upon completion and fixed asset registration
29	Municipal planning and land resources committee	Initial registration of maritime space use rights	5 working days	Public service	Yes	Inspection for acceptance upon completion and fixed asset registration
30	Municipal planning and land resources committee	Registration of changes in maritime space use rights	5 working days	Public service	Yes	Inspection for acceptance upon completion and fixed asset registration
31	Municipal planning and land resources committee	Registration of revoking maritime space use rights	5 working days	Public service	No	Inspection for acceptance upon completion and fixed asset registration
32	Municipal housing and construction bureau	Seismic fortification approval of projects for high-rise buildings exceeding the limit	20 working days	Administrative licensing	No	Construction projects planning permission
33	Municipal housing and construction bureau	Issuance of permission for construction projects	3 working days	Administrative licensing	No	Construction permission

(continued)

Table 4 (continued)

Serial No.	Enforcement agency	Item names	Time limit	Category	Fees	Execution phase
34	Municipal housing and construction bureau	Special inspection for acceptance of energy conservation in civil buildings	8 working days	Administrative licensing	No	Inspection for acceptance upon completion and fixed asset registration
35	Municipal housing and construction bureau	Shenzhen municipal construction project completion acceptance and filing."	2 working days	Public service	No	Inspection for acceptance upon completion and fixed asset registration
36	Municipal and district environmental protection department	Approval of environmental impact assessment documents of construction project	Report book: 20 working days; report tables: 10 working days	Administrative licensing	No	Construction permission
37	Municipal human settlements commission	Technical review of environmental impact assessment	12 working days	Public service	No	Construction permission
38	Municipal transport committee	Review of the design scheme of transport construction project	10 working days	Public service	No	Construction projects planning permission
39	Municipal transport committee; municipal traffic police bureau	Approval for occupying and excavating roads	Transport committee: 12 working days; traffic police bureau: 10 working days	Administrative licensing	Yes	Construction projects planning permission

(continued)

Table 4 (continued)

Serial No.	Enforcement agency	Item names	Time limit	Category	Fees	Execution phase
40	Municipal transport committee	Inspection for acceptance and filing of road project completion	5 working days	Public service	No	Inspection for acceptance upon completion and fixed asset registration
41	Municipal and district water resources department	Approval of soil and water conservation plans for production and construction projects	Approval: 20 working days; registration: on-the-spot processing	Administrative licensing	No	Construction projects planning permission
42	Municipal and district water resources department	Filing of the reports of construction project water conservation	On-the-spot processing	Public service	No	Construction projects planning permission
43	Municipal and district water resources department	Demolition and alteration of urban drainage and sewage treatment facilities	20 working days	Administrative licensing	No	Construction projects planning permission
44	Municipal water resources bureau	Approval of construction schemes for the development and utilization of tidal flats in the Pearl River Estuary not involving two or more municipal administrative regions	20 working days	Administrative licensing	No	Construction projects planning permission
45	Municipal and district water resources department	Approval of construction schemes within river management areas	20 working days	Administrative licensing	No	Construction projects planning permission

(continued)

Table 4 (continued)

Serial No.	Enforcement agency	Item names	Time limit	Category	Fees	Execution phase
46	Municipal and district water resources department	Permission for urban drainable projects	12 working days	Administrative licensing	No	Construction permission
47	Municipal and district water resources department	Inspecting for acceptance and filing of drainage facilities	8 working days	Public service	No	Inspection for acceptance upon completion and fixed asset registration
48	Municipal and district water resources department	Acceptance and filing of soil and water conservation plans for production and construction projects	8 working days	Public service	No	Inspection for acceptance upon completion and fixed asset registration
49	Municipal and district urban management bureau	Approval for the occupation of urban green spaces and the felling or relocation of urban trees	10 working days	Administrative licensing	Yes	Construction projects planning permission
50	Municipal fire department	Review of fire safety design or spot check of the filing of such designs	10 working days	Administrative licensing or public service	No	Construction projects planning permission
51	Municipal fire department	Spot check of acceptance or filing of construction project fire safety	10 working days	Administrative licensing or public service	No	Inspection for acceptance upon completion and fixed asset registration

(continued)

Table 4 (continued)

Serial No.	Enforcement agency	Item names	Time limit	Category	Fees	Execution phase
52	Municipal and district civil defense department	Review of the proposal of civil defense projects	6 working days	Administrative licensing	Yes	Construction projects planning permission
53	Municipal meteorological bureau	Review of the design of lightning protection device	5 working days	Administrative licensing	No	Construction projects planning permission
54	Municipal meteorological bureau	Review and approval of lightning protection device upon project completion	10 working days	Administrative licensing	No	Inspection for acceptance upon completion and fixed asset registration
55	District cultural relics department	Review of other construction projects within the protection scope of district-level cultural relics protection units	8 working days	Administrative licensing	No	Construction projects planning permission
56	District cultural relics department	Approval of construction project design schemes within the construction control zone of district-level cultural relics protection units	8 working days	Administrative licensing	No	Construction projects planning permission
57	Municipal culture, sports, and tourism administration	Approval of construction project design schemes within the construction control zone of municipal-level cultural relics protection units	8 working days	Administrative licensing	No	Construction projects planning permission

(continued)

Table 4 (continued)

Serial No.	Enforcement agency	Item names	Time limit	Category	Fees	Execution phase
58	Municipal health, population, and family planning committee	Review of the occupational disease hazard pre-assessment report for radiodiagnosis and treatment construction projects	8 working days	Administrative licensing	No	Construction projects planning permission
59	Municipal archives bureau	Reception and acceptance of urban construction archives	5 working days	Public service	No	Inspection for acceptance upon completion and fixed asset registration
60	Municipal market and quality supervision committee	Special equipment construction notification	On-the-spot processing	Public service	No	Construction permission
61	Municipal market and quality supervision committee	Special equipment monitoring and inspection	18 working days	Public service	Yes	Inspection for acceptance upon completion and fixed asset registration
62	Municipal safety supervision bureau	Safety condition review of hazardous chemical construction projects	Regular case: 12 working days; simplified case: on-the-spot processing	Administrative licensing	No	Construction projects planning permission

(continued)

Table 4 (continued)

Serial No.	Enforcement agency	Item names	Time limit	Category	Fees	Execution phase
63	Municipal safety supervision bureau	Review of safety facility design for hazardous chemical construction projects	Regular case: 8 working days; simplified case: on-the-spot processing	Administrative licensing	No	Construction projects planning permission

Catalogue Description:

1. There are 63 items for the declaration and registration of socially-invested construction projects, among which 25 items require approval while another 38 items may involve such approval.
2. The full process of handling the declaration and registration of socially-invested construction projects is divided into four stages, including the required approval items as follows. The first stage is the land transfer and land use planning permission which includes five items, namely, the filing of socially-invested projects, the signing of land use right transfer contracts/the signing of land use right transfer contracts (for urban renewal projects), the issuance of construction land planning permission/the issuance of construction land planning permission (for urban renewal projects); The second stage is the construction project planning permission stage which includes six items, namely, the issuance of review opinions concerning construction project design schemes (for building projects)/the issuance of review opinions concerning construction project design schemes (for building projects in urban renewal), the issuance of construction project planning permission (for building projects)/the issuance of construction project planning permission (for building projects in urban renewal), approval of soil and water conservation plans for production and construction projects, and water conservation assessment report filing for construction projects. The third stage is the construction permission which includes five items, namely, the issuance of construction permission, approval of environmental impact assessment documents for construction projects, technical review of environmental impact assessments, construction project commencement inspection (for building projects)/construction project commencement inspection (for building projects in urban renewal). The fourth stage is the inspection for acceptance upon the completion of construction projects and real estate registration which includes nine items, namely, construction project planning acceptance (for building projects)/construction project planning acceptance (for building projects in urban renewal), spot check for construction project fire safety acceptance or filing, drainage facility acceptance filing, acceptance filing of soil and water conservation facilities for production and construction projects, completion acceptance approval of lightning protection devices, construction project completion acceptance filing, first registration of land use rights, and first registration of land use rights and property ownership.

Shanghai Qingpu District Industrial Project Administrative Approval Process Flowchart (Trial)

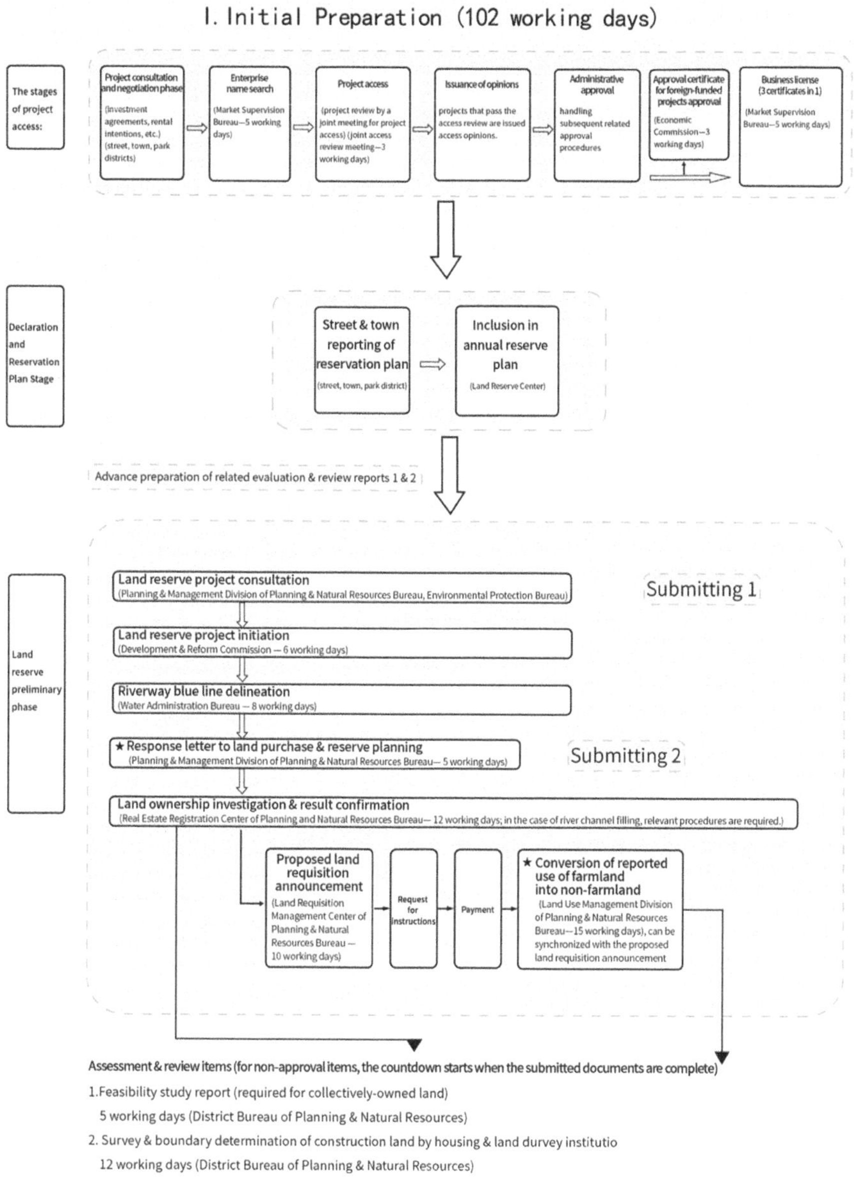

Fig. 2 .

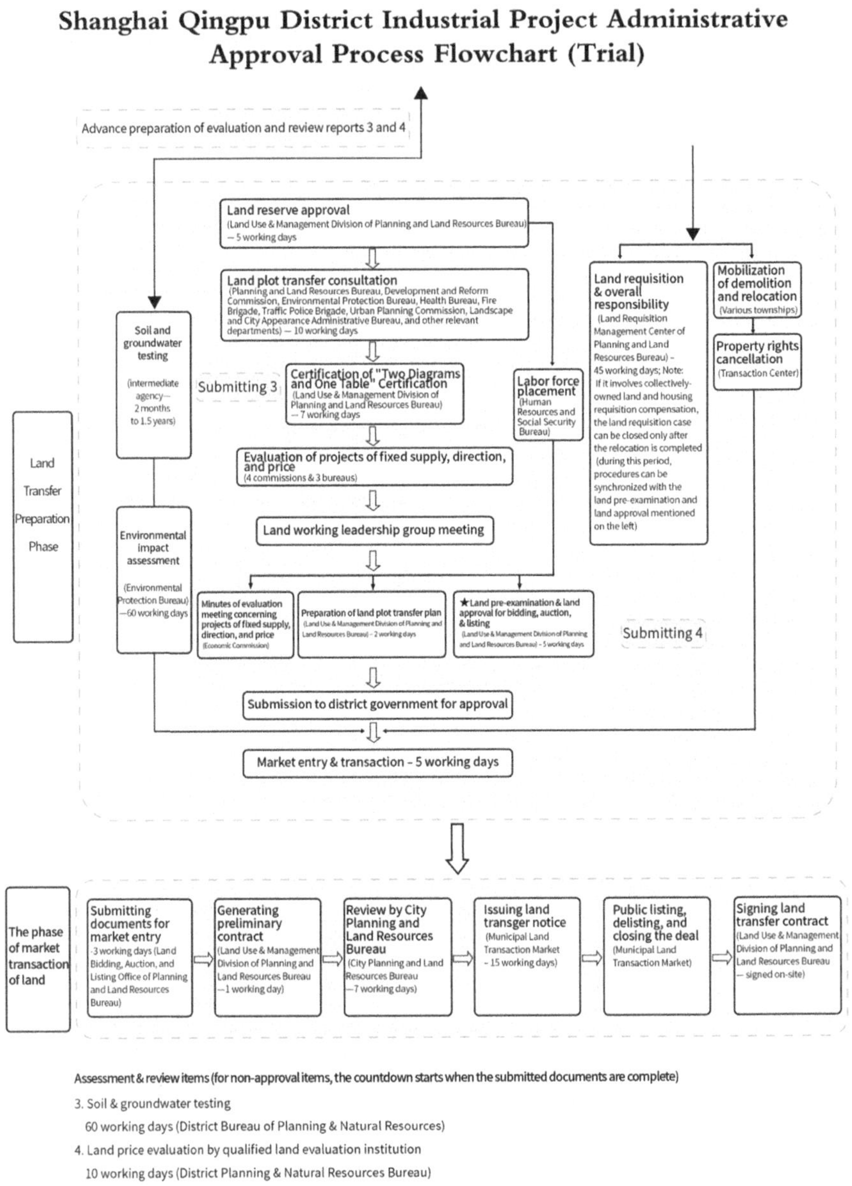

Fig. 2 (continued)

Shanghai Qingpu District Industrial Project Administrative Approval Process Flowchart (Trial)

II. Land Acquisition and Project Initiation (10 working days)

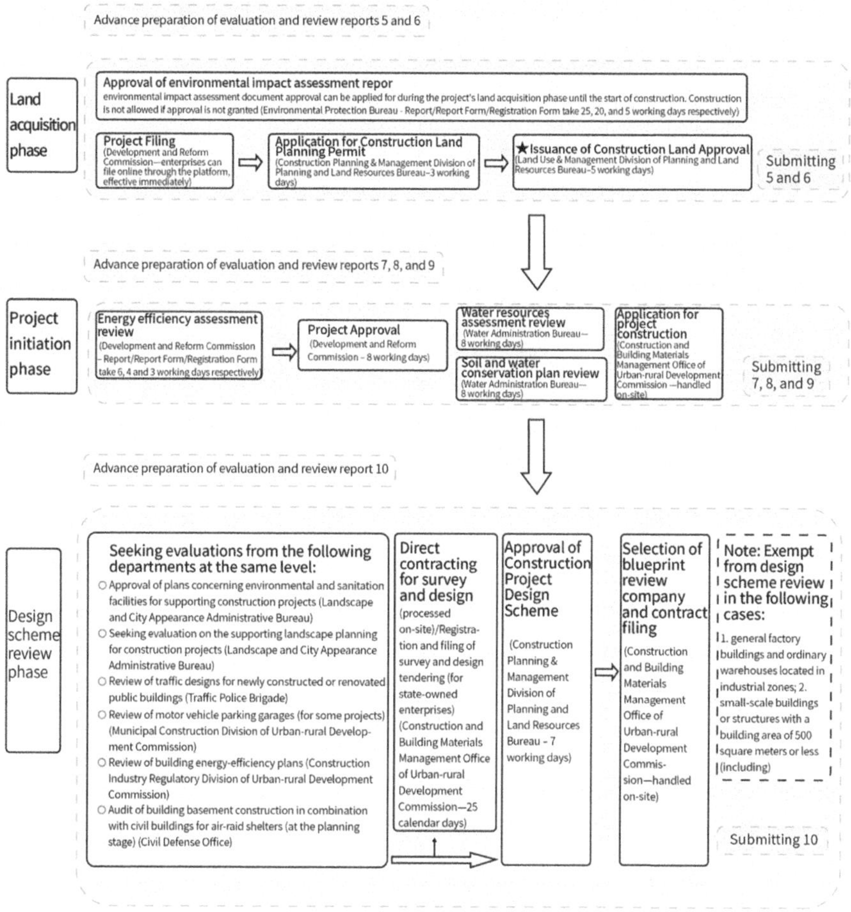

Assessment & review items (for non-approval items, the countdown starts when the submitted documents are complete)

5. Project application report—6 working days (District Development and Reform Commission)
6. Technical assessment of environmental impact assessment report—30 working days (District Environmental Protection Bureau)
7. Energy efficiency assessment—3 working days (District Development and Reform Commission)
8. Water resource study report—8 working days (District Water Administration Bureau)
9. Formulating soil & water conservation plan by qualified institutions—8 working days (District Water Administration Bureau)
10. Regional Traffic Impact Assessment—20 working days (District Traffic Police Brigade)

Fig. 2 (continued)

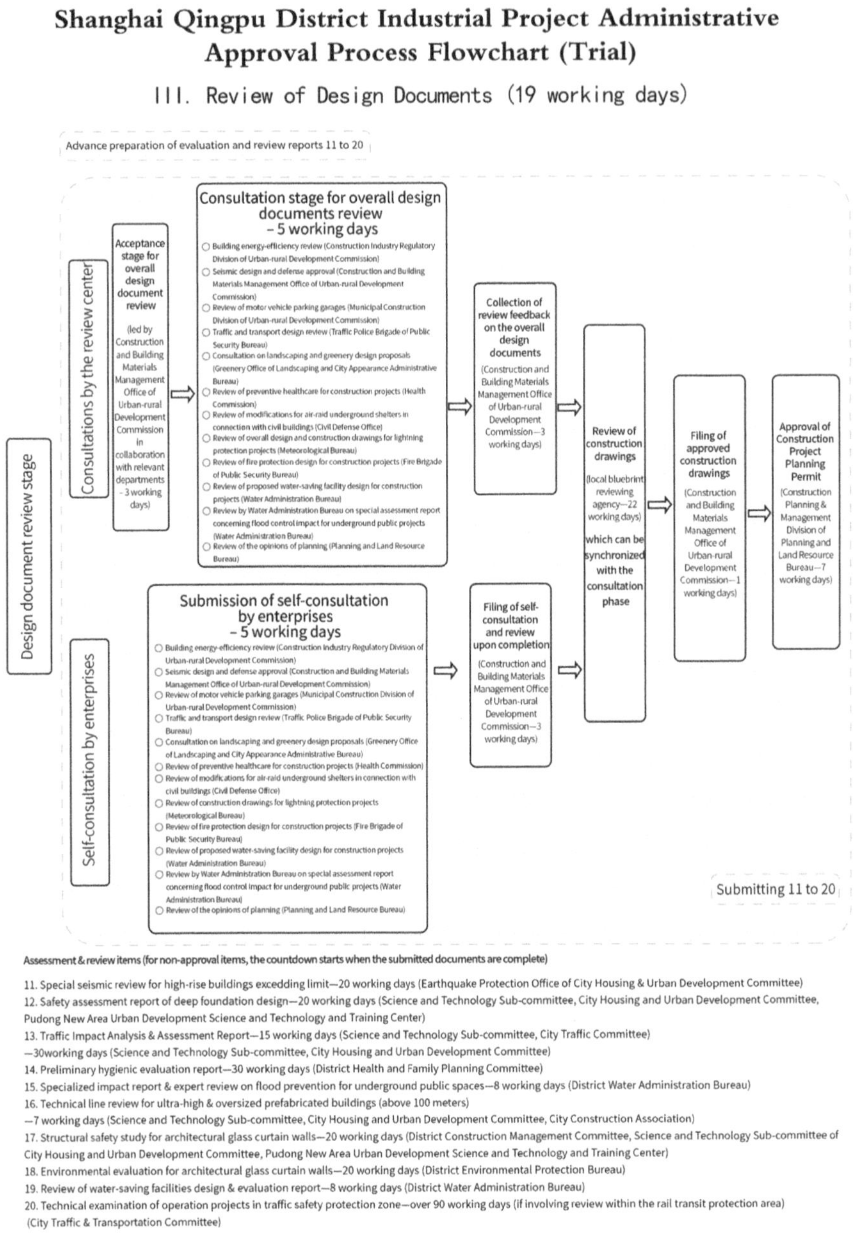

Fig. 2 (continued)

Shanghai Qingpu District Industrial Project Administrative Approval Process Flowchart (Trial)

Ⅳ. Construction Commencement Procedures (4 working)

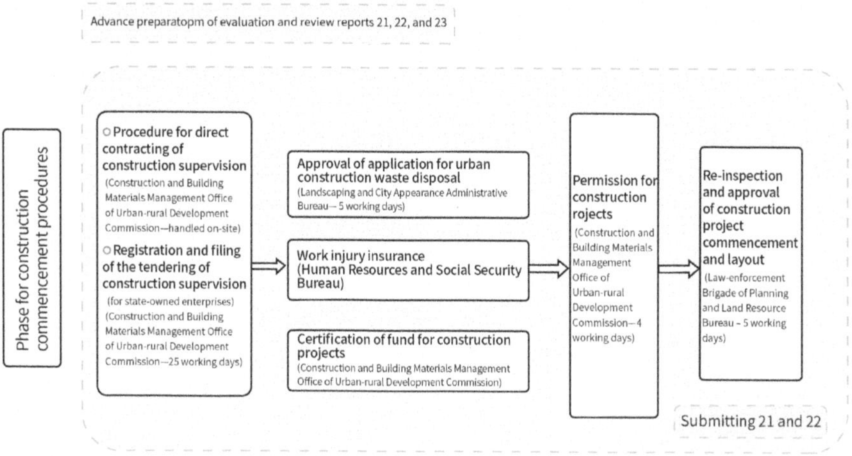

Ⅴ. Acceptance & Filing of Project Completion (18 working days)

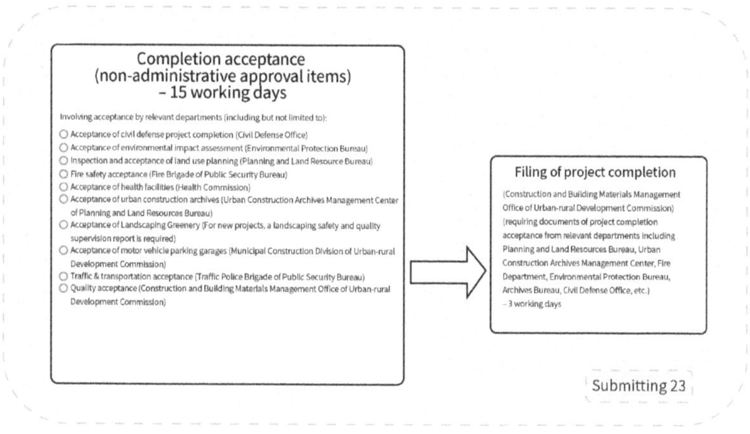

Assessment & review items (for non-approval items, the countdown starts when the submitted documents are complete)

21. Planning red lines for related roads
    —5 working days (District Planning and Natural Resources Bureau)
22. Re-inspection and on-spot check of construction project commencement and layout
    —5 working days (District Planning and Natural Resources Bureau)
23. Completion acceptance & testing report for secondary water supply
    —3 working days (District Health and Family Planning Committee)

Fig. 2 (continued)

Chapter 7
Reform of the Construction Land System

In his book "A Treatise of Taxes and Contributions," the British classical political economist William Petty argued that "land is the mother of all wealth." Land is the most basic form of natural resources and an important factor of production. As analyzed in the previous chapter, the insufficient land supply and the excessively long supply cycle tend to impose significant constraints on development. In this chapter, by reviewing the history of land systems both in China and abroad, the author expect to demonstrate that the constraints imposed on development by limited land supply are quite ubiquitous in many countries. In China, the increasing time and transaction costs for investors to obtain land for construction can be explained by two major factors. The first is the increasing number of transaction modules and the second is the growing complexity of transaction rules within each module. The overly complicated system of land administration is directly responsible for the exorbitant transaction costs for acquiring land for the construction purpose, which in turn creates constraints on land supply that directly hinders investment in fixed assets. Such constraints constitute what might be called hard constraints on China's economic development.

1 The Land System and the Regulation of Land Uses

The ability of land to generate wealth is inextricably intertwined with the land system, and different land systems have vastly different abilities to foster wealth. An overview of the historical development of land systems both in China and abroad reveals that this historical process has mainly centered on property rights and the regulation of land uses.

B. Fan, *The Rationale Behind Change*, https://doi.org/10.1007/978-981-97-8854-5_7

1. The system of land property right

Regarding what exactly constitutes the land property rights, scholars in different countries and in historical periods tend to diverge in their views. A relatively prevailing opinion at present is that land property rights refer to the exclusive rights that are immanent in land, including ownership, usufruct, leasing right, mortgage right, inheritance right, easement right, and other rights. In this chapter, we will conduct a comparative analysis on the land property systems by selecting the United Kingdom and the United States, which belong to the Common Law System, as well as Japan and China, which belong to the Continental Law System.

In the wake of the Norman Conquest in 1066, the English legal system recognized that the king was the ultimate owner of land. The king then granted land to nobles of various ranks, creating a feudal system of land ownership where land ownership and usufruct were separated. In the medieval England, the law prohibited the purchase, sale, and transfer of land, thus imposing tremendous restrictions on the development and exploitation of land. Toward the late Middle Ages, in 1290, England enacted the law of "Quia Emptores," which recognized the lawfulness of land sales and transfers, marking the advent of the private ownership of land.[1] In the 17th to the nineteenth centuries, private land ownership was legally recognized in England.

Soon after its foundation, the United States established a system of private land ownership and implemented a policy of nationalizing lands in its vast western regions. In 1785, the U.S. Congress passed the Ordinance for the Sale of Western Lands, which allowed federal public lands to be sold to private individuals without any restrictions or additional obligations such as personal restrictions, tribute, loyalty, labor, land rent, land tax, residency requirements, land use requirements, transfer restrictions, or inheritance restrictions. These legal provisions created a land system which demonstrated implicit freedom.[2] In 1787, the U.S. Constitution still did not contain any specific provisions regarding the property rights of land, but in 1791, the Fifth Amendment of the U.S. Constitution clearly stipulated that private property could not be taken for public use without proper compensations.[3] This law was tantamount to confirming the private property rights of land. In 1862, the Homestead Act was enacted, which granted free land to pioneers. Farmers who cultivated unclaimed western lands for five consecutive years only needed to pay a $10 fee for paperwork to obtain 160 acres of surveyed government land. The free land system contributed significantly to the westward expansion movement of the United States.

During its feudal period, the Japanese society went through several different stages of land ownership, ranging from the "Handen Shuju-sei" (which was a system of state ownership and allocation of land), the feudal lord manor system, and the landlord system. Before the Meiji Restoration, land was primarily owned by the ruling class

---

[1] Zhang Qiushi, "Land Legislation in the Edward I Period," *Nanjing University Law Review*, 2012, Issue 1.

[2] Lei Yao, "Historical Changes in the American Land System and Land Finance" *Zhejiang Finance*, 2020, Issue 2.

[3] Lin Muxuan, "The US Land Management System and its Instructive Messages," *Land & Resources Herald*, 2011, Issue Z1.

(consisting of the emperor, nobility, officials, and landlords). At the same time, the government prohibited the buying and the selling of land.[4] After the Meiji Restoration, in 1868, Japan abolished the system of land ownership by feudal lords, but the vast majority of the land still remained in the possession of the former feudal lords. In 1872, the Meiji government abolished the law prohibiting the buying and selling of land and allowed land transactions. In the wake of World War II, the Japanese government enforced compulsory measures to purchase lands from landlords and resell them to farmers who did not possess any lands or did not possess sufficient lands, thereby establishing the system of yeoman land ownership. Subsequent to those measures, the government passed a series of laws designed to promote the circulation of farmland,[5] relaxing the regulations on the transfer of farmland and encouraging relatively concentrated exploitation of farmland.

In China, a form of public land ownership named the "jingtian system" was implemented from the Western Zhou Dynasty to the Spring and Autumn Period and the Warring States Period, when it was claimed that "all the land under heaven belongs exclusively to the emperor," meaning that all the land in the entire country was owned by Emperor Zhou. On his part, Emperor Zhou distributed lands to nobles, who in turn allocated the lands to commoners for their use. The commoners were granted private land on the precondition of collectively cultivating the public land. Through the Shang Yang Reform, the Qin Dynasty abolished the "jingtian system" and initiated the system of private land ownership, which was to become China's longest-lasting land system extending all the way from the end of the Warring States Period to the establishment of the People's Republic of China. Under the system of private land ownership, land was owned by landlords, and farmers had to rent the land from landlords, paying the land rent and undertaking corvée labor. In order to ease the tensions between landlords and farmers, successive dynasties ranging from the Northern Wei Dynasty, the Northern Qi Dynasty, the Sui Dynasty, to the Tang Dynasty implemented the land-equalization system, in which the state distributed unclaimed land and wasteland to farmers for use.

During the Ming and Qing dynasties and the era of the Republic of China, land ownership became increasingly complicated, evolving from a single structure into a multiple structure. The land ownership and the land usufruct were no longer possessed by the same person, but were largely separated. As a result, various types of land contract documents came into existence, including those of buying and selling, pawning, pledging, property dividing, and leasing. In order to facilitate and expedite transactions, agreements tantamount to modern contracts were created. These contracts carried very detailed terms and provisions covering all the necessary points in a transaction and clearly defining and regulating the rights and obligations of both parties of the transaction. At that time, the property right of the land was divided into

[4] In 1643, the Tokugawa Shogunate implemented the "Prohibition of Permanent Sale and Purchase of Farmland."

[5] They include the Agricultural Land Law, Agricultural Land Use Promotion Act, "Law on Strengthening the Foundation of Agricultural Operations," "Law on the Promotion of Farmland Use," "Law on Promoting and Strengthening the Foundation of Agricultural Operations," "Basic Law of New Agriculture," and so on.

two components: the "*tian gu quan*" (literally, "land bone right") and the "*tian pi quan*" (literally, "land skin right"), which were also known as the "*tian di quan*" (literally, "land bottom right") and the "*tian mian quan*" (literally, "land surface right"). This meant that for the same piece of land, there could be two owners—one was the "*tian gu*" owner and the other was the "*tian pi*" owner. The difference between the two was that the "*tian pi*" owner had the autonomous rights to possess, cultivate, and transfer the land, independent of the "*tian gu*" owner.[6]

After the establishment of the People's Republic of China, China successively implemented different systems of land ownership, including private ownership, rural collective ownership, and urban public ownership. From the very outset of the newly-established People's Republic of China to the mid-1950s, China implemented an urban–rural land system with very distinctive "individual ownership." The land in rural areas belonged to farmers whereas urban land belonged to individuals. The land reform in the rural areas established private ownership of land by farmers, thus fulfilling the ideal of "every farmer in possession of his or her own land." In urban areas, the economic interests and the private property of workers, peasants, petite bourgeoisie, and national bourgeoisie were duly protected. In the mid- to late 1950s, with the completion of the socialist transformation, China launched the socialist reform of the private urban housing, which resulted in the transition of urban land ownership from private individual ownership to public state ownership. In rural areas, China successively carried out organizational reform of agricultural production through mutual aid groups, primary cooperatives, advanced cooperatives, and people's communes, which transformed rural land ownership from individual ownership to collective ownership. After launching the reform and opening-up, China implemented the household contract responsibility system in rural areas, abolished people's communes, and separated the right to contract land operation from land ownership, which greatly spurred the zeal of farmers to engage in agricultural production.

In 1982, the Constitution of the People's Republic of China unequivocally stipulated that "urban land belongs to the state," fundamentally establishing the state ownership of the urban land. Subsequently, the state implemented a system of paid transfer of urban land usufruct and a system of regulating land uses based on the principle of separation between land ownership and land usufruct, thus achieving the transformation of urban land from free allocation to paid use. After entering the twenty-first century, China obliterated the rule that "farmers are prohibited from leasing or transferring contracted land" and allowed the sub-contracting of the contracted land operation, leasing, mutual exchange, transfer, or other forms of land circulation, thus achieving the separation of the "two rights" of the farmland, that is, the right of land ownership and the right of contracting land. Since 2014, the country has deepened the reform in the land sector and proposed, on the basis of the separation of the "two rights" of the arable lands, to adhere to the collective ownership of rural land, to implement "the separation of three rights" (i.e. the right

[6] Chai Rong, "A Study of Tianpi Transaction Contracts in the Ming and Qing Dynasties," Journal of Renmin University of China, 2004, Vol. 28, Issue 4.

of ownership, the contracting right, and the right to operate land-based business), and to explore ways to extend "the separation of three rights" to the homestead land.

Based on the above analysis, the changes in the systems of land ownership in China and foreign countries can be summarized as demonstrating the following characteristics.

First, the change in land ownership remains central to the changes in land systems. In England, land ownership transformed gradually from the ownership by the king, with the nobles and lords of various ranks equipped with the land usufruct, to private ownership, creating a unified and complete system of property rights covering the land's revenue, inheritance, transaction, and use. The United States instituted private land ownership immediately after the founding of the nation and established the most liberal system of land ownership, selling and granting federal public land to private individuals without virtually any additional conditions or obligations. Japanese land ownership also underwent a drastic transformation, changing from ownership by feudal lords to private ownership, with clearly defined property rights and a fully functional land property system. China has taken a different path in the changes of its land property system. Since the establishment of private land ownership in the Qin Dynasty, private land ownership has dominated the property right of land, with relatively well-defined land ownership, usufruct, transaction right, inheritance right, etc. After the founding of the People's Republic of China, land ownership switched from private ownership to public ownership through socialist transformation and the people's commune movement. Since the reform and opening-up, although China's system of land ownership has remained largely unchanged, elements of private ownership have emerged. The right of urban residential land use remains valid for 70 years and can be extended after expiration, which is virtually equivalent to private land ownership. The long-term contracting of rural land is also in effect tantamount to private ownership. It is still highly controversial as to in which direction the land ownership will be moving in the next phase of the reform of land property right.

Secondly, for most countries, their land ownership systems have undergone a transition from non-transaction to free transaction. In England, land was always prohibited from transaction prior to the Middle Ages, and it was not until the late Middle Ages that the "Quia Emptores" was enacted, recognizing the legitimacy of land transfer and sales. In the United States, land transactions already existed before it secured independence, the land market had already reached a certain scale, and a series of relatively mature transaction mechanisms evolved. By 1785, a relatively full-fledged land market had developed. During Japan's feudal period, land was banned from any form of transaction, but as the Meiji government abolished the prohibition on land transaction in 1872, the trading of land was made possible. After World War II, the Japanese government promulgated a series of laws designed to promote the circulation of farmlands by relaxing the government regulation on the transfer of farmlands.

Since the establishment of private land ownership in the Qin Dynasty, land in China remained amenable to transaction for a long time. However, from the mid-Han Dynasty to the middle of the Tang Dynasty, private land ownership was largely incomplete. For the sake of guaranteeing state revenue and mitigating social conflicts, the government formulated various policies and laws aimed at restricting large-scale private ownership, selling, and annexation of land. From the late Tang Dynasty to the Qing Dynasty and the era of the Republic of China, government restrictions and interventions on land sales were gradually removed, and a relatively complete and free system of private land ownership was established. From the Ming and the Qing Dynasties to the Republic of China period, land ownership shifted from a single structure to a multiple structure, and land ownership and usufruct were separated. The owners of "tian gu" was entitled to land ownership, while the owners of "tian pi" enjoyed rights such as the possession, cultivation, and transfer of the land. In the early years of the New China, i.e. the People's Republic of China, private land ownership was preserved for a brief period of time and land was susceptible to transaction. Later on, the private land ownership was replaced by public ownership, with urban land being state-owned and rural land being collectively owned, and land was not tradable. After the reform and opening-up, without changing the nature of land ownership, China achieved the separation of land ownership and land usufruct. In addition, by allowing the compensated use of urban land and the lawful transfer of rural land contract rights, China legitimized the transaction of the usufructs related to land, such as the right of land use and the right of land-based business operation.

Thirdly, land rights have shifted from the pattern of a single right to a pattern of multiple rights. Generally speaking, land rights comprise of ownership, usufruct, transaction right, inheritance right, and mortgage right, among others. Taken together, these rights constitute a bundle of rights. The greater the bundle of rights, the more complicated it is to complete the transfer of land ownership in its entirety, and the higher the transaction cost. By contrast, the cost of completing the transaction of a single right is relatively low. For example, when an oil company in the United States wishes to exploit oil, it has to pay a colossal price in terms of time and cash in order to purchase the adjacent land for drilling wells. The transaction costs would be exorbitant. In general practice, most oil companies only pay cash to procure the right to exploit resources from adjacent land and share the profits with the landowner. In this way, the transaction cost of oil extraction is significantly reduced.[7] In China, while the public ownership of land remains unchanged, the usufruct of land is isolated from the urban construction land, which can be procured by developers who use the land for urban construction. In rural areas, the right to engage in land-based business operation is separated from the land contract right, and farmers could transfer the right of land-based business operation to other farmers for cultivation. After the transformation of land ownership from the pattern of a single right to a pattern of multiple rights in China, the transaction costs involving a single right are relatively low, but it is virtually impossible to subject all the rights to transaction, and the transaction costs can be said to be infinite.

---

[7] Zhang Libin, "Property Rights, Market Access, and Antitrust Law: Insights from Several Verdicts of US Energy Law for China's Energy Law," *Energy Policy Research*, 2011, Issue 3.

2. The regulation of land uses

Land is a natural ecosystem that is interconnected and remains unmovable and indivisible. To the extent that land is being used, externalities such as pollution, environmental destruction, and ecological imbalance are inevitably generated. The negative externalities that arise from land use often result in the reduced value of the surrounding land and certain social problems, making it necessary to institute measures aimed at the control of land uses. Since the nineteenth century, the accelerated industrialization and urbanization in England has caused public health and housing problems as cities could not provide sufficient standard housing for industrial workers. In particular, massive cholera epidemics erupted in 1832 and 1849, sparking dissatisfactions among all sectors of the society which demanded the government to implement public administration of urban development. In 1909, the UK established a land planning system by promulgating the "Housing, Town Planning, etc. Act." Article 54 of the Act stipulates that any land "under development or preparing for housing construction" must comply with the requirements of the housing and town planning. After 1947, the UK promulgated a series of laws,[8] developing a system of land planning and land use control. The system of land use planning in the UK operates on four levels: central planning, regional planning, county planning, and city planning, all of which are legally bounding. Government departments at all levels formulate land use plans for all the places under their respective jurisdiction. Any activities that take place on the land must first obtain the planning permission from the government. When there does arise a necessity to adjust the land planning in a certain area, a lengthy period of feasibility study would be called for. The adjustment proposal in the planning must be approved by the public before the government can make any actual adjustments.

In the early twentieth century, the United States initiated its efforts to establish a system of land use control. In 1916, New York City promulgated the first regulation on land area planning in the United States, which is entitled *The 1916 Zoning Resolution*. The regulation stipulated the use of land and buildings, the range of land development, the height of buildings, and the population density. In the early 1930s, the federal government began to establish a system of land protection, which restricted the non-agricultural use of farmland.[9] In addition, regulations were established regarding the function and utilization of urban land.[10] Currently, the control of land uses in the United States can be divided into two categories. The first is the land use control centered on controlling both the density and the volume of land use, mainly targeting at buildings and their physical layout such as building height, number of stories, scale, building lines, minimum open space requirements, building density, minimum volume ratio, and so on. The second is the land use control centered on controlling the size of cities and protecting the farmland, which are to be achieved mainly

[8] Please refer to the UK "Town and Country Planning Act," "General Permitted Development Order," "Use Classes Order," and so on.

[9] They mainly include the Farmland Protection Policy Act, the Federal Agriculture Improvement and Reform Act, the Agriculture Risk Protection Act, and so on.

[10] Please refer to the US Federal Land Policy and Land Management Act.

by imposing control on the overall number of building permits, carrying out land development in different stages and different zones, and establishing development control zones.

After World War II, in order to prevent the unlimited sprawling of cities, Japan implemented a series of laws and planning systems to restrict the abuse of private land ownership and to preserve farmland.[11] Japan divided the land in the entire country into five categories—urban areas, agricultural areas, forest areas, natural park areas, and natural conservation areas. The system of land use control consists of four main components: agricultural land control, the planning system of urban land use, forest protection system, and vacant land control. The main measures aimed at protecting farmland are designed to limit the conversion of agricultural land to other uses and to ensure that "farmland is used for farming." On the other hand, according to the "Urban Planning Law," the planning of urban land use is divided into urban construction zones and urban adjustment zones; and only residential or sports facilities are allowed to be built in the urban adjustment zones, with stringent government review and approval. Under the forest protection system, 8.8 million hectares of forest land are designated as "forest protection areas," where excessive deforestation is strictly prohibited. Among those 8.8 million hectares of forest land, 60% of these areas are listed as "national parks" exclusively owned by the state and cannot be arbitrarily encroached upon.

China's system of land use control differs significantly from those in developed countries. The systems of land use control adopted by countries such as the United Kingdom, the United States, and Japan are based on the private ownership of land and the market allocation of land resources, as embodied in Urban Growth Boundaries (UGB), zoning administration, and subdivision regulation, etc. China implements the most stringent system of land use control, based on the public ownership of land and planned administration. In China, the land usufruct that are actually susceptible to transactions is only limited to urban construction land, which accounts for less than 1% of the entire national territory (as of the end of 2016).[12] The vast majority of land cannot be traded. Control measures include the following: specifying the use of each piece of land, allocating land resources through formulating land use plans, government monopolization of the supply of construction land, implementing mandatory planning management regarding annual land supply, and using the government approval system to ensure the implementation of annual land planning.

To some extent, the government's control over land use reduces the market value of certain rights in the bundle of rights involving land ownership. Such a control weakens an individual's right of land ownership and limits the vibrancy of land-related production factors. Its concomitant negative impacts on development cannot

---

[11] They include the Land Zoning and Readjustment Act, Residential Areas Improvement Act, National Land Use Planning Act, Basic Act on Land, Agricultural Land Law, Standards for Permission for the Conversion of Agricultural Land, and so on.

[12] As of December 31, 2016, the total urban land area in China was 94.31 million hectares. The total land area of the country is calculated as 9.6 million square kilometers. http://www.mnr.gov.cn/dt/zb/2017/tdly/.

be overlooked. The planned management of land demonstrates characteristics similar to those of the administrative planning under the system of planned economy. To complete a transaction of land allocation between the government and enterprises, the precondition is to complete a series of transactions between the enterprises and the government in other areas, as well as a series of inter-governmental transactions. In other words, a significant amount of transaction cost must be incurred in conducting transactions of rights with the government in addition to the transaction costs associated with land allocation. This issue will be discussed in greater details in subsequent sections of this chapter.

After the 1960s, the British economy experienced a period of "British disease" of stagnation. The traditional system of land planning imposed excessive control over the market activities related to land development, which impeded the revival of declining industrial cities. From the late 1980s to the early 1990s, the Thatcher administration performed a series of reforms in the land planning system, which streamlined the planning procedures by introducing the Simplified Planning Zone (SPZ) system. The changes introduced included modifying the "Use Classes Order" to increase the types of development projects that did not require planning permission, and establishing special purpose zones to eliminate the unreasonable constraints on development projects exerted by overly complex planning procedures and regulations.[13] With the advent of the new century, urban researchers and policy enforcers in the United States began to ponder over an important question—whether "the regulations of land use in the United States have gone too far," such as the practice of zoning and the Land Use Regulations.[14] The establishment of zoning and land use regulations was initially meant to obviate the possible damages by industrial civilization against traditional agriculture and ecological environment. For this reason, the regulations require that there must be a certain distance between the residential, the industrial, and the commercial areas. However, these two institutions of urban planning have become increasingly complex, imposing strict controls regarding an individual building's minimum floor space, floor area ratio, open space ratio, and other aspects. Obviously, such a stringent control was contradictory to the original purpose of creating those two urban planning institutions.[15]

---

[13] Yang Jianjun, Tong Xin, and Chen Wei, "The Issue of Coordinated Planning and the Market: An In-Depth Analysis of the Practice of Simplified Planning Zones in the United Kingdom," *Journal of International Urban Planning*, 2016, Vol. 31, Issue 4.

[14] The history of zoning and land use regulation in the United States is long-standing, with only Houston currently not implementing a zoning system, while other American cities introduced zoning in the 1920s.

[15] Please refer to Shao Ting's article entitled "Has the Regulation of Land Use in the United States Gone Too Far?" http://www.chinado.cn/?p=3071.

2 Changes in China's Construction Land System

After the Third Plenary Session of the 11th CPC Central Committee, China reactivated its economic development in a comprehensive manner, and there was a substantial increase in the demand for construction land. To meet this new development, there was a gradual institutional building related to the system of construction land, which covered land requisition, transfer, land use control, planning, and regulation. As the system kept developing, there has formed a system of construction land use which is large in scale, complex in structure, abundant in rules, and stringent in administration.

1. 1979–1997: establishing the construction land system

In the early stage of the reform and opening-up campaign, China's land usufruct (referred to as the "construction land usufruct" after the promulgation of the Property Law) extended the patterns of unified allocation, free use, and prohibition of circulation which had been in existence since the era of planned economy. Thereafter, in order to be better geared to the needs of the development of commodity economy, China began its land system reform. In June 1986, the Standing Committee of the National People's Congress passed the "The Law of Land Administration," which stipulated that the people's governments on all levels are responsible for organizing the preparation of overall land use plans and the system of land acquisition for construction purposes. In 1988, the system covering both the paid transfer and the paid renewal of construction land usufruct was established.

The first major component in China's reform of its land use system was the establishment of the system of overall planning of land use. According to the Land Administration Law, "governments on all levels must develop overall plans of land use, and the overall plans of land use developed by local people's governments must be approved for implementation by higher-level governments." In addition, the law stipulates that "urban planning and the overall planning of land use should be well-coordinated, and that land use within urban planning areas should be in accordance with the urban plan."

The second major component is the establishment of the land expropriation system. In 1982, the State Council promulgated the "National Regulations on the Expropriation of Land for Construction," which was based on the 1978 Constitution but was applicable only to the expropriation of the collectively-owned land. For the first time, the "Regulations" explicitly stipulated that the principle for determining the compensations for expropriated land was to "guarantee that the income and living standards of the individuals of expropriated land will not be lowered." The "Regulations" further specified that the compensations for land expropriation included fees for land compensation, compensation for crops and trees, compensation for the property attached to the land, and compensation for re-settlement of the agrarian population. Compared with the previous land expropriation system, the standard of compensation fees was duly raised. In 1986, under the Land Administration Law, land expropriation was legally confirmed and the level of administrative approval was determined based on the scale of the expropriation. For example, if the expropriation involves over 1,000 *mu* (1 *mu* is roughly equivalent to 666.67m^2) of cultivated land or over 2,000 *mu* of other lands, it would have to be approved by the State Council. If the expropriated cultivated land is less than 3 *mu* and if the expropriated non-cultivated land was less than 10 *mu*, it would have to be approved by the county-level people's government.

The third major component was the establishment of a system for the grant and the transfer of state-owned land usufruct. The "Law of the People's Republic of China on Chinese-Foreign Equity Joint Ventures," passed in 1979, stipulated that "the investment of Chinese joint venture partners can include the right to use land for the operation of the joint venture during its term. If the use of land is not part of the investment of Chinese joint venture partners, the joint venture shall pay a use fee to the Chinese government." In 1980, the State Council promulgated the "Interim Provisions on the Construction Land of Sino-Foreign Joint Ventures," which required that "a use fee should be charged for the land used by Chinese-foreign joint ventures, whether the land is newly acquired or is used from existing enterprises." In October of the same year, the former National Construction Commission raised the issue of collecting the fees for the urban land use at a national urban planning conference in Beijing. Subsequently, Shenzhen became the first city in China to commence the collection of the fees for the urban land use in 1982, with the fees ranging from 1 to 21 yuan per square meter per year depending on the grade of the land. In 1984, Guangzhou City began collecting urban land use fees within a certain area. Fushun City in Liaoning Province also started its feasibility study and experiments with the collection of land use fees in 1984. After tentative experiments with the compensation-based grant and transfer of state-owned land usufruct in coastal areas from 1987 to 1989, the Constitution and the Land Administration Law[16] in 1988 were among the first national legislations that allowed for the transfer of land usufruct. In 1990, the system of compensation-based grant of the state-owned land usufruct was formally established, and the duration of land use for various types of construction was specified.[17] The policy of urban land use shifted from its former "gratuitous, indefinite, and non-transferable" tradition to the new practice of "compensated use." The changes are reflected in three specific aspects. Firstly, the state implemented a system for the grant and the transfer of state-owned land usufruct based on the principle of the separation between the land ownership and land usufruct. Secondly, three ways to grant land usufruct were developed, that is, through agreement, through bidding, and through auction. Thirdly, land users who have acquired the land usufruct can sell, exchange, donate, rent, or mortgage the land within the period of land use.

---

[16] On December 29, 1988, the first amendment to the Law of Land Administration was made, mainly stating that "the usufruct of the state-owned land and collectively-owned land can be transferred according to law; the state implements a system of compensated use of state-owned land according to law." These provisions laid the legal foundation for state-owned land to enter the market.

[17] Please refer to "Interim Regulations on the Offering and Transfer of Urban State-owned Land Usufruct of the People's Republic of China" (The State Council Decree No. 55, May 1990).

2. 1998–2002: establishing the framework of the management system regarding construction land

During this period, China's system of construction land administration experienced comprehensive development, especially in 1998 when The Law of Land Administration was comprehensively revised. The main changes included the following aspects: the addition of the land use control system which established the institutional framework for converting agricultural land into construction land; the addition of an annual plan for land use, which imposed control over the scale of construction land through quota management; further development of the system for compensated use of construction land, which specified that land transfer through bidding, auction, and public listing was the main mode of land grant; and significant adjustments in the approval mechanism of land expropriation. In order to help implement this law, the former Ministry of Land and Resources successively formulated a multiplicity of supporting systems.

The first is the system of land use control. With regard to the uses of land, a land is categorized into agricultural land, construction land, and the unexploited land. The state strictly restricts the conversion of agricultural land into construction land, controls the total amount of construction land, and implements special protection for arable land. For construction projects that involve the conversion of agricultural land into construction land, such projects must go through approval procedures in order to convert agricultural land into non-agricultural use. Different types of construction projects are subjected to different levels of requirements in terms of land use approval.[18] During the feasibility study of a construction project, the land administrative department may conduct review of the relevant matters related to construction land and pass review judgments.

The second is the newly-added land use planning and management system. The control of the total amount of construction land is instituted. The procedures for the preparing and approval of the annual land use plans are the same as those for the overall planning of land use, all of which must be strictly implemented after administrative approval.

The third is the establishment of the system of land bidding, auction, and public listing. In 1999, China started to enforce the nationwide system of granting the usufruct of state-owned land through bidding and auctioning, and some cities required

[18] According to Article 44 of The Law of Land Administration (revised in 1998), in the road and pipeline projects and the large-scale infrastructure construction projects approved by provincial, autonomous region, or municipal people's governments, or in the construction projects approved by the State Council, if those projects involve the conversion of cultivated land into construction land, they shall be approved by the State Council. If the conversion of farmland into construction land happens within the scope of the urban and rural construction land determined by the overall plan of land use, it shall be approved in batches according to the annual plan of land use by the original authority that approved the overall plan of land use. For the land use in specific construction projects happens within the scope of the conversion of farmland into non-agricultural land, it shall be approved by the municipal or county people's governments.

that six categories of commercial uses for land, including tourism, business, entertainment, finance, service industry, and commercial housing, must be acquired through the bidding and auction system. Since then, the system of bidding and auction has become the main way to grant the use of state-owned land,[19] and all the commercial land usufruct must be granted through bidding, auction, and public listing. Each region is obligated to prepare plans for the grant of the state-owned land usufruct, which must be made public in an opportune manner. Each bidding or auction event must be publicly announced at least 20 days before the start date. At each bidding or auction, there must be no less than three bidders, and the results must be announced publicly within 10 working days.

The fourth change involves significant adjustments in the approval process of land expropriation. The maximum sum of land compensations and resettlement allowance was increased from 20 to 30 times of the annual output value of the acquired land. The government authority in charge of the approval of land expropriation was changed from the authorities on 4 levels (the central, provincial, municipal, and county levels) to 2 levels (the authorities on the central and provincial levels).[20] In 2001, the State Council explicitly proposed that "local governments equipped with sufficient conditions should adopt a land acquisition and reserve system regarding construction land on a trial basis to enhance the government's regulatory capacity over the land market. Municipal and county governments may allocate a certain portion of their land revenue to purchase land, and financial institutions should provide credit support in accordance with the law."[21] This policy provided a basis for land reserve mechanism at the policy level.

3. 2003 to 2012: the construction land system as part of the macroeconomic regulation

In 2003, China's macroeconomic situation experienced overheated development, with economic growth excessively relying on the investment growth. In response, the Central Government introduced a series of policies to control the land supply as a means of curbing the overheated economy. Since then, land policies were incorporated, for a while, into the macroeconomic regulation system and became part of the adjustment of the economic structure. The main measures include the following.

The first was strengthening the system of the land use control and freezing the approval of the land use for new construction projects. In April 2004, the General

[19] Please refer to "Regulations on Publicly Offering the Usufruct of the State-owned Land through Tendering, Auction, and Public Listing." (Decree No. 11 of the Ministry of Land and Resources of the People's Republic of China).

[20] According to Article 45 of the Law of Land Administration (revised in 1998), the expropriation of the following categories of land shall be subject to the approval by the State Council: (1) basic farmland; (2) cultivated land outside the basic farmland exceeding 35 hectares; and (3) other land exceeding 70 hectares. For the expropriation of land beyond aforementioned three categories, it shall be approved by the people's governments of provinces, autonomous regions, and municipalities under the direct jurisdiction of the Central Government and reported to the State Council for registration.

[21] Please refer to the "Notice of the State Council on Strengthening the Management of State-Owned Land Assets" (GuoFa [2001] No. 15).

Office of the State Council issued a directive consisting of "three suspensions," which suspended the approval of new industrial construction projects, infrastructure projects, real-estates projects, etc., and intensified the magnitude of investigating and penalizing the land use that violated the law and government regulations.[22] At the end of 2006, the former Ministry of Land and Resources and the National Development and Reform Commission issued the "Catalogue of Restricted Land Use Projects" and the "Catalogue of Prohibited Land Use Projects," which restricted the use of land for construction projects. At the end of 2007, the General Office of the State Council issued another directive, which required strict implementation of the system of land use control and regulated the use of the farmers' collectively-owned land for construction projects.[23]

The second was the strict implementation of the land planning quota management. Governments on all levels was required to further strengthen the strict implementation of rural land administration system that involved farmland protection, land use planning, and conversion of agricultural land into non-agricultural use.[24] The policy of tight and strict control over the supply of construction land was to be continued,[25] and the overall planning for land use and the annual plan was to be strictly enforced to control the scale of construction land. Local governments were not allowed to exceed the limits on the land use in the approved annual plan or to modify, without authorization, the land use approved by the overall planning.[26]

The third was the strict pre-construction approval. The department of land and resources management raised the standard for checking the scale of industrial land in the stages of preliminary review and actual approval of construction land. The standard comprised of four indexes including investment magnitude, floor area ratio, building coefficient, and the proportion of administrative offices and residential service facilities. These four indicators constituted important bases for industrial enterprises and design institutions to prepare feasibility reports and preliminary design documents for industrial projects.[27] Emphasis was placed on intensifying the control on the conversion of agricultural land into construction land through measures such as land use planning and approval for the conversion of agricultural

---

[22] Please refer to the "Urgent Notice of the General Office of the State Council on Intensifying the Governance and Rectification of the Land Market and on Strict Administration of Land" (GuoBanFa [2004] No. 20).

[23] Please refer to the "Notice of the General Office of the State Council on Strictly Implementing Laws and Policies Related to Rural Collectively-owned Construction Land" (GuoBanFa [2007] No. 71).

[24] Please refer to the "Decision of the State Council on Deepening Reform and Strict Administration of Land" (GuoFa [2004] No. 28).

[25] Please refer to the "Notice on Issuing the Key Issues in the Work on Land and Resources in 2005" (GuoTuZiFa [2005] No. 1).

[26] Please refer to the "Urgent Notice on Further Strengthening Land Administration" (GuoTuZiDianFa [2006] No. 17).

[27] Please refer to the "Notice of the Ministry of Land and Resources on Issuing and Implementing the Industrial Project Construction Land Control Quotas (the Trial Version)" (GuoTuZiFa [2004] No. 232).

land into construction land, and prohibiting "land leasing as a substitution for land expropriation."[28]

The fourth involved new measures in the land expropriation system. Starting from 2008, the former Ministry of Land and Resources introduced a policy which brought into close correlation the increase and decrease of urban and rural construction land. According to this policy, the rural land plots for construction projects which were planned to be reclaimed for crop cultivation and the land plots planned for urban construction as well as other areas were put together to form areas of demolition and new construction projects. Through those measures of demolition and new construction projects, land reorganization and reclamation, the goal of increasing the effective area of cultivated land was achieved.[29] Later on, the government regulated the pilot programs and corrected problems such as exceeding the quota of land turnover.

The fifth was more stringent control of the commercial land development through planning. In 2011, the State Council issued the "National Plan for Key Functional Zones,"[30] which, based on the resource and environmental load capacity and the existing development density and potential of different zones, designed the future population distribution, economic layout, land use and urbanization pattern in a comprehensively coordinated manner. The state-owned land was divided into four categories, namely, optimized development, key development, restricted development, and prohibited development. In this way, the key function of different zones was determined, the direction of development was clarified, and the development intensity was brought under control.

4. 2013 to the present: developing a land system combining power delegation and administrative management, with greater emphasis on administrative management

Since 2013, China's land administration system has been characterized by alternations between the tightening and the relaxing of administrative control, with greater emphasis on the tightening of control measures. Starting from 2015, China has implemented the reform of "streamlining administration and delegating power, improving regulation and providing better services." The reform helped simplify the approval process for investment projects. By duly relaxing the approval and the regulation of the land use for construction projects, the land administration department somehow managed to improve the efficiency of the administrative approval. At the same time, China has further strengthened the control of land quotas and has successively introduced the systems regarding land development—the system of spatial control and the system of boundary management. As a result, during this period, the overall trend of China's land administration system has been to strengthen government regulation and control, with the tightening of control taking precedence over de-regulation.

[28] Please refer to the "Notice of the State Council on Certain Issues in Strengthening Land Control" (GuoFa [2006] No. 31).

[29] Please refer to the "Administration Measures for the Pilot Projects on the Coordinated Increase and Decrease of Construction Land Use in Urban and Rural Areas" (GuoTuZiFa [2008] No. 138).

[30] Please refer to the "Notice of the State Council on Issuing the National Plan for Main Functional Zones" (GuoFa [2010] No. 46).

Regarding the delegation of power, the measures included the following.

The first was delegating the authority concerning the preliminary review of land use in construction projects. In 2013, the National Development and Reform Commission delegated the approval authority covering 12 categories of investment projects undertaken by enterprises, cancelled the approval requirements imposed on 13 categories of investment projects by enterprises, and adjusted the administrative regulation to registration. For the 12 categories of projects whose approval authority was delegated, the provincial or the equivalent local departments of land and resources could deal with them in accordance with the principle of "peer review" for preliminary review of the land use for construction projects.[31]

The second was simplifying the contents of approval. In 2016, the former Ministry of Land and Resources revised the "Administrative Measures for Pre-Examination of the Land Use for Construction Project" and the "Administrative Measures for the Review and Approval of Construction Land Use." By focusing on key issues, adjusting time sequence, simplifying contents, and optimizing procedures, the government sought to achieve the goal of "simplified paperwork, shortened time, and reduced difficulty" in the approval of land use for construction projects. More specifically, the measures included: (1) simplifying the review of proposed projects which complied with the overall land use plan and land use standards. Regarding those construction projects which have passed the preliminary review of land use, there would be, in principle, no re-review of whether those projects complied with the overall land use plan or land use standards at the stage of land use approval. (2) simplifying the examination of supplementary cultivated land and of the compensations for the expropriated land; (3) improving the assessment of geological hazards and risks and the examination of the likelihood of construction projects overlying on important mineral resources; (4) improving the examination and approval of urban construction land use; and (5) appropriately narrowing the scope of land pre-examination so that projects that do not involve new construction land and whose land use has already been approved for construction can be exempted from pre-examination of land use for construction projects.[32]

The third was allowing the collectively-owned construction land in rural areas to enter the market, which served to increase the sources of construction land. In 2015, China launched a pilot program that allowed the collectively-owned and collectively-managed construction land to enter the market. In response to the incomplete property rights of rural collectively-owned and collectively-managed construction land, as well as problems like the lack of equal access to the market, the lack of equal property rights and of equal market price, and the urgent need to improve transaction rules, a system for the entry of rural collectively-operated construction land into the

[31] Please refer to the "Notice of the General Office of the Ministry of Land and Resources on Partially Delegating the Pre-Examination Authority of Construction Project Land Use" (GuoTuZiTingFa [2013] No. 44).

[32] Please refer to "Notice of the Ministry of Land and Resources on Improving and Optimizing the Pre-examination and Examination of Construction Project Land Use" (GuoTuZiGui [2016] No. 16).

market was established. By improving the property rights system of rural collectively-operated construction land, the system granted the rights of transfer, leasing, and equity participation to the rural collectively-operated construction land. The system also specified the scope and the approaches whereby the rural collectively-operated construction land could gain access to the market, and helped establish sound market transaction rules and service supervision system. The newly-revised "The Law of Land Administration" in 2019 stipulates that for collectively-operated construction land that has been registered according to law and whose land use has been determined in the overall land use plan or urban and rural planning as serving industrial, commercial, or other business purposes, the landowner can transfer or lease the land to the organizations or individuals for use.

Regarding the regulatory measures, they have been further strengthened. After several decades of development following the implementation of the reform and opening-up policy, a complete set of land administration systems has been established, with regulations governing a multiplicity of aspects including land development planning, land requisition and transfer, land use control, and annual planning. Due to path dependency, various administrative measures have been constantly refined and strengthened. In recent years, there has been further enhancement of the regulatory measures concerning the development and utilization of the country's land spaces.

Firstly, the control of the quotas in various categories has been comprehensively strengthened. The "National Overall Plan of Land Use (2006–2020)" issued in 2008 defined the total amount of agricultural land to be converted into urban construction land across the country. Based on this, the annual plans for land use in various regions further specified the projected annual quotas for the conversion of agricultural land into construction land, which are the total amounts of new construction land acquired through occupying the arable land in various regions on an annual basis. Since the 12th Five-Year Plan period, the quotas for new construction land have been continuously reduced. During the 12th Five-Year Plan period, the total amount of newly-added construction land in the entire country was 39.25 million *mu*, which decreased to 32.56 million *mu* in the 13th Five-Year Plan period, showing a decline of about 6.69 million *mu*. During the 14th Five-Year Plan period, restrictions on land have been further intensified, and the insistence on the "red line" of 1.8 billion *mu* of arable land was maintained. The scale of new construction land has further shrunk, reaching less than 29.5 million *mu* as compared with the 13th Five-Year Plan period, and a target of creating 275 million *mu* of high-standard concentrated and contiguous farmland was proposed.

Secondly, the red line of ecological protection has been defined. In 2014, the former Ministry of Environmental Protection issued the "National Ecological Protection Red Line—Technical Guidelines for Delineating Ecological Function Baselines (Trial Version)" and promoted its implementation nationwide in 2017. The red line of ecological protection is implemented in accordance with the requirement of prohibiting the development in designated areas. According to the requirement, all types of development activities that violate overall functional designation are strictly prohibited, so are any arbitrary changes in land use. If there is indeed a need to make adjustments due to major national infrastructure projects or major projects involving the assurance of people's livelihood, the proposal of adjustment must be reviewed by the former Ministry of Environmental Protection, the National Development and Reform Commission in association with other relevant departments which must then pass their judgment. The adjustments must be approved by the State Council.[33]

Thirdly, urban development boundaries have been delineated. In 2014, China released the "National New Urbanization Plan (2014–2020)," which called for strengthening the management and control of urban spatial development and limiting disorderly urban sprawling and inefficient expansion by reasonably defining urban development boundaries. Subsequently, the Ministry of Housing and Urban–Rural Development and the former Ministry of Land and Resources selected 14 pilot cities, including Beijing and Shanghai, to explore how to delineate the boundaries of urban development. In April 2019, the Beijing Municipal Government issued the "Beijing Ecological Control Line and Management Measures of Urban Development Boundary." According to this document, if the land for a construction project needed to make slight adjustments regarding the ecological control line or urban development boundary, the district government must publish the adjustment plan (for no less than 30 days), submit it for review by relevant functional departments, revise and improve the plan after feasibility analysis, and then submit it again for approval by the municipal government after review by the municipal department of planning and natural resources.[34] As of early 2020, more than 600 cities nationwide have carried out the delineation of the urban development boundary.

3 Transaction Costs Caused by Changes in Transaction Modules

Currently, investors need to go through five main transaction modules before they can acquire a piece of construction land: land expropriation, land transfer, spatial planning, land use control, and annual plan (please refer to Fig. 7.1). Among them, spatial planning, land use control, and annual plan are still subjected to the system of planned management system and belong to the subtype of direct planning. Under these major transaction modules, there are many sub-modules that have gradually developed with the passage of time. An examination of the evolution of this system reveals that the increase in transaction costs for acquiring construction land is primarily due to the increase in the number of transaction modules.

[33] Please refer to the "Notice on Issuing the Guidelines for the Delineation of Ecological Protection Red Lines" (HuanBanShengTai [2017] No. 48).

[34] Please refer to the "Notice of the People's Government of Beijing Municipality on Issuing the Beijing Administrative Measures Concerning the Ecological Control Line and Urban Development Boundary" (JingZhengFa [2019] No. 7).

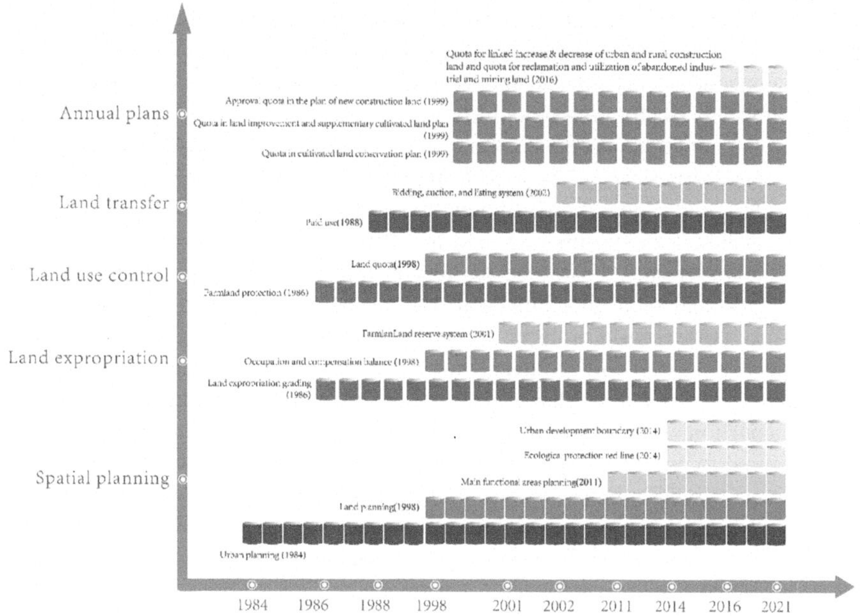

Fig. 7.1 Transaction module regarding the land use for construction projects

1. The land expropriation system

In the initial phase of the reform and opening-up, China had not yet established a system of market-oriented land transaction. The organizations that needed land for construction directly expropriated land and the expropriation was subjected to approval by the central, provincial, municipal, and county-level governments according to the scale of land expropriation. The organizations had to pay compensation fees to the holders of the land, including compensation for cultivated land, resettlement subsidies, compensation for the physical objects attached to the land, and compensation for the planted crops.[35] This was a relatively simple transaction module. From today's perspective, this mode of land expropriation was relatively simple and easy and the compensation standards were not sufficiently high.

With the development of economy, a large amount of investment in fixed assets was no longer limited to the construction activities by the state. The investment by various types of economic ownership all involved land and necessitated adjustments in the system of land expropriation. While the module of land approval was retained, new transaction modules were gradually added to the expropriation process.

The first approach is the balance between the occupation and the compensation of cultivated land. The revised "The Law of Land Administration" in 1998 emphasized the need to strike a balance between the occupation of the cultivated land and the

[35] Please refer to Article 25 of the "Law of Land Administration of the People's Republic of China" (1986).

development and reclamation of cultivated land. For non-agricultural construction projects that involve the occupation of the cultivated land, the principle of "balanced land occupation and land reclamation" requires that the organization, when occupying cultivated land for non-agricultural construction, is responsible for reclaiming the cultivated land that is equivalent in quantity and quality to the land occupied.

The second approach is the establishment of a system of land purchase and reserve. Since the 1990s, some regions have gradually transformed the original approach of directly expropriating land for construction projects into a system in which local governments assumed the responsibility of first expropriating all the potential land and then allocating it to the respective organizations which were to undertake construction projects. In 2001, the State Council proposed that local governments equipped with sufficient conditions should implement a land purchase and reserve system on a trial basis. City and county governments were permitted to allocate a portion of their land revenue to purchase land, while financial institutions were required to provide credit support in accordance with the law. This move was an indication that essentially recognized the legitimacy of this system. In 2007, the Ministry of Land and Resources, the Ministry of Finance, and the People's Bank of China jointly issued the "Land Reserve Management Measures," which unified the main contents of the land reserve system in the form of the formal regulations of those official institutions. Since then, the land used for construction projects has undergone a major change, evolving from direct expropriation to a new mechanism in which the occupation of arable lands must be balanced by newly reclaimed lands and land for construction projects must be acquired from the government agency responsible for land purchase and land reserve.

2. The paid use of land

During the period of planned economy, land was regarded as a means of production that could not enter market transaction. Construction projects could have access to land free of charge. In the reform and opening-up period, the transition from free use of land to the paid use of land represents a significant progress. But this progress is not without its price, which is the addition of transaction procedures and increased transaction costs.

The paid use of land was first implemented in coastal areas. Since 1988, China's laws and regulations have clarified and specified the paid use of land, and have stipulated the maximum term of years for the use of different types of land. The transfer of land can be carried out by means of agreements, tenders, or auctions.[36] With the implementation of the system of the paid use of land, the transfer of land through agreements was relatively high in proportion. However, the price negotiated

[36] According to Article 12 of the "Interim Regulations on the Offering and Transfer of Urban State-owned Land Usufruct of the People's Republic of China" (The State Council Decree No. 55), the maximum term for the transfer of land usufruct shall be determined on the basis of the following categories of land use: (1) 70 years for the residential use of land; (2) 50 years for the industrial use of land; (3) 50 years for the educational, scientific, cultural, health, and sports use of land; (4) 40 years for the commercial, tourism, and entertainment use of land; (5) 50 years for the comprehensive or other types of use of land.

in those agreements could not accurately reflect the supply and demand relationship or the real value of the land. There were also many cases of corruption. All those factors resulted in extensive criticisms from all walks of life in the Chinese society. To address this problem, China began to comprehensively implement the system of tender, auction, and public listing for land transfer in 2002. According to this system, various types of land transfer for commercial purposes, including business, tourism, entertainment, and commercial housing, must go through procedures of tender, auction, or public listing.[37] Competition mechanisms were introduced into the procedures of tendering, auction, and public listing; and those mechanisms have proved conducive to improving the transparency of land transactions and augmenting land value. In 2007, the procedures of tendering, auction, and public listing were further expanded to the industrial sector.[38]

The procedures for land tendering, auction, and public listing generally include the following steps. (1) publishing the land supply plan and determining the method of supply; (2) preparing and determining the auction plan; (3) evaluating the land price and determining the reserve price; (4) preparing the auction documents; (5) publishing the auction notice; (6) application and qualification review; (7) conducting the bidding or auction activity; (8) signing the auction contract and publishing the auction results; (9) issuing the construction land approval certificate and delivering the land to the buyer; (10) completing the land registration; (11) archiving the relevant documents. Different regions may have their own detailed operational procedures (please refer to Fig. 7.2).[39]

3. Land and spatial planning

To address the conflicts between large population and land scarcity, between urban and rural areas in terms of the level of development, and between the demolition of old buildings and the construction of new buildings in China's urbanization process, governments at all levels have formulated land and spatial planning programs to coordinate urban and rural spatial layout. Admittedly, for a certain period of time, these planning programs have played a positive role in balancing urban and rural development, protecting land resources, and preventing illegal land use. However, with the passage of time, the number of plans has overly increased, the government control has become overly detailed, and the execution has become increasingly rigid, thus inhibiting the vitality of production factors related to land. If we consider the contents within a certain category of planning program as a transaction module, we

---

[37] Please refer to "Regulations on Publicly Offering the Usufruct of the State-owned Land through Tendering, Auction, and Listing." (Decree No. 11 of the Ministry of Land and Resources of the People's Republic of China).

[38] Please refer to "Regulations on Publicly Offering the Usufruct of the State-owned Construction Land through Tendering, Auction, and Listing." (Decree No. 39 of the Ministry of Land and Resources of the People's Republic of China).

[39] Please refer to the "Rules Regarding Publicly Offering the Usufruct of the State-owned Land through Tendering, Auction, and Listing." (GuoTuZiFa [2006] No. 114).

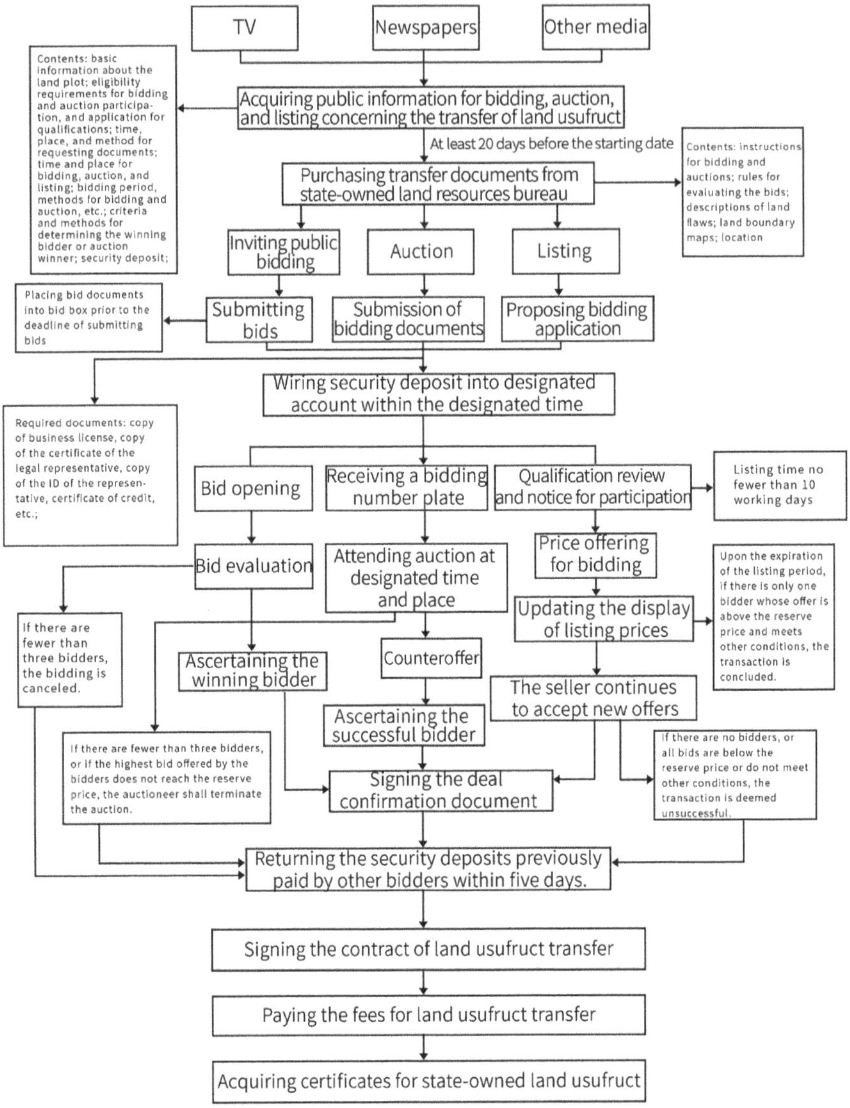

Fig. 7.2 Bidding, auction, and public listing procedures for the transfer of state-owned land usufruct[40]

will find that, since 1980s, the number of land planning modules has increased from

[40] Please refer to "The Process of Publicly Offering the Usufruct of the State-owned Land through Tendering, Auction, and Listing." https://www.51wendang.com/doc/18e11f561c1907f4606f4057.

one to six, which can be summarized as the "three zones and three lines."[41] The three zones refer to the three functional zones of urban, agricultural, and ecological space whereas the three lines refer to the three red lines of control related to ecological protection, protection of permanent basic farmland, and urban development boundaries. The land use involved in construction projects must meet all the requirements in the planning programs. The expansion of contents in this transaction module can be historically described as follows.

Firstly, in 1984, it was required that all cities must develop urban plans and that land use for construction projects within each city must comply with the plans.[42]

Secondly, in 1998, it was required that the overall plans of land use at county and township levels must chart out the protected areas for basic farmland, the land reclamation areas, the construction land areas, and the areas of prohibited land reclamation. The use of each piece of land must be specified.[43]

Thirdly, in 2011, it was required that land space in the entire country was to be divided into four categories: land for optimized development, land for key development, land for restricted development, and land for prohibited development.[44]

Fourthly, in 2014, it was required that each region should develop red lines of ecological protection and those areas under ecological protection should be managed as areas of prohibited development; any arbitrary change in the land use would be strictly prohibited.[45]

Fifthly, in 2014, it was required to determine the boundary of urban development and delineate the boundary and control areas regarding the urban and rural

---

[41] Please refer to "Several Opinions of the CPC Central Committee and the State Council on Establishing a National Territorial Spatial Planning System and Supervising its Implementation" (ZhongFa [2019] No. 18).

[42] According to Article 31 of the "Urban Planning Regulations" (1984), if any organization or individual who carries out construction activities within the urban planning area needs to use the land owned by the state or to expropriate the collectively-owned land, it must hold a construction plan, design task book, or other relevant certificates that have been approved through the procedures prescribed by the state, and submit an application for construction land to the urban planning authority. The organization or individual applying for construction land can use the land only after the urban planning authority has reviewed and approved the location, the area, and the scale of the applied land, has allocated the land, and has issued the construction land use permit.

[43] According to Article 10 of the Implementation Regulations of the Law of Land Administration of the People's Republic of China (1998), the overall plan of land use shall divide the land into agricultural land, construction land, and unused land. The overall plans of land use at county and township levels should, as necessary, designate different areas of land, including the area for the protection of basic farmland, the area for land reclamation, the area for construction land, and the area of prohibited reclamation. Among them, the overall plans of land use at the township level should also determine the use of each piece of land according to its conditions of use.

[44] Please refer to the "Notice of the State Council on Issuing the National Plan for Main Functional Zones" (GuoFa [2010] No. 46).

[45] Please refer to the "Notice on Issuing the Guidelines for Delineation of Ecological Protection Redlines" (HuanBanShengTai [2017] No. 48).

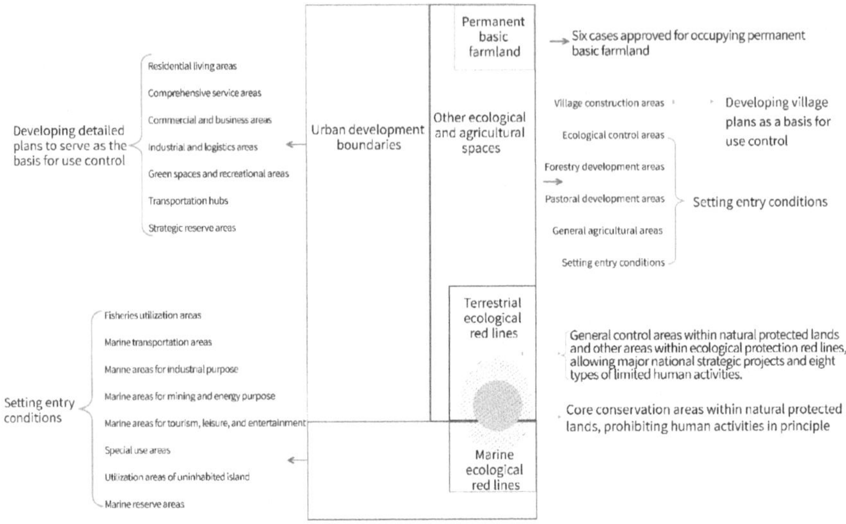

Fig. 7.3 Diagram of all-space uses control of state-owned land[47]

construction land, including the boundary of the construction scale, the boundary of expansion, and the boundary of the prohibited construction (please refer to Fig. 7.3).[46]

[46] Article 22 of "The Administration Measures on Overall Planning of Land Use" (Decree No. 72 of the Ministry of Land and Resources of the People's Republic of China) stipulates that when formulating the overall plans of urban, county, and township land use, the department of land and resources in charge shall work together with the department of environmental protection and the department of housing and urban-rural construction and take into full consideration the red line of ecological protection, permanent basic farmland, and urban development boundaries. The following urban-rural construction land control boundaries and control areas shall be properly demarcated in accordance with local conditions: (1) the boundary over the scale of urban-rural construction land; (2) the boundary over the expansion of urban-rural construction land; (3) the boundary over the forbidden urban-rural construction land; (4) the permitted construction area; (5) the conditionally-permitted construction area; (6) the restricted construction area; (7) the prohibited construction area. Article 38 stipulates that the space for the development and construction in cities, towns, villages, and industrial and mining areas should be limited to the permitted construction area determined in the overall plan of land use. Without changing the scale of the permitted construction area and without exceeding the boundary over the expansion of urban-rural construction land and the conditionally-permitted construction area, cities and counties can formulate plans for adjusting the boundary over the scale of urban-rural construction land. With the due approval from the land and resources department in charge which is at the same executive level as the government agency in charge of the approval of the overall plan of land use, the spatial layout of the permitted construction area and the conditionally-permitted construction area can be adjusted. The boundary over the expansion of urban-rural construction land cannot be adjusted. If an adjustment is indeed necessary, it must be subjected to the approval, in accordance with the regulations prescribed in this present document, by the original approval authority of the overall plan.

[47] Please refer to Qian Jing, Lan Quanyou, and Zheng Qin, "The Expanded Control of Uses: From Land to Homeland Spaces," *China Land*, Issue 7, 2020.

The specific regulations in the program of "three zones and three lines" can be found in the documents including the "Overall Land Use Planning," the "Urban and Rural Planning," "Main Functional Area Planning and Ecological Functional Zone Delineation," which are respectively compiled by the natural resources department, housing and urban–rural development department, development and reform department, and ecological and environmental department at all levels. These plans generally exhibit the following problems—long periods of planning, approval by very high administrative levels, and slow adjustment in planning. Generally speaking, the land use planning remains valid for 15 years, and the overall urban and town planning spans a valid planning period of 20 years. In the entire country, the land use planning by 106 large- and medium-sized cities and the urban planning by 108 cities must be reported via bottom-to-top hierarchies all the way to the State Council for approval. In general, any potential adjustment in the urban planning and land use planning needs to be proposed by the original planning department, and approved through the same bottom-to-top hierarchies according to the previous approval sequences. In practice, urban and rural construction, as well as linear infrastructure construction such as railways, highways, and water conservancy projects, tends to face changes in the nature of land use, such as the conversion of farmland to non-agricultural use. These cases of change would require the approval of relevant departments in the original planning programs and land use would be permitted only after the approval of the adjustments by relevant planning departments. County-level and city-level planning adjustments must be reported for approval to the provincial department in charge, and if the adjustments involve the occupation of land for more than 30 hectares of basic farmland or ordinary cultivated land, they must be reported to the State Council for approval. It might seem that planning adjustments are a transaction of rights between the land construction organization and the local planning department and constitutes a transaction module. Nevertheless, behind this, there also exist power transactions between the planning departments at the basic level and the higher levels in an effort to vie for the approval of the planning adjustments. This power transaction can be further divided into multiple transaction modules. This leads to excessively long time in making planning adjustments and creates huge transaction costs.

Starting from 2014, in order to address the constraints imposed on construction land by excessive compliance requirements, China launched the "many-in-one" pilot program in 28 cities and counties in an effort to integrate multiple land use regulations.[48] In 2019, the CPC Central Committee and the State Council proposed to integrate diverse spatial planning programs, such as the main functional zone planning, the land use planning, and the urban–rural planning, into a unified planning program of national land space, thus achieving the "many-in-one" integration.[49] At the same time, it was stipulated that local governments would no longer compile and approve

[48] Please refer to the "Notice on the Pilot Program of 'Many-in-One Integration of Regulations in Cities and Counties" (FaGaiGuiHua [2014] No. 1971).

[49] Please refer to the "Several Opinions of the CPC Central Committee and the State Council on Establishing a National Territorial Spatial Planning System and Supervising Its Implementation" (ZhongFa [2019] No. 18).

planning documents such as main functional zone planning, overall plans of land use, urban system planning, overall planning of city (town), and marine functional zone planning. Various existing provincial-level planning programs whose approved planning period extends after 2020 should be integrated into the newly-compiled land space planning programs on the same administrative level in accordance with the new planning requirements.[50] The "many-in-one" integration seeks to reduce transaction costs by reducing and merging transaction modules.

4. Land use control

After the implementation of the reform and opening-up policies, some regions saw an increase in the unauthorized use of cultivated land due to the need for economic development. In response to the rapid decrease in cultivated land, China enforced a system of land use control. The classification of land use became increasingly specific, and accordingly it became increasingly difficult to change the nature of land use. Under the "The Law of Land Administration" passed in 1986, the use of cultivated land for construction projects must be approved by government institutions. This was the preliminary form of land use control. Subsequently, the "Urban Planning Law" enacted in 1990 required that construction projects in the areas covered by urban planning must comply with the land use as has been specified in the urban planning programs.[51] The revised "The Law of Land Administration" in 1998 divided land into three categories, the agricultural land, the construction land, and unexploited land. In addition, the construction land was subdivided into the land for urban and rural residence and for public facilities, the land for industrial and mining use, the land for transportation and water conservancy facilities, the land for tourism, and the land for military facilities, etc. In order to formulate plans and to impose necessary control and approval over land use, the housing and urban–rural development department formulated detailed standards for classifying the urban land and the construction land. The urban and rural land use within the municipal boundary is divided into two major categories, nine sub-categories, and 14 minor categories whereas urban construction land was divided into 8 major categories, 35 sub-categories, and 43

[50] Please refer to the "Notice of the Ministry of Natural Resources on the Comprehensive Implementation of National Land Space Planning" (ZhiRanZiFa [2019] No. 87).

[51] According to Article 18 of The Law of Urban Planning of the People's Republic of China (1990), the preparation of urban planning generally consists of two stages: the overall planning and the detailed planning. In order to further control and determine the land use, scope, and capacity of different areas, and coordinate the construction of various infrastructure and public facilities, large and medium-sized cities can also prepare district plans based on the overall planning. Article 32 stipulates that for the construction, expansion, and renovation of buildings, structures, roads, pipelines, and other engineering facilities within the urban planning area, the applicant must hold relevant approval documents and apply to the administrative authority of urban planning. The administrative authority shall issue construction project planning permits based on the planning and design requirements proposed by the urban planning, and the organization or individual intending to engage in construction projects may apply for construction commencement procedures only after obtaining the construction project planning permits and other relevant approval documents.

minor categories.[52] This meant that the land use was classified into a total of 57 types. After the organization seeking project construction acquires the land through bidding or auction, it can develop the land only according to the designated use. If there is any change in the designated land use, the organization must seek approval by going through the previous approval process or transfer the land through tendering, auction, or public listing. Land use control exceeded the initial practice of controlling the agricultural land from being converted into non-agricultural land. The control has become a system which imposes control over all types of land use. These uses were subjectively determined by administrative agencies, and the government formulated strict regulations based on those subjectively-determined land uses when having the land transferred. When the government agencies intend to adjust land use or when actual land users want to change the land use, they all have to go through exceedingly complicated procedures in planning adjustment and in administrative approval, thus paying enormous transaction costs. Here, a random example is chosen to illustrate the approval process which involves changes in the use of construction land, as shown in the diagram publicly issued by Fengtai County in Anhui Province (please refer to Fig. 7.4).

5. The annual plan of land use

In China, land use is managed through planned administration. The quotas of land under government administration are issued annually, formulated by the Central Government, distributed in different portions to provincial and local governments, and implemented in accordance with overall planning. In the case of an insufficiency of land quota, the social and economic development of a given region will face a bottleneck. Land quotas are an important component in the transaction of rights between governmental departments. Here, we can use the number of land use quotas as an example to shed light on the trend of the increasing number of transaction modules.

In 1999, there were three quotas in the annual land use plan: (1) the quotas in the annual plan regarding the conversion of the agricultural land (including the arable land) to non-agricultural use; (2) the quotas in the annual plan regarding the minimum preservation of the cultivated and arable land; (3) the quotas in the annual plan regarding land development and arrangement.[53]

In 2004, two of the three land use quotas were further sub-divided, thus creating two sub-modules. The first was the quota regarding the conversion of agricultural land into non- agricultural use, which was sub-divided into the quota regarding the occupation of agricultural land for construction in city, town, and village, and the quota regarding the occupation of agricultural land for the key construction projects that require independent site selection, such as the construction of energy,

[52] Please refer to "The Classification of Urban Land Use and Standards for Planning Land Use for Construction" (GBJ137-90) and "The Classification of Urban Land Use and Standards for Planning Land Use for Construction" (GB50137-2011).

[53] Please refer to "The Administration Measures on the Annual Plan of Land Use" (Decree No. 2 of the Ministry of Land and Resources of the People's Republic of China, 1999).

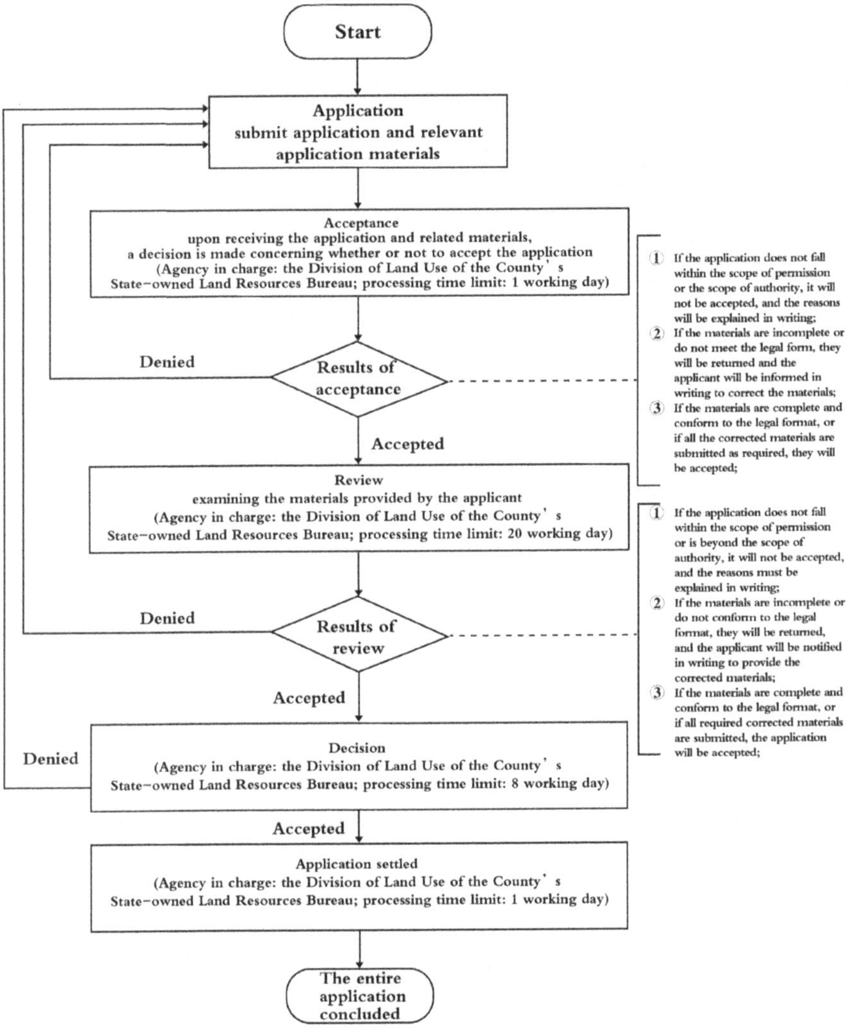

Fig. 7.4 Review and approval process involving changes in the construction land use in Fengtai County, Anhui Province[54]

transportation, and water conservancy projects. The second was the quota regarding land development and arrangement, which was subdivided into the quota regarding the compensation of arable land used for commercial land development and the quota regarding the compensation of arable land in land arrangement and reclamation. Furthermore, it was specified that local governments could add quota controls based on the actual needs on top of the three categories of land use quotas formulated by

[54] http://www.huainan.gov.cn/public/118322956/257033943.html.

the Central Government,[55] thus granting the local governments the power to create new transaction modules.

Among the three categories of land use quotas specified by the Central Government in the annual plans, the first category "the quota of the planned special use of agricultural land" was changed, in 2006, into "the quota of land planned for new construction," which included the total amount of new land for construction and the quota for both the agricultural land and cultivated land used for new construction. The total amount of new land for construction included both the agricultural land occupied for construction and the unused land. This measure expanded the scope of the quota control.[56]

In 2016, the quotas of land use in the annual plans set by the Chinese government were adjusted to include four categories, namely: (1) the quota of land planned for new construction, which included the total amount of new land for construction and the quota for both the agricultural land and cultivated land used for new construction; (2) the quota of the land planned to be compensated for the arable land through land arrangement; (3) the quota for the minimum preservation of the cultivated and arable land; and (4) the quota for the proportioned increase and decrease in the amount of urban and rural construction land and for the reclamation and exploitation of the industrial and mining waste land. Meanwhile, local governments were still permitted to establish additional quota controls on top of those set by the Central Government.[57] In the annual land use plans, the number of the quotas has increased from three categories in 1999 to four categories at present, with each category capable of being further subdivided into more specific categories. Here, we can bear witness to an important change, the change from the quotas formulated by the Central Government at the very outset to the permission for local governments to establish quota controls. With the increasingly tightened control over land supply imposed by the mandatory land plans, the local governments and enterprises have to pay increasing costs of transaction in order to secure the necessary quotas of land use.

4 Transaction Costs Caused by Changes in Transaction Rules

The transaction costs arising from the use of construction land in China have demonstrated a general trend of increase in quantity, which is caused by both the aforementioned factors of increasing transaction modules and the increasing complexity of

---

[55] Please refer to "The Administration Measures on the Annual Plan of Land Use" (Decree No. 26 of the Ministry of Land and Resources of the People's Republic of China, 2004).

[56] Please refer to "The Administration Measures on the Annual Plan of Land Use" (Decree No. 37 of the Ministry of Land and Resources of the People's Republic of China, 2006) and "Interpretation of the Revised 'The Administration Measures on the Annual Plan of Land Use'." (http://www.gov.cn/gzdt/2006-12/25/con-tent_478245.htm).

[57] Please refer to the "The Administration Measures on the Annual Plan of Land Use" (Decree No. 66 of the Ministry of Land and Resources of the People's Republic of China).

transaction rules within each module. Here, we take the sub-module of the balance between the occupation and the compensation of cultivated land as an example for analysis.

In 1997, China first proposed the idea of "the balance between the occupation and the compensation of cultivated land." According to this policy, in the case of occupying cultivated land for non-agricultural construction projects, an equivalent area of cultivated land that meets quality standards must be developed or reclaimed.[58] In 1998, this system was incorporated into the revised "The Law of Land Administration."[59] The land administration department in the local government and the land users are the main transaction entities, and the entire set of regulations regarding the balanced occupation and compensation stipulated by the Central Government constitute transaction contracts. These contracts, relatively simple at the outset, have become increasingly complex, with new contents being added over time. The first provision was "compensation before occupation." At the beginning of implementing the occupation and compensation balance policy, it was stipulated that for those construction projects that have to select sites separately outside the planned area, compensation must be made first if they involve the occupation of cultivated land. Only when the newly-added cultivated land is inspected and accepted as qualified can the land users apply for land for construction purpose.

The second provision was the balance between the occupation and compensation of cultivated land within the local area. The Department of Land and Resources Administration stipulated that, starting from 2001, the balanced occupation and compensation of cultivated land should be carried out within the city or the county itself. If it is difficult to achieve a balance of occupation and compensation within the administrative region due to the shortage of reserved resources of cultivated land, application can be made to the higher-level department of land and resources administration for the compensation of cultivated land elsewhere within the province. It is not allowed to carry out the balancing of the occupation and compensation in other provinces, regions, or cities.

The third provision was that the occupation of high-quality land must be balanced by an equal amount of high-quality land. In response to the problem of compensation with low-quality land for high-quality land in various regions, the Department of Land and Resources Administration required in 2004 that the occupation of cultivated land must be supplemented by an equivalent amount of cultivated land of the same

---

58 In 1997, the CPC Central Committee and the State Council issued a notice titled "Further Strengthening Land Administration and Effectively Protecting Arable Land" (ZhongFa [1997] No. 11), which first proposed the concept of "balance between the occupation and compensation of arable land."

59 Article 19 of the revised "The Law of Land Administration of the People's Republic of China" (1998) stipulates that the overall plan of land use should be formulated on the basis of the following principles: (1) strictly protecting the basic farmland and controlling the occupation of farmland for non-agricultural construction; (2) enhancing the land utilization efficiency; (3) arranging various types of land use in different regions in a well-coordinated manner; (4) protecting and improving the ecological environment and ensuring the sustainable use of land; (5) balancing the occupation of farmland with the development and reclamation of new farmland.

quality. The practice of land compensation with insufficient quantity and quality must be prohibited.[60] According to these transaction rules, land-using organizations need to spend time searching for suitable target land in order to compensate for the occupied cultivated land and they also need to carry out land reclamation and restoration to make the compensation. Only when the newly-added cultivated land is inspected and accepted as qualified can the land-using organizations apply for land for construction purpose. The more economically developed a region is, the scarcer is the reserve of the cultivated land with equivalent quantity and quality within that particular administrative region. This scarcity means that the organization seeking construction land needs to spend more time searching for target cultivated land or applying for the occupation-compensation balance within the province. To reduce transaction costs, the Department of Land and Resources Administration has taken some measures. One of such measures was to implement a system linking up the cultivated land reserve system and the construction project to optimize the process and reduce transaction costs.[61] A new mechanism was introduced in which local governments established, for the purpose of occupation-compensation balance, a pool of cultivated land reserve or a pool of land development, arrangement, and reclamation projects. The organization seeking construction land can access one of the pools to secure necessary quotas.

The second measure was a national coordination mechanism regarding the supplementation of the cultivated land.[62] For municipalities directly under the Central Government which face serious shortages of farmland reserve resources, where the

[60] Please refer to the "Decision of the State Council on Deepening Reform and Strict Administration of Land" (GuoFa [2004] No. 28).

[61] On November 28, 2001, the Ministry of Land and Resources issued the "Notice on Further Strengthening and Improving the Balancing of the Occupation and Supplementation of Cultivated Land" (GuoTuZiFa [2001] No. 374), which stipulates that local governments equipped with necessary conditions should allow the farmland to be developed and arranged in accordance with land development, arrangement and reclamation projects. After the projects are evaluated and accepted as qualified, the quota of newly-added cultivated land will be incorporated into the pool of the cultivated land reserve. When a land-using organization occupies farmland and needs to balance the occupation and supplementation of cultivated land, it should pay for the fee for land development and reclamation and secure a quota from the pool of the pool of the cultivated land reserve to supplement the land before occupation. In those regions that are currently not equipped with the necessary conditions to establish a pool of cultivated land reserve, When the occupied farmland needs to be supplemented in the case of a construction project, it is necessary to select, from the pool of land development, arrangement, and reclamation projects, a project that have been fully evaluated and approved and match it to the proposed construction project. A plan for supplementing cultivated land needs to be developed and the fee for land reclamation paid by the land-occupying construction organization will be used to carry out projects of land development, arrangement and reclamation to supplement the cultivated land.

[62] In 2017, the CPC Central Committee and the State Council issued the "Opinions on Strengthening Farmland Preservation and Improving the Balance of Land Occupation and Compensation" (ZhongFa [2017] No.4), proposing to explore national coordination mechanism for farmland supplementation. In 2018, the General Office of the State Council issued the " Measures for Managing the National Coordination of Inter-provincial Farmland Supplementation," which stipulated that "national coordination for supplementing farmland across provinces" refers to situations where a municipality under the direct jurisdiction of the central government or a province with severely

newly-reclaimed farmland is not sufficient to compensate for the occupied farmland or there is a gap in supplementary farmland caused by the implementation of major national construction projects, they can apply for national coordination from the State Council. The relevant provinces shall contribute the cross-province supplementary farmland funds to the central treasury according to the prescribed standards.[63]

The third measure was to introduce a mechanism of adjusting the physical interests arising from cross-regional supplementation of farmland.[64] The Central Government supports the regions that fall within the national key poverty-alleviation programs but are in possession of abundant reserves of farmland resources to engage in land arrangement in an orderly manner in an effort to increase the amount of farmland. The quotas of supplementary farmland can be re-allocated to the economically developed areas within the province which need the quotas. With the adjustments in accordance with these rules, the transaction costs between land-using organization and local governments for the sake of balancing land occupation and compensation have been significantly reduced. However, in establishing farmland reserves, applying for national coordination, and making cross-regional interest adjustments, government departments forge new transaction rules between themselves and, as a result, new transaction costs are created.

limited farmland reserve resources, which cannot supplement the farmland occupied or newly cultivated due to major construction projects, or where resources and environmental conditions severely constrain the ability to supplement farmland, can carry out the compensation of farmland in other provinces with abundant reserve of farmland resources, with the approval by the State Council.

[63] Please refer to the "Notice of the General Office of the State Council on Issuing the Measures for the National Coordination of Cross-Regional Farmland Supplementation and the Measures for the Cross-Regional Adjustment of Surplus Quotas for Urban and Rural Construction in Regulating Farmland Preservation" (GuoBanFa [2018] No. 16).

[64] The "Opinions of the CPC Central Committee and the State Council on Strengthening the Protection of Cultivated Land and Improving the Balance between Occupancy and Utilization" (ZhongFa [2017] No. 4) proposed to carry out benefit adjustment for cross-regional supplementary farmland. Under the premise of ecological conditions permitting, it supports the orderly promotion of land improvement and increases in cultivated land in national poverty-stricken areas with abundant farmland reserves. The supplementary cultivated land indicators can be adjusted to economically developed areas within the province, and the benefits from the adjustment of supplementary cultivated land indicators will be used for cultivated land protection, agricultural production, and rural economic and social development through budget arrangements by the county-level government. Provincial (autonomous region, municipality) governments should coordinate the protection of cultivated land and regional coordinated development, support areas that occupy cultivated land to provide assistance in supplementary cultivated land areas based on the payment of adjustment fees for supplementary cultivated land indicators, and stimulate the enthusiasm of supplementary cultivated land areas to protect cultivated land through various means such as industrial transfer and support for infrastructure construction.

Chapter 8
Reform of the Energy System

Two paramount factors determine the level of human energy utilization, technology and institution. In terms of energy technologies, be it the exploration and development of the primary energy or the conversion and utilization of the secondary energy, China has already developed some of the world's most cutting-edge technologies. The rapid development of the energy industry after the reform and opening-up has given strong impetus to the high-speed growth of China's economy. However, with the advent of the twenty-first century, China has frequently experienced energy supply shortages such as "power shortages," "gas shortages," and "coal shortages." For some categories of energy products, their prices are seriously mismatched with the supply and demand. Even in those cases when the prices of primary energy on the global market have plummeted, the costs of energy consumption in China remain exorbitant. Problems of this kind can hardly be attributed to China's backward conditions of energy technology or insufficiency of energy resources. The root cause must be traced to the energy system. In this chapter, an analytical framework for the energy system is proposed, and the focus of analysis is given to an institutional analysis of the two most vital industry chains in the field of energy—the coal-electricity industry chain and the oil–gas industry chain. Through this analysis, it is expected to disclose how changes in transaction costs brought about by changes in energy systems affect the supply and demand relationship.

1 Analytical Framework for the Reform of the Energy System

For the government, its primary task in energy administration and management is to ensure energy supply. Under the system of planned economy, on account of the ubiquitous "soft constraints" of budget, local governments tend to possess exceedingly

B. Fan, *The Rationale Behind Change*, https://doi.org/10.1007/978-981-97-8854-5_8

strong endogenous impulse to expand investment. Once the scale of basic construction becomes too large, it will result in nationwide shortages in the supply of coal, electricity, oil, and transportation, which will further lead to an overheated economy. The state will have to resort to necessary measures to reduce the overall scale of basic construction. Therefore, during the period of planned economy, a comprehensive plan regarding the coal, electricity, oil, and transportation was the prerequisite for formulating plans for other industrial production and basic construction. However, the seemingly meticulous plan concerning the coal, electricity, oil, and transportation failed to meet the needs of economic development and of ordinary people's livelihoods. It was often the case to provide emergency coal support and make special temporary allocations.

With the implementation of the reform and opening-up, the role played by the market in energy allocation kept increasing in considerable proportion, but the paces of reform in various energy industries were not identical. The market-oriented reform of the coal industry started relatively early, and the supply capacity grew rapidly. For a considerable period of time, the pricing mechanism demonstrated a fairly strong ability to regulate the supply-and-demand relationship. However, in recent years, an increasing number of administrative regulations have been imposed on coal mining, which has resulted in obvious constraints on coal supply. The electricity industry has been characterized by a competition pattern in which multiple entities engage in power generation and those entities belong to multiple forms of ownership. With the implementation of reform in which the power plant and the grid came to be separated, a competition mechanism was further introduced to develop the sources of electric power, which significantly alleviated the long-standing problem of power shortages that has impeded China's development. However, the traditional system of electric power, in which the power grid enterprises monopolize the purchase and the sale of electricity, has continued to exist up till this day. Obviously, electricity prices have failed to regulate the disparities in electricity's supply-and-demand relationship and "crises of power shortages" still occur from time to time. The reform of the oil and gas system has been continually promoted but the progress has been exceedingly slow. The ownership structure is not diversified, there are considerable gaps in the oil price between China's domestic market and the international market, and "gas shortages" occur periodically. The intermittent shortages of energy have kept enterprises waiting for exceedingly long time and have increased their capital cost for the sake of energy consumption.

Energy has been subjected to strict government administration since the period of planned economy, and such government control has been relaxed and tightened alternately for several times during the reform and opening-up. Up to this very day, we can still witness considerable administrative interventions. An analysis of the energy system can shed light on the fact that energy production and consumption is a matter that not only involves the transaction of rights between enterprises but also involves a large number of transactions of rights between the enterprises and the government, between the market and the government, and between different government departments. Among all those transactions, some may generate transaction costs that are necessary, but there is also a considerable part of transaction costs that could disrupt normal supply-and-demand relationship. An analysis of the energy system can be conducted according to the following framework.

The first factor in this analytical framework is the system of the property rights of the resources. Most of the primary energy sources come directly from nature. China has implemented different systems concerning the property rights of resources, including solid minerals, gaseous minerals, liquid minerals, and hydropower resources. The overall trend regarding the property rights of these resources is a transition from free allocation to paid use. During the period of planned economy, China did not acknowledge mineral resources as commodities, but as production materials that were owned by all the people. Relevant government departments were made responsible for organizing the exploration of the resources whereas the state-owned enterprises were made responsible for the mining, production, and processing of the resources according to national plans. This approach had the obvious advantage of low transaction costs, but the production scale remained small and the efficiency of resource output was low. During the reform period, China recognized the attributes of mineral resources as commodities and allowed the state-owned enterprises as well as other market entities to carry out the development of the resources. The acquisition of most mining rights underwent important changes, from free allocation and distribution during the period of planned economy gradually to paid transfer of rights upon administrative licensing. Administrative licensing is managed according to the process of first obtaining the exploration right and then the mining right. This system of managing the property rights of the resources incurred transaction costs at the very beginning of its implementation. However, compared with the value generated out of the increased number of market entities and with the revenue obtained by the state via the transfer of the resources, these transaction costs were acceptable. With the passage of time, the transaction rules for market entities to obtain exploration rights and mining rights became increasingly complicated, and the transaction costs kept rising. For instance, China manages mineral resources according to different categories of minerals. If there are different types of minerals in the land of one single geographical area, it is imperative to apply for different exploration rights and mining rights, and transaction costs will double. For another example, regarding some categories of minerals, the government has set up franchise rights for mining operations, only allowing one or two particular enterprises to engage in mining operations. Under such circumstances, other enterprises will have to incur exceedingly high institutional costs of mining transactions.

We can take coal mining as an example. Most of China's coal mines are mines of high gas concentrations. A relatively economical approach is to extract coalbed methane first and then mine the coal. However, the coalbed methane and the coal belong to different types of minerals. To mine them, it is necessary to obtain two different administrative licenses for mining at the same time. Coalbed methane mining requires franchised operations, which are virtually impossible for ordinary enterprises to apply for and obtain. Therefore, most coal companies can only mine the coal and abandon the development of the coalbed methane, thus resulting in huge wastes of resources. In other fields of primary energy, oil and gas blocks are registered and obtained by China's three major oil and gas companies, which are often called the Big Three, namely, PetroChina, SINOPEC, and CNOOC. The right to develop the hydropower of rivers is owned by hydropower development enterprises on a first-come-first-served basis. All these companies are entitled to the permanent use of such energy resources. The reform process in these fields lags far behind that in the coal field.

Under the conditions of marketization and globalization, coal, oil, and gas can rely on market mechanisms for free transaction and global allocation. Some resource-rich countries can use the revenues generated from the transfer of state-owned resources as a secondary finance. For the Chinese government which is the administrator of energy resources, to be directly involved in organizing energy production is no longer its main task; instead, its overriding mission should be to operate energy resources in such a way as to yield the proceeds that rightly belong to all the people. If this can become a new and clear consensus, for those energy resources which already require paid use, it is necessary to reduce the transaction costs for enterprises to obtain such resources. For example, in the coal mining industry, since 2019, China has tried to merge exploration rights and mining rights into a single unified category of rights, which constitutes a very encouraging and rewarding institutional exploration. For oil and gas resources as well as hydropower resources for which have not required the paid transfer, it is advisable to consider carrying out the reform oriented toward paid use. Through such a reform, more market entities can be introduced to increase the scale of primary energy supply and expand the revenue of government-operated state-owned energy resources.

The second component in this analytical framework is the industry administration. In the reform and opening-up process, the energy sector gradually abolished government-imposed quotas under the planned economy and abolished various administrative agencies in the industry, such as the Coal Department, the Petroleum Department, the Chemical Engineering Department, the Electric Power Department, and the Energy Department. For a certain period of time, the government administration of the energy industry was weakened. In recent years, however, the government administration of the energy industry has shown signs of being gradually tightened. After undergoing this process, the country's energy management has evolved from highly-centralized planned administration to decentralized planned administration, and the approach of managing the energy industry has evolved from the mode of planned management of the production quota to the mode of management characterized by the management of multiple administrative means. Correspondingly, the transaction costs between enterprises and the government have also experienced changes, from high costs to relatively low costs and then back to high costs once again.

During the period of planned economy, the planning department was responsible for formulating the production plans and allocation plans for each coal mine. Having abolished the coal production plans for many years, starting in 2004, the development and reform commission began to specify the production capacity of each coal mine.[1] The specified production capacity plan in each region must be reported to the development and reform commission, and even be reported to the State Council for approval.[2] The mining supervision department issues production plans to coal production enterprises on a quarterly or monthly basis.[3] Thus a situation worse than the planned economy develops—that the officials of coal enterprises risk criminal liabilities if they allow their coal production to exceed the stipulated capacity.[4] The contracts between the coal production enterprises and the power generation enterprises are brokered by the development and reform commission at the national conference of coal transaction and the implementation of the contracts are supervised by a special government agency. The number of generating equipment availability hours (GEAH) of the power generation enterprises must follow the power generation plans issued by the Ministry of Industry and Information Technology and by the power grid enterprises. In the case of electricity supply shortages, electricity users must follow the plan of the orderly electricity consumption formulated by the Ministry of Industry and Information Technology and the power grid enterprises. The on-grid electricity price and the sales price of power generation enterprises are determined by the development and reform commission, and any adjustment in such prices would have to seek the approval from the development and reform commission. The import of oil falls under the administration of the Ministry of Commerce, which takes the form of quota management. The planning and administration authority of the energy industry has been decentralized and distributed to various individual departments, such as the development and reform department, the department of industry and information

[1] Please refer to the "Notice of the National Development and Reform Commission on Issuing Several Provisions on the Verification of Coal Mine Production Capacity" (Development and Reform Commission [2004] No. 2544).

[2] Please refer to the "Notice of the National Development and Reform Commission on Issuing the Catalogue of Fixed Asset Investment Projects to be Reported to and Approved by the State Council (Provisional Version)" (Development and Reform Commission [2004] No. 1927).

[3] Please refer to the "Management Measures for Coal Mine Production Capacity" (State Administration of Work Safety Doc., No. 61, 2014) & (Development and Reform Commission [2006] No. 819).

[4] The Amendment XI to the Criminal Law of the People's Republic of China was implemented on March 1, 2021. A new article is added after Article 134 of the Criminal Law as Article 134-1, stipulating that (1) "If the relevant safety administration regulations are violated during production or operation and one of the following circumstances exists, which poses a real danger of causing a major accident or other serious consequences, the offender shall be sentenced to fixed-term imprisonment of not more than one year, criminal detention, or public surveillance or restriction." (2) "Any refusal to execute a decree to suspend production or operation, construction or use of relevant equipment, facilities or premises or to take immediate rectification measures to eliminate hazards due to the existence of major accident hazards as required by law, is punishable as a criminal violation." According to the "Criteria for Determining Major Accident Hazards in Coal Mines" (Decree No. 4 of the Ministry of Emergency Administration) released on November 20, 2020, Article 4 stipulates that production activities exceeding the approved production capacity can be regarded as a major accident hazard. Although the Ministry of Emergency Administration has no right to interpret the provisions contained in the Criminal Law, under the regulation of this department, coal producers generally believe that this provision can be linked with the newly revised Criminal Law and there is a risk of punishment in the case of overproduction.

technology, the commerce department, and the mining supervision department. Part of the planning and administration authority over the power generation enterprises belongs directly to the Central Government, while others belong to relevant local departments. In addition to the planned quotas, a number of other administrative measures exist in the energy industry, such as industrial policies, industry planning, emission standards, etc.

All these administration practices of the energy industry are embodied in the transaction of rights between the government and enterprises, as well as between different government departments. Once the transaction of a particular right is established as an institution, the transaction rules will become increasingly complex and transaction costs will keep escalating. Once a major gap develops between energy supply and energy demand, the production enterprises and the users cannot quickly reach an agreement, but must first go through a series of transactions between the enterprises and the government and between different government departments. For example, in the round of coal-electricity conflict that happened in 2021, when the price of coal for electricity generation spiked dramatically in August and September, the cost of coal delivered to most thermal power plants reached two to three times the breakeven point, or even higher. The production capacity of thermal power decreased, and many provinces experienced power outages. However, coal production enterprises were unable to increase supply due to limitations imposed by the government-fixed production capacities and production plans. Thanks to the coordination by the State Council, relevant government departments increased the production capacity of the coal production enterprises, adjusted production plans, and re-activated a group of coal mines that had been shut down. By November, coal prices gradually returned to normal. This process indicates that it is not that China's coal production capacity is insufficient, but that the centralized and planned administration of the industry cannot respond effectively to the changes in the market's supply-and-demand relationship.

The third component in this analytical framework is the system of ownership. Under the planned economy, almost all the enterprises which engaged in energy production and energy business were state-owned enterprises. During the reform process, some enterprises of non-public ownership found their way into the coal, electricity, and petroleum industries. In recent years, the proportion of non-public economy has once again shown a downward trend, a changing situation which is closely intertwined with the transaction costs. Energy represents a realm where there exist a large number of transactions of rights between the government and the enterprises. The transaction costs between state-owned enterprises and the government are relatively low whereas the transaction costs between the non-public enterprises and the government are relatively high. An outcome from this game of the transaction of rights is that the transaction entities suffering from higher transaction costs are eliminated while the transaction entities enjoying lower transaction costs are preserved. It was only in times of relaxed administration of the energy industry that private enterprises were able to enter the sector and achieve relatively rapid development. With the tightened administration of the energy industry, state-owned enterprises can have access to mineral resources and bank loans at lower transaction costs and pass the government inspections of production safety.

However, the behavior of state-owned enterprises does not conform to the general attributes of proper corporate behavior under the market economy. When offering explanations about the relationship between enterprises and the market, Coase pointed out that both the enterprises and the market are organizations responsible for the allocation of resources. In the market, the resource allocation is automatically adjusted under the impact of price mechanism whereas, inside an enterprise, the allocation of various resources is accomplished by the "authoritative organization" within the enterprise. The existence of allocation costs determines that they are mutually substitutive, thus the boundary of the enterprises come to be determined. In other words, when the transaction cost within the enterprise is overly high, the enterprise will remove this part of business operation and allow the market to take care of it. By contrast, when the transaction cost between the enterprises and the market becomes unbearably high, enterprises will handle this part of business operation internally. State-owned enterprises in China are responsible for accomplishing multiple goals; seeking to maximize profits has never been the single most important objective of their existence. Hence, they tend to have a greater tolerance for business operations with high internal transaction costs. As a consequence, a number of problems arise for the state-owned enterprises. They tend to become very large in scale and all-encompassing in scope whereas some might still seek to be all-encompassing in scope despite their small scale. In an atmosphere where individual initiative and contributions are not encouraged, employees are entitled to undifferentiated reward, a phenomenon which has often been vividly described as "everyone having his share from a big iron pot." In addition, they often independently operate businesses in the "third industry" and are enthusiastic about diversifying their business pattern. Finally, they are required to perform huge corporate social responsibility. These problems are ubiquitous in China's state-owned enterprises in industries such as coal, electricity, oil, and gas. In those industries, we can observe a widespread phenomenon of high transaction costs within state-owned energy enterprises and low transaction costs within private enterprises. If the ownership structure in the energy industry is increasingly dominated by a single public ownership, there is a risk of overall inefficiency in the entire industry.

The fourth component in the analytical framework is circulation. The circulation system in the coal, oil, and gas industries has also repeatedly experienced relaxation and tightening during the reform and opening-up process. When the government relaxes its administrative control over circulation, transaction costs between the government and the enterprises decrease, the market becomes increasingly active, and the magnitude of price fluctuations increases. However, price fluctuations often trigger the tightening of government control over the circulation, resulting in increased transaction costs between the enterprises and the government. For example, when coal prices rise rapidly, the coal-producing provinces would issue policies designed to restrict the transportation of coal to other provinces. In 2021, when there was a gap in the supply-and-demand relationship between coal and electricity in China, the local coal regulatory authorities in Yulin (in Shaanxi Province) and Ordos (in Inner Mongolia Autonomous Region) issued "Coal Administration Tickets" to coal mines, which were tied up with the production capacity and transportation capacity.[5] According to this ticket-based administrative measure, coal mines receive tickets from the regulatory authorities on a monthly basis and arrange for coal production, sales, and transportation according to the quantities specified in the tickets. Transaction costs in circulation are also reflected in the transaction of rights between the enterprises and monopoly industries modeled on an extensive network, such as power grids, oil and gas pipelines, and railway transportation. The network-based monopoly industries would create lower transaction costs if they provide services to users without discrimination. Conversely, if those industries use their monopolistic position to construct high thresholds for network access and network transportation, they would considerably raise the costs of their transaction with the enterprises when enterprises of electricity grids and of oil and gas pipeline network engage in the buying and selling of electricity, gas, and oil and when the railway authority imposes double-track prices on the planned and unplanned transportation capacity respectively. Currently, China's power grid enterprises are gradually withdrawing from their dominant positions as monopolistic buyers and sellers of electricity; thus, the scale of direct power transactions is expanding appreciably. On the other hand, the oil and gas pipeline networks have separated themselves from the Big Three in the oil and gas industry. However, the efficacy of the reform has not yet been fully demonstrated, and the situation of high transaction costs between enterprises and network-based monopolistic industries has not been fundamentally reversed.

The fifth factor in the analytical framework is finance and taxation. In the transition from the gratuitous use of mineral resources to the paid use of the resources, the state has levied many special taxes and fees, a measure that is entirely necessary to protect the rights and the interests of the state-owned resources. In the transactions between the enterprises and the government, the transaction costs generated by changes in the transaction rules have a significant impact on the behavior and survival of enterprises. For example, since 2017, the fees for China's exploration rights and mining rights have undergone significant changes in the way they are collected, from post-mining collection in the past to pre-mining collection at present.[6] That is to say, companies must pay the fees according to the estimated value of the mineral reserves before they can actually generate any benefits from business operations. As the actual reserves may differ from the evaluated reserves in terms of quantity, this may exacerbate the enterprise's risk of exploring and developing the mineral resources. This change in the rules has also increased the enterprise's use of the capital, and some companies have

[5] The so-called "Coal Administration Ticket" is a special kind of tickets for measuring coal sales in Yulin City, Shaanxi Province. It is printed by the Yulin City Finance Bureau and issued to enterprises by the city and county energy bureaus. The Coal Sales Administration Agency of Yulin City manages the city's coal, over-land transportation, and sales according to the "3 unified patterns" (i.e. the unified pattern of planning, the unified pattern of bills, and the unified pattern of administration system and equipment). In the Inner Mongolia Autonomous Region, the Energy Bureau of Ordos City is responsible for issuing the "Coal Administration Tickets" in areas under its jurisdiction. The bureau has a special finance & ticket division, which is responsible for organizing and supervising the printing, issuance, collection, audit, and destruction of coal administration tickets.

[6] Please refer to the "Interim Measures for the Administration of Collection of Income from Mineral Rights Transfer" (Ministry of Finance [2017] No. 35).

been unable to pay and have had to withdraw. In some areas, too low transaction costs will also make it difficult for the interests of national ownership to be fully reflected. For example, in terms of the oil and gas development, the fees for using the mining rights are only related to the area of the resources instead of to the endowment of the resources. A possible result is that the oil and gas companies may merely occupy the registered mining areas without actually mining them, thus resulting in the waste of resources.

The sixth component is investment. Like other investment projects, new construction projects in the energy industry have to be reported to local governments for administrative approval and the approval process is fraught with potential problems, such as exceedingly slow approval of land use, many repeated approvals, too many preconditions, and extremely long time spent on intermediary services. Most energy construction projects are approved by different levels of governments according to different scales. Relatively small-scale projects are approved by provincial and municipal governments, but large-scale projects must be approved by relevant departments of the Central Government. This means that in the transactions between the enterprises and the government, the transaction costs of approving small-scale projects are relatively low whereas the transaction costs of approving large-scale projects are high. Generally speaking, the scale efficiency of energy projects are quite obvious; that is, the larger the scale, the lower the unit energy consumption and pollution emissions. Setting different levels of administrative approval according to project scales often leads to the enterprises' choice of investment paths with low transaction costs. As a result, such a policy is conducive to the construction of small-scale and high-emission projects. In order to solve this problem, the state has formulated additional transaction rules regarding new construction projects of energy, including the need for capacity replacement and the need to acquire emission quotas and energy consumption quotas, etc. For example, if a coal mine submits an application for increasing production capacity, the investor of the coal mine would be required to promise that an equal amount of production capacity of old mines would be shut down. The development of new thermal power generation projects needs to be tied up with the shutting down of the installed capacity of small thermal power units. In addition, the main atmospheric pollutant emission quotas for newly-built thermal power construction projects must be balanced within a given industry and in a given region. Due to these and many other government regulations, enterprises have to pay much higher transaction costs than before to complete their investment projects.[7]

The seventh component is the level of industrial concentration. The excessively high level of industrial concentration in China's energy sectors is mainly manifested in the oil and gas sector, which is dominated by three leading state-owned enterprises, plus Shaanxi Yanchang Petroleum Group and PipeChina. As for the electric power sector, it is mainly dominated by two major power grid enterprises and several large

[7] Please refer to the "Catalogue of Administrative Review and Approval Items Published by the National Development and Reform Commission" (http://www.gov.cn/gzdt/2014-02/16/content_2605757.htm) and the "Notice of the National Development and Reform Commission on Issuing the Catalogue of Fixed Asset Investment Projects to be Reported to and Approved by the State Council (Provisional Version)" (Development and Reform Commission [2004] No. 1927).

power groups, all of which have combined to form an oligopoly. To some extent, high industrial concentration has its positive effect in being conducive to the exertion of economies of scale. However, it should also be realized that the high industrial concentration of China's energy sector is not the result of sufficient market competition, but is primarily the outcome of administrative arrangements. Since these enterprises have already divided up the market among themselves and many industries require administrative approval for market access, new market entities face higher transaction costs when they seek such market access. Therefore, the high industrial concentration in the energy sector has in some degree inhibited market competitions and reduced consumers' potential choices.

The eighth component is regulation. Paradoxically, over-regulation and under-regulation coexist in China's energy sector. The supervision imposed by various government departments on energy production capacity, output, energy consumption quotas, energy-saving levels, etc., constitutes administrative interferences in corporate autonomy, giving rise to meaningless transaction costs between the enterprises and various regulatory agencies. At the same time, in areas that do require strong regulation, such as power grids and oil and gas pipelines, special regulatory agencies have not yet been established to exercise effective management over network transportation costs; furthermore, little regulation has been imposed to facilitate non-discriminatory market access.

The final component in the analytical framework is the demand management. In recent years, China has increased and strengthened its management of the energy's demand side. This mainly includes the following measures. First, enterprises have implemented the policy of orderly consumption of electricity according to the electricity consumption sequence list developed by the Ministry of Industry and Information Technology. In addition, the government departments in charge of regulatory control have issued electricity and energy consumption quotas for some high-energy-consuming enterprises. Finally, new energy-consuming projects are subject to administrative approval within the scope of dual control targets, that is, the control over the total volume and over the magnitude of energy consumption. These measures have required enterprises to engage in transactions of rights with government departments regarding the use of energy in order to meet their production and investment demands. For the enterprises, their main transaction costs are reflected in the time of waiting for government approval. For example, when there occurred a major gap between power supply and demand across the entire country in 2021, many regions implemented the measure of orderly use of electricity, with enterprises having to "suspend production for three days and engage in production for four days" every week, or in some cases "suspend production for five days and engage in production for two days." During power outages which forced enterprises to suspend their production activities, enterprises have to pay additional wages, rent, financial costs, and compensations for the breaching of contracts. The resulting loss of business orders and missed business opportunities would be beyond calculation. For another example, many investment projects that have been formulated and planned for many years may cause investors to lose valuable market opportunities because they cannot start project construction in their seemingly endless waiting for the approval of energy consumption quotas.

Since the Keynesian revolution, major economies across the world have generally used the expansion of demands as an important means for promoting development. China has long implemented a strategy of expanding domestic demands, but man-made restrictions on energy consumption have directly suppressed the demands, impeding China's economic development due to their unreasonable nature.

2 Reform of the Entire Coal-Electricity Industry Chain

Coal represents a main proportion of energy consumption in China. Currently, coal accounts for about half of China's total energy consumption, and coal-based thermoelectric power generation accounts for nearly 70% of China's entire power generation.[8] Under the planned economy, China's supply of both coal and electricity remained gravely inadequate for a long time. After the reform and opening-up, this problem came to be alleviated. In the 1990s, there was once a surplus of coal and electricity supply in China. Since the beginning of the twenty-first century, although the total supply of coal and electricity has increased significantly, there are still periodic "coal shortages" and "power shortages," which are often called the "coal-electricity contradiction." The entire "coal-electricity" industry chain consists of three links: electricity-generating coal,[9] transportation capacity, and electric power. The upstream and downstream relationship is well-defined, the entire chain is simple, and a long-term stable supply-and-demand relationship is relatively easy to develop. Developed countries rarely experience such sharp supply-and-demand contradictions between coal and electricity as does China. It is true that China does not face constraints in terms of coal resources and power generation technology; the real problem is that the coal-electricity system is difficult to adapt to the demands of the market-oriented allocation of coal and power resources. In this chapter, by analyzing the evolution of the three systems, i.e., the systems of electricity-generating coal, electric power, and transportation capacity, as well as the impacts of relevant policies on the three cycles of coal-electricity contradictions in the new century, we can see how changes in the transaction of rights and in the transaction rules affect transaction costs and exacerbate or alleviate coal-electricity contradictions.

1. **The institutional evolution of China's coal-electricity industry chain**

During the period of planned economy, coal has to go through an entire process of production, transportation, power generation, and final consumption; both the output and the prices of all the products in this entire process were subjected to

[8] In 2020, China's total energy consumption was 4.98 billion tons of standard coal, of which coal accounted for 56.8%. In 2019, China's electricity production reached 7.50343 trillion kWh, and thermal power generation reached 5.22015 trillion kWh, accounting for 69.6% of the total power generation.

[9] "Electric coal" refers to the coal used for generating electric power. In 2018, China's coal consumption reached 3.97452 billion tons, and the intermediate consumption of coal in thermal power generation was 2.05197 billion tons, accounting for 51.6% of the entire coal consumption.

the arrangements in national plans. Every transaction between the upstream and downstream enterprises had to go through a large number of transactions of rights between the enterprises and the government, as well as between different government departments. Currently, from coal mining to electricity consumption, transactions between enterprises in the three links of coal market, transportation capacity market, and electricity market are required. However, these transactions are not entirely decided by the enterprises themselves. A large number of transactions still need to be completed through transactions between enterprises and governments or between different government departments. Exorbitant transaction costs can seriously disrupt normal price signals and the supply-and-demand relationship, and become a vital cause for coal-electricity contradictions.

(1) **The electricity-generating coal market**

The electricity-generating coal market comprised of two transaction modules: the first is the transaction between coal enterprises and the resource-managing government department whereby the coal enterprises acquire mining rights; the second is the transaction between coal enterprises and power generation enterprises whereby the coal ownership is transferred. These two modules can be divided into a series of sub-modules. Since the reform and opening-up, the coal market has experienced an evolution in which the number of transaction modules first decreased and then increased once again and, according, transaction rules were first simplified and then became complicated again. This process conforms to the trajectory of changes in the coal supply-and-demand relationship from scarcity to abundance and then back to scarcity once again.

At the beginning of the reform and opening-up, China's coal transaction preserved the practices of planned economy. After the geological department (now called the Natural Resources Department) completed its resource exploration, state-owned coal enterprises could obtain both the prospecting rights and the mining rights gratuitously. That constituted a low-cost transaction of rights between the enterprises and the government. However, since only state-owned coal enterprises were entitled to engage in coal mining, the number of transactions between the enterprises and the government was small, and the overall scale of coal mining was quite limited, a situation which proved difficult to meet the demands of economic development. After coal enterprises began their coal production, their transactions with power generation enterprises had to meet one precondition, that is, they had to first complete a considerable number of transactions of rights, such as the transaction between the enterprises and planning departments on various levels, the transaction between the planning departments and railway departments, material departments, power departments and other agencies on various levels. The coal enterprises and power generation enterprises could engage in the purchase and sales activities of the electricity-generating coal only after they had acquired the administrative approval of relevant government departments concerning the volume of transaction, the price of transaction, and the planned number of wagons for freight train transportation (please refer to Table 1). Apart from high transaction costs, this mode of operation was marred by low efficiency in matching the supply with the demand. To solve the problem of coal shortages caused by inadequate implementation of plans, the former State Economic Commission created a special coordination agency, one of whose functions was to organize emergency coal transportation to coal-deficient areas.

With the deepening of the reform of mineral resources, coal mine resources could go through paid transfer with the due administrative approval. Apart from the existing state-owned coal mines, a large number of enterprises started to engage in coal mining. Although the cost of transaction between the enterprises and the government was higher than the cost of directly granting mining rights to state-owned enterprises in the past, the scale of transaction augmented significantly, along with significant increase in the coal supply capacity. For a certain period during the 1990s, the problem of insufficient coal supply was worked out (please refer to Table 2).

Since the advent of the twenty-first century, the number of transaction modules between coal enterprises and the government in the coal mining industry has increased noticeably, including the transactions between coal enterprises and investment management departments (now development and reform departments), environmental protection departments (now ecological environment departments), land departments (now natural resource departments), and production safety supervision departments (now emergency management departments). The transaction rules in each transaction module have become increasingly complex, and the transaction costs of building new coal production capacity have increased remarkably. The transaction costs between the existing coal production capacity and these departments are also increasing. For example, some departments have raised new standards or rectification requirements for coal mines. When coal mines have to invest too much money or suspend production for too long time, they will withdraw from coal production business because they cannot afford the transaction costs. For another example, the coal mine supervision department issues production plans to coal enterprises according to the time schedule. Production beyond the plan is regarded as activities with potential production safety hazards, and the members in the top management of the enterprise risk criminal responsibilities. Furthermore, some coal management departments in the local government would issue "coal management tickets" to coal production enterprises, requiring enterprises to produce and transport coal to other provinces according to the face value of the tickets. All these measures have imposed considerable constraints on coal production capacity due to the increased transaction costs.

With the initiation of the reform and opening-up, the state abolished the direct plans imposed on the coal enterprises and power generation enterprises regarding the transaction volume and product pricing, but the so-called "shadow plans" still exist. The Development and Reform Commission would organize the National Coal Order Conference (renamed Key Coal Production and Demand Connection Conference after 2004) on an annual basis. At the conference, the transaction entities first engage in negotiations autonomously. In those cases where agreement could not be reached, the Development and Reform Commission would determine both the transaction price and the transaction volume, and industry associations would be made responsible for supervising the implementation of the arrangements. Since those contracts were not market-oriented, coal enterprises will demand price increases

Table 1 Transaction module of the coal market under the planned economy

	Transaction module		Sub-module of transaction	
Coal market	Transaction of rights	Transaction entities	Transaction of rights	Transaction entities
	Acquiring the mining right	Coal Enterprise—geological department		
	Coal output	Coal enterprise—coal regulatory department	Output plan	Coal regulatory department—planning department
				Planning department—department of material resources
				Planning department—railway department
				Planning department—department of material resources
				Planning department—electric power department
	Coal for power generation	Power enterprise—power regulatory department	Power generation plan	Electric power department—planning department
				Electric power department—regulatory departments (i.e. metallurgical department, chemical engineering department) of power-using enterprises
	Coal transaction	Coal enterprise—power enterprise	Coal transaction plan	Coal enterprise—coal regulatory department
				Coal regulatory department—planning department
				Planning department—department of material resources

(continued)

Table 1 (continued)

	Transaction module		Sub-module of transaction	
				Planning department—railway department
				Planning department—electric power department

Note It can be seen from the above table that, in order to complete transactions between coal companies and power generation companies, a series of sub-modules of transaction between coal companies, power-generation companies and government departments on the right must be completed first, which gives rise to huge transaction costs

when demand exceeds supply. If the Development and Reform Commission prohibited coal enterprises from raising prices, coal enterprises would make up for their losses with the coal of inferior quality so that the price paid by the power generation enterprises for obtaining the coal's actual calorific value would be no different from the market price. Alternatively, coal enterprises could resort to delivery delay or prioritize supplying coal to power generation enterprises that offer higher prices. Faced with this situation, power generation enterprises have to pay transaction costs arising from re-washing the inferior coal, blending coal of inferior quality with coal of superior quality, or waiting for the delayed coal.

(2) **The railway transportation capacity market**

On the spatial dimension, the production and consumption of electricity-generating coal in China are not well matched. Coal resources are abundant in the north and scarce in the south, and abundant in the west and scare in the east, mostly concentrated in the northwest regions such as Shanxi Province, Shaanxi Province, and Inner Mongolia Autonomous Region. However, the consumption of coal is mainly concentrated in regions such as the southeast coasts, the central China, and Beijing-Tianjin-Hebei region. This spatial distribution of coal has contributed to a pattern of "coal transportation from the north to the south and from the west to the east." Coal transportation involves three major transportation methods: transportation by means of highways, by railways, and by water routes. On accountant of the significant cost effectiveness of railways in long-distance and large-volume transportation, more than 60% of China's coal transportation has been undertaken by railways for a long period of time over the past.[10] During the period of planned economy, railway transportation capacity has always been a weak link in the "coal-electricity" industry

[10] The network of railway corridors includes "Seven North-South Vertical Lines and Five East-West Horizontal Lines." The "Seven North-South Vertical Lines" mainly include the Shanxi-Shaanxi-Inner Mongolia external transportation routes that cover Jiaozuo-Liuzhou Railway, Beijing-Jiulong Railway, Beijing-Guangzhou Railway, Haolebaoji-Ji'an Railway (under construction), and Baotou-Xi'an Railway. The Guizhou external transportation route covers Nanning-Kunming Railway. The Xinjiang external transportation route covers Lanzhou-Xinjiang Railway and Lanzhou-Chongqing Railway. The "Five East-West Horizontal Lines" mainly include

Table 2 Transaction module of the coal market in the late 1990s

	Transaction module		Sub-module of transaction	
Coal market	Transaction rights	Transaction entities	Transaction of rights	Transaction entities
	Acquiring the mining right	Coal enterprise—geological department		
	Coal output	Coal enterprise—planning department	Output plan	Coal regulatory department—planning department
				Planning department—railway department
				Planning department—electrical power department
	Coal for power generation	Power enterprise—planning department		
	Coal transaction	Coal enterprise—power enterprise	Coal transaction plan	Coal enterprise—planning department
				Planning department—railway department
				Planning department—electrical power department

Note After the 1990s, China gradually abolished the regulatory departments in various industrial sectors. The relevant functions were either canceled or merged into the National Development and Reform Commission and other development and reform departments (formerly planning departments). For example, the Energy Department, Textile Industry Department, and Light Industry Department were abolished in 1993; the Coal Industry Department, Machinery Industry Department, and Electronics Industry Department were abolished in 1998; and the Metallurgical Industry Bureau was abolished in 2003. The abolition and the merging of institutions served to reduce the number of sub-modules of transaction and lower the transaction costs

the Shanxi-Shaanxi-Inner Mongolia external transportation route's northern passages (Datong-Qinhuangdao Railway, Shenmu-Shuozhou-Huanghua Raiway, Mongolia-Hebei Railway, Fengtai-Shacheng-Datong Railway, Jining-Tongliao Railway, and Beijing-Yuanping Railway), central passages (Shijiazhuang–Taiyuan Railway, Handan-Changzhi Railway, central-southern Shanxi railway, and Heshun-Xingtai Railway), and southern passages (Houma-Yueshan Railway, Lanzhou-Lianyungang Railway, and Nanjing-Xi'an Railway), as well as the horizontal passages including Xiwu Railway and Bayanwula-Xinqiu Railway. Guizhou external transportation route covers the Shanghai-Kunming Railway.

chain. Since the beginning of the twenty-first century, the weak railway transportation capacity has always been a bottleneck in each of the successive coal-electricity contradictions.

After the founding of the People's Republic of China, China established the Ministry of Railways, and the railway transportation sector implemented a system of integration between administrative authorities and corporate organizations. The transportation of the electricity-generating coal from the coal enterprises to the power generation enterprises must abide by the transportation plans of the railway authorities. Such plans were the result of complicated transactions between coal enterprises, power generation enterprises, and the government authorities, with the volume and price of railway transportation being formulated all through national planning mechanisms. With the implementation of reform and opening-up, the railway authorities gradually delegated power and promoted the economic contracting responsibility system. Since the beginning of the new century, the railway sector implemented a reform of separating the government authorities from corporate organizations. In 2013, the National Railway Administration was established under the Ministry of Transport. After the Ministry of Railways was reorganized into China Railway Corporation, it was restructured into China State Railway Group Co., Ltd. (referred to as "China Railway Group").

Since the implementation of the reform, the national planning department has no longer issued mandatory transportation plans to railway enterprises. Coal enterprises and power-generating enterprises have obtained the right to engage in transactions concerning the freight wagons they need. The transactions between those two enterprises and the government during the planned economy have been changed into transactions between the enterprises and China Railway Group. In terms of the transaction rules, transportation prices are still formulated by the National Development and Reform Commission. Although the state no longer issues mandatory plans regarding transportation volume, planned management is still implemented within China Railway Group. The company's planning department collects information concerning the demands of individual enterprises for transportation vehicles, and then issues transportation plans after making necessary balances. As railway transportation prices cannot accurately reflect the changes in the supply-and-demand relationship, the plan-based transportation will inevitably cause some enterprises to pay transaction costs in the form of waiting in the case of increased coal supply.

(3) **The electricity market**

In 1997, China implemented the reform whereby government administration came to be separated from enterprise management in the electricity industry and the Ministry of Electric Power was reorganized into the State Power Corporation. A vertical and integrated pattern of management of assets and business operations was introduced, covering power generation, transmission, distribution, and supply.[11] The development of power source took the form of transactions between the State Power Corporation and the government. The transaction entities were highly limited in number and the transaction scale, which was the newly-added installed capacity of power generation annually, proved difficult to meet the needs of economic development. The sales of electric power were manifested as transactions between power companies and consumers. As there was only a single seller of electricity, electricity users had no alternative. Since electricity prices were set by the state, when the supply of electricity failed to meet demand, electricity users had to pay transaction costs for waiting, and they could not adjust the order of electricity consumption through price mechanisms. In view of those factors, China's power sector subsequently underwent two major reforms. The first was conducted in 2002 when the State Council issued a power system reform plan (referred to as "Document No. 5").[12] The second was carried out in 2015 when the CPC Central Committee and the State Council issued a new round of power system reform plan (referred to as "Document No. 9").[13] The transaction costs within the electric power system can be analyzed from the following several perspectives.

First, there is the transaction cost of power source development on the power generation side. The transaction module of power source development mainly includes transactions between power enterprises and the government, and transactions between different government departments in investment activities. With the promulgation of Document No. 5, the previous system of State Power Corporation's integration of power generation, transmission, distribution and sales, which was characterized by vertical operation and high concentration, was broken. The separation of government administration from corporate management and the separation of power plants from power grids were implemented. After the reform, the number of transaction entities for power investment increased significantly, developing a competitive pattern of five leading power generation groups and centrally-managed power generation enterprises such as Shenhua Group and China Resources Group, along with a considerable number of local, foreign-funded a swell as private power generation enterprises with multiple ownership structures. It was true that transaction costs remained roughly the same, as it was still necessary for local governments to report investment projects to the national energy management department for approval during the investment review. However, the substantial increase in transaction entities considerably expanded the overall transaction scale. Before the reform, China had 20 to 30 million kilowatts of newly installed capacity for power generation annually whereas, after the reform, this scale continued for more than ten years with

[11] Please refer to the "Notice of the State Council on the Establishment of the State Power Corporation" (State Council [1996] No. 48).

[12] Please refer to the "Notice of the State Council on Issuing the Plan for the Reform of the Power System" (State Council [2002] No. 5).

[13] The CPC Central Committee and the State Council issued the guiding document on the reform of power system "Several Opinions on Further Deepening the Reform of the Power System" (Central Committee [2015] No. 9).

an annual increase in newly installed capacity of more than 100 million kilowatts, which effectively augmented China's power supply capacity.

Second is the cost of electric power transaction. This transaction mainly includes two modules: one is the transaction between power generation enterprises and grid enterprises, and the other is the transaction between grid enterprises and power users. The reform mainly changed the transaction rules.

Document No. 5 contained the following important requirements. (1) The transaction rules between power generation enterprises and grid enterprises mainly include: power generation enterprises generate electricity according to the plans of generating equipment availability hours (GEAH) formulated by the government authorities in charge of economic operation and according to the prices formulated by the pricing authorities. Grid enterprises purchase electricity according to the on-grid electricity price formulated by the pricing authorities and allocate electricity according to the rules approved by the power regulatory authorities. (2) The transaction rules between grid enterprises and power users mainly include: grid enterprises sell electricity according to the prices formulated by the pricing authorities; there should only be one main supplier in a supply area and, in principle, users can purchase electricity only from the grid and they should not generate their own electricity or purchase electricity directly from power plants. In other words, the country's electricity is mainly purchased and sold by grid enterprises in a unified manner. Power generation enterprises often have to secure from grid enterprises more proportions of electricity to be allocated onto the grid. The amount of electricity that falls below the generating capacity and cannot be distributed onto the grid becomes a loss for power generation companies. On the other hand, power users can only purchase electricity from the grid, losing the opportunities to purchase electricity at more favorable prices from other channels and thus incurring losses in price. Since electricity prices are fixed by government authorities and the cycle of adjustment is relatively long, in the case of changes in the supply-and-demand relationship of electricity, power generation enterprises and power users have to pay transaction costs and price losses in the form of waiting for adjustments in electricity prices.

According the power system designed in Document No. 9, power grid enterprises must withdraw from their position both as the purchaser and as the seller of electricity so that power generation and consumption can be brought into direct transactions. For the power grid enterprises, their profit-making model has to face a major change, from earning the price differences between the purchasing and the selling of electricity to earning the proceeds from the transmission and distribution of electricity, that is, the revenue from the transmission of electricity through their grids. As a result, important changes happen in the transaction rules. (1) The transaction between the power generation enterprise and the power grid enterprise must follow this rule—that the power grid enterprise allocates the power generation enterprise's electricity onto the grid according to the contract between the power generation enterprise and the power consumption enterprise. (2) The transaction between the power grid enterprise and the users must following this rule—that the power grid enterprise supplies electricity to the users according to the contract between the power generation enterprise and the power consumption enterprise, and collects transmission and distribution fees contained in the electricity price. By adding a direct transaction module between the power generation entity and power consumption entity, electricity transaction is conducted directly between both parties without the intervention from government authorities. According to the power system designed in Document No. 9, government authorities would no longer formulate plans regarding the generating equipment availability hours (GEAH) or fix electricity prices, thus minimizing transaction costs between power generation enterprises, power grid enterprises, and government authorities close to zero. Power generation enterprises and electricity users can directly determine electricity prices according to market conditions, avoiding the waiting time and losses in electricity prices. Therefore, these changes in transaction rules can effectively reduce transaction costs and avoid unnecessary losses for both power generation enterprises and consumption enterprises. Admittedly, the electricity transaction system designed by Document No. 9 has not yet been fully implemented. Thirdly, there are transaction costs on the demand side of electricity. For a long time, transaction costs on the demand side of electricity have primarily been reflected in the access to electricity.[14] In recent years, new transactions of rights have taken place between new electricity users and government authorities, which mainly include the following: the measure of orderly use of electricity during tight supply-and-demand situations, the energy consumption quotas allocated to enterprises under energy consumption dual control measures, and the restrictions imposed on new energy consumption projects. These measures have led to transaction costs for companies in the form of waiting for the use of electricity and energy. The losses incurred by companies in terms of business income, market opportunities, and investment opportunities as a result of the costs of waiting are beyond estimation.

2. **An institutional analysis of the cyclical coal-electricity contradictions**

Since entering the twenty-first century, China has undergone three rounds of coal-electricity contradictions (please refer to Fig. 1). The first round was characterized by rising coal prices but delayed adjustment of on-grid electricity prices for power plants, a situation which led to general losses in the thermal power industry. The second round was characterized by sustained decline in coal prices but delayed adjustments of the prices of on-grid electricity and electricity sales. This prevented the benefits from the declined coal prices from reaching electricity consumers, who are mainly composed of industrial and commercial enterprises. The third round was characterized by severe shortages of the supply of power-generating coal and sharp rise in prices, delayed adjustments of the prices of power plants' on-grid electricity and electricity sales, and widespread losses in the entire thermal power sector. Industrial and commercial enterprises had to face large-scale power rationing and, simultaneously, face restrictions in energy use under the impact of the dual control policy on energy consumption. On the surface, the coal-electricity conflict appears to be a cyclical conflict in the supply-and-demand relationship. In essence, however, it is due to the entanglement of a large number of transactional relationships between enterprises and the government, and between different government authorities in

[14] For the related analysis, please refer to Sect. 3 of Chap. 9 in this book.

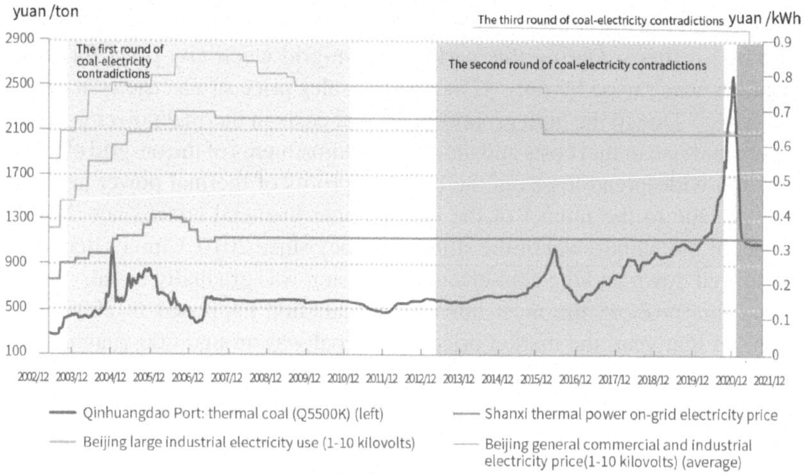

Fig. 1 Three rounds of coal-electricity contradictions since the beginning of the twenty-first century

the three transaction relations that could otherwise be autonomously market-based: the coal market, the transportation capacity market, and the electricity market. This entanglement forced enterprises to pay unnecessary transaction costs. When these transaction costs accumulate to a certain extent, a nation-wide supply-and-demand crisis would develop. However, the government authorities in charge believe that this supply-and-demand conflict is a problem in energy management that can be solved by improving management and strengthening power allocation. Therefore, administrative measures such as price adjustment, production capacity regulation, and consumption suppression have been generally adopted to deal with coal-electricity conflicts. The result is that the transaction rules between the enterprises and the government or between different government departments have become all the more complex, along with higher transaction costs. All those factors sow the seeds for the outbreak of the next round of supply-and-demand conflicts.

(1) **The first round of coal-electricity contradictions (2003–2010)**

During this period, the average price of coal in China rose from 260.5 yuan per ton in 2003 to 755 yuan per ton in June 2010, showing an increase of 1.9 times. The standard coal price of the five major power generation groups (the Big 5)[15] rose from

[15] In 2002, the reform of the power system was activated, in which the power generation assets of the State Power Corporation was divided into five major power generation groups, namely, China Huaneng Group, China Power Investment Group, China Datang Corporation, China Guodian Corporation, and China Huadian Corporation. The power generation assets held by these five groups account for half of the country's total power generation capacity. As of 2018, the total installed capacity of China Energy (established by reorganizing China Guodian Corporation and China Shenhua Group in 2017) reached 238 million kW, of China Huaneng Group 176.57 million kW, of China State Power Investment Corporation (SPIC, which was established by reorganizing the former CPI Power Engineering and State Nuclear Power Technology Company, SNPTC) 144.87

273 yuan per ton in 2003 to 656 yuan per ton in the first half of 2010, showing an increase of 1.4 times. During this period, the on-grid electricity price for thermal power plants was raised by only 32%, and the sales price of electricity was raised by only 25%.[16] Due to the high proportion of fuel costs in thermal power generation costs, the rapid rise in fuel costs and the delayed adjustments of the on-grid electricity prices led to widespread losses in the business profits of thermal power generation enterprises. Due to the impact of the international financial crisis since 2008 and the impact of the withdrawal of the stimulus policy since 2010, China's demand for energy slowed down and the coal-electricity tension was gradually eased.

During this process, the most intense contradiction happened in 2008. At the beginning of that year, the market price of the coal was around 600 yuan each ton. Within six months, the price of coal surged and was nearly 1000 yuan per ton. Nevertheless, the electricity price remained unchanged. Subsequent to this development, the state adjusted the electricity price twice in August and in September that year, with a total increase of 3.5 *fen*. In October, due to the outbreak of the international financial crisis, the coal-electricity conflict was somewhat alleviated. In 2009, coal prices remained roughly at a low level, giving the impression of having reduced the impact of the coal-electricity conflict. However, in fact, the root cause of the contradiction failed to be removed and, fairly soon, the coal-electricity conflict intensified once again. From the second half of 2009 to early 2010, coal prices exhibited an upward surge and continued to grow by more than 25%, while electricity prices remained unchanged.

In 2007, the thermal power sector experienced a profitable condition throughout the country, with a profit of 71.9 billion yuan for the whole year, with the Big 5 yielding a profit of 24.4 billion yuan. However, in 2008, the thermal power industry suffered from a loss of about 70 billion yuan, and the loss incurred by the Big 5 reached 35.6 billion yuan. In the first half of 2010, the Big 5's thermal power companies lost 4.728 billion yuan, with a loss rate as high as 56.22%. For power generation enterprises, the overall asset-liability ratio was considerably high, with the Big 5 exceeding 80%. The consequences were reflected in insufficient production and operation funds, deteriorating financial conditions, declining debt repayment ability, and severe difficulty for some enterprises even to maintain simple reproduction. The two key indicators of enterprise performance, the return on assets (ROA) and the return on equity (ROE), decreased significantly. Power generation enterprises believed that the reasons for the business losses of power plants were not only due to the impact of the economic crisis on the downstream demand but also, more importantly, due to the sharp rise in coal prices. The proportion that fuel costs accounted for in the sales revenue also increased, from around 60% in the past to 70% or 80%. The railway transportation capacity remained largely insufficient, keeping the coal

million kW, of China Datang Corporation 138.9183 million kW, of China Huadian Corporation 146 million kW (as of the end of 2017).

[16] The data concerning electricity price comes from the official website of China Electric Power News and is the arithmetic average of the benchmark electricity prices for thermal power in each region. The data on coal price comes from WIND Information.

transportation costs in a high condition. The country failed to implement the policy of coal-electricity price correlation, making it impossible to digest the factors of rising cost of power generation via corresponding price increases.

At the same time, power grid enterprises also experienced a decline in their profits. In 2008, the profit level of State Grid Corporation and Southern Power Grid Company decreased by 80% as compared with 2007. In 2009, they even began to show obvious business losses, with a loss of nearly 20 billion yuan in the first three quarters. Power grid enterprises believed that the loss could be explained by the increase in on-grid electricity prices in 2008 and by the need for grid enterprises to offer favorable prices. The National Development and Reform Commission announced that from August 20, 2008, the average on-grid electricity price for thermal power generation enterprises nationwide would be increased by 2 *fen* per kilowatt-hour whereas grid enterprises could not adjust the price of electricity that they want to sell to power users. Power grid enterprises demanded that the state should further increase the sales price of electricity and develop a mechanism for synchronously raising the on-grid electricity price and the sales price of electricity so as to reduce losses in their income.

In response to the call from power generation enterprises and grid enterprises for raising electricity prices, many electricity-consuming enterprises reported that the actual electricity prices for power users were already excessively high, even reaching the rate in some developed countries. Compared with the market demand, the supply of power generation capacity in the entire country was greater than demand, and it was reasonable for electricity prices to decline rather than to rise. Affected by the international financial crisis, many enterprises encountered exceeding difficulties in business operation. Any policy leading to price increase of electricity would further undermine the competitiveness of enterprises in the international market and may even affect the overall situation of national economy.

This round of coal-electricity contradictions came to be alleviated mainly due to the decline in the domestic and foreign demand caused by the 2008 international financial crisis and by the withdrawal of China's domestic stimulus plans after 2010. This decline in return led to a decrease in the demand for energy. In 2008, China's exports of commodities increased by 17.2% as compared with the previous year, and decreased by 16.0% in 2009. This precipitous decline in exports could be well ascribed to the global financial crisis. Although the GDP growth rate rebounded to 10.6% in 2010 as a result of stimulus policies, it started to decline year by year since then, falling to 9.6% in 2011 and further to 7.9% in 2012. The growth rate of power generation fell from 14.9% in 2007 to 5.5% in 2008, and further to 4.7% in 2012.

During this period, many administrative measures were adopted by relevant government authorities to resolve the coal-electricity tensions. These measures were all aimed at "patching up" existing policies, that is, making marginal adjustments in the rules of existing transaction modules. They exhibited obvious characteristics of path dependence. Despite the existence of coal-electricity contradictions, none of the transaction modules was restructured, and the adjustment of transaction rules only led to increased government interventions and to increased transaction costs. In the preliminary stage, transaction entities could still afford to withstand the

Table 3 Adjustments in the on-grid price and sales price of electricity in the thermal power industry from 2004 to 2010

	Timeline of adjustments	Increase in on-grid electricity price (*fen*/kWh)	Increase in sales price (*fen*/kWh)
1	January 1, 2004	0.70	0.80
2	June 15, 2004	1.71	2.20
3	May 1, 2005	1.86	2.52
4	June 30, 2006	1.39	2.50
5	July 1, 2008	2.14	2.61
6	August 20, 2008	2.00	0.00
7	November 20, 2009	0.00	2.80
	Total	9.80	13.43

Data source Edited from open sources.
Note Items in the serial numbers from 3 to 7 are the adjustments of the electricity prices since the initiation of the coal-electricity pricing linkage policy.

increased transaction costs. Therefore, these measures of marginal adjustment tended to succeed in producing certain effects on a short-term basis in some particular fields. However, with the transaction rules becoming increasingly complicated, the transaction costs incurred by transaction entities became heavier and heavier. If it had not been for the slowdown in the overall energy demand, this round of coal-electricity contradictions would have lasted longer. The administrative measures of adjustment mainly included the following two aspects.

The first is the synchronized coal-electricity pricing. In order to solve the problem of belated adjustment in the on-grid electricity prices as compared with the rise in coal prices, the National Development and Reform Commission proposed the coal-electricity linkage policy in 2004. According to this rule, the on-grid electricity price and the coal price were to be linked, so were the sales price of electricity and the price of on-grid electricity. The linkage cycle would generally last no less than six months. A coal price information system and index system was to be established, and the coal-electricity price linkage in different pricing areas according to power grid regions was to be implemented (please refer to Table 3).[17] From the end of 2004, when the coal-electricity linkage mechanism was created, to the end of 2010, coal-electricity linkage mechanism was put into operation for five times. In 2008 alone, coal-electricity pricing linkage was initiated twice. In the second linkage operation, only the on-grid electricity price was raised, and the sales price of electricity remained unchanged. In 2009, the sales price of electricity was raised whereas the on-grid electricity price remained unchanged.

Coal-electricity pricing linkage mechanism appeared to be a new policy proposed in 2004. However, in essence, it was still a form of transaction of rights between the government, the market, and the enterprises in the field of government-dominated

[17] Please refer to the "Notice on Issuing the Opinions on Establishing a Coal-Electricity Price Linkage Mechanism" (Development and Reform Commission Doc., No. 2909, 2004).

pricing. By adjusting the transaction rules, the coal-electricity pricing linkage mechanism stipulated that the price adjustment cycle should not be less than six months. This mechanism consists of two transaction modules. The first module is the transaction of rights regarding the price of on-grid electricity between the electricity market and the government's price regulatory agency, that is, the National Development and Reform Commission. Although the on-grid electricity pricing occurs between power generation enterprises and grid enterprises, it is actually a transaction of rights between the power market and the government's price regulatory agency. When there is a rise in coal price, the power market would call on the government to adjust the on-grid electricity price, and the price regulatory department would develop a price adjustment plan after making comprehensive balances. The second module is the transaction of rights between grid enterprises and the government's price regulatory agency (the National Development and Reform Commission) concerning the sales price of electricity. With the adjustment in the on-grid electricity price, grid enterprises would request the government's price regulatory department to adjust the sales price of electricity. The price regulatory department would formulate a price adjustment plan after making comprehensive balances.

Compared with the independent pricing by thermal power enterprises which purchase coal in the market according to market conditions, the adjustment in the on-grid price and the sales price of electricity is characterized by obvious belatedness and passivity. This delay and passivity arise from the time of bargaining between the market on one hand and the grid enterprises and government price regulatory department on the other. The time for waiting constitutes the transaction cost that power generation enterprises and grid enterprises have to face. While waiting, power generation enterprises cannot cover, by means of on-grid electricity prices, the increased costs due to the rise in coal prices. After the adjustment of on-grid electricity prices, power generation enterprises cannot make up for their historical losses and can, at best, only work out part of the immediate increase in costs to alleviate the coal-electricity conflict on a short-term basis. The accumulated transaction costs are converted into a source of business losses that power generation enterprises and grid enterprises have to withstand.

The second was the intervention in coal pricing. In June 2008, the National Development and Reform Commission (NDRC) issued a series of temporary intervention policies regarding coal prices.[18] More specifically, the rule was that the actual settlement price on June 19, 2008 would constitute the highest price limit for the coal supplied in that same year by coal production enterprises to power generation enterprises. The introduction of policy of price limit happened against the background of sharp rise in the price of the coal for thermal power generation at that time, and the FOB (Free on Board) price for the high-quality mixed coal from Shanxi Province at Qinhuangdao Port reached 820 yuan per ton, showing an increase of 56% as

[18] Please refer to the "Notice on Implementing Temporary Measures of Price Intervention for Power-Generating Coal" (Development and Reform Commission [2008] No. 46) and the "Notice on Further Improving Temporary Measures for Intervening in the Price of Power-Generating Coal" (Development and Reform Commission [2008] No. 248).

compared with the price at the beginning of that year. The policy of coal price intervention represented the most severe and direct measure of administrative intervention by the government in the market, signaling that the government control had spread from electricity prices to the sales prices of coal, and escalated from the shadow plans for coal production enterprises to direct administrative plans. With the implementation of the intervention measures, the mechanism of coal pricing changed from the transaction module involving the enterprises and the market to the coexistence of the transaction module between the government and the market and the transaction module between the enterprises and the market. The increasing number of transaction modules and the growing complexity of transaction rules greatly increased transaction costs, as evidenced by extreme difficulty to purchase coal, the selling of low-quality coal as high-quality coal, underground transactions, delayed delivery, etc. Coal enterprises resorted to various measures to circumvent the price intervention by the government, resulting in significantly longer time needed to achieve a balance in the supply-and-demand relationship of coal.

(2) **The second round of coal-electricity contradictions (2013–2020)**

From 2012 to 2020, as the pressure from economic downturn intensified, the demand for coal decreased, leading to a significant reduction in its price. This development resulted in improved profitability for power generation companies, thereby alleviating the traditional conflict between coal and electricity. However, the reduced coal prices failed to produce an equal decrease in the price of terminal electricity consumption. High electricity prices still affected the competitiveness of Chinese enterprises, and the contradiction between coal and electricity resurged in a new form. Here, a two-stage analysis is offered. The first stage spanned the period from 2013 to 2016, during which the price of electricity-generating coal kept declining. For four times, the National Development and Reform Commission lowered the on-grid price for coal-based electricity, with a total reduction of 7.44 *fen*/kWh. Meanwhile, in April 2015 and January 2016, the sales price of the industrial and commercial electricity and the sales price of general industrial and commercial electricity were also correspondingly reduced by 1.8 *fen*/kWh and 3 *fen*/kWh respectively. However, due to the fact that the price reduction did not cover all categories of electricity prices and all regions, the reduction in the sales-side electricity prices was less than that of on-grid electricity prices. Because of the delayed adjustment of the on-grid electricity price in response to the rise in coal price, the on-grid price and sales price of the coal-based electricity in most parts of the country remained high, roughly as high as that from 2010 to 2011 when coal prices were exceedingly high. The second stage lasted from 2016 to 2020. The country had taken measures to reduce production overcapacity in the coal industry, and the price of thermal-electricity coal rose rapidly. From 2017 to early 2021, the price fluctuated between 500 and 650 yuan per ton. In 2016, electricity prices were adjusted twice. At the beginning of the year, the average on-grid electricity price for coal-based power generation nationwide was reduced by about 3 *fen*/kWh, and the sales price of the general industrial and commercial electricity was lowered by the same amount. However, the price of industrial electricity over

315 kVA was not adjusted.[19] Another electricity price reduction happened when the preferential electricity price for producing fertilizer and other purposes was canceled. The general industrial and commercial electricity prices in 21 provinces involved in this round of price reduction were generally reduced by 1.05 *fen*/kWh on average, and the price of industrial electricity over 315kVA was generally reduced by 1.1 *fen*/kWh on average.[20] In 2017, some extra charges and funds of electric power were removed, reducing the cost of electricity for industrial and commercial enterprises by 57 billion yuan.[21] In 2018, 2019, and 2020, the average electricity price for general industrial and commercial use was continuously reduced by 10%, 10%, and 5%.

[19] In December 2015, the National Development and Reform Commission issued the "Notice on Reducing the On-Grid Electricity Price of Coal-Based Power Generation and the Price of Electricity for General Industrial and Commercial Use" (Development and Reform Commission [2015] No. 3105), which contains the following provisions. (1) The average on-grid electricity price for coal-based power generation is to be reduced by about 3 *fen* per kilowatt-hour (including tax) on a nationwide basis, and the sales price of electricity for general industrial and commercial use is to be reduced by the same amount to support ultra-low emission upgrading of coal-based power plants and renewable energy development. Special funds for the structural adjustment of industrial enterprises are also established. (2) The average sales price of electricity for general industrial and commercial use nationwide is to be reduced by about 3 *fen* per kilowatt-hour, and the price of electricity for large-scale industrial use is not adjusted to reduce the burden on small- and medium-sized enterprises. The pricing authorities in each province (including autonomous region and municipality) shall formulate and issue specific plans for adjusting on-grid prices and sales prices of electricity in their respective provinces (autonomous regions, municipalities) in accordance with the average adjustment rates specified in the attached document, and report them to our Commission to be put on record. (3) As there is still room for reducing the price of on-grid electricity produced via coal-based power generation, this can be used to create a special fund for the structural adjustment of industrial enterprises to support local placement of laid-off workers in the elimination of outmoded production capacity in coal and steel industries. It is further specified that the adjustment of electricity price will be implemented from January 1, 2016. Electricity of general industrial and commercial use refers to the use of electricity for commercial purpose and the use of electricity for industrial purpose on a small scale, with a transformer capacity below 315 kVA. The use of electricity for industrial purpose on a large scale refers to the following cases involving the transformer capacity of 315 kVA or above: (1) the use of electricity in industrial production as primary power or for smelting, baking, welding, electrolysis, electroplating, or electric heating; (2) the use of electricity for production activities of railways (including subways and light rails), shipping, trams, petroleum (natural gas, thermal power) pressurization stations; (3) the use of electricity in production activities of tap water supply, industrial experiments, electronic computing centers, garbage treatment, sewage treatment, etc. For more detailed information, please refer to "Notice of the National Development and Reform Commission on Relevant Questions Concerning the Classification Structure for Adjusting the Sales Prices of Electricity" (Development and Reform Commission [2013] No. 973).

[20] Please refer to the "National Development and Reform Commission's Briefing on Deepening the Reform of Price Mechanism and Reducing the Cost of the Real Economy," http://www.gov.cn/xinwen/2016-06/28/content_5086469.htm.

[21] Since 2017, China has adopted the policy consisting of "one reform, two reductions, and three cancellations" regarding electricity prices in order to reduce electricity costs. The "reform" refers to the second and third round of reform of the prices of electricity transmission and distribution, which helped reduce 38 billion yuan. The "two reductions" refer to the reduction of 25% in the electricity fee charged for major water conservancy projects construction and late-stage resettlement support in large- and medium-sized reservoir projects, which reached 16 billion yuan. The "three cancellations" refer to the cancellation of urban public utility surcharges collected via electricity price, the cancellation of electricity prices for electric railway loan repayment, and the cancellation

To some extent, these measures aimed at adjusting electricity prices alleviated the burden of downstream general industrial and commercial enterprises but failed to significantly reduce the burden of industrial enterprises consuming electricity over 315kVA.

The coal-electricity contradiction in this round demonstrated its usual characteristic—that the electricity price adjustment still lagged considerably behind when the coal price had already fluctuated. The precipitous drop in coal prices substantially reduced the variable costs of power generation enterprises, but this cost-lowering factor was not rendered accessible to electricity consumers. In response to the call from the electricity consumption market, the state reduced some of the sales prices and canceled some of the extra charges in electricity price. The government's regulatory authorities could not tolerate the sharp drop in coal prices and believed that the price decline was a manifestation of production overcapacity. As a result, the authorities artificially intervened into the production capacity. These policy adjustments were made under the framework of the transactions of rights between the government and the coal market, between the government and the power generation market, and between the government and the power consumption market, and they covered adjustments of the transaction rules regarding production output and price. Here, an analysis can be performed concerning the changes in transaction costs brought about by several major policies.

The first is the electricity price adjustment. The policy of coal-electricity price linkage formulated in the previous round of coal-electricity conflict was a policy design featuring one-way price increase, which did not take into account the possibility of a sharp drop in coal prices. Even when the price of coal plummeted, the adjustment of electricity's on-grid price and sales prices could be delayed. The coal-electricity price linkage policy has ceased to exist. Therefore, it could be safely asserted that this policy had already ceased to exist in reality despite its existence in name.[22] The transaction costs arising from the delay in the price adjustments were converted into the electricity cost burdens for downstream industrial and commercial enterprises, and its impact was all-pervasive. When the government's regulatory department recognized this problem, it enforced a series of measures to intervene in the sales price of electricity, which included reducing general industrial and commercial electricity prices, canceling some extra charges and funds of electricity. These

of special funds for the structural adjustment of industrial enterprise collected from power generation enterprises. These three cancellation programs involved different amounts of reduced expenditure. Urban public utility surcharges were reduced by 35 billion yuan, the electric railway loan repayment was reduced by 6 billion yuan, and the special funds for industrial enterprise structural adjustment was reduced by 39 billion yuan. Through these price-reduction measures, a total expenditure burden of 100 billion yuan was reduced.

[22] In September 2019, the State Council executive meeting decided to cancel the coal-electricity price linkage mechanism and accelerate the establishment of a market-oriented electricity pricing mechanism through reform. Starting from January 1, 2020, the benchmark on-grid electricity price mechanism will be changed to a market-oriented mechanism of "benchmark price plus floating price" by canceling the coal-electricity price linkage mechanism. The benchmark price is determined based on the current benchmark on-grid electricity price for coal-based power generation in each region, with a fluctuation range of up to 10% upward and generally not more than 15% downward.

measures reflected the adjustment of rules in the transaction between the government and the industrial and commercial enterprises. However, this change in the transaction rules was quite different from the price reduction caused by changes in market supply-and-demand relationship, which tends be the result of mutual agreement between both parties. In reducing electricity price, the government demonstrated obvious preferences of allowing or not allowing certain entities to benefit from the related price reduction. For example, in 2018, 2019, and 2020, only general industrial and commercial electricity price was reduced on the sales side whereas the price of industrial electricity over 315kVA remained constant. For another example, in 2016, while the on-grid price and the sales price of electricity were reduced, only general industrial and commercial electricity prices were reduced on the sales side, excluding the price of industrial electricity over 315 kVA. The funds derived from this part of un-reduced prices were used to establish funds for the structural adjustments in industrial enterprises to support local governments' effort to make compensations to the laid-off workers in the process of eliminating backward production capacity in coal and steel industries.[23]

The second is the reduction of production capacity in the coal industry. Since 2016, a drastic adjustment was introduced into the rules governing the coal production capacity by the government and the coal market. The plan was to reduce production capacity by about 500 million tons over a period of 3 to 5 years starting from that particular year. It was expected that, by significantly reducing the coal production capacity, the country would moderately reduce the number of coal mines. Starting in 2016, the production capacity of coal mines was re-determined on the basis of a new standard: no more than 276 working days per year, and in principle no production was to be scheduled on statutory holidays and Sundays in principle.[24] In 2019, the National Development and Reform Commission and other departments demanded that efforts should be made to accelerate the elimination of backward and unsafe coal mines. In that year, coal mines producing less than 300,000 tons per year in the four regions of China, including Shanxi Province, Shaanxi Province, the Inner Mongolia Autonomous Region, and Ningxia Autonomous Region, were generally closed. Strict regulations were imposed on the access of newly-constructed coal mines or renovated or expanded mines.[25] To comply with those rules, coal companies needed to spend time restructuring their business operations and making new investments. Companies that could afford these transaction costs might stay in business while those that could not had to withdraw from the industry. By the end of 2020, about a total of 5500 coal mines had been closed nationwide, with more than 1 billion tons of outdated

---

[23] Please refer to the "Notice on Reducing the On-Grid Electricity Price of Coal-Based Power Generation and the Price of Electricity for General Industrial and Commercial Use" (Development and Reform Commission [2015] No. 3105).

[24] Please refer to the "Opinions on Resolving Overcapacity in the Coal Industry and Achieving Sustainable Development through Poverty Alleviation" (State Council [2016] No. 7).

[25] Please refer to the "Notice on Properly Reducing Overcapacity in Key Areas in 2019" issued by National Development and Reform Commission, Ministry of Industry and Information Technology, and National Energy Administration (Development and Reform Commission [2019] No. 785).

coal production capacity eliminated on an annual basis.[26] These were merely the transaction costs for coal mine access. In addition, in their actual operation, coal mines had to produce coal according to the plans issued by the regulatory authorities of the mining industry on a quarterly or monthly basis. There were risks of criminal liability for mining beyond the production plans or exceeding the designated production capacity. In this way, transaction cost for coal mine access and the transaction cost for mining operation were merged. Although this effectively contributed to the policy objective of reducing production capacity, it also laid the foundation for the next round of coal-electricity contradictions.

(3) **The third round of coal-electricity contradictions (2021)**

The year 2021 witnessed the resurgence of the coal-electricity conflict. While thermal power enterprises suffered from large-scale losses, most provinces had to take drastic measures in using electricity, such as avoiding using electricity at the peak hour, staggering the peaks of electricity use, stopping electricity supply, or restricting the use of electricity. This round of coal-electricity conflict was both a continuation of the past conflict and a new development, whose main characteristic was an evolution from the previous supply constraint to the dual constraints of supply and demand. The supply constraint was manifested in the insufficient coal production and rapid price increase. As the cost of thermal power rose, the power plants incurred growing losses, and their willingness to generate electricity decreased, resulting in substantial power shortages. The thermal power units in many provinces could have used local coal, but now had to rely on coal transported from other provinces because of the reduction in coal production capacity in the previous stage. Due to high coal prices, coal-based power plants generally faced cost inversion, and the on-grid electricity price could not even cover fuel costs. Under the pressure of business losses, temporary maintenance of units significantly increased, the gap of power supply increased, and it became increasingly difficult to distribute electricity in a balanced manner. According to the investigations conducted by the author, as of the end of September 2021, the coal-based electricity industry in Zhejiang Province incurred an estimated business loss exceeding 10 billion yuan. The statistics from Jiangsu Province indicated that the companies affiliated to three leading power generation groups of the country, China Huaneng Group, China Resources, and China Energy, in Jiangsu Province were expected to lose 2.5 billion yuan, 2.8 billion yuan, and 1.2 billion yuan respectively for the whole year. According to data from the Inner Mongolia Autonomous Region, the thermal power companies in the western part of Inner Mongolia's power grid lost 5.5 billion yuan in the first eight months of the year whereas, in Shanxi Province, 42 main thermal power companies under the coordination of the provincial government reported a net loss of 5.4 billion yuan in the first eight months, with a loss rate of 83%.

Constraints on demand were manifested in various forms. In some regions, due to the restrictions imposed by the policy of dual energy consumption controls and

---

[26] Please refer to the article "About 5,500 Coal Mines Shut Down Nationwide," http://m.people.cn/n4/2021/0304/c1274-14869721.html.

the policy of orderly use of electricity, enterprises faced restrictions in their energy consumption and in their production output. Among the provincial-level administrative regions that were surveyed, 25 regions implemented measures of peak-staggering and power-restricting measures. Only Beijing, Shanghai, Ningxia, Hainan, Tibet, Xinjiang Autonomous Region and its Production and Construction Corps maintained a balance between the supply and demand of electricity. Constraints on demand mainly fell into two categories. The first was to implement the orderly use of electricity in response to insufficient power supply. In Guangdong Province, for example, the maximum peak-staggering load in September exceeded 20 million kilowatts, and industrial enterprises in various regions and cities were generally forced to "operate production for three days and suspend production for four days" within a single week, or even "operate for two days and suspend for five days." In Tianjin, the maximum daily measures of power balancing involved an increasing number of electricity-consuming industrial enterprises, from 24 on September 17 to 3394 on September 22. In Guangxi Province, 3103 companies participated in peak-staggering in July, and in August the maximum number reached more than 6000. In Anhui Province, starting from September 22nd, 1200 enterprises of high energy consumption were arranged to participate in the orderly use of electricity, with a maximum staggering peak load of 2.56 million kilowatts. In Hunan Province, during the peak season of summer, more than 6800 industrial enterprises were affected by the restricted use of electricity, accounting for 38% of the province's industrial enterprises above the designated size. In Liaoning Province, in order to implement the "rigid execution of external power transmission," from September 10th to the 23rd this year, a total of 10 rounds of the measures of orderly use of electricity were implemented, covering all the 14 prefecture-level cities and involving a total of 27,523 users. The second category was the orderly use of electricity and the restriction both of energy consumption and of production due to the constraints imposed by policies like the energy consumption dual controls and the related quotas. On August 17th, 2021, the National Development and Reform Commission released the "The Performance Review of Achieving Energy Consumption Dual Control Targets in Various Regions in the First Half of 2021." Concerning the reduction of energy consumption magnitude, level-1 warnings were issued to nine provincial administrative regions, level-2 warnings were issued to ten regions, and level-3 warnings were issued to eleven regions. Regarding the control of total energy consumption, level-1 warnings were issued to eight provincial administrative regions, level-2 warnings were issued to five regions, and level-3 warnings were issued to seventeen regions. The warnings covered almost the entire country. Local authorities formulated their individual measures of energy consumption dual controls. Some measures directly limited electricity use while others limited energy consumption by means of suspending production activities or restricting production capacity.

The most immediate cause of this round of coal-electricity conflict was the excessive implementation of the policy of production capacity reduction in the previous round of coal-electricity conflict. As the adjustment of coal production was not conducted according to market conditions of supply and demand but was arbitrarily planned and decided, the result was that, in the case of a coal supply shortage in the market, coal enterprises could not augment their production in a timely manner but must wait for adjustments in the state's plans. The transaction costs incurred during this waiting period would be turned into comprehensive losses for coal-electricity enterprises and comprehensive power shortages for industrial and commercial enterprises. The response measures that were adopted primarily replicated previous patterns, mainly making adjustments in the transaction rules between the government and the three other entities, that is, the coal enterprises, the power generation enterprises, and power consumers. As the transaction rules became increasingly complicated, more obvious constraints were imposed on the entire industry chain.

The first constraint was the intervention in the price of electricity-generating coal. In December 2020, in reaction to the rapid rise in coal prices, the National Development and Reform Commission required power companies to purchase coal at a price not exceeding 640 yuan/ton. If the price exceeded that rate, it must be reported individually to the National Development and Reform Commission. In October 2021, the Pricing Department of the National Development and Reform Commission developed specific measures at a special session to intervene in coal prices. The standard price limit was that the benchmark price of power coal at the mine site was uniformly formulated by the National Development and Reform Commission, with a tax-containing price of 440 yuan/ton and a maximum floating rate of 20%, that is, 528 yuan/ton.[27] Meanwhile, government authorities tightened interventions in the long-term coal agreements, requiring both the supply side and the demand side to reach agreements according to the guidelines developed by the regulatory authorities, who in return would supervise the implementation of the agreements.[28] The previous market-oriented electricity and coal transactions were restored to the transaction module between the government and the coal enterprises according to the government-fixed prices. This measure was very similar to the practice during the first round of coal-electricity conflict.

---

[27] Please refer to the "National Development and Reform Commission Responding to the News of Setting Price Ceiling on Power-generating Coal: Specific Measures for Intervening in Coal Prices are Still under Study." https://baijiahao.baidu.com/s?id=1714862857433872256&wfr=spider&for=pc.

[28] Here, the long-term contract of power-generating coal in 2021 can be cited as an example. The "Notice of the General Office of the National Development and Reform Commission on Properly Managing the Signing and Implementation of Medium- and Long-Term Coal Contracts in 2021" (Development and Reform Commission Office, No. 902, 2020) requires that if both supply and demand parties can reach a consensus on price in their medium- and long-term contracts, the contracts shall be implemented according to the agreement that both parties have reached. If a consensus cannot be reached, the coal price will be determined according to the principle of "benchmark price plus floating price." As for the benchmark price, the benchmark price of coal transported over water is to be determined first through consultation between both parties. If they cannot reach an agreement, the price will have to follow the rates in 2020. The benchmark price of the coal transported directly via railway should be determined by two factors, the average on-site coal price (that is, the benchmark price of coal transported over water whose transportation and miscellaneous other expenses have been deduced), and the average monthly transaction price of both supply and demand parties in 2020, with each factor accounting for 50% weight. As for floating prices, the floating prices of the coal transported over water and the coal transported directly via railway can be comprehensively determined according to the Bohai Rim Coal Price Index, CCTD Coal Price Index at Qinhuangdao Port, and China Coastal Coal Procurement Price Index.

The second constraint was the intervention in electricity price. As in the past two rounds of the coal-electricity contradictions, the state tried to remove the factors triggering changes in power plants' cost as a result of the fluctuating coal prices by adjusting electricity prices. On October 11, 2021, the National Development and Reform Commission updated its decision. Previously, the range of the fluctuations for the market transaction prices of the coal-generated electricity included the upper limit of no more than 10% and lower limit (in principle) of no more than 15%. In the updated policy, the range of fluctuations was no more than 20% in principle, both for the upper limit and the lower limit, and for the enterprises of high energy consumption, the market transaction price of electricity would not be subjected to an upper limit increase of 20%.[29] Essentially speaking, these measures had no difference from the past adjustments of transaction rules between thermal power companies and grid companies or between grid companies and end users.

To fundamentally solve the problem of exorbitant transaction costs caused by delayed adjustments in electricity price, it is imperative to establish a transaction module that allows direct transactions between power generation companies and power users. In seeking to address this round of coal-electricity tension, while continuing to make price adjustments via administrative measures, the state has been taking steps to create new transaction modules. The National Development and Reform Commission required that all industrial and commercial users across the country be encouraged to enter the electricity market by purchasing electricity at market prices. The catalogue of the sales prices of electricity for the industrial and commercial sector was to be annulled.[30] Of course, the establishment of a new transaction module has merely been proposed as a future vision, and it will take quite some time before it can be fully implemented.

The third constraint involves the demand-side management. The orderly use of electricity[31] seems to be a transaction rule between grid companies and power users, but in actuality what it reflects is a transaction of rights between the government and

[29] Please refer to the "Notice of the National Development and Reform Commission on Further Deepening the Market-oriented Reform of On-grid Electricity Prices for Coal-based Power Generation" (Development and Reform Commission [2021] No. 1439).

[30] Users who have not yet entered the market should all enter if they are 10 kV and above. Other users should also enter the market as soon as possible. For users who have participated in market transactions and adopted the agent service of electricity purchase via power grid enterprises, their prices shall be implemented at 1.5 times the price that power grid enterprises offer to other users in their agent service of electricity purchase. For more detailed information, please refer to the "Notice of the National Development and Reform Commission on Further Deepening the Market-oriented Reform of On-grid Electricity Prices for Coal-based Power Generation" (Development and Reform Commission [2021] No. 1439).

[31] The term "orderly use of electricity" refers to a mode of managing the use of electricity by lawfully controlling part of the electricity demand through administrative measures, economic means, and technical methods to maintain a stable order of the supply and demand in cases of insufficient power supply and emergencies. Please refer to the "Notice of the National Development and Reform Commission on Issuing the "Administration Measures of the Orderly Use of Electricity" (Development and Reform Commission [2011] No. 832).

the electricity consumption market. When power supply is insufficient, the government develops an order of priorities in power consumption based on its own judgment of the relative importance of the industries and enterprises, and grid companies are made responsible for the actual implementation of the policy. For some enterprises, their use of electricity is guaranteed whereas for others they have to pay transaction costs in the form of waiting. In the absence of a power market, that is, when there is no direct transaction module between power generation companies and power users, the latter cannot purchase electricity at high prices from power generation companies in times of scarcity of electricity resources. The policy of the orderly use of electricity has gradually evolved from an emergency measure to deal with power shortages to a means employed by the government to regulate diverse industries. Changes in transaction rules have substantially increased the transaction costs between the government and the market in terms of the transaction of rights in using electricity.

3. **The spreading of constraints in the coal-electricity industry chain: from a local segment to the entire industry chain**

Here it would be useful to make a summary concerning the transaction modules and main sub-modules of the "coal-electricity" industry chain (please refer to Table 4). In undergoing three rounds of coal-electricity contradictions, the government has mainly responded by adjusting transaction rules within the existing institutional framework. In the first round of coal-electricity contradictions, rules were adjusted in the two sub-modules of the electricity transaction module, namely, the on-grid electricity price and the sales price of electricity. Apart from that, rules were adjusted in the two sub-modules of the coal transaction module, namely, the transaction volume and the transaction price. In the second round of coal-electricity contradictions, the adjustments of the rules for the on-grid price and the sales price of electricity in the previous round of coal-electricity contradictions was repeated, and a new measure was added to adjust the rules contained in the transaction module of coal production capacity. In the third round of coal-electricity contradictions, the adjustments of the rules for electricity's on-grid price, sales price, coal production capacity, and coal transaction in the previous two rounds of coal-electricity contradictions were repeated. The newly-added measure was to adjust the rules for the orderly use of electricity and power consumption quotas.

A careful examination of this process indicates that, in response to coal-electricity contradictions, the regulatory measures adopted by the government exhibit important changes. Instead of the previous two transaction modules, now there are three transaction modules; and rather than the previous four sub-modules of transaction, there are currently seven sub-modules of transaction. More and more transactions between enterprises require that transaction costs between enterprises and the government and between different government departments be paid in the first place. The government's regulation of the coal-electricity industry chain has spread from the supply side to the demand side, from constraints on particular segments to constraints on the entire industry chain. Coal and electricity resources have become increasingly allocated by means of administrative decrees of the government authorities. The entire

Table 4 The transaction modules and sub-modules in the "coal-electricity" industry chain

	Transaction modules		Sub-modules of transaction	
Coal market	Transaction rights	Transaction entities	Transaction rights	Transaction entities
	Acquiring mining right	Coal enterprise—government department in resources administration		
	Coal production output	Coal enterprise—mining regulatory authorities		
	Coal transaction	Coal enterprise—power generation enterprise	Coal transaction volume	Coal enterprise—the development & reform department
			Coal transaction price	Coal enterprise—the development & reform department
Railway transportation capacity market	Transportation plan	Enterprise—state-owned railway company		
Electric power market	Power source development	Power generation enterprise—government	Project review & approval	Government—government
	Electric power transaction	Power generation enterprise—grid enterprise	Generating equipment availability hours (GEAH)	Power generation enterprise—the department of industry and information technology
			Price of on-grid electricity	Power generation enterprise—the development & reform department
		Grid enterprise—electricity users	Sales price of electricity	Grid enterprise—the development & reform department
				Electricity users—the development & reform department
			Orderly use of electricity (right to electricity)	Electricity users—the department of economic operation regulation (the development & reform department or the department of industry and information technology)

(continued)

Table 4 (continued)

	Transaction modules		Sub-modules of transaction	
			Electricity consumption quotas	Electricity users—the development & reform department
		Power generation enterprise—electricity users	Allocation of electricity	Power generation enterprise & electricity users—grid enterprise

industry chain presents signs of moving toward direct planning, which runs counter to the trend of reform in which the market plays a decisive role in the allocation of resources.

3 Reform of the Entire Oil–Gas Industry Chain

Compared with coal, oil and gas represent an energy source of considerably superior quality. Since the 1950s, oil and gas have gradually replaced coal as the main energy source in the world's primary energy. Developed countries have mostly completed their transition from the era of coal to the era of oil and gas. After the founding of the People's Republic of China, significant progress has been made in the petroleum and chemical-engineering industry, providing strong support for China's economic and social development. However, by international standards, China's oil and gas consumption ratio is relatively low in primary energy consumption, and it is rather costly to produce and utilize oil and gas. The transition from the era of coal to the era of oil and gas has not yet been completed (please refer to Fig. 2). Institutionally, the transaction costs to gain market access in China's oil and gas business are considerably high, and the number of market entities has been slow to grow. The oil and gas transactions between enterprises contain a large number of transactions between the enterprises and the government, and between the market and the government. All the accumulated transaction costs have found their way into the supply capacity and prices of oil and gas. With the shale gas revolution in the United States, a new landscape of the world's oil and gas supply has developed, characterized by supply by multiple regions and by over-supply. However, the Chinese consumers have found it exceedingly difficult to share in a timely manner the benefits generated out of the continuous decline in international oil and gas prices. After years of reform of the oil and gas system, transaction costs have been reduced in some transaction links in the oil and gas industry chain, but high transaction costs are still preserved in some links. The oil and gas industry chain has come to a crossroad, with the possibility of either evolving toward a fully market-oriented industry chain or returning to a fully planned condition of the entire industry chain due to the spreading of constraints.

1. **Key problems**

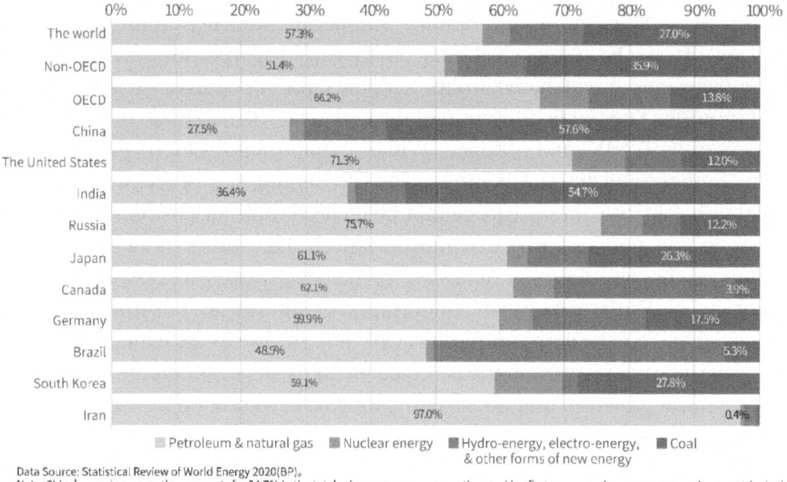

Data Source: Statistical Review of World Energy 2020(BP)。
Note: China' s coal consumption accounts for 54.7% in the total primary energy consumption, ranking first among major energy-consuming countries in the world. It can be said that China is still in the coal era. Developed countries entered the oil and gas era very early. The proportion of oil and gas consumption in OECO countries' primary energy consumption is as high as 66.2%, while coal accounts for only 13.8%.

Fig. 2 The structure of primary energy consumption by top 10 countries in the world in 2019

For a long time in the past, China made significant efforts to enhance its petroleum and natural gas self-sufficiency, but the result has not been very encouraging in actuality. In 1993, China became a net oil importer and, ever since then, imports and dependence on external sources have kept rising. In 2020, China imported 542 million tons of crude oil, and its external dependence reached as high as 73.5%.[32] The decline in the domestic oil and gas security can be directly explained by the low exploration rates of petroleum and conventional natural gas, which are only 30% and 14% respectively.[33] These two rates indicate that China has merely gone beyond the early stage of petroleum exploration and in the field of gas exploration China is still in the preliminary stage.[34] They remain far below the average rates of oil and gas exploration in other parts of the world, which are about 40% to 50%.

While the growth of domestic oil and gas production remained sluggish, the importation of international oil and gas has come under considerable restriction. Although crude oil is currently the largest freely-traded commodity in the world, only a limited number of enterprises in China are licensed to engage in its transaction. In terms of importation of crude oil, China still implements the management pattern of state-owned trade, allowing only an extremely small amount of non-state-owned trade. The total amount of crude oil imported by five state-owned enterprises, namely CNPC

---

[32] *Report on the Development of China's Domestic Petroleum Circulation Industry in 2020,* http://www.mofcom.gov.cn/article/tongjiziliao/sjtj/jsc/202105/20210503063494.shtml.

[33] China Geological Survey Bureau, *100 Achievements in China's Geological Survey*, Geological Publishing House, 2016 edition, p. 31.

[34] According to international standards, an exploration stage can be designated as "early" if the degree of exploration is less than 30%, as "intermediate" if the degree of exploration is between 30% and 60%, and as "final" if the degree of exploration is greater than 60%.

(China National Petroleum Corporation), Sinopec (China Petroleum & Chemical Corporation), CNOOC (China National Offshore Oil Corporation), Zhuhai Zhenrong Company, and SinoChem Group, accounts for more than 90% of the total crude oil imports. The crude oil imported through state-owned trade must be refined and processed by CNPC and Sinopec. Without state-owned enterprises' necessary documents concerning the production plans of refining and processing, the crude oil imported by private enterprises cannot be cleared through customs, and railway authorities would not authorize its transportation. The result of this institutional arrangement is that entities other than state-owned enterprises are restricted from the oil market access. With respect to the importation of natural gas, it is true that the state has not issued any clear-cut prohibitions; nevertheless, due to the exclusive nature of import infrastructure, private enterprises face virtually insurmountable difficulties in importing natural gas from abroad. Usually, they have to rely on the "Big 3" oil and gas companies to import gas on their behalf.

Regarding the wholesale and retail business, the state has granted Sinopec and CNPC the exclusive right to engage in the wholesale and retail of finished oil products. All finished oil products produced by refineries across the country must be sold only by the wholesale enterprises of Sinopec and CNPC. Refineries themselves are not allowed to sell finished oil products. All the new gas stations are constructed at the total expense of Sinopec and CNPC, who are the exclusive share-holders of these stations. Although this tight control has been somehow relaxed in recent years, Yanchang Oil and Gas Company has entered the retail industry, and CNPC, Sinopec, and CNOOC have initiated cooperation with private enterprises, these state-owned enterprises still dominate the vast majority of the market share in the wholesale and retail business, making it difficult for other market entities to enter freely.

2. **Oil and gas exploration and development**

Oil and gas exploration and development primarily consist of two transaction modules, which can be listed according to the order they appear. The first module contains the transaction between the oil–gas enterprises and the government authorities in charge of resources administration whereby the enterprises acquire the exploration right and the mining right. The second module pertains to the transaction between the oil–gas enterprises and the government authorities in charge of resources administration whereby the enterprises acquire the right to explore for new mineral resources. At the beginning of the reform and opening-up, China's exploration, development, and sales of oil and gas resources were all carried out according to national plans. Within this system, the former Ministry of Geology (now the Ministry of Natural Resources) was responsible for exploring petroleum resources, and the former Ministry of Petroleum Industry was responsible for more in-depth petroleum exploration and development. Those two government agencies were typical examples of the mixture of government administration and corporate operation. After the 1980s, China undertook reforms of the oil and gas resource system to separate the government from enterprises. CNPC, Sinopec, and CNOOC (usually referred to as the "Big 3″ or "Three Giants") were established as leading entities of oil and gas exploration and development. The "Three Giants" acquired the mine exploration right and mining right by entering deals with the former Ministry of Geology. The key transaction rules include the following. The first is the registration and the transfer of mining rights. China implements the mine right registration system, which allows a few state-owned enterprises to acquire the right to oil and gas exploration free of charge through "prerequisite application." The second is the low cost of holding the exploration and mining rights. For the registered exploration right, only a maximum of 500 yuan/square kilometer per year is required as the fee for wielding the exploration right. On the other hand, the fee for using the mining right is paid annually according to the size of the mining area, with a rate of 1000 yuan/square kilometer per year.[35] The consequence produced by these transaction rules is that only a very limited number of enterprises (currently only the Three Giants and Yanchang Petroleum Group) can acquire and hold the oil and gas mining rights at relatively low transaction costs, who hold possession of the oil and gas resources without actually developing them. Due to the very limited number of transactions between the enterprises and the government, there has been very slow growth in the overall scale of oil and gas development, thus limiting the increase in domestic supply.

With the passage of time, changes were introduced into the transaction rules in 1998. First, potential oil and gas companies can apply to the State Council for the administrative approval of establishment. Second, to apply for the registration of the mine exploration right, it is necessary to obtain exploration qualification in the first place.[36] According to these new rules, exploration qualification has become a prerequisite and in the oil and gas field, only the Three Giants and Yanchang Petroleum Group have the exploration qualification. This qualification also requires the review and approval by the State Council. Enterprises which are latecomers generally do not have the condition to apply for the survey and exploration qualifications, nor can they establish survey and exploration enterprises before applying for the qualifications. Although the conditions for the market access for oil and gas exploration and development have been relaxed, the market entities other than the Three Giants and Yanchang Petroleum Group will have to incur unimaginably high transaction costs, which are totally beyond the affordability of private enterprises.

Witnessing the success of the shale gas revolution in North America, China has also taken steps to promote the development of shale gas. In order to allow new market entities other than the Three Giants and Yanchang Petroleum Group to gain market access, the former national land and resources department established shale gas as a new mineral resource. The transfer of this mining right came to constitute a new transaction module, and its main transaction rules can be summarized as follows. Firstly, the mine exploration right is transferred by means of bidding, auction, and public listing and the highest bidder wins the right. Secondly, it is necessary for

---

[35] Please refer to the "Administration Measures for Mineral Resource Mining Registration" (State Council Executive Order, No. 241).

[36] As stipulated in the "Administration Measures on Registering Mineral Resource Exploration Blocks," an enterprise applying for exploration of oil and natural gas must also submit documents indicating the approval by the State Council regarding the establishment of an oil company or conducting oil and natural gas exploration, in addition to the certificate of legal person qualification of the applicant.

a potential entity to have the qualification to explore petroleum and natural gas or gaseous mineral resources or, in the absence of such qualification, to cooperate with enterprises in possession of such qualifications.[37] Thirdly, the enterprise applying for the mine exploration right must make formal pledges to the former Ministry of Land and Resources concerning exploration responsibilities and obligations, including capital input, physical workload, exploration process, comprehensive survey, block exit, and the willingness to be held responsible for the violation of contracts and acts of dishonesty. Fourthly, the Three Giants and Yanchang Petroleum Group must withdraw from the shale gas mining areas if they take no action to develop the resource after having acquired their mining right. The Ministry of Land and Resources will have to set up the exploration right of shale gas mines.

Compared with the acquisition of the traditional rights of oil and gas exploration and development, the transfer of the shale gas mining right is relatively easy, as the applicants face less stringent requirements to obtain necessary qualifications, thus lowering transaction costs of market access. However, the potential holders of the shale gas mining rights have to make higher commitments than those required of the Three Giants in registering the right to occupy the mining areas, thus reflecting high transaction costs for holding the shale gas mining rights. Since the Three Giants have already registered the occupation of most, if not all, of the shale gas blocks with sound conditions, if they are made to withdraw from those blocks, the Ministry of Land and Resources would have to engage in a new transaction of rights with the Three Giants. Then, the Ministry will have to set up mining rights once again and have them transferred to other market entities. This inevitably means higher transaction costs. These transaction rules, formulated in order to attract other market entities, ignore the fact that the transaction costs necessary to implement those rules are beyond the affordability of those other entities. This factor constitutes the main institutional reason why China's newly established shale gas mining rights have failed to produce the desired results (please refer to Table 5).

3. **Transportation via pipeline networks**

The oil and gas pipeline networks fall into two categories, the long-distance trunk pipeline network and the urban gas pipeline network. Here, we mainly focus on the transportation via long-distance trunk pipeline network. In 1998, when the State Council re-structured the national petroleum industry, part of the upstream business was allocated to Sinopec whereas part of the downstream business was allocated to PetroChina. Among all the businesses, PetroChina was made responsible for managing a larger proportion of oil and gas trunk pipelines. Each of the two corporations succeeded in establishing a mode of integrated vertical management. At that time, some experts suggested that the management of pipelines should be independent of petroleum companies. However, due to the small scale of pipeline network

[37] Please refer to the "Notice of the Ministry of Land and Resources on Strengthening the Exploration, Development, Supervision, and Administration of Shale Gas Resources" (Ministry of Land and Resources [2012] No. 159).

Table 5 Diagram of China's shale gas development and transaction model

Transaction entities	Mining rights		
	Transaction rules	Transaction costs	
Three giants—Ministry of Natural Resources	1. Registration	Low	Low
	2. The fee to use the mine exploration right	Low	Low
	3. The fee to use the mining right	Low	Low
		$\sum t$	$\sum C$
Transaction entities	Exploration and development access		
	Transaction rules	Transaction costs	
Enterprises—The State Council	1. Oil & gas exploration qualification	Very high	
		$\sum t$	$\sum P$
Transaction entities	Exploration and development access of new mineral resources		
	Transaction rules	Transaction costs	
Enterprises—Ministry of Natural Resources	1. Oil & gas exploration qualification or cooperation	Relatively high	Relatively high
		$\sum t$	$\sum P$

construction in China, pipeline assets were still retained within several leading corporations and it was believed that the integrated management of the upstream, middlestream, and downstream business would facilitate the rapid growth of enterprises and could ensure those enterprises' strong investment in pipeline network construction. As of the end of 2020, China built a total of 144,000 km of long-distance oil and gas pipelines. This figure included approximately 86,000 km of natural gas pipelines, approximately 29,000 km of crude oil pipelines, and approximately 29,000 km of refined oil pipelines.[38] Before the institutional reform of the oil and gas industry in 2017, the long-distance pipeline networks were primarily controlled by the Three Giants, who operated their businesses independently of one another.

There have been three transaction modules in the field of oil and gas transportation via long-distance pipeline networks. (1) The pipeline network companies of the Three Giants provide their internal subsidiaries with pipeline transportation services. (2) The pipeline network companies of the Three Giants provide other market entities with pipeline transportation services. (3) After the establishment of the independent PipeChina, it provides pipeline transportation services to various market entities.

With the integrated operation of the upstream and downstream business, oil and gas pipeline transportation services become part of a corporation's internal transaction and are subject to the arrangements under the corporation's overall plans. The cost of this internal transaction can also be regarded as management expenses.

[38] Gao Peng, Gao Zhenyu, Zhao Shangxin, and Liu Guangren, "New Progress in China's Oil and Gas Pipeline Construction in 2020," *International Petroleum Economics*, Issue 3, 2021.

After 1992, China significantly reduced the categories of oil and gas products that were subjected to government planning, and the number of market entities in the oil and gas industry increased. More and more enterprises have managed to obtain licenses for operating oil and gas business, and there has been increasing market demand for pipeline transportation. For example, private enterprises purchase LNG from abroad and other state-owned enterprises produce natural gas by means of coal gasification projects. This portion of LNG and natural gas needs to be transported via pipeline network. As a result, in addition to the existing internal transactions within the Three Giants, a new transaction module has been created consisting of the transactions between the pipeline network companies affiliated to the Three Giants and the market consignors. For the market consignors, in order to obtain pipeline transportation services from the Three Giants, they need to submit applications to them. The pipeline network companies affiliated to the Three Giants would naturally prioritize the satisfaction of the needs of internal transportation business and would not treat external commissions and internal transportation plans on an equal basis. For the consignors, in addition to paying pipeline transportation fees, they need to pay additional transaction costs, that is, the time for waiting.

In 2019, the state stripped the Three Giants of their transportation business related to pipeline network and established the national pipeline company PipeChina. A third transaction module of pipeline transportation came to be developed, and PipeChina engages in transactions with consignors. With the creation of PipeChina, the existing pipeline transportation services within the Three Giants have changed from internal transactions to external transactions, and those three corporations are placed on the equal footing with other market entities. They are all consignors of pipeline transportation services whom PipeChina must treat equally. For consignors other than the Three Giants, their transaction costs could be expected to decrease drastically as compared to those before the reform.

4. **The circulation system**

Since the reform and opening-up, the state has tried to impose administrative control, tightening and relaxing alternately over time, over the circulation of oil and gas, gradually evolving from completely planned allocation to market-oriented allocation of resources. The transaction rules for engaging in the oil and gas circulation business have also gradually changed, from strict market access to relatively free access. The costs of transaction between the enterprises and the government have gradually decreased. However, the transactions between the government and enterprises have been preserved to some extent and oil and gas, as commodities, are not yet fully free-flowing.

(1) **The crude oil**

There are three transaction modules regarding the crude oil circulation. (1) Enterprises engage in transactions with the government to secure market access. (2) Enterprises engage in transactions with government authorities such as commerce department or the development and reform department to obtain import quotas. (3) The government engages in the transaction of rights with the market and enterprises regarding pricing.

The transaction rules for market access have gone through a complicated process, passing from simplicity to complexity and then back to simplicity. In the crude oil sector, China has long implemented a pattern of planned circulation, characterized by unified purchasing and unified sales, where there was no separation between the government and enterprises, and market access was distributed entirely according to government plans. Like other products in the planned economy, to participate in the circulation of the crude oil, enterprises could engage in transactions with one another only after a considerable number of transactions had been completed between the government and enterprises, and among various government departments themselves. It would take a long time for oil companies to secure crude oil, and transaction costs were exceedingly high. After the reform and opening-up began, China started to develop a crude oil circulation market. Enterprises engaged in crude oil circulation business can operate their business without having to apply for administrative approval from the government. The number of market entities has increased substantially while the time required for oil companies to obtain crude oil has been shortened and transaction costs reduced. However, in 1994, crude oil procurement was monopolized by Sinopec,[39] and the threshold for crude oil circulation access was drastically raised. Under such circumstances, it was very difficult for market entities to acquire access to crude oil circulation, the number of operating entities decreased, and the level of difficulty for oil companies to acquire crude oil increased again. In 2001, as upon joining the World Trade Organization (WTO), China pledged to open up its crude oil circulation market. In 2006, the transaction rules were adjusted. Enterprises applying for crude oil sales must have a registered capital of no less than 100 million yuan, with long-term stable channels of crude oil supply and sales and an oil storage capacity of no less than 200,000 cubic meters.[40] In 2015, the transaction

[39] Please refer to the "Notice of the State Council on Approving and Issuing the Opinions by the State Planning Commission and the State Economic and Trade Commission on the Reform of the Crude Oil and Refined Oil Circulation System" (State Council [1994] No. 21).

[40] "Measures of Crude Oil Market Administration" (Executive Order by Ministry of Commerce [2006] No. 24) stipulates in Article 6 that enterprises applying for crude oil sales license should meet the following conditions. 1. The applicant must have the status of a Chinese corporate legal person with a registered capital of not less than RMB 100 million. 2. The applicant must have a long-term and stable crude oil supply channel. More specifically, this supply channel refers to: (1) crude oil mining enterprises that have obtained the "Petroleum Mining License" approved by the State Council and are generating real production output; or (2) import enterprises that possess business qualifications of crude oil import, with an annual import volume of more than 500,000 tons; or (3) signing a crude oil supply agreement for more than one year with an enterprise which meets the requirements of both Clause (1) and Clause (2) in this section, with the oil supply commensurate with the business scale of the applicant. 3. The applicant must have a long-term, stable, and legal sales channel of crude oil. 4. The applicant must have an oil storage capacity of not less than 200,000 cubic meters, and the construction of oil storage facilities complies with local urban and rural planning, oil storage physical layout planning, and has passed the evaluation by administrative departments in land resources, planning construction, safety supervision, fire protection for public security, environmental protection, meteorology, quality supervision, and other related areas.

rules were adjusted again and the requirement of registered capital was removed.[41] In July 2020, China abolished the qualification restrictions on crude oil circulation access, and various market entities such as private enterprises and companies of foreign capital can all engage in crude oil circulation business.[42]

The transaction rules governing the enterprises' attempts to acquire the right for obtaining trade quotas have become increasingly simplified. With the relaxation of the otherwise stringent transaction rules, transaction costs have been reduced. At the beginning of the reform and opening-up, China's crude oil trade was exclusively monopolized by Sinochem Corporation. Other companies needed to import crude oil through Sinochem Corporation. During that period, transactions of the crude oil import quotas were conducted between the state-owned oil and gas companies and Sinochem Corporation. As a result, China's domestic oil companies, apart from transactions with their international counterparts which could be conducted directly, had to pay additional transaction costs in purchasing and waiting for import quotas. After the 1990s, an increasing number of state-owned companies acquired the crude oil trade monopolies, creating a pattern in which five state-owned enterprises, namely, CNPC, Sinopec, CNOOC, Zhuhai Zhenrong Company, and Sinochem Group, are made responsible for China's petroleum import and export business. Enterprises which use imported crude oil could have more choices, the difficulty for them to obtain quotas decreased, and transaction costs were somehow lowered as compared with before. After joining the World Trade Organization (WTO), China gradually relaxed its state-controlled crude oil trade and allowed a certain number of non-state trade entities to engage in import business apart from the state-managed trade. Private enterprises which engage in crude oil import business must abide by the following rules. Firstly, they must obtain non-state trade import qualifications approved by the Ministry of Commerce. Secondly, they must obtain the qualifications to use imported crude oil approved by the National Development and Reform Commission. Thirdly, they must obtain a production scheduling plan and purchase agreements from CNPC and Sinopec (that is, written documents indicating that oil refining enterprises will use crude oil of non-state quotas and arrangements have been made for production). In order to meet these three conditions, private enterprises need to spend exceedingly long time waiting and invest large amounts of fund. Faced with such forbidding expenses, private enterprises often have to give up importing crude oil on their own. Therefore, China's current crude oil trade is still dominated by state-controlled trade, and oil companies need to pay additional transaction costs to intermediaries for importing crude oil.

The pricing of crude oil requires the transaction of rights between the market and the government. Although the transaction rules have been relaxed, transaction costs still remain overly high. At the beginning of the reform and opening-up, China still relied primarily on planned economy and organized crude oil production according to

[41] Please refer to the "Measures of Crude Oil Market Administration" (Executive order by Ministry of Commerce [2006] No. 24, revised in 2015).

[42] Please refer to the "Decision of the Ministry of Commerce on Abolishing Certain Regulations" (Executive Order by Ministry of Commerce [2020] No. 1).

administrative plans. In 1981, the state began to relax its administrative control. The State Council approved that the crude oil produced beyond the required minimum could be exported according to international market prices. In 1983, the State Council further approved that petroleum produced beyond the state plans could be sold at a higher price domestically, thus gradually forming a dual-track system of crude oil prices that encompassed state pricing and market-regulated pricing. Oil companies which chose to use planned oil could enjoy lower prices but had to face longer waiting time, whereas they could wait for shorter periods of time but would have to face higher prices if they chose to use crude oil outside the government plans. In 1994, the state implemented unified pricing of both the planned and the non-planned crude oil and refined oil, and the dual-track system was terminated. However, the price was not market-oriented; it was still decided by the state. In 1998, the National Development and Reform Commission released the "Reform Plan of Crude Oil and Refined Oil Pricing," which clearly stated that the purchase and sales price of crude oil was to be negotiated by CNPC and Sinopec. The purchase price of crude oil, ex-factory price of refined oil, wholesale price, and retail price were no longer decided via government directives; instead, they were to be independently decided based on government-recommended prices. This pricing mechanism has been preserved even until this day. The institutional reform of crude oil pricing has gone through a number of stages, passing from planned pricing, dual-track pricing, the merging of dual-track prices into a single-track government pricing, and finally to the autonomous pricing by enterprises with the authorization of the government. The pricing by enterprises with the authorization of the government, which eventually came to be adopted, is actually an act of administrative authorization, which essentially means that the enterprise exercises its authority of pricing on behalf of the government. Therefore, in terms of pricing, there has always been a transaction of rights between the market and government, and between the enterprises and the government. Such transactions are indispensable to all the oil companies. Transactions purely between enterprises themselves simply do not exist.

(2) **The refined oil**

There are two transaction modules for the circulation of refined oil. The first module is the transaction conducted by enterprises for the sake of gaining market access. The second module is the transaction conducted by the government with the market and enterprises regarding government pricing. Since the reform and opening-up were implemented, the scale of China's refined oil circulation market has gradually been expanded, and the government's regulation of this market has undergone changes in several phases, passing from relatively liberal regulation, to tight control, and then back to relaxed management. The circulation of refined oil has also gone through an evolution, characterized by an increasing number of transaction modules and varying complexity of transaction rules, starting with relative simplicity, replaced by growing complexity, and eventually returning to simplicity.

For more than 3 decades prior to the 1980s, China implemented a mode of planned administration of refined oil, which was a system of unified purchase and sales of oil products. There was a three-tier wholesale mechanism, with fixed wholesale channels, fixed supply range, and fixed discount rate. Since the reform and opening-up, in the crude oil sector, a large number of market entities have gained free access to the market of refined oil circulation. In the 1990s, the number of private enterprises engaged in refined oil circulation increased significantly, and the market scale expanded rapidly. After 1998, it was stipulated that CNPC and Sinopec were to handle all the domestically-produced refined oil products.[43] Gas stations had to purchase refined oil from these two large groups and various gas stations and the two large groups constituted transaction entities. In 2001, the state formulated the following transaction rules regarding the refined oil. Firstly, refined oil was to be wholesaled exclusively by CNPC Group and Sinopec Group. Secondly, all the new gas stations must be constructed by CNPC and Sinopec entirely at their own expenses and the gas stations would become their wholly-owned or controlled subsidiaries.[44] Due to the state ownership of the sales channels of refined oil, both the access to the refined oil circulation market and the number of gas stations were subjected to strict state control. The transaction costs for private gas stations to obtain refined oil increased rapidly. Phenomena such as unstable oil sources and frequent "oil shortages" kept occurring and the subsequent ramifications reached their peak from 2003 to 2005. Many private enterprises had difficulties in operating their business due to long-term oil shortages and had to sell or shut down their gas stations.

Upon joining the World Trade Organization (WTO), China promised to gradually open up the access to refined oil circulation. The transaction rules for market access underwent several rounds of adjustment led by the Ministry of Commerce. (1) In November 2004, it was stipulated that the authority for approving the wholesale licenses for refined oil belonged to the Central Government and the Ministry of Commerce was authorized for the license approval. On the other hand, the storage or the retail licensing of refined oil belonged to local government authorities and their approval were to be granted by the commerce department at the provincial level.[45] (2) In 2006, the license approval of refined oil storage was no longer an authority that belonged to local government but to the Central Government and must be granted by the Ministry of Commerce. This showed an obvious tightening of the market access.[46] (3) After 2015, the license approval of refined oil wholesale and storage business was cancelled, and the approval of refined oil retail license

---

[43] In 1998, the State Planning Commission issued the "Crude Oil and Refined Oil Price Reform Plan" (Planning Commission [1998] No. 52), which stipulated that gasoline and diesel sales were to be entirely organized by two group companies for distribution to terminal retailers, implementing uniform urban and rural prices.

[44] Please refer to the "Notice of the General Office of the State Council on Issuing the Opinions on Further Rectifying and Regulating the Order of the Refined Oil Market Developed by the State Economic and Trade Commission and Other Departments" (State Council General Office [2001] No. 72).

[45] Please refer to the "Interim Measures for the Administration of the Refined Oil Market" (Executive Order by Ministry of Commerce [2004] No. 23).

[46] Please refer to the "Measures for the Administration of the Refined Oil Market" (Executive Order by Ministry of Commerce [2006] No. 23).

was delegated from provincial government authorities to regional or municipal-level people's governments, and the market access was somewhat relaxed.[47] (4) In July 2020, the existing measures of refined oil market administration were abolished, and commerce departments at all levels were no longer responsible for approving wholesale and storage licenses. Nevertheless, the approval of retail license was still reserved by local governments.[48] The rules for accessing the refined oil circulation business have undergone a simplifying process. The approval of wholesale, retail, and storage business of the refined oil by the Central Government or provincial governments was gradually abolished, and the approval was changed into the approval by regional or municipal-level governments. Along with the simplification of transaction rules has come the gradual decrease in transaction costs.

The transaction of rights regarding the refined oil pricing has been mainly conducted between the market and the government's price regulatory department. At the very outset of the reform and opening-up, as in the market of crude oil, a dual-track system of government pricing and market-regulated pricing existed in the refined oil market. In 1994, the state implemented unified pricing for all planned and non-planned crude oil and refined oil.[49] The pricing rules have undergone a number of changes. (1) After 1994, all the refined oil was priced by the state. (2) In 1998, refined oil pricing was changed and the pricing was to be based on the government-recommended prices. It was stipulated that domestic crude oil and refined oil prices were to be determined according to the changes in the oil prices in the Singapore market. When the cumulative price changes in the gasoline and diesel transaction in the Singapore market exceeded 5%, the National Development and Reform Commission would adjust the standard retail prices of gasoline and diesel.[50] (3) In 2001, domestic refined oil pricing mechanism was changed once again. Previously, the price was determined solely according to price fluctuations in the Singapore market. Now, oil price was to be determined according to petroleum market prices in Singapore, Rotterdam and New York. The range of fluctuations in gasoline and diesel retail prices was expanded from 5 to 8%.[51] (4) In 2006, another change was introduced. The domestic refined oil retail benchmark price was determined on the basis of the ex-factory price, plus the price variations in the circulation process. Enterprises were allowed to fix their respective retail prices within an 8% fluctuation range. (5) In 2008, regarding the gasoline and diesel retail benchmark price, the previous mechanism of

[47] Please refer to the "Opinions on Accelerating the Development of Circulation and Promoting Commercial Consumption" (State Council General Office [2019] No. 42).

[48] Please refer to the "Decision of the Ministry of Commerce on Abolishing Some Regulations" (Executive Order by Ministry of Commerce [2020] No. 1).

[49] Please refer to the "Notice of the State Council on Approving and Issuing the Opinions by the State Planning Commission and the State Economic and Trade Commission on the Reform of the Crude Oil and Refined Oil Circulation System" (State Council [1994] No. 21).

[50] Please refer to the "Crude Oil and Refined Oil Price Reform Plan" (Planning Commission [1998] No. 52).

[51] Please refer to the "Notice of the State Planning Commission on Improving the Method of Petroleum Price Convergence and Adjusting Refined Oil Prices" (Planning Commission [2001] No. 96).

upward and downward fluctuations was replaced by the mechanism of imposing an upper limit on retail price. (6) In 2009, it was stipulated that when the average crude oil price changes in the international market for a period of 22 consecutive working days exceed 4%, domestic refined oil prices could be adjusted accordingly. When crude oil price in the international market falls below $80 per barrel, refined oil price is to be calculated on the basis of normal processing profit margins. When the crude oil price in the international market rises above $80 per barrel, the processing profit margins are to be deduced until refined oil prices are calculated based on the zero processing profit margins. When crude oil price in the international market exceeds $130 per barrel, gasoline and diesel prices will not be raised in principle, or will be raised only slightly.[52] (7) In 2016, an upper limit and a lower limit were imposed on the refined oil prices (no price adjustments would be made when oil prices are below $40 per barrel or above $130 per barrel), and the adjustment cycle was shortened from 22 to 10 days.[53] This rule remains valid up to this day.

The pricing of refined oil has gone a long way, from the dual-track pricing, to government pricing, and finally to government-recommended pricing. The pricing cycle has been shortened, and the range of fluctuations of government-recommended prices has increased. It seems that the time for the market to wait for price adjustments has been shortened and this constitutes a measure to reduce transaction costs. However, no matter what changes are introduced into them, these transaction rules are the pricing rules of a simulated market in the framework of the existing pricing mechanisms of the planned economy. They cannot accurately reflect the real supply-and-demand relationship of the refined oil market. The so-called reform of the refined oil pricing is merely marginal institutional adjustments under the condition of path dependence and, essentially, there has been no change in the high transaction costs. In the case of precipitous declines in the global oil prices, China's domestic refined oil prices have remained high and have not decreased accordingly. High transaction costs are directly reflected in high oil prices (please refer to Fig. 3).

(3) The natural gas

Since the reform and opening-up, the circulation of natural gas has undergone important changes, from the absence of any transaction modules to the creation of transaction modules. Currently, it consists of three transaction modules. The first is the transaction of rights between the government and the pipeline network companies affiliated to the Three Giants regarding the pricing of ex-factory natural gas. The second is the transaction of rights among the pipeline network companies affiliated to the Three Giants, gas-consuming enterprises, and the government regarding the retail price of natural gas. The third is the transaction between market entities and the

[52] Please refer to the "Notice of the National Development and Reform Commission on Issuing the Petroleum Price Administration Measures (the Trial Version)" (Development and Reform Commission-Price [2009] No. 1198).

[53] Please refer to the "Notice of the National Development and Reform Commission on Further Improving the Issues Related to the Formation Mechanism of Refined Oil Prices" (Development and Reform Commission-Price [2016] No. 64).

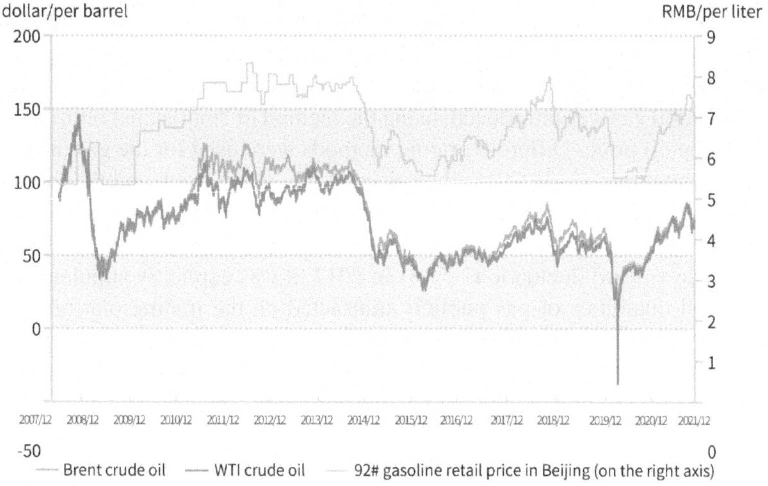

Fig. 3 Comparisons of international oil prices and Chinese gasoline prices

national pipeline company whereby to access the pipeline transportation services. The third transaction module has been discussed earlier and the first two transaction modules will be the focus of our following discussions.

Compared with the consumption of coal, electricity, and oil, China's consumption of natural gas started relatively late and grew rapidly only after the turn of the century. The module of natural gas pricing has undergone institutional evolution, from complete government pricing to an increasing proportion of market-oriented pricing. The Three Giants mainly engage in transactions with the government over the ex-factory price of natural gas. The changes in their transaction rules can be described as follows. (1) At the beginning of the reform and opening-up, government pricing was implemented, using the method of "cost plus a certain degree of profit margin." (2) After 1992, a dual-track pricing system was launched. Apart from the government pricing, government-recommended pricing was imposed on the natural gas sold by the gas producers themselves at the production site. (3) In 2005, a uniform government- recommended pricing was imposed on all the ex-factory natural gas and natural gas prices were allowed to fluctuate within a certain range.[54]

[54] The "Notice of the National Development and Reform Commission on Reforming the Formation Mechanism of Natural Gas Ex-factory Prices and Appropriately Raising Natural Gas Ex-factory Prices in the Near Future" (Development and Reform Commission-Price [2005] No. 2756) clearly states that it is important to adhere to market orientation and introduce changes into the pricing model. In order to increase the flexibility of government pricing and better reflect market supply and demand, the ex-factory price of natural gas is to be changed into a unified government-guided price. Among them, the first-tier ex-factory price of natural gas can be negotiated by both supply and demand parties within a floating range of plus or minus 10%, based on the state-prescribed ex-factory benchmark price. The second-tier ex-factory price of natural gas has a 10% increase based on the state-prescribed ex-factory benchmark price, and there is no limit on the price decrease.

Later on, the transaction of rights concerning natural gas pricing went through several changes in content, with ex-factory prices gradually being replaced by retail prices. The changes in the transaction rules are as follows. (1) In 2013, the retail price of natural gas was introduced, using the method of "market net return" that was linked to the oil price. Different pricing methods were used for the gas in stock and the incremental gas. (2) In 2015, the prices of the gas in stock and the incremental gas were merged. When urban gas companies purchased natural gas from the Three Giants, the retail prices could fluctuate between "a 20% upward fluctuation and unlimited downward fluctuation."[55] (3) In 2017, it was explicitly stipulated that the prices of all quantities of gas publicly transacted on the trading platform were to be determined via market transactions. Within this pricing mechanism, more than 50% would be entirely market-oriented, and about 30% would be based on a flexible mechanism of "20% upward fluctuation and unlimited downward fluctuation." (4) In 2020, the government-recommended retail prices of natural gas were removed from the Central Government's pricing catalog.[56]

The changes in transaction rules for natural gas, ranging from government-fixed ex-factory price to the flexible retail price and then to the prices decided by open transactions on trading platforms, have increased the proportion of market-oriented pricing as well as the range of price fluctuations. A considerable number of enterprises can obtain natural gas at market prices without waiting for gas supply at the government-fixed prices, thus reducing the transaction costs ensuing from waiting. However, in China's natural gas transactions, it is still quite disconcerting that certain state-owned enterprises have monopolized natural gas pricing under government authorization, and the pricing model which produces high transaction costs still exists.

5. **Refining**

In the oil refining industry, China has always advocated "the shutting down of small refineries and the building of large refining bases for the development of the economies of scale." Within this transaction module, there are three major sub-modules. The first is the transaction conducted by the enterprises with the government to secure the administrative approval for engaging in investment projects. The second is the transaction conducted by the enterprises with the government to obtain the administrative permits to use oil. The third is the transaction conducted by the enterprises with the government to avoid administrative sanctions.

---

[55] Please refer to the "Opinions on Promoting the Reform of Price Mechanism" (Central Committee [2015] No. 28).

[56] The "Central Government Pricing Catalogue" has an annotation which states, "The price for the imported pipeline-carried natural gas put into operation after 2015 is to be decided by the market. The retail price of other domestic over-land pipeline-carried natural gas and imported pipeline-carried natural gas put into operation before the end of 2014 is to be temporarily managed according to the current price mechanism, and will be determined by the market when the reform process of natural gas marketization makes due progress."

At the beginning of the reform and opening-up, China's refining industry was chiefly state-owned and local refineries gradually developed as a result of the development of oil fields. After 1992, with the significant reduction of planned administration in the oil and gas fields, China's downstream refining industry achieved rapid development, and transaction costs for accessing the refining industry were exceedingly low. In order to enhance the level of industrial scale of the refining sector, China formulated strict provisions concerning investment access. For example, new refineries and expansion projects of primary oil refining were to be approved by the investment regulatory department of the State Council. Among them, expansion projects that have been included in the national energy development plans and the development plans of the petrochemical industry were to be approved by provincial governments. The approval of new refining projects and the expansion projects of the primary oil refining refers to the administrative approval that falls within the authority of the National Development and Reform Commission, with a total of 33 approval items (please refer to Table 6).[57] This means that there are at least 33 sub-modules of transaction under this transaction module for the construction of new refineries. The transaction costs for new refinery projects have increased markedly as compared with those at the beginning of the reform and opening-up.

The rules for enterprises to engage in transactions with the government to secure the oil use permits include the following. (1) The amount of oil consumption by the newly-added oil-consuming enterprises is determined on the basis of a certain proportion among several factors, the capacity of outdated equipment eliminated by the enterprises themselves, or the enterprises merged and restructured, and the scale of gas storage facilities that are constructed. (2) To obtain foreign oil, local refineries cannot import directly from foreign market but have to import through major agencies, that is, five enterprises that include CNPC, Sinopec, CNOOC, Sinochem Group, and Zhuhai Zhenrong Co., Ltd. In their actual business operation, local refineries undoubtedly have to pay high transaction costs in order to abide by these transaction rules. Obviously, those enterprises that cannot afford these costs will be eliminated from the market.

In dealing with those potentially undesirable transaction modules, the state formulated a series of standards about business scale. The evolution of the transaction rules includes the following steps. (1) In 2005, small-scale refining units which produced gasoline, diesel, and kerosene with an annual output of 1 million tons or less were eliminated.[58] (2) In 2009, inefficient and outdated refining units with an annual output of 1 million tons or less were eliminated, and local governments should make active efforts to make the refineries with an annual output of 1 to 2 million tons to shut down, or to merge, or to transform.[59] (3) In 2011, the atmospheric-vacuum distillation units with an annual output of less than 2 million tons were eliminated, and local refineries

[57] Please refer to the "Notice of the State Council Concerning the Catalog of the Government-Approved Investment Projects (2014 Edition)" (State Council [2014] No. 53).

[58] Please refer to the "Guiding Catalogue for Industrial Structure Adjustment (2005 Edition)" (Executive Order by the Development and Reform Commission, No. 40).

[59] Article 3 (7) of the "Plan for the Adjustment and Revitalization of the Petrochemical Industry" (State Council [2009] No. 16) stipulates that efforts should be made to accelerate the elimination

Table 6 Catalogue for approving new oil refining projects and expanding the primary oil refining projects

I. The review and approval stage	
Entities of enforcement	Items for approval
The regulatory department of land and resources	Preliminary review of land use of construction projects (not involving newly-added land; no review will be required of the projects whose renovation and expansion take place on the land whose use has already been approved)
The regulatory department of environmental protection	The approval of the documents regarding the environmental impact of the construction projects (excluding the construction projects of nuclear and radiative facilities)
The regulatory department of urban–rural planning	Site-selection evaluation document (mandatory only for projects whose usufruct of the state-owned land is acquired via government allocation)
The regulatory department of maritime administration	The approval of the environmental impact report concerning the maritime construction projects (mandatory only for maritime projects)
The regulatory department of maritime administration	The approval of the development and exploitation of uninhabited islands which have been ratified by the State Council (mandatory only for maritime projects)
The regulatory department of maritime administration	The preliminary approval of the maritime utilization (mandatory only for maritime projects)
The regulatory department of traffic and transportation	Evaluation of the navigation route conditions and navigation safety
The department of river valley administration	Approval of the construction plans regarding the projects that are within the range of waterway administration (mandatory only for the projects that are within the range of waterway administration)
The regulatory department of water administration	The approval of the water source feasibility report of construction projects
The regulatory department of water administration	The approval of the water and soil conservation in production and construction projects
The department of river valley administration	Flood impact evaluation (mandatory only for the non-anti-flood construction projects in the flooded area or flood-modulation area)
The regulatory department of water administration	Approval of water acquisition for construction projects (mandatory only for those projects which acquire water directly from rivers, lakes, or underground sources by means of water-acquisition projects or facilities)

(continued)

Table 6 (continued)

I. The review and approval stage	
Entities of enforcement	Items for approval
The regulatory department of earthquake prevention	Review of the earthquake safety evaluation report and anti-earthquake measures (mandatory only for major construction projects and for those projects which might trigger serious secondary damages)
Relevant people's government & the regulatory department of cultural relics	Approval of other construction projects that are within the range of protection by cultural relics protection agencies or those construction projects involving explosion, drilling, digging, and other operations (mandatory only for projects related to cultural relics)
Relevant people's government & the regulatory department of cultural relics	Approval of construction projects located in the areas of construction control by cultural relics protection agencies (mandatory only for projects related to cultural relics)
Relevant people's government & the regulatory department of cultural relics	Approval of archaeological survey, exploration, and excavation within the area of construction projects (mandatory only for projects related to cultural relics)
Relevant people's government & the regulatory department of cultural relics	Approval of the cultural relics protection plans involving protection on the existing site, relocation, or demolition concerning the immovable cultural relics due to construction projects (mandatory only for projects related to cultural relics)
National Development and Reform Commission	Evaluation and review of energy conservation in fixed-assets investment projects
National Development and Reform Commission	Approval of the fixed-assets investment projects developed by enterprises, government-affiliated institutions, and social organizations
II. Post-approval and pre-construction stage	
Entities of enforcement	Items for approval
The regulatory department of land and resources	Review of the use of rural lands for non-rural purposes and of land expropriation
The regulatory department of land and resources	Approval of construction projects that cover important mineral deposits

(continued)

Table 6 (continued)

II. Post-approval and pre-construction stage	
Entities of enforcement	Items for approval
The regulatory department of maritime administration	Approval of the construction and laying of submarine cables and pipelines (mandatory only for sea-related projects)
The regulatory department of maritime administration	Approval of the right of sea area use (mandatory only for sea-related projects)
The regulatory department of maritime administration	Investigation of the routing of submarine cables and pipelines (mandatory only for sea-related projects)
The department of safety supervision	Approval of safety condition of construction projects
The department of safety supervision	Review of the design of occupational disease prevention and protection facilities for construction projects with potential hazards of serious occupational diseases
III. Post-construction and pre-completion stage	
Entities of enforcement	Items for approval
The regulatory department of environmental protection	Review of construction project's compliance with environmental protection standards upon completion (excluding the construction projects of nuclear and radiative facilities)
The regulatory department of maritime administration	Evaluation of environmental protection facilities in maritime construction projects upon completion (mandatory only for sea-related projects)
The regulatory department of maritime administration	Inspection and ratification of the "three synchronizations" regarding the environmental protection facilities in maritime construction projects (mandatory only for sea-related projects)
The regulatory department of maritime administration	Inspection and acceptance of the reclamation projects upon completion (mandatory only for sea-related projects)
The regulatory department of water administration	Inspection and acceptance of the water and soil conservation facilities in production and construction projects

(continued)

Table 6 (continued)

III. Post-construction and pre-completion stage	
Entities of enforcement	Items for approval
The department of safety supervision	Inspection and acceptance of occupational disease prevention and protection facilities in the completed construction projects with potential hazards of serious and very serious occupational diseases
The department of safety supervision	Inspection and acceptance of occupational disease prevention and protection facilities in the completed construction projects with potential hazards of regular occupational diseases

Note According to open sources, as of 2015

that failed to meet requirements concerning production scale and equipment were eliminated.[60] Under this sub-module, transaction rules have become increasingly harsh and the threshold for refining facilities was raised from 1 million tons to 2 million tons. In order to meet the requirements imposed by the National Development and Reform Commission, enterprises across the country have been obliged to devote considerable time and expenditure to upgrade their equipment, thus incurring high transaction costs.

6. **The market-oriented reform of the entire industry chain**

In general, the oil and gas system underwent a reform process in which the government's administrative control alternated between tightening and relaxation, and different levels of progress were achieved in the reform of various segments in this industry chain. The reforms carried out in upstream exploration and development, in crude oil circulation, and in pipeline transportation are relatively slow, demonstrating the constraints imposed on the supply side. Although the circulation of the refined oil and of natural gas, which is the downstream of the industry chain, has not been completely liberalized, the degree of marketization has kept increasing. With regard to refining, the complete absence of access restrictions has been replaced by the creation of exceedingly high access thresholds. From the very beginning of the reform to the present, there have been few changes in terms of transaction modules

---

of outdated production capacity. Production capacity with outdated technological process, of poor product quality, serious safety hazards, and serious environmental pollution must be eliminated. For the refining industry, the method of equal-amount replacement in a given region is to be adopted to eliminate inefficient and low-quality refining units with a capacity of 1 million tons or less. In addition, active steps are to be taken to promote the shutdown and transformation of refining units with a capacity of 1 million to 2 million tons and to prevent new refining projects from being built under the name of asphalt and heavy oil processing.

[60] Please refer to the "Guiding Catalogue for Industrial Structure Adjustment (2011 Edition)" (Executive Order by the Development and Reform Commission [2011] No. 9).

and transaction entities in various segments in the entire industry chain. The institutional changes are mainly reflected in the changes in transaction rules, and the government has always been a stakeholder in all the transactions of rights. The transactions of rights are mainly embodied in the government's intervention in both the volume and the price of transaction. In order to allow oil and gas to regain their commodity attributes, the key is to achieve free trade between upstream and downstream enterprises, who can engage in autonomous transactions in whatever quantity and at whatever price they choose to, thus eliminating the transactions between enterprises and the government as a prerequisite for inter-enterprise transactions. Of course, this mode of free transactions does not exclude government regulation over the price and the level of openness of the monopolized business in the oil and gas pipeline industry, nor does it exclude necessary government regulation over environmental protection and production safety. Such regulation is precisely what is vacant and deficient in the transactions between the government and enterprises. In this sense, the entire oil and gas industry chain in China can be characterized as still being subjected to serious constraints. As far as the market-oriented reform of this entire industry chain is concerned, it still has a long way to go.

Chapter 9
Reform of the Business Environment

In the present-day world, regions which boast sound business environment tend to demonstrate unparalleled advantages in attracting capital investment, the best human talents, and many other production factors. The World Bank conducts annual surveys to evaluate business environments in countries across the world. Time constitutes the paramount norm in its assessment. Such assessments serve as an indisputable case in which the transaction costs can be measured in terms of time. However, comparative studies of the temporal dimension alone are insufficient to disclose the reasons underlying different indexes of the business environment. This deficiency undermines the value of applying such evaluations to institutional reforms. In this chapter, transaction modules will be utilized as an analytical method to demonstrate how to systematically identify flaws in the business environment, thus creating a foundation for formulating systematic plans with which to reform the business environment.

1 The System of Assessment Indexes

Currently, the business environment evaluation systems that are widely recognized by the international community mainly include "Doing Business" released by the World Bank, the "Global Competitiveness Report" by the World Economic Forum, the "Index of Economic Freedom" by the American think tank Heritage Foundation, the "IMD World Competitiveness Yearbook" by the International Institute for Management Development (IMD) in Switzerland, and the "Corruption Perceptions Index" by Transparency International, etc. Among these publications, the World Bank's "Doing Business" has produced a particularly significant impact on improving China's business environment, and a considerable number of Chinese local governments have assimilated its evaluation methods. However, if we conduct our analysis in terms of transaction costs, the evaluation methods employed by the World Bank also exhibit considerable limitations.

B. Fan, *The Rationale Behind Change*, https://doi.org/10.1007/978-981-97-8854-5_9

From 2002 to 2020, the International Finance Corporation, which is affiliated to the World Bank Group, conducted annual surveys of global business environments through its "Doing Business" project. The World Bank is convinced that the business environment can be gauged by the extent of difficulty or convenience in launching and operating business in any given country or region, and the factors for measuring the business environment mainly include the conditions of time and costs that businesses have to spend in order to comply with policies and regulations in aspects such as launching and operating business, engaging in trade activities, paying taxes, executing contracts, and shutting down a company, etc. The system of business environment evaluation indexes adopts two major methods, questionnaire-based surveys and case studies, and seeks to measure the soundness of the business environment in various countries through objective perspectives. The World Bank chose 10 primary indicators with which to measure time and costs. These indicators range from initiating a business, dealing with construction permits, obtaining the use of electricity, registering property rights, acquiring credit loans, protecting the minority of the investors, paying taxes, engaging in cross-border trade, executing contracts, and resolving insolvency. Among those ten indicators, eight use time as the criterion of measurement. Taking Shanghai as an example, in 2020, it took at least nine days to start a new business, with five days spent on company registration and applying for business licenses, one day on making the company seal, two days on acquiring tax control equipment and financial invoices, and one day on handling "five insurances and one fund" (namely, endowment insurance, medical insurance, unemployment insurance, employment injury insurance, maternity insurance, and housing provident fund) for employees (please refer to Tables 1 and 2).

Based on continuous evaluations over a period of time, we can observe the trend of changes in the business environment. We can cite the example of enterprises' tax payment in Shanghai. In 2006, a typical enterprise in Shanghai spent an average of 832 h per year preparing, declaring, and paying taxes, with the requirement of making 37 payments. By 2020, these indicators had been reduced to 138 h and 7 payments on an annual basis. Out of the 138 h, 52 h were spent on paying "five insurances and one fund," 46 h on paying value-added tax (VAT), and 40 h on paying income tax. This system of indicators measures the time required to prepare, declare, and pay three major types of taxes and fees. The preparation time includes the time needed to collect all the information required to calculate payable taxes and the amounts due. The declaration time includes the time to complete all the necessary tax return forms and to submit relevant forms to the tax authorities. Finally, the payment time refers to the time needed to pay taxes and fees either online or in person.

The World Bank established various indicators regarding the business environment, based primarily on the concerns that enterprises tend to develop in their business operation. The statistical findings associated with these indicators are not counted as transaction costs. On the other hand, previous studies in economics and institutional research did not conduct any practical work in this area either. Essentially speaking, however, the time and costs that enterprises have to pay in their business operation are indeed transaction costs. If we follow the analytical methodology concerning the transaction modules proposed in Chapter Three, it becomes quite obvious that

Table 1 World Bank "doing business" evaluation index system

Primary indicators	Secondary indicators
1. Starting a business	1.1 Procedures
	1.2 Time
	1.3 Cost
	1.4 Minimum registered capital required for starting a company of limited liabilities
2. Dealing with construction permits	2.1 Procedures
	2.2 Time
	2.3 Cost
	2.4 Building quality control index
3. Getting electricity	3.1 Procedures
	3.2. Time
	3.3. Cost
	3.4. Power supply reliability and billing transparency index
4. Registering property	4.1. Procedures for property transfer registration
	4.2. Time for property transfer registration
	4.3. Cost for property transfer registration
	4.4. Quality of land management system
5. Getting credit	5.1 Movable collateral law index
	5.2 Credit information system index
6. Protecting minority investors	6.1 Information disclosure index
	6.2 Director liability index
	6.3 Shareholder litigation convenience index
	6.4 Shareholder rights protection index
	6.5 Ownership and control protection index
	6.6 Corporate transparency index
7. Paying taxes	7.1 Number of times for companies to pay taxes
	7.2 Time required for paying taxes
	7.3 Total tax rate
	7.4. Post-taxation practices process index 7.4.1 VAT refund claim time 7.4.2 Time needed to receive tax refunds 7.4.3 Time for filing corporate income tax audit 7.4.4 Time for completing corporate income tax audit
8. Trading across borders	8.1 Time for reviewing export customs declaration
	8.2 Time for export customs clearance
	8.3 Cost for reviewing export customs declaration
	8.4 Cost for export customs clearance

(continued)

Table 1 (continued)

Primary indicators	Secondary indicators
	8.5 Time for reviewing import customs declaration
	8.6 Time for import customs clearance
	8.7 Cost for reviewing import customs declaration
	8.8 Cost for import customs clearance
9. Enforcing contracts	9.1. Time for resolving commercial disputes
	9.2. Cost for resolving commercial disputes
	9.3. Quality index of judicial procedures
10. Resolving insolvency	10.1 Recovery rate
	10.2 Protection index of legal framework regarding insolvency

the time and the costs examined by the World Bank only account for a very small proportion in the entire transaction costs of doing business.

The 10 indicators chosen by the World Bank for analysis are primarily designed to evaluate the executive activities by the government, which can be viewed as transactions between the government and the enterprises. In each transaction module, the government's administrative actions create rights, the relevant regulations formulated by the government are the contracts, and the time and costs that enterprises have to pay in order to obtain these rights constitute transaction costs. Each transaction module can be divided into a number of sub-modules. What the World Bank measures is just one or a few of the many sub-modules, not the aggregate transaction costs in a given project. For local governments in some regions in China, they deliberately lower the standards associated with those indicators in order to cope with the evaluations conducted by the World Bank or by domestic evaluation agencies. However, they might increase sub-modules elsewhere or increase the number of transaction rules in some sub-modules. As a result, the overall transaction costs remain unchanged. In actually developing the business environment report, if the government merely focuses on improving the performance of relevant indicators in the report and rather than reducing the overall transaction costs, it is highly unlikely that reforms of this sort will ever achieve the expected result of improving the business environment. In the subsequent sections, we will select a number of areas to analyze how to comprehensively investigate the transaction costs created by the government's administrative actions.

Table 2 Procedures for starting a new business in Shanghai in 2020

	Procedures	Time for completion	Costs
1	Registering the company and applying for a business license Agency: Shanghai Market Supervision Administration (MSA) Founders of corporate organizations must register their companies and obtain business licenses (the Industrial and Commercial Business License) issued by Shanghai Market Supervision Administration. Applications must be prepared and submitted online at the website of the State Administration for Market Regulation (http://yct.sh.gov.cn). The availability of company names can be checked when submitting the applications Previously, five other approval certificates were required, namely, the business license, the organizational code certificate, the tax registration, the statistical registration, and the social welfare insurance registration. These approval certificates have now been merged into one license only. Upon receiving the application, Shanghai Market Supervision Administration submits the documents to relevant departments for registration. After submitting their applications, founders of corporate organizations go to the counter of Shanghai Market Supervision Administration to collect the business licenses and submit the following documents: 1. Application form 2. The company's articles of association 3. Personal identity documents of shareholders 4. The authorization letter 5. Photocopy of the office property certificate (signed by the property owner) 6. The registration form of supplementary information	5 days	Free
2	Making the company seal Agency: the seal making company The company seal is to be made by a designated company holding the "Shanghai Special Profession License." The cost of making the seal ranges from 300 to 1000 yuan, depending on the design and quality of the seal	1 day	400 yuan

(continued)

Table 2 (continued)

	Procedures	Time for completion	Costs
3	Acquiring tax control equipment and applying for authorization to print or purchase financial invoices Agency: Municipal Taxation Authority The required tax control equipment is also known as the tax control disk. There are two authorized manufacturers of this equipment, and new companies preparing to launch their businesses can freely choose to use the products by either of the two manufacturers. The equipment price is 200 yuan, with an annual maintenance fee of 280 yuan, as stipulated by the National Development and Reform Commission's Notice on Reducing the Price of VAT Tax Control System Products and Maintenance Services (NDRC No. 1243 [2017]). Activation of tax declaration devices and approval from the taxation authority are required before the newly-founded company can issue VAT invoices, including general and special invoices. Applications can be submitted online at https://www.tax.sh.gov.cn/xbwt/. Upon approval by the taxation authority to grant the company this qualification, an invoice purchase book is issued. Applicants must go to Shanghai Municipal Tax Service, State Taxation Administration, to collect the letter of approval and submit the following documents: 1. Tax registration certificate 2. Tax personnel identity card 3. Application form 4. Invoice seal model 5. Company seal	2 days	200 yuan for the encryption device, along with 280 yuan for the annual maintenance of the encryption device
4	Registering employees with the Social Insurance Center Agency: the Social Insurance Center Within 30 days of hiring employees, employers must register with the Shanghai Municipal Human Resources and Social Security Bureau (the local social insurance agency under the Ministry of Human Resources and Social Security) Purpose of registration: to establish the obligation to pay social insurance on behalf of employees. Relevant application forms can be downloaded electronically or obtained from local offices, filled out, and submitted via the following website: https://zzjb.12333sh.gov.cn/zzjbdl/jsp/login.jsp. After receiving the company's registration information, the Social Insurance Center will issue a notification, and open a social insurance account for the company. The company then must submit application for opening an insurance collection account at a bank. After receiving the bank account opening notification, the local social insurance center will issue a social insurance registration card to the company, enabling it to start paying social insurance for its employees	1 day	Free

2 The Commercial System

The concept of "commercial system" first appeared in an official document issued by the General Office of the State Council in 2020[1] and has achieved wide currency in practice ever since then. There is scarcely any precise definition of this concept in existing laws and academic literature. Judging from the context in which it is used, we will find that it refers to the institutional arrangements by the government for managing the entire lifecycle of enterprises, involving various institutional regulations concerning the establishment, existence, and exit of enterprises. A commercial system consists of a number of transaction modules, which encompass registration, cancellation, and production permits of enterprises. Among all these transaction modules, the government and enterprises are the transaction entities, the various rights derived from the government's administrative actions are the objects of transaction, and the various laws and regulations formulated by the government, which are aimed at governing the enterprises, are the transaction contracts. Each of these transaction modules can be divided into a considerable number of sub-modules.

In recent years, by conducting reforms in the country's system of company registration, China has significantly reduced the time and costs spent on starting a business, and the transaction costs in the sub-modules of enterprise registration within the commercial system itself have apparently decreased. However, apart from registration, a considerable number of rights are involved in the transactions with the government throughout the entire lifecycle of a company, and the transaction costs in these sub-modules of transaction are still rather substantial. A case in point is the supervisory system during the lifecycle of an enterprise. China has gone through two phases—the annual inspection system and the annual report system. The annual inspection, a mechanism established in 1988, is a short form for annual examination. According to regulations, the annual inspection period for enterprises spans from March to June every year. During the inspection, the enterprise registration authority (formerly the Industrial and Commercial Administration) conducts reviews, according to different categories of enterprises, regarding the registration, capital contribution, licensing, and conditions of business operation (please refer to Table 3).[2] If an enterprise refuses to undergo the annual inspection as required or if an enterprise refuses to tell the truth or commits fraudulence during the inspection, it will be subjected to penalties, either fines or the revoking of its business license.

As a matter of fact, many of the contents in the inspections and reviews basically fall within the enterprises' scope of business autonomy and do not entail the government's administrative intervention, such as whether shareholders have actually contributed the registered capital, whether an enterprise has changed its place of business operation, whether an enterprise's business licenses regarding individual

[1] Please refer to the Notice of the General Office of the State Council on Deepening the Reform of the Commercial System to Further Unburden Enterprises and to Stimulate Corporate Vitality (General Office of the State Council [2020] No. 29).

[2] Please refer to the "Enterprise Annual Inspection Measures" (Executive Order by the State Administration for Industry and Commerce, No. 23, Feb. 2006).

Table 3 Requirements for company annual inspection and review

Whether the company is using its name as per regulations and whether, in the case of any change in name, the alteration has been registered as per regulations
Whether, in the case of any change in company address, the alteration has been registered as per regulations
Whether, in the case of any change in the company's legal representative, the alteration has been registered as per regulations
Whether the company has falsely declared its registered capital; whether shareholders or company initiators have contributed their capital as per regulations; and whether there are any acts of withdrawing the contributed capital or evading the contribution of the capital
Whether the licenses and approval documents for business items specified within the range of business operation, which require administrative permission before enterprise registration, have been revoked, suspended, or have expired; whether the business activities are kept within the registered range of business operation
Whether, in the case of any transfer of equity by shareholders or company initiators, the alteration has been registered as per regulations
Whether the term of business operation has expired
Whether the alterations in the company's constitution and the changes in directors, supervisors, and managers have been filed as per regulations
Whether the establishment of branch companies has been filed as per regulations; whether there have been cases in which any branch companies have been revoked, legally ordered to close, or had their business licenses revoked
Whether the liquidation group, in the case of the company initiating the liquidation process, has filed the liquidation as per regulations
Whether a natural person has invested in establishing multiple single-member companies of limited liabilities

items remain valid, whether business activities conform to the registered scope of business operation, etc. However, all these matters are covered by the annual review, and the authorities of industrial and commercial administration can impose penalties on companies and may even suspend and revoke their business licenses in some cases. Under this system of annual inspection, all the enterprises across the country have to invest a certain amount of manpower, physical resources, and time every year to deal with the review performed by the authorities of the industrial and commercial administration. All these invested resources constitute the transaction costs to the existence and continuation of an enterprise. The authorities of the industrial and commercial administration are equipped with the decisive power over the destiny of enterprises. In some places, power rental runs rampant, resulting in obvious deterioration of the environment for doing business. In some other places, as there are too many enterprises, authorities of the industrial and commercial administration cannot conduct substantive review of individual enterprises one by one, rendering the system of annual inspection essentially dysfunctional and pointless. As a consequence, the system of annual inspection, originally intended to preserve and safeguard the order of market economy, has backfired by moving into the opposite direction, evolving into a system that hinders the healthy development of market entities.

By drawing on the regulatory approaches practiced in foreign countries, China abolished the system of annual inspection in 2014, replaced by the system of annual report. From January to June each year, enterprises submit annual reports to the authorities of the industrial and commercial administration. The contents in the reports to be submitted are not significantly different from the information filled out under the system of annual inspection. The documents for the annual inspection feature five categories, namely, registration, record-filing, foreign investments, establishment or revocation of branches, and operational status. Now, the contents of in the annual report has increased to include seven items, namely, the basic information, existence status, investment by the enterprise, capital contribution by shareholders, equity changes, enterprise website information, and operational status. For each category, it is necessary to fill out detailed information under many indicators. The data in the annual report do not need to be reviewed or approved by the market supervisory authorities (formerly the authorities of the industrial and commercial administration), but are publicly disclosed and accountable to society. Under such circumstances, an enterprise does not face the yearly risk of having its license revoked, a penalty which is equivalent to a "death sentence" for the enterprise. This abrupt change in transaction rules has reduced the opportunities for market supervisory authorities to intervene in the business activities of enterprises and lowered the cost of transactions between the enterprises and the government.

After the system of annual report was established, there have been continuous marginal adjustments, resulting in the gradual increase in transaction costs. A punitive module regarding the overdue annual reports has been added to the system of annual report, specifying that businesses that are late with their reports will be placed on the list of abnormal business operations. These companies on the list will be restricted or prohibited from participating in government procurements, project biddings, transfers of state-owned land, receiving honors from the government, etc. They further face restrictions and prohibitions from engaging in financial services such as credit, investment, and guarantees. Those companies which have been on the list of abnormal business operations for three consecutive years and have still failed to fulfill their public disclosure obligations will be placed on the list of seriously illegal and dishonest enterprises. The legal representatives or persons in charge of the companies placed on the list are disqualified from serving as legal representatives or CEOs of other companies for a period of three years. Enterprises listed as seriously illegal and dishonest are forbidden from applying for removal from such a list for a period of five years. Under the system of annual inspection, the administrative penalties for non-compliances are mostly fines in monetary terms and the payment of the fines can terminate the penalties and enterprises would be allowed to re-engage in normal business operations. By contrast, under the system of annual report, the punishments for failing to file timely reports are both deeper and broader, making the chances for resuming normal business operations rather slim. The time consumed in the entire process contributes to the overall transaction costs. In this sense, compared to the system of annual inspection, the system of annual report merely represents a nominal advancement; it can hardly be characterized as a form of substantive advancement.

Company cancellation, or deregistration, also constitutes a transaction module with extremely high transaction costs. The "Company Law" stipulates that, when a company declares bankruptcy, or is acquired by another company, or discontinues business operations by the time the stipulated business term expires, or when the company is dissolved internally, deregistration must be carried out.[3] In the deregistration module, the main entities involved in the transaction are the government and the company, the transaction right is the administrative permission by the government allowing for the termination of the legal person status, and the transaction contract is the process of statutory deregistration.

The increased transaction costs for company deregistration stem from the progressive increment of transaction rules. According to China's Company Law, in the wake of company liquidation, the liquidation report should be submitted to the company registration authority in application for the cancellation of the company's registration and for publicly announcing the termination of the company.[4] Many people might assume that the company registration authority only has a simple function to play, that is, to publicly announce the termination of the said company upon the reception of the liquidation report. However, the "Regulations on Company Registration Management" have expanded the enterprise deregistration process to include six major steps, which include reporting about the liquidation group to the registration authority in advance, submitting deregistration application form, resolutions or decisions concerning deregistration, documents of court judgment or arbitration, business licenses, and other relevant documents.[5] In actually processing the deregistration, the registration authority, based on the last requirement in the "Regulations on Company Registration Management" which is the submission of "other relevant documents," further requires the deregistering company to complete a total of nine procedures by submitting authorized letter of attorney, documents confirming the liquidation report, tax clearance certificates, liquidation group filing notices, copies of the written announcement of deregistration in newspapers, etc.

Evidently, although registering a company might be easy, it is far from easy to deal with the authorities of market regulation at various stages throughout the lifecycle of a corporate organization. In particular, once a company runs into problems in its business operation, it has to face exorbitant transaction costs in order to resume normal operations. In real economic life, a great many complicated reasons might contribute to a company's failure to submit its annual report in a timely manner, and not all of those reasons are intentional. In many cases, a lot of companies have the strong intention to maintain their business operation, but once a company is listed as

[3] Please refer to Articles 73, 142, 179, and 188 of the Company Law of the People's Republic of China.

[4] Please refer to Article 188 of the Company Law of the People's Republic of China.

[5] Article 41 of the Regulations on the Administration of Company Registration of the People's Republic of China stipulates that the liquidation group shall file a record with the company registration authority concerning the list of members and the person in charge of the liquidation group within 10 days of its establishment.

a severely illegal and untrustworthy corporation, its legal representatives and CEOs often find it extremely difficult to start a business once again due to high transaction costs. To make matters worse, in the process of company deregistration, companies whose business licenses have been revoked need to carry out taxation deregistration within 15 days. However, virtually none of such companies can paying off the arrears over the past as well as the delayed taxes of the year, thus rendering it difficult to complete the deregistration process. As the arrears and delayed fees continue to accumulate, these failed business owners will face forbidding administrative fines and penalties for bad faith or dishonesty, making it almost impossible to re-start a business.

3 Electricity Supply

A fundamental condition for a hospitable business environment is that this environment must ensure that businesses can have convenient access to electricity and a safe and reliable supply of electricity. Currently, power grid companies in China still predominate over the purchase and the sale of electricity. To put it in another way, in most of circumstances, the power grid companies purchase electricity from power generation companies and then sell the electricity to potential end users, earning a profit margin in the process. Although the reform of the electricity system over the recent years has made possible direct transactions between power generating companies and electricity users, with the power grid companies only collecting a fee for electricity transmission (electricity transmission and distribution price), such direct transactions still account for a relatively small proportion. This chapter primarily focuses the cases in which users purchase electricity from the power grid companies. All the power grid companies in China are state-owned enterprises which, in accordance with the requirements of the state, perform the responsibility of providing general services. The transactions between the power grid companies and electricity-using companies are akin to the transactions between the government and the businesses, where the electricity-using companies acquire the right to use electricity from the power grid companies, and the transaction rules consist of the workflow of power grid companies and the rates for charging the fees formulated by the government. Transaction costs are incurred by the electricity-using enterprises when they apply to the power grid companies for the right to use electricity.

Here, we can take Shanghai as an example. All the applications, made by the non-resident users of low-voltage electricity, for new installations, increased capacity, and other business expansion services are handled by power grid companies alone. If the services applied for consist of two items, the application for the use of electricity and the installations of meters upon the completion of construction projects, it will take no more than 10 days.[6] Of those 10 days, the time limit for the government's administrative approval shall not exceed 2 days, and users incur no cost in obtaining access to electricity. If we consider only the process of electricity access itself, Shanghai definitely stands in a leading position globally, with its minimal time consumption and cost. However, when we introduce the analytical approach that involves the transaction module, we will find that this is merely one of the sub-modules within the larger module of electricity access transaction. For different users, that is, resident users and non-resident users, and for users at different voltage levels, different transaction modules employing different transaction rules are applied.

For large industrial users of medium and high voltage levels, the electricity access employs a transaction module with longer approval time and higher fees; accordingly, transaction costs are higher. After prospective users of medium and high voltage levels have applied for electricity access, the power grid companies will inspect the site for supply conditions on the next working day at the earliest, and will provide a formal reply regarding the power supply plan within 15 working days (30 working days for customers of dual power sources). The power grid company is responsible for the construction of the external line project (the project outside the property demarcation point), and users themselves need to complete the construction of the power reception project (the project inside the property demarcation point) before the completion of the external line project. Users are independently responsible for purchasing the equipment and materials that meet technical standards and choosing qualified construction companies to complete the customer's project of power reception. After the power reception project is completed, the user submits an application to the power grid company for project completion inspection, and the power grid company must complete the inspection within 5 working days. After completing the inspection, the power grid company installs meters and enables the electricity access within another 5 working days. The installation and accessing costs are calculated according to the varying levels of voltage, with a fixed fee-charging rate of 850 yuan per kVA for projects at the 35 kV voltage level and 1006 yuan per kVA for projects at the 10 kV voltage level.

The procedures and the timeline for the above-mentioned electricity access projects applied by users of medium and high voltages are specified in written documents. However, in actuality, the execution of the procedures may exceed the stipulated time, and the transaction cost of electricity access arising from prolonged transaction time often becomes a point of criticism by businesses. In addition, the financial costs incurred by enterprises are also very high. In most places, users of medium- and high-voltage power need to complete their own power reception projects (including external power supply projects and power reception facilities). Since electricity access ultimately has to seek the approval by power grid companies, it is common for these companies to directly or indirectly, or in a roundabout manner, issue mandatory instructions concerning the project design, project construction, and

[6] Please refer to the "Shanghai Municipality's Measures for Further Optimizing the Business Environment for Electricity Access." (Shanghai Municipal Development & Reform Commission-standards [2019] No. 15)

equipment suppliers. To expedite the electricity access process and reduce further costs in operation and maintenance, some electricity users may even transfer the electricity distribution assets that they built to the power grid companies, entirely free of charge. If we take into consideration the overall transaction costs at all voltage levels, China's international ranking is not quite encouraging.

Once a power-consuming enterprise is connected to the power grid, it implies that the grid should provide the enterprise with long-term services of reliable electricity supply. Unreliable power supply can not only lead to the deterioration of perishable products, damage to sensitive equipment, and loss of production efficiency, but may also impose additional transaction costs on enterprises as they have to wait for renewed power supply. Additional transaction costs include the time spent on waiting and the concomitant costs ensuing from employee wages, rent, and financial expenses incurred during the waiting. In China, in the case of defaults on the part of the power grid companies, there is no compensation for the direct financial losses incurred by users. Other opportunity losses caused by power outages, such as the defaults due to the manufacturer's inability to deliver products on time, reduction in production capacity, and the losses caused by the missing of trade orders, would be impossible to calculate and thus to be compensated for.

Whether or not the user can have access to reliable supply of electricity actually constitutes another transaction between the government and enterprises, which can be designated as the transaction module of power reliability. China has long implemented demand-side management in terms of electricity supply and in cases of insufficient power supply or emergencies, the state makes arrangements for achieving power balance in the following sequence, first staggering peak times, and then avoiding peak times, followed by power restrictions, and finally the suspension of power supply. In recent years, due to various factors such as reduced coal combustion, declining water levels in reservoirs, wind power generators being covered with ice in winter, and reduced long-distance power transmission, many regions cannot meet power load demands during peak times in summer and winter. These regions would implement the policy of orderly use of electricity, that is, restricting power consumption according to the government's plan of power suspension according to pre-arranged order or sequence. The government decides which enterprises are given priority for the power supply and which have to stagger the peak times in order to be eligible for electricity use. Enterprises required to stagger the peak times must operate during the non-peak periods, or on weekends and during the night. If peak-staggering power consumption still cannot meet electricity demand, enterprises must then face restricted or even suspended use of electricity by following specified sequences, for instance, "3-day suspension and 4-day operation" or "4-day suspension and 4-day operation" in each week.

Here, it might be useful to take Shanghai in 2020 as an example. The Shanghai Municipal Commission of Economy and Information Technology developed the "Shanghai Peak-Staggering Plan for the Orderly Use of Electricity in Winter," whose implementation covered a total of 89 days from December 14, 2020 to March 12, 2021. During this period, power cuts were scheduled according to approximately 17.5% of the predicted peak load (with a maximum reducible load of 4.8 million kilowatts). If intermittent supply gaps appeared in the entire Shanghai power grid during the day, the headquarters of Baosteel Co., Ltd., along with its stainless steel and special steel companies, would have to temporarily avoid the peak times and cut the use of electricity by 250,000 kilowatts. Meanwhile, in accordance with the existing fast protocol, 18 super-large power-consuming enterprises must take peak-staggering measures by cutting the use of electricity by 250,000 kW. In this way, a total of 500,000 kW was cut in the use of electricity. Should the Shanghai power grid experience foreseeable supply gaps for multiple days, for a week, or for a continuous period, measures such as peak-staggering, rotational day-off, power yielding, and power restriction could be implemented, with a maximum reducible load totaling 1 million kilowatts (please refer to Table 4).

Based on the above analysis, it is possible to assess the business environment of power supply by measuring transaction costs. Of electricity access and power supply reliability, either of these two factors can serve as an indicator to compare the varying levels of power security in different regions and use it as an important frame of reference for investors' decision-making. When various regions seek to improve the business environment for power supply, they should develop a genuine understanding of their local power systems, conduct a comprehensive investigation of the transaction modules related to the use of electricity in the entire lifecycle of the enterprises, and make a comparative analysis of the transaction costs after calculating the total costs incurred. Only in this way can a panoramic view of power supply be accurately presented.

4 Building Permission

In China, the institutional framework for managing the activation of construction projects can be traced back to 1979 when the former State Planning Commission and the State Basic Construction Commission established a reporting system for the commencement of basic construction projects.[7] Under that system, prior to the

[7] According to the Notice of the State Planning Commission and the State Construction Commission on Properly Managing the Preliminary Work of Basic Construction (issued on May 10, 1979), the following prerequisites are required for project commencement: (1) Preliminary design approved, complete construction drawings ensuring normal construction needs; (2) Site report approved, land requisition completed, and site leveling and demolition completed; (3) Construction teams in place and construction plans compiled; (4) Funds secured, and the project included in the annual construction plan; (5) Production materials, fuel, power, and important transportation conditions secured and all the relevant agreements signed; (6) Building materials and construction machinery secured and in place; (7) Major production equipment secured, and arrangements made in advance for large specialized equipment with long manufacturing cycles or needing trial production; (8) External collaborative projects like power transmission, communication lines, water supply, drainage, roads, and living services facilities secured and related agreements signed; (9) "Three accesses (water access, power access, and road access) and one leveling (ground leveling)" completed at the construction site, and temporary facilities for production and living basically completed; (10) Project management team established and becoming operational.

Table 4 Shanghai municipality's plan for the orderly use of electricity 2020

Serial No.	Plan names	Reducible load (unit: 10,000 kW)
	Level-IV Plan (Routine emergency-response plan, total reducible load of 500,000 kW)	50
Plan 1	Peak avoidance plan of Baosteel Co., Ltd	25
Plan 2	Peak avoidance plan of the agreement-participating users	25
	Level-III Plan (Temporary emergency-response plan, total reducible load of 3,200,000 kW, including the load in Level-IV Plan)	270
Plan 3	Temporary power restriction plan (for 30 min)	270
	Level-II Plan (Emergency-response plan during low-temperature period, total reducible load of 3,800,000 kW, including the load in Level-III Plan)	60
Plan 4	Peak avoidance plan for entertainment venues on low-temperature days	1.07
Plan 5	Peak avoidance plan for business office buildings on low-temperature days	31.17
Plan 6	Peak avoidance plan for multi-functional commercial buildings on low-temperature days	4.17
Plan 7	Peak avoidance plan for hotels and restaurants on low-temperature days	10.11
Plan 8	Peak avoidance plan for public utility business premises on low-temperature days	4.27
Plan 9	Peak avoidance plan for government office buildings on low-temperature days	0.32
Plan 10	Peak avoidance plan for urban landscape lighting and outdoor advertising facilities on low-temperature days	8.89
	Level-I Plan (Special emergency-response plan, total reducible load of 4,800,000 kW including the load in Level-II Plan)	100
Plan 11	Electricity yielding plan (arranging for industrial enterprises characterized by "high input, high energy consumption, high pollution, and low economic outcomes" to discontinue production during winter peak periods)	22
Plan 12	Peak staggering plan (arranging for industrial enterprises of non-continuous technological processes to re-schedule their 2-day weekends to workdays from Monday to Friday)	31.66
Plan 13	Days-off Rotation Plan (arranging for industrial enterprises of non-continuous technological processes to re-schedule their one-week working hours in winter to two-day weekends in spring and autumn)	46.34
	Sum total from the plan for the orderly use of electricity	480

activation of medium-scale or large-scale projects, the company which invests in the construction of buildings, in conjunction with the contractor which undertake the actual construction of the buildings, must jointly submit a commencement report about the construction project. Only after obtaining the administrative permission can the construction project formally commence.

In 1984, the former State Planning Commission relegated its authority of approving the reports of construction commencement, making various departments and provincial governments responsible for the approval. However, it was still required that records be filed with the State Planning Commission.[8] After 1995, there emerged a period of over-heated investment. In an effort to strictly control the initiation of new construction projects, the state used the approval system regarding commencement reports as a crucial mechanism to regulate the pace of fixed-assets investment.[9] By the late 1990s, the former State Planning Commission ceased approving commencement reports, and urban and rural construction departments established a construction permit system.[10] Under this system, construction projects whose investment volume exceeds 300,000 yuan or a building area over 300 m^2 must apply for a construction permit. The housing and urban–rural development commissions under provincial governments could allow adjustments in the building area limits according to local circumstances and must file the records with the Ministry of Housing and Urban–rural Development under the State Council. As per the regulations stipulated by the Ministry in 2014, preconditions for the commencement of a construction project covered a number of approvals in the process of seeking commencement report approval and applying for construction permit, including the approval of construction planning, the approval of land use, and the approvals related to environmental conservation and energy efficiency.[11]

[8] Please refer to the National Planning Commission's Notice on Simplifying the Approval Procedures for Basic Construction Projects (JiZi [1984] No. 1684).

[9] Please refer to the State Council's Notice on Strictly Limiting New Projects and Strengthening the Control of Capital Sources for Fixed Asset Investment' (GuoFaMingDian [1995] No. 6), the Notice on Strictly Controlling High-End Real Estate Development Projects (GuoFa [1995] No. 13), and the National Planning Commission's Notice on Reaffirming the Strict Implementation of Basic Construction Procedures and Approval Regulations (JiTouZi [1999] No. 693).

[10] Please refer to the Management Measures Regarding Building Permits for Construction Projects (Ministry of Housing and Urban-Rural Development, Executive Order No. 18, Oct. 2014).

[11] According to the Management Measures Regarding Building Permits for Construction Projects (Ministry of Housing and Urban-Rural Development of the People's Republic of China, Decree No. 18), the following conditions must be met before a construction company can apply for a building permit. (1) For construction projects that legally require land approval procedures, these procedures have been completed. (2) For construction projects in urban and town planning areas, a construction project planning permit has been obtained. (3) The construction site is basically ready for construction; for projects requiring house expropriation, the progress of expropriation must meet construction requirements. (4) Construction enterprise has been determined. (5) Technical materials sufficient for construction needs and construction design documents have been reviewed and approved as required. (6) Specific measures to ensure project quality and safety are in place. (7) For projects requiring supervision, supervision measures have been arranged. (8) Construction funds is secured.

In the discussions in Chapter Four on the investment system, an analysis has already been conducted on the transaction costs of the majority of approval mechanisms. In the following part, our discussions will be primarily focused on the transaction costs incurred by enterprises in obtaining building permits. This includes the time and costs associated with acquiring construction permits, completing the necessary notifications and inspections, and obtaining access to public utilities and infrastructure.

Shanghai, recognized as one of the cities with the best business environment in China, has undergone several rounds of reform in the procedures for obtaining building permits. Currently, the entire process of obtaining building permits has been reduced to 18 steps, the processing time has been cut to 125.5 days, and the cost is approximately 70,000 RMB. In 2020, Shanghai further proposed to reduce the entire process from 18 steps to 4, shorten the time from 125.5 days to approximately 23 days, and decrease the cost to about 550 RMB. In the entire process, it takes 9 days to obtain a construction permit, 1 day for a joint supervisory inspection, 7 days for comprehensive inspection upon project completion and real estate registration, and 6 days for accessing the water supply and drainage system.[12]

The specific reform measures include the formulation of differentiated reform initiatives based on varying levels of project risks. For instance, among all the projects funded by non-government investments, the scope for the low-risk projects was defined, extending from below 3000 to 10,000 m^2. Those low-risk projects are further categorized into industrial and non-industrial projects, each undergoing different approval processes. With the implementation of the reform, the time and costs consumed for acquiring building permits for low-risk industrial projects have been significantly reduced, making it possible to align with the objective of reducing the entire procedural sequence to 23 days.

In essence, the post-2020 reforms in Shanghai have divided the transaction module of acquiring building permits into multiple sub-modules, progressing from building permits to building permits for low-risk projects and eventually to building permits for low-risk industrial projects, with transaction costs decreasing in each sub-divided module. The transaction module used for the World Bank evaluation is the one with the lowest transaction costs among all the sub-modules. The reforms are undoubtedly effective for such projects. However, reforms of this kind are unlikely to reflect the actual changes in the overall transaction costs for acquiring building permits, thus one should not be overly optimistic about the outcomes of the on-going reforms.

Another reform implemented in Shanghai is the integrated inspection and approval of the completion of the construction projects. Apart from the abolishment of the fire department's inspection, the four-party inspection mechanism[13] was also cancelled, thus allowing the company investing in the construction project to implement the inspection by itself. Concerning the inspection and approval of the construction

[12] This does not include the approval for road excavation and occupation.

[13] The four parties involved in the acceptance inspection include the site inspector, the designer, the builder, and the supervisor.

completion participated by the relevant government departments, the low-risk industrial projects fall within the authority of construction management department and the department of planning and resources, led and organized by the approval and review center. Regarding other construction projects, they might also involve the inspection by the health, greenery, civil defense, traffic, traffic police, and meteorology departments, etc. In the transaction module of completion inspection, the main entities involved in the transaction are relevant administrative departments and enterprises, the rights being transacted include various types of inspection approvals, and the rules of the transaction are the various regulations and standards stipulated for the completion inspection. The transaction costs include, at least, the time spent on waiting for the inspection and, also possibly, the cost for modifications and improvements. If we analyze Shanghai's transaction module of integrated completion inspection by applying the analytical method of transaction modules, we will find that eliminating some of inspection mechanisms will significantly reduce the number of sub-modules of transaction. However, the fact that the approval and review center is made responsible for leading and organizing multi-departmental inspections does not reduce sub-modules of transaction; rather, due to the need to coordinate the timing of on-site inspections by multiple departments, it is more likely to increase the time waiting for inspections and thereby increase transaction costs.

Shanghai, in promoting governmental services, created a mechanism of "one-stop paperwork acceptance and the completion of review within stipulated timeframe" and established the approval and review center. Various administrative departments would have to select staff to be stationed at the center; however, individual departments carry out their approvals and supervisions in line with their own specific functions. Superficially, this "one-stop" service has only one reception window at the front end to accept review applications, but at the back end, each approval process is still to be completed by respective departments. For example, the back end of the "one-stop service" of construction investment approval includes such functionary departments as the development and reform commission, the bureau of natural resources and planning, the water conservancy bureau, the urban and rural development bureau, the transportation bureau, the housing management bureau, the marine and fishery bureau, the meteorological bureau, and the bureau of ecology and environment. Only when the application materials are complete and comply with legally-stipulated forms will the application be accepted at the window of "one-stop service" and "the countdown" activated. However, the approval process does not include the time spent on all the necessary procedures prior to the acceptance of application materials, such as multiple-party consultations, planning adjustments, review of materials, as well as various reviews, evaluations, public notifications, hearings, measurement, and on-site prospecting. As a mechanism, "the completion of review within stipulated timeframe" reflects a reduction in transaction costs, but it only pertains to the transaction costs "inside the window" at the Approval Center when all the documents are complete, while the time consumed in the processes "outside the window" constitutes the main part of the transaction costs. Thus, there are substantial limitations in using "the completion of review within stipulated timeframe" to reflect the efficiency of the business environment.

A legitimacy review of building permits reveals that certain government departments have set up transaction modules for projects that legally do not actually require building permits, thus adding extra transaction costs. According to China's "Building Law," the sub-module of the right to trade building permits only involve "the construction of various buildings and their ancillary facilities and the installation of supporting lines, pipes, and equipment."[14] The "Measures for Managing the Building Permit for Construction Projects," formulated by the housing and construction department in accordance with the "Building Law," have added two more sub-modules of transaction, namely, the "Decoration and Refurbishment" module and the "Urban Municipal Infrastructure Projects" module.[15] This implies that nearly all the construction projects in urban areas need to apply for building permits.

By putting together the analyses of all the aforementioned transaction modules, we can discover that different transaction rules can be devised for obtaining construction permits for various types of investment projects. Optimization can be performed concerning the rules in each category of transaction modules to minimize transaction costs as much as possible. Imposing an undifferentiated requirement on all the construction projects to acquire building permits certainly increases the transaction costs for the investment activities of a whole society, resulting in constraints on the institutional supply of investments.

5 Sanctions Against Dishonesty

The spirit of the contract is the cornerstone of market economy. Without any exception, investors prefer to cooperate with business partners who have good credit; likewise, investors love to operate business in places with a positive credit environment. However, in the development of the credit system, if the boundaries between the public and the private rights, and between moral constraints and legal regulations, are not clearly defined, the outcome may backfire on the original intentions of this institutional construction.

In the construction of the credit system in China, we can see that credit and personal integrity are somehow inseparable and exchangeable. Both credit and personal integrity share the quality of honesty. Credit pertains more to the commercial context, emphasizing the ability of repaying credit loans in good faith. On the other hand, personal integrity is more related to interpersonal relationship, stressing the personal attribute of trustworthiness. In Chinese judicial practice, those individuals subject to enforcement are not included in the list of dishonest judgment debtors if they lack the ability to perform the duty of repaying the credit. Only those who deliberately refuse to perform legal obligations and act unlawfully are subject

[14] Please refer to Article 2 of the Construction Law of the People's Republic of China (revised in 2019).

[15] Please refer to the Management Measures Regarding Building Permits for Construction Projects' (Ministry of Housing and Urban-Rural Development, Executive Order No. 18, Oct. 2014).

to punishment and sanctions.[16] Therefore, legally speaking, whether one is deemed dishonest is based on unlawful facts and the consequences of infringement, instead of on moral qualities of being good, just, or honorable. While morality and law are closely related, they have clear regulatory boundaries, and legal judgments cannot be made on the basis of moral standards.

Initially, the subjects of credit sanctions were all those listed in the Supreme People's Court's Database of Dishonest Persons Subject to Enforcement as well as those others to whom were issued High Consumption Restriction Orders by the People's Courts (hereinafter collectively referred to as "dishonest persons subject to enforcement"). When the dishonest persons subject to enforcement, the term refers to the concerned persons themselves. When it refers to corporate organizations, it includes their legal representatives, principal persons in charge of the corporate organizations, and those directly responsible for the execution of debts.[17] The Supreme People's Court would send the List of Dishonest Judgment Debtors to all contracted parties. By issuing orders of high consumption restriction to dishonest persons subject to enforcement on the "National Courts' Information Publication and Inquiry Platform Regarding Persons Subject to Enforcement," the Supreme People's Court collaborates with related departments to restrict the dishonest debtors' acts of high consumption and implement other credit sanctions.[18] By December 2020, a total of 7.51 million dishonest persons subject to enforcement nationwide had fulfilled their obligations due to the pressure of credit sanctions, with the rate of voluntary fulfillment of valid legal documents increasing annually and the overall difficulty of law-enforcement gradually easing.[19] Subsequently, the range of credit sanctions gradually expanded, and various departments began to establish their own lists of dishonest debtors for law-enforcement, deviating from the original intention of this institutional design and leading to significant institutional alienation.

As of the end of 2019, at the level of the Central Government, there was no legislation by the National People's Congress or administrative regulations from the State Council regarding the building of the credit system. Nevertheless, various government departments had started to implement joint punitive measures in the

[16] Please refer to the Decision of the Supreme People's Court on Amending the Several Provisions on the Public Announcement of the List of Information of Dishonest Judgment Debtors (Judicial Interpretation [2017] No. 7).

[17] Please refer to the Notice on Issuing the Memorandum of Cooperation on "Promoting Credit and Penalizing Dishonesty" by the Central Civilization Office, the Supreme People's Court, the Ministry of Public Security, the State-owned Assets Supervision and Administration Commission of the State Council, the State Administration for Industry and Commerce, the China Banking Regulatory Commission, the Civil Aviation Administration of China, and the China Railway Corporation (Civilization Office [2014] No. 4).

[18] Please refer to the Several Provisions of the Supreme People's Court on Restricting High Consumption of Dishonest Judgment Debtors (Judicial Interpretation [2010] No. 8) and the Several Provisions on the Public Announcement of the List of Information of Dishonest Judgment Debtors (Judicial Interpretation [2013] No. 17).

[19] Liu Guixiang, "7.51 Million Dishonest Judgment Debtors Forced by Pressure to Fulfill Obligations," http://jszx.court.gov.cn/main/SupremeCourt/284530.jhtml.

form of memoranda, with a total of 34 "memoranda of cooperation on joint regulatory and punitive actions against dishonesty" published. Originally, administrative departments' memoranda were archival documents used for internal record-keeping and they only served as a foundation for internal administrative actions. However, in developing the credit system, relevant departments, for the first time on a large scale, used the memoranda to regulate and discipline the administrative counterparts. The legitimacy of such a practice is highly questionable. Administrative actions can be categorized into internal and external administrative actions. Internal administrative actions are valid only internally and are not applicable externally. This means that they are not legally binding with respect to social counterparts.[20] In developing China's credit system, related departments have systematically employed internal actions against external cases, thus avoiding the legally-established procedures required for formulating formal administrative regulations and decisions. For example, there would be no need for record registration or review by judicial departments or for supervision over the administrative law-enforcement, thus leading to the lack of necessary checks and balances. Many provisions contained in these memoranda have produced substantial adverse consequences on administrative counterparts. To a certain extent, such a phenomenon has become quite widespread.

In a survey conducted by the author of this book in October 2020, it was discovered that, in various regions across China, there was a widespread rush and abuse of credit sanctions in their efforts to develop the credit system. Generally, local government departments tend to use credit evaluations of their administrative counterparts as a new method to execute their administrative responsibilities. Credit has virtually become a "basket" into which one can throw everything. Some municipal governments have over 50 departments participating in the construction of the credit system, issuing more than 100 administrative documents. Worse still, even some towns have issued their own documents for developing the credit system. An overview of the existing practices in building the credit system reveals the following major problems.

Firstly, there are too numerous and overly-broad credit standards. Administrative departments at all levels, such as those in charge of housing construction, taxation, market supervision, ecology and environment, public security, and transportation, are all involved in credit evaluations regarding enterprises. They employ graded classifications and implement differentiated supervisions. However, the evaluation standards and classifications vary among different departments. For example, the taxation department might classify enterprises into five levels, A, B, M, C, and D respectively, based on the results of taxation credit evaluations. On the other hand, the market supervision department might classify enterprises into five major categories: excellent credit, good credit, ordinary credit, bad credit, and very bad credit. Furthermore, the department of ecology and environment might divide enterprises into four broad categories in terms of environmental protection: outstanding, good, warning, and poor.

Secondly, there is a high proportion and substantial risk of enterprises being evaluated as violating public honesty and trustworthiness. As too many administrative

[20] Hu Jianmiao, *Administrative Law*, Law Press, 2015 Edition, p. 176.

departments are involved in credit evaluations, enterprises can easily be designated as "dishonest" for slight missteps. For example, a 2020 survey in a city, named N, randomly selected from a province along the southeast coast, showed that out of 80,733 enterprises publicized by the city's Market Supervision and Administration Bureau, 11,540 were classified as demonstrating "bad credit" or "very bad credit," accounting for 14.3% of all the enterprises in the city. Additionally, the city's Taxation Bureau publicized 10,657 enterprises with lower credit ratings of C and D, accounting for 17.6% of the total 60,625 enterprises.

On November 25, 2020, the State Council held a regular executive meeting to examine issues related to the building of the credit system. Subsequently, the General Office of the State Council issued Document No. 49, calling for promoting the construction of the social credit system in a prudent and moderate manner that conforms to laws and regulations. The contents included in public credit information, the range of information sharing and disclosure, the determination of the list of dishonest entities, the punishment and rectification of dishonest behavior, all these must all have legal and regulatory basis. The State Council required all the relevant departments in various regions to promptly review and rectify the measures already introduced for the identification, recording, disclosure, and punishment of dishonest behavior that do not comply with the newly-published requirements.[21] Subsequently, credit legislation was launched nationwide, and local people's congresses in multiple provinces and municipalities have passed laws and regulations regarding social credit. In September 2021, the author of this book conducted another survey. In this survey, a group of samples were randomly selected from the "Credit China" website in G Province, interviews were conducted with some of the involved parties, and discussions were held with relevant administrative departments of the province. The survey has identified the following problems.

Firstly, unjustifiable measures of the dishonesty constraint have not been adequately cleared up. By tracking the process of rectifying the measures of dishonesty constraint in Province G, it was revealed that, among a total of seven regimes of rules and regulations to be revised and modified by various departments, only one has actually been rectified, and only about one-third of the over 30 regimes planned to be revised by individual districts and cities have been completed. Some measures aimed at penalizing dishonesty, which lack a legal or regulatory basis, have not been included in the rectification list and are still being enforced. For instance, it is stipulated by the Department of Natural Resources that credit entities on the blacklist should be subjected to disclosure on the Social Credit Management Platform for Natural Resources, and they must be restricted from acquiring publicly-owned natural resources and from participating in natural resource projects funded by the government's financial allocation. Moreover, some punitive measures against dishonesty that lack legal and regulatory basis are still being formulated, such as

[21] Please refer to the Guidelines by the General Office of the State Council on Further Improving the Dishonesty Constraint System and Building a Long-term Mechanism for Promoting Credit (General Office of the State Council [2020] No. 49).

the "Blacklist Notification System for Dishonest Companies in Financing Guarantee" currently being formulated by the Financial Regulatory Bureau, which plans to expose in the industry itself the financing guarantee institutions included in the blacklist. As a technical term, the concept of "blacklist" has never been employed in the existing laws and regulations of China, and there is no legal basis to establish such a blacklist or to put any individual or entity on such a blacklist.

Secondly, the difficulty to remedy dishonesty still persists. According to the credit restoration measures for dishonest entities in Province G, the departments that identify dishonest entities should, upon accepting applications for credit restoration, provide feedback and issue decision documents within seven working days and in complex situations, the delay should not exceed seven working days. However, the actual situation is far from being so simple and straightforward. From the survey, it is found that currently, the procedures and difficulties for businesses to restore their credit have largely remained unchanged as compared with the period before the issuing of Document No. 49 by the State Council. Companies that have been subjected to administrative penalties generally have to apply to the administrative authorities making the penalty decisions for credit restoration immediately after the shortest disclosure period expires on the credit website, and only after passing the application approval can the penalized companies have the relevant information of dishonesty withdrawn. Once subjected to administrative penalties, all the sanctioned companies would be automatically listed as demonstrating dishonest behavior, regardless of the severity of the dishonest behavior or whether such behavior is intentional or inadvertent. However, the information about dishonest behavior will not be removed automatically from the list of dishonesty upon the expiration of the disclosure period; instead, penalized companies have to go through extremely complicated procedures of credit restoration. Typically, the entire process involves going through many different stages, such as making credit commitments, completing rectifications in credit, undergoing special education, submitting credit reports. Restoration will be deemed completed only after passing the credit check by multiple departments.

Thirdly, the blacklist system exacerbates the difficulties already faced by struggling businesses. Despite the promulgation of Document No. 49 by the State Council, most regions have not stopped developing various blacklists that are devoid of legal and regulatory foundation, and companies which were previously illegally included in the blacklist are not removed from the blacklist, thus the negative impacts on these victimized companies persist. According to the findings from the survey, some companies were included in the Safety Production Blacklist established in a certain municipality. The related dishonest information was published by the municipality's emergency management bureau and on the municipality's leading newspaper and official website, etc. At the same time, the information was forwarded to relevant departments and organizations in the fields of investment, land resources, construction, transportation, banking, securities, insurance, state-owned asset management, industry and commerce, and labor union. The affected companies would be strictly restricted from receiving policy-based fund support for business projects and from acquiring policy support in seeking administrative approval for their own new projects or in bidding for projects. In addition, they would be accorded differential treatment when applying for bank loans, thus incurring severe consequences on their production activities and business operations.

Fourthly, there is an unreasonable rush for local credit legislation. In less than a year, 17 provincial, municipal, and local people's congresses across the country have passed social credit regulations. Some departments have also accelerated the legislative process regarding their departmental rules and regulations. However, despite the lack of legal foundation from national legislation or administrative regulations of the State Council, a plethora of credit statutes have been introduced in many regions, prematurely incorporating into local laws and regulations many immature contents on which no consensus has been reached either in theory or in practice. Worse still, there are even contents that violate the national constitution and the law. A considerable part of these contents infringe upon the basic rights of citizens, including personal freedom, personal dignity, and property rights, as well as the civil rights of legal persons.[22] The enforcement of these credit sanctions does not require court trials; instead, some simple administrative procedures would suffice. In most cases, there are no or few relief measures. Any objections and applications for relief raised by the involved parties do not affect the execution of the sanctions.

Fifthly, the legitimate rights and interests of the involved parties tend to be overlooked.

In this regard, the first problem is that the procedure of imposing credit sanctions is unfavorable to the parties involved. In the absence of procedural justice, there will be no guarantee for fair outcomes, and this principle applies equally to the imposition of credit sanctions. If we are to break down the procedure for credit sanctions into sub-categories, it would include several phases: information acquisition, decision-making concerning sanctions, enforcement of the sanctions, and oversight of the sanctions. Typically, these administrative actions are completed by one particular department or by entities delegated by that department, and there is a lack of checks and balances throughout these different phases. It thus becomes highly likely that certain unjustified credit sanctions will go unchallenged and will also render it exceedingly difficult to rectify erroneous sanction decisions once they are made. In China, increasing emphasis has been placed on procedural provisions in the legislation regarding the administrative procedural law. However, in the current local and departmental legislation on credit regulations, there generally lacks specificity in procedural provisions. No operable provisions have been formulated for the protection of the rights concerning the significant interests of the parties involved, such as public notification, removal from the list of discredited entities, and the right to defense and appeal.

The second problem is that the rights to personal dignity of the parties involved are overlooked. Rights to personal dignity include the basic rights of a citizen such

[22] The measures roughly fall into three categories: restricting citizens and legal persons from participating in certain economic activities, such as market entry, stock issuance, obtaining credit, bidding and tendering, obtaining natural resources, enjoying policy preferences, etc.; restricting the personal freedom of citizens and legal persons, such as travelling by air or by high-speed trains, and staying in certain hotels; impairing the personality of citizens and legal persons, such as disclosing credit records, limiting participation in the selection of honors and awards, etc.

as the right to reputation, the right to honor, and the right to privacy. For any society, not resorting to humiliating means in punishing those who have committed illegal or criminal acts is an important symbol of humanity's rejection of barbarism and a symbol of progress toward civilization. For example, criminals should not be paraded in the streets, tattooed on the face, or made to wear identifying markers. Calling the list of discredited entities a "blacklist" on credit websites and exposing the listed entities through public media undermine the dignity of citizens and the commercial reputation of businesses. Moreover, the information disclosure in the dishonest sanctions tends to contain substantial personal information of the involved parties, thus infringing upon the citizens' right to privacy. In the majority of the existing credit legislations, no provisions have been established to protect the citizens' right to personal dignity. Some of such legislations only have principled provisions, lacking substantive contents and thus remaining inoperable.

The third problem is that the punitive measures tend to exceed necessary and reasonable bounds. At the very outset, the joint punishment imposed on dishonest behavior was meted out mainly to the "hardened deadbeats," that is, those inveterate defaulters, who refuse to repay debts after court judgments. As the development of the credit system deepens, the scope and the entities of punishment have come to cover almost all the subjects of administrative penalties, including the individuals and enterprises publicly designated as violating the regulations of individual administrative departments. The penalties are primarily aimed at impairing personal rights, property rights, and the right to personal dignity, as well as imposing certain duties. Since the penalties are executed on the basis of the lists, without differentiating the severity of dishonest actions, all the listed dishonest acts face the same consequences of punishment. For example, those subjected to administrative penalties valued at tens and thousands of yuan are named in the same list as those subjected to administrative penalties valued at tens of yuan. For the latter, a minor misstep can lead to serious and long-lasting consequences. In particular, in the age of the Internet, the damages produced on the reputation of an individual and an enterprise can be irreversible. Therefore, imposing sanctions on dishonesty via legislation must be undertaken with caution and moderation, taking into full consideration the long-term impacts of the punitive consequences.

Sixthly, some administrative departments tend to expand their authorities by means of legislation. In 2021, various government departments, such as the Ministry of Ecology and Environment, Ministry of Transport, General Administration of Customs, State Administration for Market Regulation, General Administration of Sport, Energy Bureau, and Civil Aviation Administration, issued new departmental regulations and provisions in an effort to construct their credit systems. Some of these departments have seized the opportunity of credit legislation to expand their power. A case in point is the revision undertaken by the Administration for Market Regulation of the existing credit regulations. In December 2015, without the support from upper-level legislation, this Administration for Market Regulation created the concept of "seriously illegal and dishonest enterprises" in the "Interim Measures for the Management of the List of Seriously Unlawful and Dishonest Enterprises," and used this list to impose credit constraints, administer joint departmental penalties, and make credit information disclosure. Even after the issuance of Document No. 49 by the State Council, instead of abolishing or amending the interim measures, the Administration issued the formalized "Measures for the Management of the List of Seriously Illegal and Dishonest Enterprises" in July 2021, changing "the entities subject to regulation" to "the parties concerned." This change of name means that the entities included in the list have been expanded to include natural persons and almost all market entities. This regime of regulations also created new power for the Administration's various functional departments to enforce credit sanctions, including food safety supervision, supervision of drugs, medical devices, cosmetics, quality safety supervision, consumer rights protection, and fair competition supervision. Under this Administration, the government departments on all levels, from the level of Central Government to the level of provincial and local governments, can wield these powers and include administrative counterparts in the credit punishment list. This Administration's practice to expand its own power obviously contradicts the State Council's executive order to develop the credit system in a lawful manner.

If we perform our analysis from the perspective of institutional evolution, we will discover that a form of institutional alienation has occurred in the gradual changes of the formal constraints of the credit system. In the transaction of rights regarding the credit supervision, the principal actors or entities of the transaction are the government and the enterprises, the rights being traded are the government's credit evaluations of the enterprises, the rules of the transaction are the government-established system of social credit evaluation and the supervisory mechanisms with respect to the enterprises, and the transaction costs are the time and the expenses that enterprises spend for the sake of obtaining and restoring the government's credit ratings. The institutional alienation in the credit system is reflected in the expansion of the regulatory scope of the transaction rules, in which the mechanism's original function to assess an enterprise's capability to repay credit loans has been extended to an evaluation of the enterprise's honesty and trustworthiness. For instance, the new system requires market entities to make credit commitments to the society on their own accord. It enables government departments to conduct credit ratings concerning enterprises based on tax payment, standardized management, and honest business operation. It can also serve as the basis for government departments to implement joint incentives for the enterprises' honest operation and joint punishments for the enterprises' dishonest operation. Moreover, it also makes an enterprise's financing efforts critically dependent on government ratings. In establishing this honesty-based financing evaluation system, the government uses moral evaluation to measure debt repayment ability. All these honesty evaluation mechanisms significantly increase the time and expenditure with which enterprises have to deal with government assessments, raising transaction costs and backfiring on the efforts to improve the business environment.

Once an enterprise is identified as a distrusted entity, it faces punishments for its dishonesty. The sanctions for dishonesty fall into three major categories. The first is administrative measures. Implemented legally and according to regulations by administrative agencies, these measures curtail the rights or increase the obligations of distrusted entities. Examples include restrictions on market access or industry access, restrictions on taking up positions or holding office in certain organizations, restrictions on consumption, restrictions on going abroad, and restrictions on acquiring more advanced education. The second is management measures. Implemented by administrative departments based on the need to perform their respective functions, these measures include restrictions on applying for funding projects supported by government fiscal policy, restrictions on participating in evaluations and selections for outstanding individuals or enterprises, restrictions on enjoying preferential policies and convenience measures, inclusion in the list of seriously dishonest entities, public disclosure of dishonesty information, and identification as focal objects of supervision. The third are the measures autonomously implemented by organizations other than administrative agencies, such as inclusion of enterprises in market-oriented credit or rating reports, and stricter scrutiny in granting credit loans. In regions where local regulations have special provisions for dishonesty sanctions, the government department in charge of the local social credit system can work together with related departments (or institutions), based on local regulations, to develop a supplementary list of dishonesty sanctions applicable only to that particular region.[23]

Imposing sanctions on dishonesty is immune from the "Administrative Punishment Law." On the other hand, nearly all the activities susceptible to administrative penalties are subject to additional credit sanctions. This means that acts of violating administrative rules are equated, in a rather simplistic manner, with acts of dishonesty and penalties are imposed on dishonesty as a form of violating the law. Two sets of penalty systems, both interrelated and conflicting, have emerged in the administrative law. The main entities involved in these penalty systems are the relevant government departments and the enterprises. The rights being traded are the rights of enterprises to engage in normal business operation, and the transaction cost is the time and expenses spent by companies on resuming normal business operation in each of the two penalty systems. Evidently, in enforcing the credit sanction system, an additional transaction module is superimposed on the existing administrative penalty module. There is no essential difference between these two systems, as the entities and the rights involved in the two transaction modules are entirely identical. The rights being traded have experienced a "price hike" for no apparent reasons. The transaction costs necessary to restore credit constitute the increased cost in the overall transaction costs.

In the transaction of the rights involved in credit restoration, the enterprises and the government departments are the principal entities engaged in the transaction. The rights being transacted encompass the cessation of public disclosure of relevant information such as administrative penalties, and transaction rules comprise of the procedures to restore and reinstate corporate credit. The transaction module of credit restoration can be divided into a number of sub-modules. For instance, enterprises

[23] Please refer to the National Development and Reform Commission's "Basic List of Measures for Penalizing Dishonesty" (2021 Edition) (Draft Version). Although this document is yet to be formalized, the descriptions contained in it regarding the measures for punishing dishonesty reflect the current actual situation.

are obliged to restore their credit by clearing up the administrative penalty records on the Credit China website, on the portal credit websites of local governments, in the credit information disclosure systems, and even on certain enterprise information platforms. To rescind the public disclosure of all such information in all these sub-modules of transaction compels enterprises to incur transaction expenses. As a matter of fact, information related to administrative penalties can still be retrieved on the Internet even after all the restoration procedures are completed in these sub-modules. Apparently, once the dishonesty information is disseminated, the transactional costs required to fully restore a company's reputation are infinitely great.

6 Administrative Penalties

Administrative penalties refer to actions taken by administrative authorities in accordance with the law against citizens, legal persons, or other organizations that violate the order of the government's administrative management. These penalties take the form of either diminishing the rights and privileges or imposing additional obligations.[24] In China, imposing administrative penalties is a law-enforcement measure widely adopted by administrative agencies. The administrative penalties cover such a wide range of punishable matters, contain so broad stipulations, and are executed so randomly that they profoundly impact local business environments, triggering a multitude of social conflicts. In recent years, with the intensified endeavors on the part of party committees and governments at all levels to foster clean administration and promote law-based governance, instances where local governments impose penalties without legal basis have been significantly diminished. However, instances of barbaric law-enforcement persist, and the fairness and justifiability of many penalties are called into question. At the same time, administrative penalties have also engendered a plethora of rent-seeking and corruption activities, substantially augmenting transaction costs on the part of enterprises and affecting the credibility of the CPC and the government to the general public. Some of the principal problems can be identified as the follows.

The first major problem is the excessive quantity of punishable matters. In China, the liability for violating various laws and regulations predominantly entails administrative penalties, especially in economic activities where administrative penalties pervade numerous facets of the government's administration. The exact number of matters susceptible to administrative penalties nationwide is currently difficult to quantify. A random sampling of publicly available information on the official website of Province H's government reveals that, amongst 2831 administrative management matters that fall under the provincial government, as many as 1709 matters are subject to potential administrative penalties in the case of violations (accounting for 60%). A total of 35 government departments are authorized to mete

[24] Please refer to Article 2 of the "Law of the People's Republic of China on Administrative Penalties" (revised in 2021).

out administrative penalties. By contrast, there are only 322 administrative licensing matters in the same period (representing 11%). Most of these administrative penalties are targeted at economic activities, focusing on fields such as market supervision, drug supervision, emergency management, public health, water resources, culture, tourism, natural resources, agriculture, and forestry. An investigation that the author of this book conducted in 2018 at the State Administration for Market Regulation revealed that the bureau was legally authorized to impose administrative penalties over 1200 matters. To impose those penalties, 121 laws, 207 administrative regulations, and 326 departmental rules are involved, while administrative licensing matters are only above 70. A sample survey of the penalty documents on the official website of the State Administration for Market Regulation indicated that the primary entities subjected to administrative penalties are micro and small enterprises and self-employed individuals.

The second problem is the alarming tendency to use administrative fines as a means of generating revenue. Those regions with fewer sources of taxation and greater financial pressure are often more likely to "substitute administration with administrative fines" and "expanding revenue through penalties," using the income from the fines and confiscations to compensate for fiscal insufficiency. Data from the Ministry of Finance shows that the income from fines and confiscations in China's public fiscal revenue is on the rapid rise. In 2008, the total income from fines and confiscations nationwide was 898 billion yuan, amounting to 68 yuan per capita. By 2018, the total sum rose to 2,659 billion yuan, reaching 190 yuan per capita. During that period, both the total and per-capita income from fines and confiscations increased by more than 2.6 times. In a 2019 investigation in a county in Province M, the author of this book found that from January to August, public budget income decreased by 21.1% year on year, while income from fines and confiscations increased by 2.5 times, primarily derived from areas of traffic police department (by 3.8 times), use of state-owned land (by 2 times), environmental protection (by 4.7 times), and transportation (by 3.6 times). Despite the Central Government's repeated decrees stipulating that income from fines and confiscations should not be retained by or returned to the local administrative departments, or used for departmental expenses and benefits, the practice of increasing revenue through penalties, which used to overt, has become increasing covert in recent years. In real practices, there are countless instances in which departmental budgets are still linked to the income from fines and confiscations.

The third problem is the unlawful establishment of administrative penalties. The current "Law on Administrative Penalties" authorizes the imposition of four types of penalties (divided into six forms), namely, admonitory penalties (warnings), financial penalties (fines, confiscation of illegal gains, confiscation of illicit property), behavioral penalties (orders to cease production or business activities, temporary seizure or revocation of administrative approvals, and temporary seizure or revocation of licenses), and personal penalties (administrative detention). Beyond these categories of penalties authorized by the law and regulations, various areas and local administrative departments have made it a point of creating new forms of penalties, such as those affecting reputation and credit. For instance, China's blacklist system for tax law violation began to be implemented in 2014, based on the document released by the State Taxation Administration—"Measures for Disclosing the Information of Major Tax Violation Cases (Trial Version)." However, this document regarding the disclosure measure is a departmental document by the Administration itself and its upper-level law, the "Law on Tax Collection Management" and its detailed implementation regulations do not contain any provisions regarding the establishment of the "blacklist." Similarly, the market supervision and regulation department has formulated the "Interim Measures for the Management of the List of Seriously Unlawful and Dishonest Enterprises." The upper-level law upon which it is based, the "Interim Regulations on Enterprise Information Disclosure", does not contain any authorization for penalizing "serious violations of law or acts of dishonesty." Nevertheless, market supervision and regulation departments have included into the "list of seriously unlawful and dishonest enterprises" those which demonstrate business operation anomalies, fail to file their annual reports in a timely manner, and are subjected to administrative penalties. The penalties are meted out in the form of public disclosure or prohibition of individuals from serving as legal representatives or persons in charge of enterprises. In other words, by means of their own regulations, these departments have created penalty liabilities that exceed the provisions of the "Law on Administrative Penalties."

The fourth problem is the increasing magnitude of penalties. When some regions and local government departments formulate specific rules for implementing administrative penalties in accordance with the law and regulations, they often exceed the scope and the intensity of penalties as stipulated by the law and regulations. Government departments on different levels tend to escalate the severity of penalties and prefer stringency over leniency. A case in point is the "Construction Law," which stipulates that engaging in construction activities without applying for a construction permit can result in fines. This law defines "construction activities" as "the construction of buildings, their auxiliary facilities, and the installation of associated lines, pipes, and equipment." However, the housing and construction department, in formulating the measures for managing the building permits based on the "Construction Law," expanded the scope of "construction activities" to include "decorations" and "urban municipal infrastructure projects." In so doing, the department succeeded in increasing the number of matters punishable by administrative penalties. The administrative penalties stipulated in the "Construction Law" are only targeted at the corporate organizations involved, but the housing and construction department has expanded the entities with liabilities for punishable violations of construction permits to include individuals and at the same time added two more forms of penalty, namely, fines and public notifications.[25]

[25] The "Management Measures Regarding the Building Permits for Construction Projects" stipulates that when imposing a fine on a construction company, the directly responsible person in the top management of the company and other directly responsible personnel shall be fined between 5% and 10% of the total amount of the fine imposed on the company. When the company and the related persons in charge are penalized, the penalties would be publicly announced as a record of bad behavior.

The fifth problem is the excessive discretionary power in meting out penalties. Many laws and regulations provide rather general and abstract descriptions of administrative penalties, lacking concrete and objective standards. The amounts of monetary penalty can range from ten thousand yuan to several million yuan or from one time to ten times the illegal income, thus creating immense space for the power rental of corrupt government officials. Whether to penalize or not to penalize and whether to minimize penalties or to maximize penalties, these issues are all at the discretion of administrative law-enforcement officials. Even regarding the same illegal act, the standards for the penalty are inconsistent across different laws and regulations. Many penalty clauses also set catch-all provisions such as "other acts," "other means," "other ways," and "other forms," which render the imposition of penalties all the more arbitrary.

In March 1996, China enacted its first Law on Administrative Penalties, which served to standardize and restrain the widespread and chaotic administrative penalties at the time. However, this legislation also established a basis for certain administrative penalties that were otherwise unreasonable. Later on, the Law on Administrative Penalties underwent several rounds of amendment, but the principal problems regarding the administrative penalties have remained unresolved. In January 2021, the Standing Committee of the National People's Congress revised the Law on Administrative Penalties for a second time. This recalibration prominently reflects considerations related to transaction costs in several areas. For instance, proposed supplementary provisions stipulated that when establishing administrative penalties, extensive feedback should be solicited through hearings and deliberative meetings, and written explanations should be provided to the legislative body. These provisions also grant the concerned parties the right to request a hearing. Elaborate provisions were also formulated concerning the procedural details of such hearings. These stipulations, in essence, increase the transaction costs on the part of legislative bodies and law-enforcement agencies when exercising their power and serve to protect the legitimate rights and interests of the administrative counterparts.[26] Additionally, the new law required that a comprehensive administrative enforcement system be established in fields such as urban management, market supervision, ecological environment, cultural market, transportation, emergency management, and agriculture so that the power of administrative penalty are executed in a relatively integrated manner.[27] This integration of the administrative penalty power helped put together transaction modules that used to be distributed discretely across various government departments. By putting transaction entities closer together and making transaction contracts better coordinated, this mechanism has helped reduce the transaction costs on behalf of the administrative counterparts. However, some provisions in this revised law may further augment the transaction costs incurred by administrative

[26] Please refer to Articles 11, 12, 44, 58, and 63 to 65 of the Law of the People's Republic of China on Administrative Penalties (revised in 2021).

[27] Please refer to Article 18 of the Law of the People's Republic of China on Administrative Penalties (revised in 2021).

counterparts due to administrative penalties. Below are the analyses of several main amendments in this revision.[28]

Firstly, there is an expansion in the legislative power among legislative entities. The original Law on Administrative Penalties stipulates that the legislative entities are the National People's Congress and its standing committee, the ministries and committees under the State Council, the People's Congresses of the provinces and of the municipalities directly under the Central Government and their standing committees, the People's Governments of the provinces, autonomous regions, and municipalities directly under the Central Government, and the municipal people's governments where the People's Governments of the provinces and autonomous regions are located, as well as the relatively large municipal people's governments approved by the State Council.[29] The renewed Law on Administrative Penalties provides the administrative laws and regulations as well as local laws and regulations with the expanded authority to establish administrative penalties. It has added the provision that if the upper-level law does not prescribe any administrative penalties against certain illegal acts, administrative laws and regulations as well as local laws and regulations can, for the purpose of enforcing the upper-level law, establish supplementary administrative penalties. Legislative entities are the designers and formulators of institutions (i.e., institutional builders), and expanding the legislative power of the legislative entities means these legislative entities are endowed with the authority to establish more administrative penalties or to adjust rules of penalty. The creation of any new administrative penalties or the introduction of any supplementary provisions into administrative penalties can generate new rights ready to be transacted, inevitably resulting in new transaction costs between the government's administrative agencies and the enterprises in the actual process of enforcement. There are 354 administrative agencies in China endowed with local legislative power.[30] Given the fact that there have already been an excessive and chaotic number of administrative penalties, it is likely that continuing to grant these administrative agencies excessive legislative power regarding administrative penalties may lead to an overly rapid increase in transaction costs.

Secondly, the authority to impose penalties is delegated to administrative bodies on lower levels. It was stipulated in the original Law on Administrative Penalties that administrative penalties were to be imposed by administrative organs at or above the

[28] Please refer to the article by Zhang Guilong, level-1 inspector of the Administrative Law Division of the Legislative Affairs Commission of the Standing Committee of the National People's Congress, "Main Modifications in the Law on Administrative Penalties," http://www.npc.gov.cn/npc/c30834/202102/e4dca001adea4d27afb27d0d9637382a.shtml.

[29] Please refer to Articles 9, 10, 11, 12, 13, and 14 in the Law of the People's Republic of China on Administrative Penalties (revised in 2017).

[30] On March 11, 2018, the Government's Work Report at the First Session of the 13th National People's Congress stated that the Central Government has granted local legislative power to all the municipalities where regions are established. The subjects entitled to local legislative authority increased from the original 31 provinces (autonomous regions, municipalities directly under the Central Government) and 49 larger cities to an additional 274, including 240 municipalities where regions are established, 30 autonomous prefectures, and 4 prefecture-level municipalities where regions are not established.

county level.[31] The current Law on Administrative Penalties stipulates that, under certain conditions, the power to impose administrative penalties can be delegated to agencies at township and even sub-district levels.[32] In China, a great variety of matters can be subjected to administrative penalties in an equally great number of categories, and the enforcement of different administrative penalties have different requirements for personnel qualities, equipment, procedures, and technology. The enforcement capabilities vary significantly from place to place. In particular, when the mechanism of checks and balances on the exercise of administrative penalty power at the basic level is not well developed, delegating the law-enforcing authority to agencies at township and sub-district levels may lead to more frequent and pervasive infringements upon the rights of administrative counterparts, making it harder for the penalized entities to have access to necessary relief. Administrative counterparts will incur more transaction costs than before in their efforts to seek exemption or relief from penalties and to resume normal business operation.

Thirdly, new categories of penalties are added. The original Law on Administrative Penalties stipulated the following categories of penalties: warning, fine, confiscation of illegal income and illicit property, orders to suspend production or business operation, temporary or permanent revocation of licenses or permits, administrative detention, and other administrative punishments as prescribed by the law and administrative regulations.[33] The revised Law on Administrative Penalties has established additional categories of penalty that include public censure, downgrading qualifications, restrictions on conducting production and business activities, orders to shut down business, and restrictions on engaging in business.[34] These changes reflect the over-generalization of the sanctions against the administrative counterparts, such as the restriction of the rights and the confiscation of property, which used to be confined to some special laws. Local legislative bodies can add new types of penalties for the same unlawful behavior, and the law enforcement agencies can also expand their means of imposing penalties. Due to the alteration in the punitive mechanism of the transaction rules, one possible result is that the administrative counterparts will have to face more severe punitive consequences and thus incur higher transaction costs.

---

[31] Article 20 of the Law of the People's Republic of China on Administrative Penalties (revised in 2021) stipulates that "Administrative penalties shall be under the jurisdiction of administrative organs equipped with administrative penalty authority at or above the county level where the illegal act occurred, unless otherwise provided by laws and administrative regulations."

[32] Article 24 of the Law of the People's Republic of China on Administrative Penalties (revised in 2021) stipulates that "provinces, autonomous regions, and municipalities directly under the Central Government may decide, based on actual local situations, to delegate the administrative penalty authority urgently needed for administration at grass-root levels, which is invested in the departments of county-level people's governments, to township people's governments and sub-district offices which can effectively enforce such administrative penalties. In such cases, regular assessments should be organized."

[33] Please refer to Article 8 of the Law of the People's Republic of China on Administrative Penalties (revised in 2017).

[34] Please refer to Article 9 of the Law of the People's Republic of China on Administrative Penalties (revised in 2021).

Fourthly, the administrative bodies may establish discretionary benchmarks for administrative penalties in accordance with the law. Both the legislation by the National People's Congress and the regulations by the State Council regarding administrative penalties tend to be relatively principled. The revised Law on Administrative Penalties allows administrative bodies to formulate discretionary benchmarks for administrative penalties.[35] For instance, with the newly-established provisions concerning the administrative penalty procedures related to epidemic control, administrative bodies have the legal foundation to rapidly and severely penalize behaviors violating emergency response measures. In order to conduct effective administrative management, the standards set by administrative bodies to determine illegal behavior tend to be rather stringent. This can easily lead to widespread violations of law by administrative counterparts, providing administrative law enforcement agencies with substantial discretionary space to enforce the law selectively. For example, some regions have set lower speed limits on highways, making it easy for motor vehicles to be fined for speeding. Similarly, some areas have established excessively high emission standards in the field of environmental protection, subjecting the majority of enterprises to penalties for their failure to comply with such standards. The alterations in the transaction rules expand the scope of applicability of the Law on Administrative Penalties, forcing more enterprises to incur transaction costs in order to have their rights restored.

[35] Article 34 of the Law of the People's Republic of China on Administrative Penalties (revised in 2021) stipulates that "Administrative organs may formulate discretion benchmarks of administrative penalties according to law and exercise administrative penalty discretion in legally responsible manners."

Conclusions and Prospects

Without any exception, all the economic activities of mankind are located within specific economic institutions or systems. This book has made tentative efforts to modify and improve the institutional theory in economics and to answer an essential question about institutional economics—how do institutions determine development?

1. **Key findings**

In the institutional studies in traditional economics, transaction costs were measured solely in monetary terms. This book suggests that time should also be used to measure transaction costs, positing that both time and money together form the standard for measuring transaction costs. In the study of institutional evolution, time is more important than money as a standard of measurement.

Traditionally, economic studies of transactions have been confined to the transfer of property rights. This book argues that the rights derived from the government's administrative actions share the same characteristics and attributes as property rights. The transfer of such rights constitutes a transaction, which can be measured in terms of transaction costs.

The genesis of institutions is the result of either rational construction or spontaneous evolution. Once established, institutions incur increasing transaction costs through marginal adjustments, leading to deviations from their initial objectives in the course of implementation. The laws underlying institutional evolution can be summarized as follows: firstly, institutions evolve amidst the paradox of decreasing efficiency and institutional alienation under the condition of path dependence; secondly, the existing institutions won't perish until their productivity is fully unleashed; finally, without external factors, internal factors alone cannot lead to radical changes in institutions.

Both neoclassical economics and new institutional economics have made homogenous assumptions about the state and the government, as well as about various kinds of economic systems. Within their doctrines, the function of the state is assumed to be homogenous across different contexts. The system of planned economy and the system of market economy have their inherent and fixed characteristics respectively.

B. Fan, *The Rationale Behind Change*, https://doi.org/10.1007/978-981-97-8854-5

Concerning this issue, this book has offered a dichotomous analysis regarding the government and various types of economic systems. It breaks down the government into different administrative entities which have different rights, face different rules, and incur different transaction costs when engaging in different transactions. The system of planned economy, the system of market economy, and the dual system can be further divided into subtypes. This entire array of issues necessitates comparative analysis within institutional research.

To delineate the trajectory of institutional evolution more clearly, this book has constructed a new analytical framework. Every transaction is treated as a transaction module consisting of three components: rights, contracts, and costs. Transactional entities complete their dealings through these modules, encompassing transactions between the government and the businesses, between the government and the market, between one government agency and another government agency, and between the businesses with the market. The analysis of institutional evolution includes a series of steps, namely, defining the transaction module, identifying the transaction entities, delineating transaction rights, clarifying transaction rules, calculating transaction costs, identifying factors affecting transaction costs, and proposing ways to optimize a given economic institution.

By making use of the transaction cost theory, laws of institutional evolution, and the method of transaction module analysis, this book examines how, over the past 40 years of China's reform and opening-up, the country opted for the market economy amidst its competition with the planned economy. It explores how China managed to untangle the "three bindings"—the bindings of ownership, of the mode of resource allocation, and of the method of wealth distribution with the social system. The untangling of the "three bindings" has served to reduce the excessively high transaction costs under the planned economy, stimulate market entities to engage in more activities of low-cost transactions, and generate significant institutional dividends. As a result, there has been a drastic growth in social wealth over a short period of time. This could be aptly described as the "secret" behind the so-called "the China Miracle."

While a country may enjoy institutional dividends, it is also possible that such dividends could be eroded. In China's economic system at the current stage, transaction rules are becoming increasingly complex, transaction costs are gradually increasing, and the government's constraints on the market and enterprises are continuously growing. As a result, we can observe what can be called the spreading of constraints, which can happen either vertically, throughout a given industry chain, or horizontally, throughout a particular industrial sector. This situation is not unique to China. Other developed market economies have also experienced similar challenges during the evolution of their economic systems.

Investment, the use of land for construction projects, energy, and business environment, those are the fields which have significant impacts on economic development. An analysis of the changes in the transaction costs brought about by the institutional changes in these areas reveals that since the reform and opening-up were initiated, there have been clear institutional dividends. However, there have also been efficiency decline and institutional alienation in varying degrees. In the process of deepening the reforms, most of the institutions still rely on the existing paths to make marginal adjustments in the transaction rules. The changes in the transaction costs have been mixed and, currently, a large number of transaction costs remain exceedingly high.

Any institutional reform should follow a path that reduces transaction costs, moving from a system of higher transaction costs to one of lower transaction costs. In China, reforms can be undertaken in three realms. The first are the reforms with a general purpose, such as reforms in finance and taxation, banking, investment, and market regulatory systems. The second are the reforms focusing on a specific field or region. The third are the reforms of the entire industry chain, reforms along the upstream and the downstream of industry chains like those of coal and electricity, oil and gas, real estate, and others.

2. **Some insights**

Institutions determine development, but they can also determine non-development. The crux lies in the kind of choice that is made regarding institutions. Institutions arise from rational construction as well as spontaneous evolution. For China, rational construction is backed up with unique advantages. However, if utilized inappropriately, such rational construction can backfire. Theoretical research on institutions should not only emphasize the importance of institutions but also illuminate how institutions are to be constructed. The state constitutes the primary provider of institutions. Before formally establishing institutions, the state should mobilize resources to launch in-depth assessments concerning the pros and cons of institutional changes. Having completed my tentative research in this book concerning institutional changes, I venture to share the following thoughts with the researchers of institutions, constructors of institutions, and the operators of institutions.

Firstly, caution must be fully exercised in establishing new institutions. At the very outset of the reform and opening-up, driven by the pioneering spirit at the grassroots level, China set up some new institutions, which became the starting points for many nationwide institutions. In their early stages, these institutions performed quite effectively so that their effective performance could completely offset the newly-emerged transaction costs. Currently, however, regulations have been established in virtually every economic field, and the space for creating entirely novel institutions based on grassroots wisdom has become quite limited. In the government's efforts to promote economic development, we often hear about phrases like "institutional innovations," with many government organizations both at the central and local levels claiming to be involved in seeking institutional innovations and innovations being made year after year. As demonstrated by the foregoing analyses and cases, once an institution is established, it presents characteristics of path dependence, diminishing efficiency, and institutional alienation. In most cases, the so-called institutional innovation is merely a form of making "patches" in the existing institutions. Marginal adjustments in transaction rules often result in the increase, rather than the decrease, in the transaction costs, unable to reverse the trend of diminishing efficiency. Without the powerful intervention by external forces, an institution can only sustain itself by continually "patching up," and the increase in the transaction costs in the institutions will negatively impact the country's efforts to preserve economic vibrancy.

Secondly, it is imperative to guard against the overlapping of transaction rules during institutional construction. In the pursuit of particular policy objectives, various administrative organizations tend to draft their own set of transaction rules. Once transaction rules are established, they invariably lead to transaction costs. These administrative organizations typically interact with the same market and with the same category of enterprises. While the transaction costs resulting from the rules of a single administrative organization might be bearable, the cumulative transaction costs due to the overlapping of the transaction rules can be very overwhelming. This can easily give rise to the fallacy of composition, resulting in the reduced efficiency in the economic activities of both the market and the enterprises. The more administrative organizations are involved in the transactions of rights and the more transaction rules are established, the higher will be the transaction costs incurred by the enterprises and the market. To reduce the transaction costs of institutions across all the economic activities of the society, it's crucial to reduce the number of the transactions of rights and to streamline and optimize transaction rules.

Thirdly, institutional operators should be prevented from overstepping their bounds in institutional construction. By definition, reform means the restructuring and adjustment of formal institutions. As the primary supplier of institutions, the state should entrust specialized bodies with the tasks of constructing rights and formulating rules. Likewise, marginal adjustments in institutions should be undertaken by institutional constructors. As for the operators of institutions, while they might also promote the formation of some informal constraints during their operation, they shouldn't become the primary entities for institutional restructuring and rule adjustment. For instance, legislative bodies formulate laws and regulations, whereas administrative bodies enforce the formulated laws and regulations; this defines the proper relationship between institutional constructors and institutional operators. If an administrative body creates additional provisions beyond the authority of the higher-level laws during its enforcement of the laws and regulations, such an act is not only unlawful but also will impose additional transaction costs on the administrative counterparties. In practice, it's prevalent for administrative organizations, in their operation of the institutions, to arbitrarily expand their power and adjust transaction rules without the endorsement of institutional constructors. Such unauthorized alterations have remained largely unchecked by institutional constructors. The so-called reforms, driven by the vested interests on the part of the institutional operators, have led to rising transaction costs. In some fields, this practice has reached a most alarming extent. Genuine reforms should allow qualified entities to construct new institutions and adjust existing ones, rather than allowing the operators of institutions to act arbitrarily, at their own free will.

Fourthly, it is crucial to address the proliferation of constraints, characterized by both the vertical spreading throughout a given industry chain and the horizontal spreading throughout a particular industrial sector. After more than four decades of reform and opening-up, virtually all economic activities in China have come to be governed by corresponding regulatory systems. Under the impact of the laws of institutional evolution, these systems inevitably face problems of diminishing efficiency and institutional alienation. A salient manifestation of this phenomenon lies in the transformation of regulations, initially designed to address a specific problem within a particular segment of an industry chain, into comprehensive regulations that encompass the entire industry chain. Such examples can be found in the coal-electricity industry chain and the real-estates industry chain. In addition, regulatory measures targeted at specific behaviors often evolve into regulations that impact all administrative counterparts, which either increase their obligations or diminish their rights, as evidenced by cases of excessive credit supervision and administrative penalties. A notable aspect of the spreading of constraints is the predilection of numerous government organizations at the central and local levels to adopt patterns of administration reminiscent of the planned economy to regulate the market and the enterprises. The traditional pattern of the highly centralized planned economy has morphed into discrete segments of planned economy, manifesting themselves in sectors such as finance, banking, land management, investment, and energy and within certain local governments. In breaking down and allocating production quotas, the administrative bodies, rather than resorting to the traditional approach in the planned economy, the approach of "comprehensive balancing through top-to-bottom and bottom-to-top processes," break down and allocate such quotas in a once-and-for-all manner, exhibiting the characteristics of "the economy of mandatory commands" worse than the traditional planned economy. As the most important provider of institutions, the state bears the responsibilities of not only establishing institutions but also upgrading and restructuring the existing institutions. For the state itself, it is vital to implement robust reform measures in the key sectors that yield macro-level transaction costs.

Fifthly, transaction costs should be incorporated as a benchmark for selecting reform initiatives. Different administrative organizations, acting in their own interests, often propose institutional designs and adjustments from their own individual perspectives, which frequently lead to difficulties in reaching a consensus on reform plans. A common solution to this dilemma is to design reform initiatives that take into account the perspectives of all the concerned administrative organizations, even when these views might be in conflict with one another. This amalgamation of disparate viewpoints within a single reform initiative is sometimes even lauded by some policymakers as a "balancing act" or "holistic coordination." In actuality, this approach means that, regarding a given market or enterprise, multiple administrative organizations formulate overlapping rules that will only serve to compel the market or the enterprise to double the time, efforts, and monetary costs in order to acquire the desired rights. By introducing transaction costs, we can establish a relatively objective criterion for evaluating different reform initiatives. Any efforts to adjust the rights and the rules of transaction should follow three important principles—the principle of reasonableness and necessity, the principle of proportionality, and the principle of minimal detriment. This means that unless there is sufficient reason and necessity, the rights and rules of transaction should not be established. In addition, the transaction costs incurred by transaction entities should be commensurate with the benefits that they can gain. Finally, when there are multiple reform alternatives to choose from, reformers should opt for the one that minimizes the time and monetary costs for the transaction entities, which is essentially the one with the lowest transaction costs.

Sixthly, utmost efforts should be made to extend the duration of institutional dividends. The dividends derived from the establishment of a new institution have temporal constraints. Transaction costs are inversely correlated to institutional dividends: the higher the transaction costs, the smaller the institutional dividends; conversely, the lower the transaction costs, the greater the institutional dividends. To extend the duration of institutional dividends, it's crucial that institutional constructors, operators, and overseers remain independent entities while exercising reciprocal checks and balances. When institutional constructors engage in rational construction of institutions or make dynamic adjustments in an existing institution, it's essential to make thorough feasibility studies concerning their potential plans to ensure that the new institution will operate with high efficiency at lower transaction costs. Meanwhile, effective oversight of institutional operators must be undertaken to prevent them from making unwarranted adjustments in the institution on their own. Such supervision may reduce the space for increasing transaction costs due to informal constraints.

Seventhly, institutional constructors must maintain a proactive stance towards reform. Institutions do not change without the impact of external forces. This determines that, for the institutional constructors, the completion of an institution's construction is not the end of the previous task but rather the commencement of a new one. In this new task, institutional constructors must keep track of the evolution of the institution and make timely adjustments, rather than relegating the power of adjustment entirely to the institutional operators. It is true that China and the Western countries differ in organizational approaches to institutional construction; nevertheless, all institutional constructors are committed to building institutions that are efficient. The only problem is that, historically, the existing research has all failed to employ transaction cost as a method of analysis.

Eighthly, we must value the time of taxpayers. In order to maintain administrative order, government agencies often impose higher transaction costs on administrative counterparts by adjusting transaction rules. For example, by establishing certain administrative permits, penalties, and credit sanctions, government agencies require administrative counterparts to spend additional time and make extra efforts to acquire the rights that inherently belong to them. While the staff in administrative agencies may be impervious to the value of time, the market and businesses are highly sensitive to it. During the construction and adjustment of institutions, the government seldom considers the economic consequences of wasting the time of the market and the enterprises. While wasting taxpayers' money is visible, wasting their time often goes unnoticed and, hence, the damage resulting from the wasted time is immeasurable. If converted into monetary terms, the cost could be far greater than the visible financial costs. In essence, unnecessary transaction costs force the market and the businesses to spend their time on meaningless matters, preventing them from engaging in more valuable and productive activities. To truly emancipate the invisible hand of the market, the key lies in restraining the visible hand, specifically the government's administrative action of increasing transaction costs by means of its administrative power.

3. Issues that warrant further discussions

This book focuses on studying the laws underlying the relationship between institutions and development. The theory of institutional economics posits the state as the primary provider of institutions. In adopting this theoretical legacy, this book primarily addresses the actions of the government in the construction and adjustment of institutions. While the government constitutes part of the state and can largely represent the actions of the state, the state itself is broader than the government, encompassing realms such as legislation, the judiciary, and politics. It is always advisable that theoretical studies adhere to the order proceeding from the simple to the complex and moving from the specific to the general. In the future, the theory of transaction costs, as well as the analytical framework of transaction modules and systemic subtypes, can also be employed to analyze the institutions in the fields outside the government.

Regarding transaction costs, this book has engaged in analysis that is largely theoretical. Due to limitations in the availability of data, most of the contents in this book have not been subjected to quantitative analysis. However, I am convinced that the optimal solution to transaction costs can be discovered through quantitative analytics when reformers formulate specific reform programs.

With respect to the three entities, namely, the government, enterprises, and the market, this book analyzes the costs of transactions between the government and enterprises, between the government and the market, and amongst different government agencies. It is pointed out in this book that, concerning the transactions between the enterprises and the market, further discussions are no longer necessary as new institutional economics has already conducted thorough research on the subject. However, the methodologies and frameworks employed by new institutional economics differ from those utilized in this book. For instance, this book has sought to measure transaction costs in terms of time and to analyze the transaction of rights by using transaction modules. There are other differences, too. In the future, novel approaches to the analysis of transaction costs can be applied to further study the relationship between the enterprises and the market, thus contributing to a unified framework for analyzing economic institutions.

The theories and analytical frameworks as developed in this book are not only applicable to China but also to other countries as well, constituting a theoretical and methodological architecture of important instrumental rationality. For instance, when imposing economic sanctions, some countries do not entirely resort to prohibition measures. Instead, they allow their governments to conduct review and approval concerning the import and export of certain enterprises or products or concerning the market access. In this way, these countries can manage the degree of sanctions by controlling transaction costs. In developed countries, the government's behavior of inefficient approval has also been subjected to criticisms and censures. At its core, such discontent arises from the government's administrative actions that have escalated transaction costs on the part of the enterprises and the general public.

The relationship between institutions and development is a universal and enduring topic, which has vital implications for the entire world.

Epilogue

In my entire professional career, I have been inextricably linked with institutional changes and reforms. When I began my career in 1991, I joined the Investment Research Institute of the State Planning Commission. My initial research focused on the system of investment in fixed assets, which was heavily reminiscent of the planned economy, as well as on macro investment regulation. Shortly thereafter, in 1992, the 14th National Congress of the Communist Party of China (CPC) was convened and China established its reform objective of transitioning to a socialist market economy. This required a fundamental shift in the work of government-dominated planning, and the reform of the investment system became one of the focal issues on the reform agenda. In 1994, I was transferred to the Policy Research Office under the State Planning Commission, where I worked chiefly on the reform of the planning system at the Division of Economic System. Compared with my previous role in the field of investment research, my new work covered a considerably broader scope and carried more important macroeconomic implications. In 1998, the State Planning Commission was re-named the State Development Planning Commission. The new name incorporates the important concept of "development." Subsequently, I switched from the Division of Economic System to the Division of Comprehensive Research and the Division of Development Research. Development became a reigning concept, as evidenced in such doctrines as "Development is of paramount importance" and "Development is the key to solving all problems." Thus, how to promote development constituted a pivotal subject of research for me and for my colleagues during that period.

In 2003, the State Development Planning Commission was re-named the National Development and Reform Commission, combining the ideas of "development" and "reform" in a single name. In May that year, as the SARS epidemic raged on, I was transferred to the Research Office of the State Council. There, I liaised with over a dozen departments under the State Council, had opportunities to conduct research overseas, and undertook frequent field studies in various provinces across China. As my vision and perspectives broadened, I authored a large number of policy research reports. These reports covered a vast array of fields, including development planning, macro-regulation, industrial development, the reform of state-owned enterprises

B. Fan, *The Rationale Behind Change*, https://doi.org/10.1007/978-981-97-8854-5

(SOEs), energy, ecology, regional economy, and opening up to the outside world, among others. These reports were informed by three fundamental aims, namely, to elaborate on problems, analyze their underlying causes, and recommend possible solutions. Many challenges faced by China in the process of its development could often be attributed to institutional factors. Consequently, any policy recommendation inevitably involved reform. The relationship between development and reform became the rationale underlying all policy research.

In 2017, I concluded my tenure at the Research Office of the State Council and was transferred to a new position. The year 2018 marked the 40th anniversary of China's reform and opening-up campaign. In that year, I published a collection of reports that I had authored over nearly a decade and the book is entitled *Unbinding the Invisible Hand*. This work addresses a whole range of topics on both the macro and the micro levels, issues related to the economy of the country and the livelihoods of ordinary citizens, as well as issues in domestic economy and in opening up to foreign markets. In addition, it discusses the issue of market reform across multiple sectors. Having completed this book, I have kept reflecting on questions like "what are the laws underlying the changes of economic institutions?" and "how do institutions determine the development?" To answer these questions, I re-studied the classics in economics, with hopes to find insights. I came to realize that the existing theories in economics concerning institutions have done a great job in analyzing the evolution of micro entities, but have failed to furnish satisfactory explanations concerning the evolution of the economic system of an entire nation. China's practices in the reform and opening-up can provide an abundance of samples for the study of economic systems. By capitalizing on the existing findings in the economic theories on institutions, I have sought to construct a new theoretical framework and analytical method and my endeavors have come into fruition in the form of this present book *The Rationale Behind Change: Institutions, Development, and Principles of Economics.*

Here, I would like to express my heartfelt gratitude to all the dear ones in my family for their sacrifices and invaluable contributions. My wife, Wang Shu, is a medical professor who, with profound love and understanding, has fully endorsed my deep commitment to research, which often encroaches upon the time which I might otherwise devote to the family. I truly appreciate her immense encouragement and support. The paradigms and insights from medical research have shed important light on my institutional studies. For instance, the idea of institutional sub-types is derived from descriptions of physiological phenomena. Our son, Fan Dechen, who is currently a student at high school, has already begun engaging with me in discussions about the relationship between the history of economic development and economic thoughts, a fact which fills me with pride. My father was an economist from an older generation, and my mother-in-law was a writer. Their expectations and assistance have been invaluable to me. My mother was a professor of economics, and my father-in-law was a philosopher. Although they have all passed away, their spirit of intellectual inquiry as dedicated scholars exerts profound and enduring influence on me. Throughout my research, I have been generously supported by Jin Aiwu, Chen Rui, Liu Yongxiang, Huang Fuli, and many others. I would also like to extend my sincere thanks to Zhang Songfeng and Lu Liyun, who have meticulously proofread and edited this book's Chinese version. It is their invaluable contributions that have made this book possible.

Fan Bi

December 20, 2021

Explicating How Institutions Determine Development

A commentary on Fan Bi's *The Rationale Behind Change: Institutions, Development, and Principles of Economics*

Zheng Xinli

Institutions can determine development; they can also determine the non-development, with the outcome hinging on the choice of the institutions. The achievements of China's development over the past four decades following the country's reform and opening-up have surpassed those in any previous eras, reaffirming the determining role that institutions play in development. However, it is undeniable that China's current economic system is not without its flaws, as some institutions pose impediments to development. How, then, should we assess the merits and demerits of economic institutions? How can we construct institutions that foster development? Addressing these questions necessitates research and judgment that can either stem from practical, case-by-case analysis or from theoretical research, applying the principles of institutional evolution to infer and evaluate the advantages and disadvantages inherent in different institutions. The former approach is commonly employed in our work, while the latter has been less satisfactorily explored, reflecting the deficiencies in economic studies regarding the laws of institutional evolution. In the field of institutional economics, although scholars like Coase, North, and Williamson have been widely recognized and been awarded with Nobel Prizes, the theory's contributions have remained limited in guiding the institutional transformations in China and in other countries undergoing transitions.

Recently, the book *The Rationale Behind Change: Institutions, Development, and Principles of Economics*, authored by Mr. Fan Bi, addresses three important issues from the perspective of transaction costs, namely, how institutions determine development, what are the laws governing institutional evolution, and how to choose institutions beneficial for development. Mr. Fan Bi initially worked at the Policy Research Office under the State Planning Commission, focusing on the reform of the planning system and development policies. He witnessed China's institutional transformation from a planned economic system to a socialist market economic system during his

B. Fan, *The Rationale Behind Change*, https://doi.org/10.1007/978-981-97-8854-5

12 years of work there, coinciding with the change of the State Planning Commission first to the State Development Planning Commission and subsequently to the National Development and Reform Commission. Following this, he spent another 13 years working at the Research Office of the State Council, serving consecutively in the Department of Macroeconomics and the Comprehensive Economic Department. As his former immediate superior, I have kept myself well-informed of his research achievements. He possesses an insider's knowledge of many core business patterns of China's major economic sectors and has authored numerous policy research reports. In analyzing development issues, he has invariably sought institutional explanations and proposed policy recommendations for improvement. His research articles are mainly collected in books like *Unbinding the Invisible Hand* and *Reform of China's Energy Market*. In recent years, he has been concentrating on studying the general laws underlying institutional evolution. By deriving crucial empirical support from a substantial number of case studies, he has succeeding in completing this latest book *The Rationale Behind Change: Institutions, Development, and Principles of Economics*. The book is most valuable for opening up new horizons for the long-stagnant field of institutional studies in economics.

I. Transaction costs determining institutional evolution

Institutional economics has evolved through several phases, passing from the Institutional School, through the Neo-Institutional School, and finally to the New Institutional Economic School. The Institutional School, which emerged around the end of the nineteenth century and the beginning of the twentieth century, was the first to study economic institutions, positing that economic and social development stems from various institutions related to economic life, but such development can be equally constrained by these institutions. The publication of *The Nature of the Firm* by Ronald H. Coase in 1937 marked the birth of the new institutional economics. His theory of transaction costs unveiled the substitutive relationship between firms and markets. Subsequently, the new institutional economics developed three main theoretical tools: the theory of property rights, the contract theory, and the theory of transaction cost. According to the new institutional economics, reducing transaction costs is the core objective of institutional reform, necessitating the design and adjustment of property rights and contracts centered on the minimization of transaction costs. Although transaction costs are a central theme in the theory of new institutional economics, scholars differ widely regarding both the intension and the extension of this concept while the issue of measuring transaction costs has also remained unresolved. By analyzing the limitations inherent in institutional economics, *The Rationale Behind Change* constructs a new framework for institutional analysis using transaction costs and transaction modules as tools. It proposes the measurement of transaction costs in terms of time and explains institutional evolution by means of transaction costs.

In discussing transaction costs, the author broadens the scope of analysis concerning what constitutes a "transaction" in institutional economics. Traditionally, transactions in institutional economics referred to the exchange of rights over various materials and services derived from property ownership. The author contends that a transaction is essentially a transfer of rights, arguing that the rights generated by governmental administrative actions can be transferred in the same way that property rights are transferred; thus, such rights can also become the proper objects of transactions. For example, when the government grants a company a franchise, the government transfers, through its administrative action, the derived right to the company and this act constitutes a transaction of right between the government and the enterprise.

For economics, theories can stand under certain assumptions; any breakthrough in assumptions can often lead to significant theoretical advancements. Neoclassical economics made a homogeneous assumption of "complete rationality" regarding firms, an assumption that Coase challenged. New institutional economics views the state as the paramount or supreme provider of institutions, seeing the state from the same perspective as neoclassical economics views firms, both of which are characterized by homogeneity. For instance, the state can create institutions, define and protect property rights, and coordinate relationship among different interest groups. However, the author of this book breaks with the new institutional economics' assumption of homogeneity about the state, pointing out that the rights produced by different state organs, such as administrative, legislative, judicial, and national defense entities, can be different. The book performs an anatomic analysis of the state as an institutional provider, focusing specifically on the administrative actions by the government in managing economic activities.

New institutional economists, when analyzing simple economic activities, can measure transaction costs in monetary terms. However, many transaction costs generated by institutions cannot be measured in monetary terms. The result is that, in practice, economists have to rely on qualitative descriptions whenever the concept of transaction cost is involved. The author suggests that transaction costs can be measured in terms of time so that both time and money can constitute the standards for measuring transaction costs. Time is objective and can be viewed as the most powerful and impartial judge. Indicators such as labor, interest, and efficiency which are used to measure economic activities all involve time. If we posit the existence of a total social labor time, it includes time spent on transaction costs. The less time from the total labor time is devoted to transaction costs, the more time is available for creating wealth. Although previous economic theories have never tried to measure transaction costs in terms of time, the governance of countries and the business operations of enterprises have all been informed by a unanimous and spontaneous effort to save time.

Once we begin to measure transaction costs in terms of time, the study of economic institutions becomes markedly clearer. For instance, Chinese scholars frequently debate whether reform should be conducted abruptly or gradually, or whether it is better to have rational construction or spontaneous evolution. By measuring transaction costs in terms of time, it becomes easier to determine which mode of institutional change is more conducive to development. We can take the "Household Contract Responsibility System" as an example. In 1980, the Central Government of China formally decided to implement this reform, which could be seen as a rational institutional construction. Prior to this decision, many places had already been secretly experimenting with that system. If the Central Government had delayed its reform decision and allowed the household contract responsibility system to evolve spontaneously in various regions, the widespread implementation of this system would have inevitably taken much longer. The Central Government's decision to implement this system saved transaction costs, which solved China's problem of food shortages within a short period of time. Similar inferences can be made about the reforms in other areas.

Using transaction costs as a tool, the author has managed to develop a broad picture about the characteristics and laws of institutional evolution, including path dependency, diminishing efficiency, and institutional alienation. Specifically, "patching" existing institutions can be an effective way to save on transaction costs, but it can lead to the common phenomenon of path dependency in institutional change. Once an institution is established, it faces continuous marginal adjustments, resulting in inevitable increases in transaction costs and leading to diminishing institutional efficiency. As transaction costs accumulate and institutions deviate further and further from the envisioned objectives, institutions often stray from the original purposes with which they were established and end up in institutional alienation.

To discuss the relationship between institutional evolution and development, it is necessary to analyze the countless transactions of rights that occur at every moment. Faced with such a plethora of complex institutions, the author proposes the analytical method of transaction modules, setting each transaction of right as a module that includes three components: the right, the contract, and the cost. All transaction entities complete their exchanges through particular transaction modules. To study the impact of institutions on development, it is necessary to discusses four major types of transactions of rights: the transaction between the government and the enterprises, the transaction between the government and the market, the transaction between different government departments, and finally the transaction between the enterprises and the market. A major deficiency of the new institutional economics is that it has only analyzed the transactions between the enterprises and the market, overlooking the transactions that involve the government as a transaction entity. This unexplored area is exactly what this book aims to address.

II. Why choosing the market economy

Having constructed his theoretical framework, the author uses the transaction cost as an important perspective and explores, based on transaction modules, why China chose the system of market economy during its reform and opening-up. The author posits that the competition between different economic systems essentially boils down to a competition in transaction costs. China's reform commenced with the reform of the system of planned economy, which was characterized by high transaction costs. The book simulates the process through which two enterprises complete a transaction under the planned economy: the planning department first needed to collect data concerning the categories of the products which were demanded, as well as the quantities of products and the production capacities of enterprises. Then, following the "two top-to-bottom processes and one bottom-to-top process" or the "two top-to-bottom processes and two bottom-to-top processes," the planning department sought to balance the supply-and-demand relationship nationwide, draw up plans, and then arrange for production and manufacturing. In formulating and implementing plans, every submission of a report to a government department on the higher level and every issuance of an administrative directive to the government department or an enterprise on the lower level could be seen as a transaction module in which a transaction of right happened between the enterprise and the government, or between different government departments. Naturally, each transaction would incur transaction costs. Balancing the supply and demand on a nationwide scale of human resources, material resources, and financial resources meant undergoing countless transactions of rights and incurring high transaction costs. In the 1980s, the annual national planning meeting would often last one to two months during which plans were developed and balanced. Under the market economy, enterprises can trade directly with each other, eliminating the cost of transactions between enterprises and the government and between different government departments. Unlike that of the former Soviet Union, China's system of planned economy never achieved complete coverage of all the economic activities. At the very outset of the reform and opening-up, market transactions that bypassed the state planning kept expanding in areas where the planned economy was weak, and the scope of economic activities covered by state planning kept shrinking. Accordingly, a dual system came into existence where government planning and marketization coexisted and competed with each other. With the convening of the 14th CPC National Congress in 1992, China established the goal of reforming towards the system of socialist market economy. This marked the triumph of the system of market economy, characterized by lower transaction costs, over the system of planned economy which was phased out due to its high transaction costs.

By using transaction cost as an analytical framework, the author further explains how China succeeded in unbinding the three bindings between production relations and the social system, thus reconstructing China's economic system. First, in terms of resource allocation, the binding between the planned economy and the social system of China as a socialist country was abolished to establish the system of socialist market economy. Second, in terms of ownership, the binding between the public ownership and the social system was exterminated, replaced by a basic economic system where the public ownership remains predominant but is supplemented by the co-development of multiple forms of ownership. Third, in terms of income distribution, the binding between distribution according to labor and the social system was eradicated and a new system was established, where labor, capital, technology, management, and other factors of production participate in the distribution of wealth according to the varying contributions of individual factors. In the process of "unbinding" these three bindings, the market and non-public sectors regained their status as transaction entities, creating an incentive mechanism for reducing transaction costs. The overall scale of societal transactions grew significantly, the average transaction cost decreased, and a large number of economic activities with low transaction costs emerged. As a result, China's economic vibrancy significantly increased, creating "considerable institutional dividends." The author is convinced that this can be considered as the "secret" behind the rapid economic development of China following the reform and opening-up.

III. Why do good institutions hinder development?

With the advent of the reform and opening-up, China initiated reforms in nearly all economic sectors. The author observed that many of the economic institutions which underwent reform in the early stages indeed facilitated economic development. But as time went by, they came to pose hindrance to economic development. This phenomenon is characterized by the author as the spreading of constraints. The reason behind this is that once the government imposes administrative regulation on a particular area, tradable rights are generated, and transaction costs arises when the government department engages in the transactions of rights with the market, the enterprises, or other government departments. Dictated by the law of path dependence, new institutions continually face diminishing efficiency, transaction costs keep accumulating, and eventually institutions become alienated. In the book, the author describes two types of the spreading of constraints.

The first is the spreading of constraints "from a particular segment through an entire industry chain." Most of the contradictions in modern economic life can be attributed to certain segments within an industrial chain, especially the supply-and-demand contradictions, where problems are manifested in a particular transaction segment, but the causes often stem from multiple segments in both the upstream and the downstream of an industry chain. The government's regulation of economic activities tends to spread along the industry chain from one particular segment to other upstream and downstream segments, moving from "segment constraints" (regulatory interventions in a specific segment) to "chain constraints" (interventions through the entire industry chain). For example, the "coal-electricity" industry chain mainly consists of coal mining, transportation, and electricity generation. The regulatory controls imposed on electricity generation and electricity prices have led to "electricity shortages." To solve the contradiction in the supply-and-demand relationship of electricity as well as the smog problem, the government intervened in coal production and sales by imposing controls over production capacity and sale prices. Later on, government regulation escalated into interventions in demand, not only restricting coal production capacity but also implementing the mechanism of the so-called "orderly use of electricity." The contradiction in the supply-and-demand relationship of energy evolved from supply constraints, through the tight supply-demand balance, and finally to dual constraints on both the supply and the demand. The result was that the demand shrank, the supply came under severe impact, and the expectations were weakened. In the industry chains of real estates, oil and gas, and even of some consumer goods, the government began by addressing local supply-and-demand contradictions and gradually adopted more and more administrative measures such as government pricing, production capacity regulation, and consumption suppression in the upstream and downstream of the industry chains. For instance, to solve the problem of traffic congestion, the government would implement the policy of car purchase restriction; to curb housing price hikes, the policy of housing purchase restrictions could be adopted, ultimately affecting the sustained and healthy development of the automobile and construction industries. Short-term opportunism in dealing with long-term strategies often ends up in the continuous accumulation of transaction costs, constraining the development of entire industry chains. Such a practice constitutes an important reason for the increasing pressure of economic downturn in recent years.

The second is the spreading of constraints "from a particular segment across an entire sector," where certain regulatory measures which were initially targeted at specific market entities are expanded to cover more entities or even all market entities in pursuit of regulatory strength or efficiency. The credit regulation is a case in point. The mechanism was initially a punitive measure adopted to address difficulties of law enforcement in judicial cases. However, in building the credit system, various government departments began to establish their own lists of the so-called credit-violating entities, and credit punishment covered nearly all the subjects of administrative penalties, as well as individuals and enterprises violating the regulations of various administrative departments. This has greatly increased the transaction costs for businesses and individuals to re-start and operate businesses. The spreading of constraints "from a particular segment across an entire sector" is prevalent in various administrative activities such as production capacity control, market supervision, and administrative licensing.

To analyze the effects of changes in transaction costs on development, the book selects and focuses on areas with significant impacts on economic growth, such as fixed-asset investment, land use for construction projects, energy, and business environment. By reviewing the history of China's reform of the investment project approval system, the author describes how the transaction costs arising from the approval process have followed a trajectory from high to low costs and then gradually back to high costs once again. Currently, the fact that investment has become increasingly ineffective in stimulating China's economy is not due to the failure of the multiplier effect of investment but because the transaction costs introduced by the approval process have made the project construction excessively time-consuming. While it is necessary to strengthen the protection of arable land and promote the economical and intensive use of land, the overly complicated system of land management has led to excessively high transaction costs for investors to obtain construction land, thus creating constraints on the land supply. From primary products to intermediate products and finally to end-users, China's energy sector is subject to administrative regulation arising from property rights system, industrial policies, industry management system, ownership, circulation, fiscal and tax policies, and supervision. The excessively high transaction costs contribute to constraints on both the supply and the demand of energy. Market entities, when engaging in business activities such as launching and operating businesses, paying taxes, executing contracts, and shutting down corporations, must meet government compliance requirements. After several years of reform in streamlining administration, delegating powers, and improving services, the business environment in China has improved; in particular, the reduced time for starting businesses and the reduced number of required administrative permissions have helped to lower transaction costs. However, if we examine the full lifecycle of a firm, the transaction costs reduced in some areas have rebounded in other areas. These analyses conducted by the author can to some extent shed light on the institutional reasons behind the continuous slowdown of China's economic growth rate in recent years.

IV. Reshaping the reform path with low transaction costs

Based on the new framework of institutional analysis, the author reflects on how China can construct economic institutions most conducive to development. Essentially speaking, the excessively high transaction costs generated by institutions mean that they divert huge amounts of time which otherwise belongs to the market and businesses to meaningless activities, hindering them from engaging in other more meaningful activities. To reduce institutional transaction costs, the author advocates that the adjustment of transaction rights and rules should follow three important principles, i.e., the principle of reasonableness and necessity, the principle of proportionality, and the principle of minimal harm. This means that transaction rights and rules should be set with sufficient reasons and necessities, transaction costs incurred by transaction entities should be proportional to the potential benefits that they might gain, and when multiple reform options are available, reformers should choose the one that causes minimal losses of time and money to the transaction entities, i.e., the option with the lowest transaction costs.

Faced with the current situation where some local governments use reform as a pretext for expanding their administrative power, the author suggests that the construction of new institutions should be undertaken with considerable caution. The state has already established regulations across all economic sectors, leaving very little room for creating entirely new institutions based on the innovations at the basic levels. The formulation and adjustment of transaction rules by numerous administrative organs tend to result in increased transaction costs. The accumulation of transaction rules framed by various administrative agencies leads to substantial transaction costs that affect economic development.

In identifying three groups of individuals, respectively, institutional constructors, institutional operators, and institutional supervisors, the author advocates that while these three groups remain independent of one another, they should implement mutual checks and balances. In China, the institutional constructors at the national level are the CPC Central Committee and the State Council, while various government departments and local administrative agencies act as institutional operators. In practice, it is quite common for institutional operators to expand their administrative power on their own and adjust transaction rules without the due approval from institutional constructors. In future reforms, the construction of new institutions and the adjustment of existing institutions must be undertaken by appropriate decision-making bodies so that institutional operators would be prevented from overstepping their bounds and acting arbitrarily. When institutions are constructed, there needs to be supervisors to effectively monitor institutional operators, preventing unnecessary adjustments in the existing institutions. In this way, the government's administrative actions that increase transaction costs through administrative power would be brought under effective control.

For a long time, the policy research in China has primarily focused on solving specific problems in reform and development. Many researchers, when proposing solutions to practical issues, often recommend expanding government functions and increasing regulatory controls, overlooking the increased institutional transaction costs that such actions impose on economic activities. Mr. Fan Bi, in his "*The Rationale Behind Change*," has made commendable contributions by presenting original insights regarding the principles underlying the relationship between institutions and development, along with solid empirical analyses. Under the leadership of the CPC, China boasts significant advantages in the rational construction of institutions, but poor utilization of such advantages would prove counterproductive. Therefore, institutional constructors should continue to maintain a high level of reform initiative, be insightful in identifying the laws of institutional evolution, and effectively apply these laws to the construction and marginal adjustment of institutions.

The manufacturer's authorised representative in the EU is Springer Nature Customer Service Centre GmbH, Europaplatz 3, 69115 Heidelberg, Germany. If you have any concerns regarding our products, please contact ProductSafety@springernature.com

Printed and bound by CPI Group (UK) Ltd, Croydon, CR0 4YY
01/10/2026
02225941-0005